Pluralism, Property, and Radical Transformation

Pluralism, Property, and Radical Transformation

Matthew Kruger

LEXINGTON BOOKS
Lanham • Boulder • New York • London

Published by Lexington Books
An imprint of The Rowman & Littlefield Publishing Group, Inc.
4501 Forbes Boulevard, Suite 200, Lanham, Maryland 20706
www.rowman.com

86-90 Paul Street, London EC2A 4NE

British Library Cataloguing in Publication Information Available

Library of Congress Cataloging-in-Publication Data Available

ISBN: 978-1-66696-839-2 (cloth : alk. paper)
ISBN: 978-1-66696-840-8 (ebook)

∞™ The paper used in this publication meets the minimum requirements of American National Standard for Information Sciences—Permanence of Paper for Printed Library Materials, ANSI/NISO Z39.48-1992.

Contents

Acknowledgements

Francis Antonie, Christopher Pierson, Lawrence Hamilton and, in particular, Leif Wenar, each of whom is responsible in their own ways for the possibility of this book becoming a reality, thank you. To my editors at Bloomsbury, Jana Hodges-Kluck and Lauran Jones, thank you for all your generous help during the publication process. To the anonymous reviewer, your comments and suggestions certainly made for an improved final product, thank you.

More than 15 years before the first volume of *Capital* was published, Marx wrote to Engels: 'I am so far advanced that I shall be finished with the whole of the economic shit in five weeks.' I imagine Engels smiled when he read the letter. At times, my friends, who were subjected to my ideas about property for almost a decade, will hopefully also have smiled – not grimaced – when I said many times that I was nearly finished with this book. In particular, Dave, Graham, Jacob, Rachel, Terrina, Tom and Quentin, you more than anyone suffered me over the years. You each listened to, encouraged, criticised and guided my thoughts. The pages of this book embody our times together. I am and forever will be grateful for all that you did.

The importance of attitudes is a red thread that runs through this book's argument. Attitudes do not just shape how we perceive and understand and make sense of the world. They also open up horizons, they bring whole worlds into being, they make possible the experience of goodness itself. Because of my family, there are two attitudes that I hold dear – humility and courage. All too often, I do not do them justice, but I try, and it was through and in that trying that I wrote this book. Mom, Dad, Wes and Bruce, due to you, a little world, a horizon scattered with words, now exists. If anything is good in it, it comes from you.

Prologue

This book about property is a work of ethics, political economy and jurisprudence. What it says is general. Its criticisms, proposals and interpretations are not limited to one political community or legal system. Most of what is said applies as much to my home, South Africa, as it does to the community where it was conceived and mostly written, the United Kingdom. It was written with South Africa in mind, though, and its last two chapters demonstrate how the theory developed in the preceding chapters has real-world practical relevance.

This relevance motivates and guides this book's theoretical arguments. This is only right, for whilst it has become a commonplace, it is true and important that theory and practice are related. In 2015, Johan Froneman, a Justice of South Africa's Constitutional Court, expressed this point as follows:

> The question of property is fiercely contested in South African society. There is, as yet, little common ground on how we conceive of property under section 25 of the Constitution, why we should do so, and what purpose the protection of property should serve. This exposes a potential fault line that may threaten our constitutional project.[1]

Not many South Africans would have disagreed with the assessment of Froneman J at the time. Now, in 2024, after Covid and the political-economic response to it, the number will probably be even fewer. Importantly, for a book that sees itself as having general relevance, it may also find a sympathetic international audience, who have arrived at similar conclusions about their communities, if the long-unfolding political-economic 'crises' revealed in, for example, Brexit and Trump were not themselves sufficient.

Like every existential threat, or at least threats that appear imminent, the need to tackle it is urgent. To do so adequately, we must understand its nature. Of course, South Africa suffers from many problems, and these are hardly unique to it: poverty, inequality, inefficiency, greed, fraud, incompetence, cowardice, and so on. We are all familiar with these problems, and of course they must be identified, exposed and dispatched. Froneman J, however, did not have these problems in mind when he issued his judicial warning, or at least not immediately so. For the threat faced by South Africa's constitutional project is not just economic, social, political, cultural, technical and bureaucratic in nature. It also has a conceptual and ethical dimension.

To see what I mean, let us unpack this proposition. South Africa's Constitution has often been described as being a long-term project to transform the country's political and social institutions and power relationships. The text, it is said, aims to facilitate a reconstruction of society through a redistribution of power and property. To effect this change, we are told, we must alter the logic of existing relations and distributions. These statements abound. That the Constitution demands meaningful change is certain. What is not clear, however, is what all this familiar talk amounts to in practice. What do we mean, structurally and substantively, by transformation? We should alter property relations, but how, according to what conceptual framework, and in pursuit of what end or ends? As I understand Froneman J, it is the lack of any shared answers to these conceptual and ethical questions – that is, a property theory – that threatens South Africa's now generation-long constitutional project with extinction.

The dire state of our property talk and the existential challenges that it generates reach well beyond South Africa's borders. This problem is shared by many political communities, including those who have reached 'the end of history' or for whom 'there is no alternative'. And, I argue in this book, we all share this problem because the theories of property available to us, despite their unique and particular genius, are not adequate to the strongly plural and therefore tragic world in which we find ourselves.

* * *

After a chapter in which I articulate two concepts that sit in the heart of this book, that is, pluralism and property, where, following Joseph Raz, I distinguish weak from strong goods pluralism and offer a Waldron-cum-Hohfeld conception of property, this book is divided into three parts. Each part has a particular emphasis: critical, constructive and interpretative.

Part I is critical in that it strives to reveal the premises that inform our dominant traditions of property theory. In chapters 2 to 4, I consider the property theories offered by Locke, Bentham, Hayek, Hegel and Marx. I argue that our tradition's most original, influential theorists start alike. Despite many differences in content, their theories are structured by what non-property theorists call the anthropological question: What is Man? Beginning with the more or less self-conscious premise that we can answer the practical question 'What is to be done?' if we first answer a more basic theoretical one about 'Man', they prescribe functionalist and essentialist property schemes. For each, property's function is to promote particular essential goods: life for Locke, security for Bentham, information-use for Hayek and forms of expressive relational unity for both Hegel and Marx. Whilst other concerns shape their concrete allocative schemes, their more significant and enduringly relevant differences emerge from their conflicting views about what is important in or for the life of man.

In some or other form or combination of forms, we still move in the shadows cast by these men, we still work within their anthropologically structured way of thinking about property, the formal outlines of which I set out in the opening paragraphs of part I.

As Michael Walzer demonstrates in his *Spheres of Justice*, though, which I consider in detail in chapter 5, the problem with the anthropological structure is its essentialism – or what I call in this book, the use of 'models'. By insisting on an absolute principle, or an internally coherent or abstractly ordered set of principles, they distort the content of their theories and disable efforts to realise goods and frustrate bads in practice. In doing this, they deprive us of the tools, conceptual and institutional, that we need to manage peaceably and resolve, for a while at least, the practical conflict that always arises whenever we ask allocative questions. Walzer, however, neglects the inevitability of conflict. This neglect frustrates his radical effort to overcome the anthropological approach to property. So, part II of this book, which is constructive in nature, follows Walzer by setting aside anthropology, the use of models. It proposes an alternative that aims to do justice to the plurality of logically incompatible goods that constitute our lives. In offering this alternative, however, chapters 5 to 8 depart from Walzer by situating the inevitability of conflict in its heart. According to this approach, chapter 5 explains, rather than with prescriptive models and around an ultimate question about man, we ought to organise our thinking about property around three deflated and descriptive alternatives, where we ask after forms, relations and rights.

Like anthropological theories, a theory structured by these questions will be functionalist in form. By remaining close to the ground, it provides practical routes or responses to diverse goods and bads. Unlike our tradition, though, it will not privilege one good or bad as decisive when we are allocating property, nor will it aim for an internal coherence or abstract ranking of goods and bads. For this reason, it will not, since it cannot, prescribe particular rights-allocations or structures for doing so. As I illustrate in chapters 6 and 7, faced with incompatible goods and bads that theory cannot rank, all it will do is describe or articulate their qualitative structures – the internal relations among qualities that constitute them – for the sake of identifying the property rights that we must allocate to facilitate or frustrate them. From this, it follows that when we are faced with the question 'What is to be done?' there is limited value in turning to philosophers. Whilst their skills matter, they are narrow. Rather than redesigning, rethinking, reframing, reimagining, and so on, some or other blueprint, paradigm, template, lens, and so on, and then proposing a research agenda, or outlining a theory of improvement, or prescribing moral guidelines to be implemented either in a particular community or universally, philosophers must limit themselves to describing existing or possible worlds. Through these descriptions, they might sometimes let our allocative options be seen more clearly, but that is all that they can do.

Ultimately, when we strive to manage the tragic conflict that emerges through and in all our property talk and practice (chapter 8), we can only look to ourselves and each other (epilogue). Property is a political and therefore legal problem, not a theoretical one. It is political even at the level of structure, for allocative conflict is not just contingent, it is also logical (chapters 1, 6, 7), with the conflict only capable of resolution through the exercise of particular concrete judgments by differently situated persons, the outcome of which is therefore contingent (chapters 1, 5). And it is legal because one of law's functions is to settle, for the time being, those agonising political conflicts that theory cannot (part III). In other words, property is ultimately a political and legal question because, in the ethical sense that I unpack conceptually in chapter 1 and then develop in the chapters that follow, we live in a world of strongly plural goods.

Whereas parts I and II are critical and constructive in form, part III is interpretative. In part III, I analyse the legal settlement embodied in South Africa's Constitution. This text, I argue in chapter 9, not only recognises the fact of strong goods pluralism, it also embraces an ethics that seeks to do justice to the logically diverse, incompatible goods that constitute South African life. It embodies a concrete judgment according to which every exercise of public power must strive to respect, protect, promote and fulfil the diverse forms and relations that diverse South Africans judge good.

Flowing from this is a radical and transformative approach to property. It is transformative, which means it is radical, because it rejects our tradition's prescriptive anthropology in favour of an embrace of the diversity of goodness. It understands that the conflict internal to allocations of property rights means that there will often be a need for new exercises of public power to settle disagreement. It recognises that exercises of this power will often result in change that is effected by grasping matters at the root – that is, by altering the logic of the relations that are facilitated or frustrated by the rights that attach to or obtain in objects, by altering the rights to some mutually exclusive set of rights. A radical and transformative approach to property, though, does not mean extreme, nor can it entail either hubris or vanity. It means precisely the opposite, since it requires striving to do justice to all sides of any conflict – and this does not merely mean recognising all who are involved and facilitating a fair decision-making process, but also striving to make up for all the diverse goods that will tragically always be lost whenever law performs its authoritative, allocative function. In chapter 10, we reveal that this duty is nowhere more pronounced than in the setting of Parliament's original power to expropriate property and its context-sensitive duty to compensate all affected parties when it does.

Nothing internal to the logic, or if you prefer, internal to the point of view, of South Africa's approach to property, its constitutive embrace of strong goods pluralism, calls for any particular changes to the existing system of property, like those longed for by prescriptive anthropologists. If regard is had to South Africa's past and still normative theoretical tradition, however, it seems to me that substantial transformation is not just likely but a near certainty. This anticipated result moved me to write this book. It is why I argue we must let go of the anthropologically structured approach to property. It is also why, despite refusing in this book to prescribe theoretically 'What is to be done', I can coherently call this theoretical change liberating. Once it is effected, we will reflectively judge it as being for the good – or to be more precise, we will recognise that, having freed ourselves from the distorting and disabling effects of the anthropological structure, we will be in a position where we together can freely judge and do good.

NOTE

1. *Shoprite Checkers (Pty) Ltd v MEC for Economic Development, Eastern Cape and Others* 2015 (6) SA 125 (CC) para 4.

Abbreviations

JEREMY BENTHAM

EL	An Essay on Language
FG	A Fragment on Government
FO	A Fragment on Ontology
IPML	An Introduction to the Principles of Morals and Legislation
PCC	Principles of the Civil Code
PL	Principles of Legislation

MARTIN BUBER

BMM	Between Man and Man
EG	Eclipse of God: Studies in the Relation between Religion and Philosophy
IT	I and Thou
PTW	Pointing the Way: Collected Essays

FRIEDRICH HAYEK

CL	The Constitution of Liberty
CRS	The Counter-Revolution of Science: Studies on the Abuse of Reason
FC	The Fatal Conceit: The Errors of Socialism
IEO	Individualism and Economic Order

LLL	Law, Legislation and Liberty: A new statement of the liberal principles of justice and political economy
NSP	New Studies in Philosophy, Politics and Economics
RS	The Road to Serfdom
SPPE	Studies in Philosophy, Politics and Economics

GEORG WILHELM FRIEDRICH HEGEL

EPR	Elements of the Philosophy of Right
ETW	On Christianity: Early Theological Writing
PhS	Phenomenology of Spirit

JOHN LOCKE

ECHU	An Essay Concerning the Human Understanding
TTG	Two Treatises of Government

KARL MARX

CCHPR	A Contribution to the Critique of Hegel's 'Philosophy of Right'
CGP	Critique of the Gotha Programme
CHPR	Critique of Hegel's 'Philosophy of Right'
CM	The Communist Manifesto
CSF	The Class Struggles in France: 1848-1850
CVI	Capital: A Critique of Political Economy, Volume I
CVII	Capital: A Critique of Political Economy, Volume II
CVIII	Capital: A Critique of Political Economy, Volume III
EB	The Eighteenth Brumaire of Louis Bonaparte
EPM	Economic and Philosophic Manuscripts of 1844
ET	Karl Marx: Early Texts
GFCPE	Grundrisse: Foundations of the Critique of Political Economy
GI	The German Ideology
OJM	On James Mill
OJQ	On the Jewish Question
PP	The Poverty of Philosophy
TF	Theses on Feuerbach
WLC	Wage Labour and Capital

MARTHA NUSSBAUM

AAF	Anger and Forgiveness: Resentment, Generosity, Justice
CC	Creating Capabilities: The Human Development Approach
FJ	Frontiers of Justice, Disability, Nationality and Species Membership
MAB	Mill between Aristotle and Bentham
PE	Political Emotions: Why Love Matters for Justice
TFG	The Fragility of Goodness: Luck and Ethics in Greek Tragedy and Philosophy
THJ	Bernard Williams: Tragedies, hope, justice
UT	Upheavals of Thought: The Intelligence of Emotions
WHD	Women and Human Development: The Capabilities Approach

Chapter 1

Pluralism and Property

In the heart of this book lie two concepts: pluralism and property. As my argument unfolds, we see that their meaning and significance are bound up not only in their internal relation, in that each only acquires its fully articulated meaning together with the other, but also in their relation to this book's political economy, ethics and jurisprudence. Despite this interconnectedness, to grasp the initial stages of my argument, we must start with general and stipulated – and, I admit right at the outset, for that reason, both dense and abstract – definitions of both.

There are many conceptions of these ideas. In essence, nothing said in this book turns on my definitions being 'right'. As it happens, I agree with theorists who think talk of uniquely true and false definitions of ethical terms and concepts does not have, in any deep sense, proper meaning. At most, they can be more or less adequate in describing our experiences of the world, better and worse in clarifying our understanding of the phenomena that constitute our reality. Whatever the outcome of these disputes about bivalence,[1] though, my limited aim here is to offer a vocabulary that enables us to analyse radically different property theories – different in what each advocates, how each argues, and indeed what each says at all. For this reason, more important than whether my definitions fit others, is that they internally cohere and clarify more than they obscure.

TWO FORMS OF GOODS PLURALISM

Let us begin with the concept of pluralism. Immediately, I must narrow my focus and then draw a distinction. The narrowness concerns the type of pluralism I define: ethical. For reasons soon to be given, I shall refer to it as goods pluralism. Regarding the distinction, it is between weak and strong forms: weak goods pluralism (WGP) and strong goods pluralism (SGP).

In distinguishing between WGP and SGP, I am following Joseph Raz and Miles Tucker,[2] and in articulating their content, I will broadly adopt Raz's account. First, however, a quick word on my use of 'good' rather than the more common 'moral value'. In this book, good should be read as broadly as possible, as referring to anything 'valuable, worthy, admirable, of whatever kind or category'.[3] The term bad has an equal breadth. The reason for my choice of terms is simple but important. The words we use can often smuggle into the premises of our arguments more or less concrete answers to controversial ethical questions that definitions must help us tackle. Whereas moral and value can have humanist, Kantian, Marxian, economic, etc., connotations,[4] the highly formal good and bad do not suggest even the most abstract ethical commitments. True, in part II, I articulate the outlines of a strongly plural approach to property theory, which I then illustrate a little more concretely in part III, but I should not, through definitional fiat, improve my chances of persuading you to adopt this approach by loading the dice in favour of it.

Turning now to the idea of goods pluralism. I begin with WGP, identifying three conditions that must be met for it to be true, in the sense of it being a more accurate description of our world than theories that deny it. Then I identify four further conditions that must, in addition to the first three, be satisfied for SGP to be true in this descriptive sense.

Weak: Three Conditions

Following Raz in his deeply rich book *The Morality of Freedom*, we can say that for weak goods pluralism to be true, three conditions have to be met.[5] First, there must exist incompatible forms of life. Second, each form must be ethically acceptable. Third, the forms must be capable of being pursued for their own sake. In the main, I think that Raz's analysis of WGP is right, but there are parts of his account that require refinement or clarification.

The first condition provides that there must be different, incompatible forms of life. For Raz, forms are incompatible if 'they cannot normally be exemplified in the same life'.[6] He offers and contrasts two examples to illustrate this idea. Whereas an individual can be both an ideal family person and an ideal teacher, he explains, it is normally not possible to live a life of contemplation and a life of action. It is not immediately clear what is distinctive between the two cases. Before offering an explanation, we should address a definitional concern.

Why does Raz condition the truth of weak goods pluralism on the existence of incompatible forms of 'life'?[7] As he elsewhere explains,[8] this is not the only option when we analyse objects. We might consider incompatible actions, mental states, conditions, etc. If he intends to make this distinction, as it seems he does,[9] why privilege a whole life over its constitutive moments? This is not an idle question. As many since Hegel argue, whilst for individuals in particular moments situations can seem tragic, when later reflecting on the experiences in the context of their 'whole life', they can sometimes lose this quality. In time, when an individual looks back on their life, it can assume a degree of formal coherence, with its apparent conflicts resolving themselves within the temporally extended structure of their 'life story'. For Hegel, this narrative unity can even, in fact ideally should, define communal life. Narrative unity, however, is contentious. Not everyone agrees that having an 'integrated' life, as Raz puts it, is essentially or absolutely or lexically more important than the 'isolated' or 'immediate' experiences that constitute it.[10] Indeed, in the wake of Martin Heidegger, Michel Foucault, Jean Baudrillard, etc., many now resist the distancing that is internal to its cognitive and reflective perspective, rather privileging life's moments, situations, impressions or events, despite or even because of their hurly-burly nature.

That philosophers disagree on this issue, though, is my point. I am not arguing, nor did Raz,[11] that the narrative perspective always never or only sometimes reconciles momentary conflicts. My point is the more modest one that this is an open question. If so, it is also an open question that cannot be solved by definition, whether WGP is best defined by the incompatibility of wholes or constitutive parts. For this reason, it seems to me, both analytical prudence and humility require a definition that makes space for both: incompatibility that arises over whole lives (diachronic) and incompatibility that arises in those particular moments that constitute these lives (synchronic). In light of this, let us reformulate WGP's first condition: there must exist incompatible forms of experience, where the form of the incompatibility is such that the experiences cannot be realised diachronically or synchronically.

Distinguishing between incompatibility in moments and lifetimes helps to make sense of the distinction between Raz's two examples: why he says there is no incompatibility between being an ideal family person and a teacher, but there is between lives of contemplation and action. The suggestiveness of their distinction is rooted in their wording and in Raz's formulation of the first condition. Because incompatibility for Raz relates to forms of life, not its constitutive moments, a contemplative life appears to be incompatible with a life of action, but no incompatibility arises between the momentary experiences of teaching during the day and then caring for a child after dinner. If we were to alter the wording of these examples, however, we would reach the opposite conclusion. Just as someone committed to a life of teaching cannot commit to a family life, so a person can, as Marx memorably advocates, act during the day and then contemplate after dinner. These observations do not undermine Raz's argument for WGP, but they do suggest difficulties with his formulation of the first condition, reinforcing the reasons provided above for adopting the reformulated, more general and temporally open version just outlined.

Like Raz's, though, this formulation situates humans at the centre of good. Whilst his use of 'life' and examples suggests human life, my use of 'experience' might be read as referring only to human experiences. Delimiting our definition in this way is impermissible. Just like moral and value, which suggest ethical and political conclusions, the idea that what is good or bad is tied to humans smuggles in conclusions. Much of what matters only matters because there are creatures like us, either because we are the source of goodness or are required to complete its actualisation. The 'humanistic principle',[12] though, the idea that we are essential to the good, is a controversial one. More concretely, imagine two worlds. In both, no people exist. In one, the world is empty. In the other, there are savannas, packs of lions and herds of antelopes. If asked by a stranger, 'Which world has greater worth?' some will identify the latter. Even without humans to experience these forms, they will tell us, goods exist, such as life and sociality. Others will object that this answer is confused. To even talk about the good, they will say, is necessarily to situate the objects of this judgement in a human world. The first group, though, will see little problem here. They will point their interlocutor to the difference between epistemology and ontology – between knowing about life and sociality and the fact that they exist. Humans may be required for there to be knowledge of these forms, they will explain, but we are not necessary for these forms to exist at all – and so their argument will continue.

Given my purpose, which is to offer a vocabulary for analysing theorists who disagree about matters like this, prudence dictates that we must not exclude either position through definitional fiat. This will reap rewards in chapter 7, where I broach the idea of a 'protected area', but for now what matters is that our definition of WGP should allow for the possibility that good exists apart from our experience. To decentre humans in this way, to avoid the charge of anthropocentrism,[13] we must reformulate the first condition for the final time as follows:

> GP1: There exist incompatible forms of being – actions, mental states, conditions, processes, states of affairs, etc. – where the incompatibility is such that these forms cannot all be realised, either diachronically or synchronically.

Let us move to the second condition stated by Raz, as adjusted by GP1. Formally, this condition is straightforward:

GP2: The forms are ethically acceptable.

The second condition excludes forms like fascistic power, robber barons and torture. These are not acceptable; they are bads, so if their manifestation is incompatible, either diachronically or synchronically, is irrelevant to WGP's truth or falsity. What must be incompatible are ethically acceptable forms. Whilst sometimes it can appear easy to identify bads,[14] this is not always so. And as we shall see in part I, the identification of goods is often a source of controversy.

Like GP2, the third condition is not difficult to formulate:

GP3: Each form matters for its own sake.

The diverse forms of being (GP1) must not only be acceptable (GP2), they must be more than just instrumentally good. Each must itself be good. They must be good for their own sake, that is, all things being equal, their reality must be worth facilitating or respecting, regardless of any further good consequences they might bring. A world with these forms must be worthy of bringing into being, no matter whether anything else good, of whatever kind or category, either flows from or accompanies their actualisation.

What matters for its own sake, of course, is rather controversial. In part I, we consider some historically favoured possibilities: life, pleasure, preference-satisfaction and forms of expressive relational unity. In chapters 6 and 7, we consider a few more. And as will become plain, not only do our tradition's great philosophers articulate diverse accounts of the good, but the forms for which they plump are also incompatible. Nowhere do these differences play out more than in their resulting property theories.

Strong: Four More Conditions

In part I, we learn that Locke, Bentham, Hayek, Hegel and Marx are weak pluralists. Whilst they privilege particular forms above other ethical concerns (GP3), each recognises that internal to their concerns is a diversity that can generate incompatibility (GP1).

For both Hegel and Hayek, this diversity lies at the heart of their theories, in the forms of our conflicting particularities or preferences. Similarly, Locke knows that despite the preservation of life being his first law of nature, limited resources mean that sometimes feeding my family might come at the expense of yours. But as Marx understands, even if we broke the bonds of nature and eliminated social strife, there will still be times when we must choose. Time is finite: if I fish in the morning, I am left with the afternoon to hunt; if I rear cattle in the evening, then I must delay criticising Hegel until after dinner.

And even Bentham, the least secure of the philosophers who form the critical backbone of this book, and therefore the least tolerant of conflicts, admits that utility takes opposing forms: subsistence and security can conflict, so sometimes we must make calculated sacrifices. Indeed, you would struggle to find many who do not subscribe to WGP. It affirms an almost trivial truth: for reasons of time or space we must often choose between goods. Pluralism, however, can take a stronger form: SGP. To do so, four additional conditions must be satisfied: GP4 to GP7. Only when these further conditions exist, along with GP1 to GP3, can we properly describe our world as strongly plural.[15]

WGP says that there exist ethically acceptable (GP2) forms that matter for their own sake (GP3), which are spatio-temporally incompatible (GP1). Some pluralists, like Raz, think that in addition to these conditions, forms can sometimes display distinct 'virtues' or 'dispositions', like loyalty, courage, honesty or commitment.[16] When they do, their incompatibility is not spatio-temporal, it is logical, in the sense that these qualities function to exclude each other.

The proposition that good forms of being can exclude each other is essential to SGP. Strong pluralists claim more than the obvious but contingent truth that we often cannot do two things at once (GP1). Yes, it is true that we cannot whistle and drink at the same time; and it is also true as well as important that scarce resources can sometimes force agonising funding choices between, say, dialysis machines and HIV medicine. But these conflicts are contingent, for we can imagine spatio-temporal fixes, for example, a better publicly funded healthcare system, where choices of this kind do not arise. Not all forms of incompatibility are resolvable in this way. Incompatibility between forms is sometimes logical – necessary, universal – for they are characterised by what Raz dubs 'constitutive incommensurabilities'.[17] For a goods pluralist who takes this view, Isaiah Berlin is right: 'That we cannot have everything is a necessary, not a contingent, truth.'[18]

Apart from Raz, logical incompatibility has been broached by various theorists. Ruth Chang offers help in her remarks about 'individuation',[19] as does Tucker who notes that certain forms cannot be analysed in the terms that we use to analyse others.[20] Similarly, Chantal Mouffe talks about the 'constitutive outside',[21] that is, some forms are 'by definition incompatible' and that it is 'exclusion' that constitutes each form.[22] There are also insightful remarks by Bernard Williams,[23] John Gray[24] and Judith Butler.[25] For clarity and depth, though, I have learnt the most from Charles Taylor. In his work, but especially in his *Sources of the Self*, he provides concrete descriptions of diverse forms, revealing what makes them 'qualitatively distinct'.[26] When Raz talks about forms displaying incompatible virtues, we must, as the section in his book concerning 'social forms',[27] which he leverages in his account of constitutive incommensurabilities,[28] suggests, interpret him as employing something like Taylor's concept of qualitative distinctiveness.

Whilst all qualities matter when determining whether forms are incompatible, it might clarify things if we focus on qualities that often conflict: modes, attitudes, concepts or categories. Taylor and Raz's point is that forms can exist in incompatible modes, display incompatible attitudes and be understood through and in incompatible concepts or categories. Put formally:

> GP4: The forms are logically incompatible, constituted by mutually exclusive qualities, e.g., (a) modes of existence; (b) attitudes; or (c) concepts or categories.

In chapters 6 and 7, we see that because forms exist as wholes, as the ensembles of qualities that constitute them, the existence of (a) or (b) or (c) can satisfy GP4. For now, though, let us contrast forms that are incompatible in all three ways. Like Hegel and Marx, in whose dialectics Taylor's idea of qualitative distinctiveness is rooted,[29] let us contrast love and markets,[30] for now putting aside the possibility that markets might only have instrumental goodness.

On their accounts of love, when in love, you are connected with another. In the idiom of GP4, its initial mode of existence (a) is internal or subjective, for it is experienced as an emotion. Your being-towards your beloved is such that you vest significance in their desires or ends, in that you want them satisfied or realised for their own sake, not for any reasons external to your relation with them. So, a loving relation is also constituted by a particular attitude (b): the commitment to helping satisfy and realise another's desires and ends. You are committed not because this might promote your own interests, but because you share their interests. Whilst their having a particular desire or end might be useful to you, to love them is to internalise their desires and ends as your own. Therefore, love is also constituted by an immediate and non-instrumental relation between persons, for it is through and in these concepts or categories (c) that you understand your relation with those whom you love: it is how you perceive, feel, think, judge, and so on, when in love. Each of these constitutive qualities, which on their own mean little but together function to constitute the relational form of love, excludes those that form markets. First, markets cannot just be subjective: it is only through and in the externalisation of desires or ends that they come into being. So, their mode of existence (a) is objective. Second, they can only exist if desires or ends conflict. Instead of sharing desires or ends, I approach you as the bearer of conflicting ones: I oppose you and you oppose me, for in the act of exchange we adopt a competitive attitude (b). Third, in a market, we relate instrumentally, for we truck, barter and exchange not for the joy that can arise when being-with another, but because we hope that it will enable and mediate a good external to the relation, for example, profit. So, the market is formed through and in a particular understanding, that is, concepts and categories (c), which include instrumentality and mediated value.

In summary, love and markets are constituted by incompatible modes (subjective/objective), attitudes (share/compete), and concepts or categories (non-instrumental/instrumental). To refer to incompatibility as logical is to observe that qualities are mutually exclusive. With these forms, it is not that we do not have enough time or space to realise both. Rather, when *in* love, you cannot *be* a market actor. In part II, we describe the incompatible qualities that constitute diverse forms, many of which are not, as the market might be, just instrumentally good but matter for their own sake (GP3). Recognising this conflict, though, does not take us far beyond WGP. This should be expected, since our descriptions of love and markets were Hegel and Marx's, who recognise this conflict but are weak goods pluralists. In chapter 4, we reveal how their responses to GP4 divide them, but sketching them here will help to reveal the content of SGP's fifth condition.

For Marx, whilst markets were initially necessary to facilitate the technological development and social organisation by means of which we can free ourselves from nature's yoke, their value was only instrumental. They did not matter for their own sake (GP3). Since reaching the stage of potential freedom, though, they have lost even this utility. Now, markets just frustrate freedom's actualisation, so their continued existence is bad. Living in the present, therefore, faced with the logical conflict between love and markets, Marx denies the market's acceptability (GP2). Despite recognising GP4, with his initial instrumentalisation and later rejection of markets, he remains a weak pluralist. Hegel offers a more challenging response. He does not escape conflict (GP4) by denying the acceptability of either member of the pair. For him, love and markets are acceptable (GP2) and matter for their own sake (GP3), since each is a necessary form through and in which 'spirit' unfolds into its ideal form: the ethical state. Neither exists for the sake of something else, as markets do for Hayek, for whom they are informational systems that facilitate our preference-satisfaction. For Hegel, both love and the market are expressive, constitutive embodiments of the relational whole that he calls spirit. Rather than rejecting the acceptability of one form (Marx) or reducing either to the role of instrumental good (Hayek), Hegel says that both of them matter for their own sake, but denies that either is ultimately good.

Essential here is Hegel's distinction, drawn by Raz too,[31] between those goods that matter for their own sake (GP3) and ultimate good. With an ultimate good, the source of its mattering for its own sake does not emanate or 'derive',[32] as Raz puts it, from a logically distinct form of being.[33] The source of its being good lies in itself, rather than from its constitutive 'contribution to something else',[34] for example, spirit, by virtue of which we explain or justify its goodness.[35] Therefore, for SGP to be true, it is not enough that there exist incompatible (GP1, GP4) acceptable (GP2) forms, each of which matters for its own sake (GP3). A fifth condition, the nature of which we find in both Hegel and Raz, must also be met:

> GP5: Each form is ultimately good, for the source of its being good lies in itself.

We have nearly arrived at SGP. Two conditions remain, each concerning ranking:

> GP6: The forms cannot be ranked, at the level of theory, relative to each person or group or situation.

> GP7: The forms cannot be ranked, at the level of theory, by any impersonal criterion that holds for all persons and situations alike.

The critical part of the conditions is their qualifying clauses: they reject theoretical ranking. SGP rejects both relativistic and universal ethical theories. The reason why has three parts. First, SGP rejects propositions that take the form: whilst X is good for person/group/situation A, Y is good for person/group/situation B. Second, SGP rejects propositions that take the form: only Z is good for all persons and situations alike. The reason why SGP rejects propositions that take these two forms is that it claims, without distinction between persons or situations, that these diverse (GP1, GP4) forms of being are all acceptable (GP2), important for their own sake (GP3), and ultimately good (GP5). Third, and this is our focus below, SGP rejects propositions that these forms can be ranked by theory – first X, then Y, then Z, etc. – for each person, group or situation (GP6), or for all persons and situations alike (GP7).

Neither GP6 nor GP7, though, denies that we can concretely rank forms. This is fortunate, as we often make such judgements.[36] Right now, having been in a 3-week lockdown for 14 weeks, it is plain to me that I would rather be in the pub with friends than sitting in my lounge typing this sentence. Further, my ranking of the joy of beer-soaked friendship over self-study or intellectual clarity hardly feels mysterious: ordinarily, we just judge what should be done in a given situation. Even when this inconspicuous enterprise of judging breaks down, forcing us to detach ourselves from the activity and think more formally about the facts, we know how to go about deciding: we identify the options, evaluate the reasons for and against each, identify the availability or efficacy of the relevant means, and then just decide based on our evaluation of the facts.

Given all this, what is meant by the claim that we cannot theoretically rank ultimate (GP5) but incompatible (GP4) forms? To answer, we must introduce the concept of incomparability. Whilst the best account of this concept is disputed, the outcome of this dispute is not relevant here.[37] So, I will follow Raz by defining it as follows: there is incomparability if it is not true that X or Y is better or worse than the other, nor true that they are equal.[38]

To grasp the concept's significance, we must clarify it in three ways. First, the two judgements in the definition are false not because we lack clarity about X or Y or other facts, say, the effects of choosing one.[39] To claim incomparability is to assert the falsity of the comparisons. So, falsity cannot be due to vague, incomplete or imprecise definitions, nor due to lack of data. It cannot be due to conceptual or epistemic defect because to claim incomparability is to deny the truth of the ranking. Incomparability, in this field's idiom, is not indeterminacy[40] or ignorance.[41] Second, it does not refer to small 'gaps' between forms.[42] Struggling to rank forms concretely because their constellation of qualitative and/or quantitative differences frustrates the drawing of a meaningful distinction and ranking is another problem. Practical reason might 'run out' here, but this issue is not one of incomparability. Judgements of rough equality or parity,[43] in this field's idiom, pertain to circumstances in which concrete rankings seem especially 'hard'. Incomparability, contrarily, in the sense that I am using it,[44] concerns theoretical, not practical, reason, and it does not say that the ranking of forms is hard, it says that it is false. Third, to say that one cannot say whether X or Y is better, worse or equal, is not to say that no judgements are possible. Incomparability concerns 'abstract' judgement.[45] To claim incomparability is to say we cannot decide, at the level of theory, if X or Y is better or worse or equal. It does not say we cannot decide this in a particular context. As Raz explains,[46] it is intelligible to say that friendship and money are incomparable and to say that in a particular context we should pursue the latter and sacrifice the former.[47] Incomparability concerns theory's limits. It claims that we cannot rank forms at the level of ideas, not that we can never rationally decide between them. For as Bernard Williams puts it, 'theory and prejudice' are not the only options when deciding,[48] there is also practical reason.[49]

To see why theoretical reason cannot rank forms, recall GP4: logical incompatibility. Often, there is something internal to one form (X, love) that frustrates the actualisation of another form (Y, markets). This 'something' is that each is constituted by conflicting modes, attitudes, etc. So, logically, we cannot apply the conflicting ensembles of qualities that constitute each form to the same relation: when you enter the market you cease to be a lover. In large part, this book is about unpacking the theoretical and practical implications of this idea for property. One implication for theory is to expose its limits. Incompatibility means theory cannot tell us that one ultimate (GP5) form is better nor can it judge them equal. When it does, when it prescribes, its claims are false, not because of indeterminacy, ignorance, etc., but rather because of the incompatibility (GP4) of the ultimate (GP5) forms that it claims to order. Together, GP4 and GP5 generate GP6 and GP7, for they mean that there is nothing, qualitatively speaking, either between or outside of the forms on which one could rationally base their abstract ranking. Let me explain.

Because the forms are logically incompatible – constituted by mutually exclusive qualitative ensembles of modes, attitudes, concepts or categories – they cannot be analysed and understood in one another's terms. Their definitions exclude each other. This means that their constitutive or formal relation is defined negatively: it is one of exclusion. Whilst the relation is essentially one of exclusion, because each of the forms is good there is what Ruth Chang calls a 'covering value' or 'covering consideration' that relates them, namely, 'goodness'.[50] When the forms that exclude each other are ultimately good, however, this covering value is absolutely abstract. Recall that, as ultimates, the source of their being good lies in themselves, rather than deriving from something else in respect of which they are constitutively contributory parts. In other words, their covering value of goodness is populated entirely by the forms themselves.[51] For this reason, the forms lack a 'positive value relation'.[52] Whilst they may share certain qualities, as relational forms they each exist as wholes – as the ensembles of their constitutive qualities – which means they also exclude each other as wholes. This is why their relation is negative: on entering the market, you cease to be a lover, even if the relations share some qualities. Because they exclude each other as wholes and also exist as their own sources of goodness, there is nothing, qualitatively speaking, between or outside of them on which rationally to base their relative evaluation as regards their covering value of goodness. Their abstract ranking, therefore, is incoherent (GP6, GP7).

We might make this argument easier to understand if we consider how people who advocate what each takes to be ultimate but incompatible goods often seem to talk past each other. Since the vocabularies – the ensembles of qualities – that constitute each form are mutually exclusive, in a sense they do talk past each other. For so long as she insists on 'talking money' and he only speaks 'the language of love', they cannot occupy the same conceptual space and so cannot make sense of each other's views. Because the argument of each cannot be translated into the language of the other, together they become lost in translation. Hence the appeal of 'silencing the enemy'. Delegitimising another's language, removing their platform or obliging them to kneel, will often be easier than the persuasion that is necessary to move them to enter into one's own world; and it is always easier than, as Heidegger puts it, 'keeping silent', really 'listening' to and so 'hearing' them,[53] and thereby opening oneself up to the possibility of inhabiting, and therefore constituting the space necessary for making sense of, their apparently unthinkable one.

If SGP is true, then incomparability, at least with theoretical reason, is true. With ultimate but incompatible goods, neither X nor Y is better or worse, nor are they equal. Put differently, the two relational forms are incommensurable but radically so,[54] for the inability to measure them against each other is rooted in their ultimate, qualitatively distinct natures. Without providing the person evaluating a context, which theory cannot do, without situating them in concrete space and time, where reasons for action can arise and take hold, it makes as much sense to commend love over markets as it does to commend chalk over cheese. An evaluative context is essential, and different contexts often urge upon different people different judgements. Without first grounding options in reality, without first knowing, say, if we are before a cheese or a chalkboard, or are intolerant or inclined to what lies before us, it makes no sense to rank them: personally relative to an abstract particular (GP6), or impersonally and universally in respect of an abstract all (GP7).

As I noted at the start of this chapter, I recognise that this conceptual analysis is rather dense and abstract. Hopefully, later chapters, in particular chapters 6 and 7, will illuminate the meaning of SGP. And, of course, many do not agree with its initial premise (GP1 to GP3), its more radical form (GP4), its significance (GP5) or its conclusion (GP6, GP7). We address some objections in chapter 5. For now, though, let us conclude this section by providing the concept of strong goods pluralism with an integrated definition:

> SGP: There are diverse, ethically acceptable forms of being, each important for their own sake, but also ultimately good, which forms are logically incompatible, that theory cannot rank, either relative to each person or group or situation, or by some impersonal criterion that is applicable to all.

PROPERTY: RIGHTS TO OR IN OBJECTS

Even more than pluralism, the concept of property is contested. It has evolved over time and is a standard subject of dispute amongst lawyers and philosophers. Despite trying to avoid it, South Africa's Constitutional Court has not escaped this controversy. In *Shoprite Checkers*, a case from that Court, we find three definitions. Each has merits: Froneman J stresses property's functional nature;[55] Moseneke DCJ worries about any definition that treats every interest as property;[56] and Madlanga J reasons that property is constituted by 'something', that is, rights, 'in hand'.[57] Below, I argue that we should, for reasons similar to those that informed our definition of pluralism, adopt a definition that does justice to each. Bar a quick adjustment and two lengthy clarifications, it has already been provided by Jeremy Waldron.

An Ecumenical Definition

For Waldron, at its most abstract, property refers to those rules that regulate the 'allocation' of objects that can satisfy some 'human need or want'.[58] All our talk about property involves asking 'who is to have access to which resources for what purposes and when'.[59] This definition reflects each concern in each judgement in *Shoprite Checkers*. It ties the concept of property to a function: to satisfy human needs or wants. It does not extend the concept to all conceivable interests since the rights to vote or to assemble, for example, do not concern objects but activities. And it makes the point that property refers to those objects in which we can have rights, like access. Despite its initial merits, there is an aspect of this definition that we must excise: its latent anthropocentrism. It might eventually turn out that we only want property to serve the needs and wants of humans, but we should not assume this from the outset, for doing this would burden our definition with a controversial ethical claim, something we must studiously avoid.

This adjustment made, let us now clarify it. This definition of property has two basic features. First, internal to the concept of property is the concept of right.[60] Second, the concept of property refers to objects. Therefore, taken together, when we refer to property, we are always referring to the rights that attach to or obtain in objects.

The nexus between rights and objects is central to this definition. Waldron distinguishes the rights that attach to or obtain in objects, and the more general rules regulating their use. Not all of the latter qualify as the former.[61] The right to use a kitchen knife or a laptop, for example, is a property right, but the rules prohibiting killing or defaming others with them are not. Waldron is right in the sense that if we are to give property its own meaning and avoid dissolving it into the general concept of rule, as Moseneke DCJ feared, we have to distinguish those rights that attach to or obtain in objects from the background rules that structure all interpersonal relations. Not all these structuring rules are essentially concerned with objects, and only the latter can ever qualify as property. Formally put:

> Property: Rights that attach to or obtain in objects.

This definition is highly formal. This is deliberate. As Marx notes, we often find 'smuggled' into definitions the allocative property schemes that a defining theorist thinks best.[62] As we shall see in chapter 10, this is the difficulty with the method of Froneman J, who defines property not just functionally, but by the function that is embodied in his model of the person. If we are to reject the method of models, however, we must also reject definitions of property that, through 'verbal legislation',[63] purport to resolve the conflicts between diverse functions.

Conscious of this, let us quickly stipulate six qualities that recommend this definition. First, it does not limit what can count as property to material objects or treat rights in 'things' as primary. On this definition, if it can be an 'object of' regulation,[64] it can be property, which means that it can include corporeal and incorporeal objects and also rights *in rem* and *in personam*. Second, it allows for individual, collective and communal property. Third, it does not favour those theorists who think that property is good due to its instrumental value or those who think that it is required to be a person at all. Fourth, by referring to rights that 'attach to' and 'obtain in' objects, it is not dependent on a realist or an anti-realist ontology. Fifth, it does not exclude particular conceptions of property by, say, equating property with commodities. And finally, it does not fix whether the rights must be *de jure*, *de facto*, customary, moral, etc. in nature.

From a South African perspective, would such an inclusive definition not frustrate necessary regulatory state measures and hinder property transformation?[65] No. Just because something fits the definition of property does not mean that we cannot alter the rights that constitute it as such. If this alteration is a deprivation, provided it is effected through a general law and is not arbitrary, we can deprive at will.[66] And as I explain in chapter 10, if a law expropriates, provided it is for a public purpose or is in the public interest and is accompanied by just compensation, we are again free to do as we will.[67] Yes, we often disagree about what is arbitrary or just. But just as we must not avoid conflicts about the functions of property by relying on models, we should not reject an analytically useful definition merely because we want to avoid difficult judgements about what is worth protecting. We cannot escape making judgements. So, we will either do this under cover of darkness, by stipulating abstract definitions, or openly when evaluating diverse courses of action. And since concepts are tools that we use to grapple with difficult ethical questions, not weapons for bludgeoning people with whom we disagree, we should embrace an ecumenical definition of property that strives to be ethically abstemious and explanatorily wide-ranging.

In short, what is property and what property is worth protecting are different questions. Each must be answered on its own terms. The result of conflating and confusing them, as Marx puts it, can be nothing but 'an illusion of metaphysics or of jurisprudence'.[68]

Hohfeld and the Concept of Right

Let us turn to the second clarification of our Waldronian definition. Internal to this concept of property is the concept of right. To make sense of the argument in this book, we need an adequate grasp of its meaning. For our purposes, sufficient work on this issue has already been done, so we can be relatively brief. For the same reasons informing our analysis of pluralism and our decision to adopt a Waldronian definition of property – ethical abstemiousness and explanatory breadth – we must adopt W. N. Hohfeld's concept of right,[69] as modified by Leif Wenar.[70]

The concept of right is internally complex. It has four components or incidents, which alone or together describe different relational forms. To say that somebody has a right might mean that they have a liberty, claim, power or immunity, or some combination of these distinct Hohfeldian incidents. To complicate matters, whilst each incident is distinct in the sense that it can exist by itself, each incident also has a relational pair within the larger structure of right. Whereas we can pair liberty with claim, power can be paired with immunity. The way that these members of each pair relate is as jural correlatives and jural opposites.[71] Again, this is rather abstract. To give it a more tangible meaning, let us begin with the first pair of incidents: liberty and claim.

What relates the two incidents within the larger internal structure of right is that each is what H. L.A Hart calls a 'primary rule'.[72] A primary rule functions to require a person to perform or to refrain from performing a particular action. As such, the concept that unites the incidents is duty. Let us unpack this further, focusing first on liberties. Liberties, sometimes called either privileges or licences, have two distinct types.[73] The first type is an exemption: it permits people to do what they have a general duty not to do.[74] The second type is a discretion: it entitles people to choose whether to perform a particular action. The correlative of liberty is no-claim and the opposite of liberty is duty. By way of illustration:

Exemption:

1. If X has a licence to sell alcohol from her store, then Y has no-claim that X not sell alcohol from her store.
2. If the licence of X is not renewed by regulator Z, then X has a duty not to sell alcohol from her store.

Discretion:

1. If X is entitled to paint her house whatever colour she chooses, then Y has no-claim that X does not paint her house purple.
2. If body corporate Z only allows houses to be painted blue or green, then X has a duty not to paint her house purple.

Having sketched the nature of liberties, let us now turn to the second Hohfeldian incident: claim. A claim can have distinct functions: perform, provide or protect. The correlative of claim is duty, and its opposite is no-claim. By way of illustration:

Perform:

1. If X has a claim that Parliament enacts legislation that facilitates her access to land, then Parliament has a duty to do so.
2. If Parliament's duty does not include ensuring acquisition of land rights, then X has no-claim that Parliament enact legislation to this effect.

Provide:

1. If X has a claim that Parliament enact legislation to ensure that X's tenure in land is made legally secure, then Parliament has a duty to provide X with these legal rights.
2. If Parliament's duty can be fulfilled either by providing rights in land or by adopting comparable measures, then X has no-claim that Parliament provide her with any legal rights in land.

Protect:

1. If X has a claim not to be deprived of her property arbitrarily, then Y has a duty not to deprive X of her property in this manner.
2. If a bill before Parliament would rationally deprive X of her property, then X has no-claim that Parliament not enact the bill into law.

Liberties and claims require people to perform or to refrain from performing actions. The other incidents have a different function, for powers and immunities are 'secondary rules',[75] in Hart's sense. As 'higher-order' incidents,[76] they determine how, if or when a right is created or altered. As Wenar explains, they are 'rights over rights'.[77] So, whereas the concept that unites liberty and claim is duty, the concept that unites power and immunity is authority. Let us unpack each of the incidents in turn.

Power refers to the ability within an existing set of rights to alter rights held by you or held by another. To have power is to have authority. It is exercised by creating, waiving or annulling rights.[78] Power can be non-discretionary or discretionary. Its correlative is liability (to the rights being altered) and its opposite is disability (to alter rights).[79] By way of illustration:

Create:

1. If Parliament enacts a law entitling persons who satisfy prescribed conditions to apply for and obtain an exemption to mine, then regulator X is liable to grant an exemption to Y if Y applies and meets the prescribed conditions.
2. If the exemption may only be granted after an environmental impact assessment, then regulator X is disabled from granting the exemption absent an assessment.

Waive:

1. If X may waive its claim against Y that Y transfer to X rights in land, then Y is liable to its duty to transfer these rights being annulled.
2. If corporate entity X may not dispose of property without the consent of its members, then X is disabled from waiving these rights absent their consent.

Annul:

1. If X has the power to expropriate Y's property, then Y is liable to the exercise of this power.
2. If X may not expropriate Y's property absent the payment to Y of just and equitable compensation, then X is disabled from annulling Y's rights absent the payment of this compensation.

Immunities limit the scope of power. They serve a protective function against authority.[80] The correlative of immunity is disability and its opposite is liability. By way of illustration:

1. If X may not evict Y without first obtaining a court order, then Y has an immunity and X is saddled with a disability.
2. If regulator Z may restrict the types of business that can be conducted at X's house, then X is liable to the exercise of this power.

All this remains quite abstract, in no small part because whilst each of these Hohfeldian incidents has been articulated and illustrated separately, as I explained at the start of this section, they can and in practice often do exist in complex combinations, where more than one of them attaches to or obtains in objects. That said, I hope that this broad overview is sufficient to prepare the reader for the argument to come and that as this book proceeds, what I have outlined above will become more concrete. For in parts II and III, we shall see that an adequate grasp of the internal structure of the Hohfeldian concept of right is required to reveal the many incompatible demands made on property by ultimate (GP5) but incompatible (GP1, GP4) goods (GP2, GP3). Its relevance at this stage, however, is for our Waldronian definition of property. For to say that property refers to the rights that attach to or obtain in objects, is to say that it refers to the liberties, claims, powers and immunities that attach to or obtain in objects.

Equipped with this minimal and abstract vocabulary – weak and strong goods pluralism, and property – let us turn to our tradition.

NOTES

1. On bivalence, see Lee Braver, *A Thing of This World: A History of Continental Anti-Realism* (2007) 19–21.

2. Joseph Raz, *The Morality of Freedom* (1986) 395–97 and Miles Tucker, 'Two Kinds of Value Pluralism' 28(3) *Utilitas* (2016) 333.

3. Charles Taylor, *Sources of the Self: The Making of Modern Identity* (1989) 92.

4. This is not how it is used in Raz (n 2) 134–36, who uses it in the same sense that I am using the term 'good' (397).

5. Ibid., 395–96. My division differs from Raz's. I sit GP4 in SGP, but he treats 'display of distinct virtues' as part of WGP. Nothing turns on this, for as he notes, 'there are further ways of refining and subdividing them' (396).

6. Ibid., 395.

7. For other references to 'form of life' when discussing pluralism, see Raz (n 2) 133, 161–62, 401, 406–07 and 425. Other times he refers to 'style of life' (343, 371, 395 and 425).

8. Ibid., 288–94.

9. Ibid., 292–93.

10. Ibid., 292.

11. Ibid., 369–71.

12. Ibid., 194.

13. Charles Taylor, *The Ethics of Authenticity* (1991) 81–91.

14. The relative ease of identifying bads informs diverse traditions, for example, Judith N. Shklar, *Political Thought & Political Thinkers* (ed. Stanley Hoffmann, 1998) 3–20, Stuart Hampshire, *Justice is Conflict* (2000), and Raymond Geuss, *A World Without Why* (2014) 68–90.

15. Raz (n 2) 396–99.

16. Ibid., 353–57 and 397.

17. Ibid., 345–53. On logical versus contingent conflict, see Bernard Williams, *Problems of the Self, Philosophical Papers 1956–1972* (1973) 166–86.

18. Isaiah Berlin, *Liberty* (ed. Henry Hardy, 2002) 215.

19. Ruth Chang, 'Value Pluralism' in Wright, *International Encyclopedia of the Social & Behavioral Sciences* (2ed, 2015, vol. 25) 21.

20. Tucker (n 2) 338.

21. Chantal Mouffe, *The Democratic Paradox* (2000) 12, 21 and 32–33.

22. Chantal Mouffe, *The Return of the Political* (2005) 127.

23. Bernard Williams, *Ethics and the Limits of Philosophy* (2011) 174–75.

24. John Gray, *Two Faces of Liberalism* (2000).

25. Judith Butler, *Frames of War: When is Life Grievable?* (2016).

26. Taylor (n 3) 19–30 and 53–98.

27. Raz (n 2) 307–13. In addition to the 'symbolic significance' of 'attitudes', key to his analysis of constitutive incommensurability (345–53), social forms 'consist of shared beliefs, folklore, high culture, collectively shared metaphors and imagination, and so on' (311).

28. Ibid., 344–57.

29. Charles Taylor, 'Marxism and Empiricism' in *British Analytic Philosophy* (eds. B Williams and A Montefiore, 1966) 227–46.

30. A similar task is performed in Raz (n 2) 345–53.

31. Ibid., 177–81 and 200.

32. Ibid., 177–78 and 397.

33. My thinking here was assisted by Christine Korsgaard, 'Two Distinctions of Goodness' 92(2) *Philosophical Review* (April, 1983) 169, dealing with Kant's 'good will'.

34. Raz (n 2) 177 fn 1.

35. Ibid., 200.

36. Ibid., 336.

37. Ruth Chang, 'Introduction' in *Incommensurability, Incomparability, and Practical Reason* (ed. Ruth Chang, 1997) 4–7. I adopt the 'Trichotomy Thesis', to which she adds a fourth relation: 'on par' (4–5 and 25–27). For the same reasons provided in respect to the Trichotomy Thesis, theory also cannot rank forms as being 'on par'.

38. Raz (n 2) 322.

39. Ibid., 323–38.

40. Ruth Chang, 'Are Hard Cases Vague Cases?' in *Value Incommensurability Ethics, Risk, and Decision-Making* (eds. Henrik Andersson and Anders Herlitz, 2022) 50–64.

41. Ignorance can be contingent or conceptual, for example, there is no 'common unit of value', in which case incommensurability is 'cardinal' (Ruth Chang, 'Parity, Imprecise Comparability and the Repugnant Conclusion' 82(2) *Theoria* (2016) 182–214, 186–89).

42. Raz (n 2) 328–31.

43. Ruth Chang, 'Hard Choices' 3(1) *Journal of the American Philosophical Association* (2017) 1–21.

44. My concern is with a subset of incommensurability, that is, its constitutive form (Raz (n 2) 345–53).

45. Ibid., 336.

46. Ibid., 352–53. Ruth Chang, 'Against Constitutive Incommensurability or Buying and Selling Friends' *Philosophical Issues*, Vol. 11, *Social, Political, and Legal Philosophy* (2001) 33–60, 41–48, criticises Raz from the perspective of practical reason. It does not extend to my argument, for my concern is theoretical reason.

47. Raz (n 2) 340–35.

48. Williams (n 23) 103–32.

49. For a defence by a strong pluralist, see Gray (n 24) 35–68.

50. Chang (n 37) 7.

51. Raz (n 2) 344.

52. Ruth Chang, 'Are Hard Choices Cases of Incomparability?' *Philosophical Issues*, Vol. 22, Action Theory (2012) 106–26, 111–13.

53. Martin Heidegger, *Being and Time* (tr. J Macquarrie and E Robinson, 1962) 203–10.

54. The terms are used interchangeably by Raz (n 2) 322.

55. *Shoprite Checkers (Pty) Ltd v MEC for Economic Development, Eastern Cape and Others* 2015 (6) SA 125 (CC) paras. 57–71.

56. Ibid., paras. 104–115.

57. Ibid., para. 143.

58. Jeremy Waldron, *The Right to Private Property* (1988) 31.

59. Ibid., 32.

60. Ibid., 26–30.

61. Ibid., 32–33.

62. GFCPE 87.

63. Raz (n 2) 166.

64. *Ethekwini Municipality v Mounthaven (Pty) Ltd* 2019 (4) SA 394 (CC) para. 19.

65. *Law Society of South Africa and Others v Minister for Transport and Another* 2011 (1) SA 400 (CC) para. 83.

66. Section 25(1) of the Constitution.

67. Sections 25(2) and (3) of the Constitution.

68. PP 168.

69. Wesley Newcomb Hohfeld 'Some Fundamental Legal Conceptions as Applied in Judicial Reasoning' 23 *Yale Law Journal* (1913) 16.

70. Leif Wenar, 'The Nature of Rights' 33(3) *Philosophy and Public Affairs* (2005) 223–52.

71. Hohfeld (n 69) 30.

72. H.L.A. Hart, *The Concept of Law* (3ed, 2012) 80–81 and 91–94.

73. Wenar (n 70) 226.

74. In *Ex parte President of the Republic of South Africa: In re Constitutionality of the Liquor Bill* 2000 (1) SA 732 (CC) para. 55, this is called 'permission'. And in *Shoprite Checkers* (n 55) paras. 14, 26 and 122, it is called a 'bare permission'.

75. Hart (n 72) 80–81 and 94–98.

76. Wenar (n 70) 230.

77. Ibid., 233.

78. Ibid., 231.

79. Leif Wenar, 'Rights' in *The Stanford Encyclopaedia of Philosophy* (ed. Edward N Zalta, Spring 2021), available at https://plato.stanford.edu/entries/rights/; and Quentin du Plessis, 'A Hohfeldian Analysis of the Bill of Rights' 139(3) *South African Law Journal* (2022) 577, 579.

80. Wenar (n 70) 232.

Part I

THE ANTHROPOLOGICAL QUESTION

In her *Lectures on Kant's Political Philosophy*, Hannah Arendt writes: 'You all know the famous three questions whose answer, according to Kant, constituted the proper business of philosophy: What can I know? What ought I to do? What may I hope?'[1] Arendt then later remarks that in his lectures Kant would often add a fourth 'anthropological' question that 'sums up' these first three questions: 'What is Man?'[2]

The humanist conviction that we can derive answers to questions like 'What ought I to do?' or 'What is to be done?' if we first have an answer to this more 'ultimate' anthropological one,[3] has structured much modern thought about ethical and political questions. As a starting point for reflection, both critical and constructive, anthropology informs schools ranging from Kantians to Hegelians, Marxians, utilitarians and pluralists, and it is equally at home in our older traditions, like liberalism, communitarianism, conservativism, and romanticism, as it is in our modern ones, analytic and continental.[4] For example, Marx asserts that: 'To be radical is to grasp matters at the root. But for man the root is man himself.'[5] J. S. Mill remarks: 'The first question in regard to any man of speculation is, what is his theory of human life?'[6] Isaiah Berlin asks rhetorically who can seriously 'deny that political problems, e.g. what men and groups can or should be or do, depend logically and directly on what man's nature is taken to be?'[7] And whereas Ellen Meiksins Wood, Roger Scruton and Jeremy Waldron make plain that questions about the nature of persons sit at the heart of the Western tradition of political and ethical thought,[8] Chantal Delsol laments their eclipse in more recent thought.[9]

What does this have to do with property? Our traditional 'idioms of moral conduct', Michael Oakeshott observes, are distinguished less by what they tell us what we should do than by their 'interpretations of what we in fact are'.[10] By this, Oakeshott means that if we are to understand why different theorists prescribe particular norms, we will do well not to look at what the norms require, but rather at the more abstract set of conceptions or understandings that structure, guide or animate their prescription of these particular norms. More than this, we can best categorise or distinguish philosophers if we look to how they think human beings essentially relate, or but for some contingent fact would relate, with themselves, others and the world. We must look to these interpretations of man, in Kant's idiom, since they structure our judgements and evaluations about past, present or future, exerting power over our more context-dependent thoughts about what has been done, is being done or should be done.

So put the relation between anthropology and property might be familiar. As others observe, contemporary debates about property, say, between liberals and communitarians, can readily be understood as being rooted in disagreements about what we in fact are.[11] Far less has been said, though, about the debts that these conflicting 'discourses' or 'narratives' owe to tradition,[12] and little if any progress has been made on how to deal meaningfully with the interpretative conflicts that arise when property is dealt with anthropologically.[13] The ahistorical nature of most present-day theory and lack of meaningful theoretical progress is not contingently related. If a historical awareness can dissolve the prejudices of the present,[14] then an ignorance of history can entrench the present's parochialism. Part I partly addresses this historical deficit through criticism of our theoretical tradition. Drawing on this criticism, part II proposes a way to deal with interpretative conflict. The proposed solution is a therapeutic one: we must *let go* of the felt need to interpret, ontologically and prescriptively, what we in fact are.

In part I, we shall explore two Oakeshottian categories: individualistic and communalistic. In each, we identify more concrete interpretations of man or models of the person. In chapters 2 and 3, we consider three individualistic models: Locke, Bentham and Hayek's. In chapter 4, we then contrast Hegel and Marx's communalistic models. In doing so, my purpose is to demonstrate that each of them allocates property according to their models of the person – their interpretations of what we in fact are.

Before I begin with Locke, let us state formally the meaning of model, in its anthropological and prescriptive sense. My original inspiration is Berlin,[15] but the same idea can be derived from otherwise rather different thinkers, from otherwise rather different traditions.[16] For Berlin, and so for us, the concept of a model is capacious. The style of any particular model, whether expressed in poetry, prose, symbols, imagery, mathematics, and so on, is not important for our purposes. Nor is it important for our purposes to distinguish between the origins of a model. Often, whether a model is derived from metaphysics, politics, sociology, linguistics, and so on, will be quite important. In part I, however, origins do not matter. More important is what each model, despite their diverse styles and origins, shares in common. Formally, each is defined by the following triadic anthropological structure:

> AS1: Each identifies particular qualities of or facts about persons that they deem worthy of ethical concern, for their own sake and/or for instrumental reasons.
>
> AS2: They abstract from and privilege – i.e., they essentialise, ontologise – the facts or qualities, by, for example,[17] making a single fact or quality absolute, or making multiple ones internally coherent, or abstractly ordering them.
>
> AS3: Equipped with an abstraction, each prescribes structural and/or actual allocations of property in a way that facilitates or frustrates their privileged object(s) of concern.

To say that modern thought about property is structured by the anthropological question is to say that the theories that still shape concrete rights-allocations, no matter their fierce disagreements, share this triadic anthropological structure. Despite their many important theoretical and practical differences, Locke, Bentham, Hayek, Hegel and Marx unite in their use of models, since each of them prescribes property according to AS1 to AS3.

This interpretative claim requires much work to make it persuasive. In part, this is because the interpretations provided below, though faithful to key texts and therefore defensible on this basis, strive to articulate the basic structures of these theories. For this reason, they will inevitably gloss over nuances that specialists will think, for the most part rightly so, rather important. In response to scholarly concerns of this nature, I can only say that I hope that what is lost is compensated by any insights that are gained. A second reason persuasion is required is less a scholarly one than it is rooted in one purpose of this book: to persuade you to let go of our traditional way of thinking about property. To realise this end, it is necessary to deflate the systematic, prescriptive property theories advocated by the still decisive founders of this tradition. In doing this, I hope to disclose their contingent and so stipulated natures, and therefore their 'limited value',[18] as Nietzsche puts it in a related context, to any effort to build an adequate theory of property. To concerns that take this second form, I can only answer by pleading that deflating our model philosophers in this way seems to me to be a point in favour of the approach that is advocated in this book. John Gardner, as always, puts the point well:

> Philosophy is not the art of compiling as many little thoughts as possible into as few big thoughts as possible, but the art of wearing every thought down to its rightful little size and then keeping it in its rightful little place. So [our mission is] *unbundling*: separating out disparate thoughts that have often been regarded, mistakenly, as part of some package deal.[19]

In chapters 2 to 4, we criticise or unbundle Locke, Bentham, Hayek, Hegel and Marx. We do this not to reject them entirely and then substitute something new in their place. This would not be a reasonable ambition. Far more reasonable than supposing that one or more of them was 'entirely mistaken',[20] is to recognise instead that whilst each got something or even many things right, all then proceeded to obscure what ultimately (GP5) matters (GP3) by letting their important little truths outgrow their rightful little places.

NOTES

1. Hannah Arendt, *Lectures on Kant's Political Philosophy* (1989) 12.
2. Ibid., 20.
3. Hannah Arendt, *The Promise of Politics* (2005) 33–34.
4. Stephen Mulhall and Adam Swift, *Liberals & Communitarians* (1992) and Daniel Chernilo, *Debating Humanity* (2017).
5. CCHPR 137.
6. J.S. Mill, 'Bentham' in *Essays on Ethics, Religion and Society* (Collected Works of John Stuart Mill, Vol. 10) 94.
7. Isaiah Berlin, *Concepts and Categories: Philosophical Essays* (ed. Henry Hardy, 1999) 167.
8. Ellen Meiksins Wood, *A Social History of Western Political Thought* (2022) 3, Roger Scruton, *On Human Nature* (2015) 109 and *The Soul of the World* (2014) 72, and Jeremy Waldron, *One Another's Equals: The Basis of Human Equality* (2017) 84–127.
9. Chantal Delsol, *Icarus Fallen: The Search for Meaning in an Uncertain World* (tr. R. Dick, 2003) 121–37.
10. Michael Oakeshott, *Hobbes on Civil Association* (1975) 81. See also his *Morality and Politics in Modern Europe* (ed. Shirley Robin, Letwin, 1993) 16–28.
11. Charles Taylor, *Philosophical Papers: Volume 2, Philosophy and the Human Sciences* (1985) 289–317, Shlomo Avineri and Avner de-Shalit (eds.), *Communitarianism and Individualism* (1992), Mulhall and Swift (n 4), Margaret Jane-Radin, *Reinterpreting Property* (1993), Joseph William Singer, *Entitlement: The Paradoxes of Property* (2000), and Lorna Fox O'Mahony and Marc L. Roark, *Squatting and the State: Resilient Property in an Age of Crisis* (2022).
12. The great exception, who I shall consider in chapter 5, is Michael Walzer, *Spheres of Justice: A Defense of Pluralism and Equality* (1983). For a more recent exception, see Fox O'Mahony and Roark (n 11) 23–199.
13. For example, despite identifying the contingency of models, Fox O'Mahony and Roark (n 11) cannot resist the temptation to offer a 'universal' (218–20), which in relation to other models they criticise as a 'grand' (56 and 410), theory of their own: 'Resilient Property' (203–30).
14. Quentin Skinner, *Liberty before Liberalism* (2012) 101–20.
15. The idea runs like a thread through his corpus, but for a clear statement see Berlin (n 7) 1–11.

16. Martin Heidegger, *Being and Time* (tr. J. Macquarrie and E. Robinson, 1962), Hannah Arendt, *The Human Condition* (2ed, 1998), Louis Althusser, *For Marx* (tr. B. Brewster, 2005), Jean Baudrillard, *The System of Objects* (tr. James Benedict, 2005) and *The Mirror of Production* (tr. Mark Poster, 1975), Richard Rorty, *Philosophy and the Mirror of Nature* (1979), and Charles Taylor, *Sources of the Self: The Making of Modern Identity* (1989).

17. Other methods, discussed mainly in passing in parts II and III, include abstractly balancing goods, rendering goods complementary, defining conflict away, and excluding relevant reasons for action from the choice-structure.

18. Friedrich Nietzsche, *The Birth of Tragedy and Other Writings* (eds. R. Geuss and R. Speirs, 1999) 147.

19. John Gardner, *Law as a Leap of Faith* (2012) v.

20. Aristotle, *The Nicomachean Ethics* (tr. D. Ross, 2009) 1098b28-30.

Chapter 2

For the Public Good

What is important in life, Locke says, is being alive. In this bare or biological sense, life does not just enable what is good, it is good itself (GP3). Sure, we must try to enjoy its comforts and ease its burdens (GP1), but first (GP7) we should do all that we can to preserve our own family's lives and, after that (GP7), the lives of others. For this reason, when relating to nature, what is important is facilitating this ideal. To do so, our relations to objects must be immediate and instrumental in form. For when we act on nature's material, we preserve life best when we understand our labour as transforming it from a simple heap into concrete things that are useful in satisfying or realising existing, that is, immediate, desires or ends. For this reason, nature's objects only have meaning for us when so used. When neglected, they lose the instrumental identity we give to them. When not used appropriately, their concrete forms dissolve, they return to nature, for they cease to be what they were when in our hands. No longer food, game or farmland, now objects existing-out-there as works of nature – as simple substances, like apples, deer or virgin territory.

Grasping Locke's interpretation of the person and her basic relation to the world is essential if we are to understand his property theory. It is because we are concerned, or at least should be, with preserving life (AS1) above all else (AS2), that the initial right that Locke prescribes (AS3) is for the sake of promoting this end. Each individual, he says, initially had an exemption to use nature's objects and human instruments being used to enhance comfort, to preserve their lives. Bare life also informs two further rights that he prescribes. First, an individual has an exclusive claim-right in objects on which he labours. Second, every individual has a duty to labour, which duty is enforceable by others. Whatever happens after rights and duties are allocated in this way, whatever complex of property rights emerges through and in the passage of time, Locke thinks, is not ultimately of any concern. Of course, the more comfort the better, but provided that life is maximally preserved, then property has done its job.

Whilst it is indebted to others, this interpretation is not standard.[1] Reading Locke's theory in this way, however, is justified for two related reasons. First, it is consistent with his model of the person. Second, it is supported by a reading together of his two principal texts: the *Two Treatises* and *Essay*. What this interpretation yields is: it makes sense of difficult aspects of his theory, like his talk of mixing labour with objects, self-ownership, and the claim that we have property in our actions; it explains why he is not a proto-desert or efficiency theorist; and it renders sensible and coherent features of the *Two Treatises* with which even his best interpreters struggle.

A CORPOREAL RATIONAL CREATURE

In this section, I draw connections between four features of Locke's model – equality, freedom, rationality and life – then explain how they ground his initial prescription of property.

We are all, Locke tells us, formally equal and free. Our equality is rooted in the fact that we are born to 'the same advantages of Nature, and the use of the same faculties',[2] in the sense that we share the capacities for desire, sense and rationality. And freedom is rooted in our equivalent rational faculties.[3] Because we all share these qualities, he says, it follows that we have a natural negative freedom,[4] with individual men born to 'a *State of perfect Freedom* to order their Actions and dispose of their Possessions, and Persons as they think fit'.[5] Because freedom is '*grounded*' in '*Reason*',[6] however, its exercise is subject to natural law.[7] Natural law is '*the Voice of God*',[8] 'the Voice of Reason',[9] 'Senses'[10] and 'desire',[11] which means that its content can be learnt by all 'who will but consult it'.[12] Identifying these laws, which bind free, equal individuals, reveals a constitutive feature of Locke's model of the person, which model lies at the root of his property theory: his privileging of bare life.[13]

According to Locke, the '*Fundamental Law of Nature*'[14] is that every individual has a duty to '*preserve himself*'[15] and his family.[16] In addition to this fundamental law, we all have a negative duty not to frustrate the efforts by others to comply with their fundamental duty to preserve their family's lives.[17] Moreover, there is an 'Obligation to mutual Love amongst Men', which grounds certain 'Duties [that we] owe one another', namely, 'the great Maxims *of Justice* and *Charity*',[18] which we fulfil by doing 'as much as [we] can, *to preserve the rest of Mankind*'.[19] These second and third laws, however, are subordinate to the duty of self- and familial-preservation. They only apply when they are not 'in competition' with our first duty.[20] Locke's distinctions between and ranking of laws seem to be rooted in the fact that even when the preservation of life is privileged, conflicts might still arise. Sometimes, this will be because individuals breach the law of nature,[21] but it might also rise when natural events or luck force individuals to privilege their own families over others. Whilst only a spatio-temporal conflict (GP1), it is nonetheless one for which Locke's ethics seeks to cater.

Indeed, it is one of two such attempts. In addition to the internal conflict that can arise within the shared obligation to preserve all life, he recognises another good: comfort or convenience.[22] Like life, comfort or convenience matters for its own sake (GP3). For Locke, though, this good is lexically subordinated to the fundamental duty to preserve life (GP7). Therefore, whenever there is conflict (GP1) between life and comfort or convenience, our duty is always to act in a way that promotes the former. In Locke's ethics, therefore, there is a nested ordering of goods. In addition to the contingent conflict (GP1) internal to his privileged concern for life and the related priority (GP7) that he affords to familial survival, when the preservation of life conflicts with comfort or convenience (GP1), the former always trumps the latter (GP7).

In all this, Locke's emphasis on the individual is striking. Ethically, we see it in the emphasis he places on 'self-preservation'.[23] Ontologically, it emerges in the fact that his primordial unit is 'Man', who exists prior to any constituted social whole. It is this individualism that animates his belief that the state of nature, constituted by a natural negative freedom, was exited only because, when we are left to ourselves, we often fail to act as the law of nature directs.[24] When we interact in this world, we live '*singly and solely by our selves*', with all our '*Defects and Imperfections*', and we continue to do so until we consent to form a political society.[25] This society is formed by the free consent of individuals,[26] existing only as a framework of laws to regulate the relations of 'distinct Persons',[27] and it should only and always function '*to preserve and enlarge Freedom*',[28] that is, 'Lives, Liberties and Estates',[29] of the individuals who belong to it.[30]

Recognising that for Locke, free, rational and equal individuals, each duty-bound to preserve life, exist prior to social wholes, is necessary to make sense of his politics. For example, freedom and equality mean that each individual in the state of nature had the natural power to enforce the duties prescribed by natural law. Apart from this, however, there existed no other ethical powers over others.[31] We will have occasion to develop this point, but for reasons that become important in later sections, we must first note the force that these constraints on power exert on his concept of parental authority, contrasting it with political authority.

Whilst parents have natural power over children, Locke says, it is 'temporary' and it cannot be exercised capriciously, for this power is not rooted in a 'right of Nature',[32] but is derived from a parent's 'Duty' to preserve their children and raise them to the age of 'Reason', at which point each becomes a 'Freeman too'.[33] As free and equal adults, contrarily, individuals exist naturally 'without Subordination or Subjection'.[34] For this reason, he says, parental and political power are '*perfectly distinct* and separate'.[35] He derives two ideas from this basic premise. First, legitimate political power by its nature rests on the consent of individuals.[36] Second, only when individuals choose to exit the state of nature and identify as parts of a community, does politics, positive law and political duty come into being.[37] These twin ideas form the basis of Locke's famous defence of the right to revolution when: legislative,[38] executive,[39] or governmental[40] powers are exercised in a way that is contrary to the end for which they exist; individuals are ruled without consent;[41] or government is ineffective.[42] When this power is legitimate and effective, however, individuals delegate their power to judge and enforce natural law.[43] We do not delegate it absolutely,[44] for it is based on 'Trust',[45] and it is granted to bodies that must create and apply laws that are general, public, equal and stable.[46] When these bodies create and enforce positive law, they must conform to natural law, which is to say, they must pursue the end for which they exist: to preserve the lives of free and equal individuals toiling to survive in a harsh world.[47]

It is these features of Locke's model – many formally equal, free and rational individuals, all toiling to preserve their lives and, if possible, the lives of others – that inform the first feature of his property theory. In the state of nature, he says, there was a common ownership of resources.[48] Ownership was not a shareholding. It included a claim-right not to be excluded,[49] but something else too. Since life-preservation (AS1) is primary (AS2), originally individuals had an exemption to use nature to sustain themselves and their families (AS3). We all had this exemption because the use of nature is necessary to comply with the law to preserve life.[50] If we do not drink, eat or find shelter we inevitably die, so if others had dominion over nature,[51] if they had a claim-right to exclude others from using objects, efforts by an individual to preserve life would be frustrated. This exemption follows from Locke's '*first and fundamental natural Law*' (AS2),[52] preserve life (AS1), and was prior to other rights that could be held in objects,[53] for it could be exercised over objects in which others had non-subsistence rights (AS3).

Locke's property theory, however, strives for more than an exemption. He wants to justify a claim-right held by individuals to exclude others from use,[54] absent consent of this right-holder.[55] In fact, for Locke, the defining feature of property is this right not to be deprived.[56] In Hohfeldian terms, therefore, this claim-right serves a protective function, for it imposes on others a duty not to frustrate a right-holder's use of his property. In arguing for it, Locke's property theory evolves from a straightforward and externally instrumental one – property is to preserve life – to one that in certain respects foreshadows the expressivist self that we shall encounter in Hegel's and Marx's theories, albeit one that is still ultimately rooted in his concern for bare life.

LABOURING CONSUMER

The first move in his argument for individual claim-rights is the assertion that 'every Man has a *Property* in his own *Person*'.[57] It is because we have property in our persons (AS1), he says, that we have rights not to be deprived of objects (AS3). This claim prompts questions: What is meant by 'Person' and 'Man'? What does he mean when he says that 'Person' is 'a Property' of 'Man'? Why is it 'his' (Man's) property rather than someone else's or everyone's?

To answer the first question, we must note Locke's distinction between objects and subjects. In doing so, we start to reveal the essentially instrumental and immediate form of his conception of object-relations. The faculty of reason, Locke says, gives each individual a degree of freedom from nature. It empowers us to transcend nature's forces and to direct our actions as we consider best. The exercise of this power, he argues, transforms men from objects into subjects. Whilst we can rationally transcend nature, though, we do not quite reach the level of 'Angels',[58] for we also have bodies to which we must attend. In short, we are always both subjects and objects. For this reason, it might be tempting to read 'Man' and 'Person' as referring to the individual *qua* object and subject. As James Tully and Jeremy Waldron explain, though, this would be a mistake.[59] To see why, we have to introduce a third term: 'Body'. In the *Two Treatises* and *Essay*, Locke uses each of these terms to refer to three distinct ideas. Whereas 'Body', at least when he talks about, as we shall see below, the 'Labour of his Body', refers to the individual *qua* object, and 'Person' refers to them *qua* rational agents with memories about their past actions,[60] that is, with an identity, the term 'Man' refers to individuals insofar as they are both 'Body' and 'Person'.[61]

Let us move to the second and third questions. What does it mean to say that this 'Person' is 'a property' of 'Man'? Why 'his' property, not another's or everyone's? To answer this, we must turn to Locke's account of how we moved from an original community of property in the state of nature to a world in which an individual can have exclusive claim-rights in objects. After he says that 'every Man has a *Property* in his own *Person*', he says:

> This no Body has any Right to but himself. The *Labour* of his Body, and the *Work* of his Hands . . . are properly his. Whatsoever then he removes out of the State that Nature hath provided, and left it in, he hath mixed his *Labour* with,

> and joyned to it something that is his own, and thereby makes it his *Property*. It being by him removed from the common state Nature placed it in, it hath by this *labour* something annexed to it, that excludes the common right of other Men . . . no Man but he can have a right to what that is once joyned to, at least where there is enough, and as good left in common.[62]

This argument has two related parts. First, when an individual labours or acts on nature's unused objects,[63] they mix their labour with it. Second, by acting on it, through their rational industry,[64] they remove it from nature. In doing this, it is '*made* his *Property*',[65] for it becomes 'his, *i.e.* a part of him'.[66] Of the many attempts to understand Locke's ideas, two interpretations seem to me to offer most promise. One is advocated by Karl Olivecrona, and there are versions of the other advocated by Tully and Gopal Sreenivasan. Below, I shall argue for an interpretation that lies somewhere in between the two.

According to Olivecrona, Locke believes that all objects essentially function as extensions of personality. When a person identifies with an object in an intimate way, they comes to value it to such a degree that it takes on an especial significance for him, that is, becomes 'a part of him'.[67] For this reason, they must have a claim in the object, for unless others have the correlative duty not to deprive him of its use, this existentially important relation will be insecure. One significant merit of this interpretation is that it helps to make sense of perhaps the most notorious of Locke's ideas in the *Two Treatises*: his assertion that we mix, annex and join our labour with objects when we labour on them. When using these terms elsewhere in this text, Locke is referring to a conceptual relation between two distinct entities: between persons;[68] parts of the state;[69] power and duty;[70] inheritance and duty;[71] and law and penalty.[72] In each case, there exist analytically distinct but conceptually related entities: free men and authority; democracy, oligarchy and monarchy; parent and child; land and responsibilities; and crime and punishment. Whilst they are conceptually distinct, Locke says, the existence of one entity, say, parent or crime, for ethical reasons implies the existence of the other, namely, child or punishment.

Locke's idiom – mixing, joining and annexing – has been a cause of consternation for certain analytically minded theorists. Once we understand that he is using these terms in this conceptual and normative sense, however, their concerns seem less pressing. Indeed, in the *Essay*,[73] a work of epistemology published a year after the *Two Treatises*, the terms annex and join are used in this same way.[74] And he uses a term of art, 'mixed mode', sometimes together with the other two,[75] to refer to normative ideas, like property,[76] which exist as 'creatures of the understanding, rather than the works of nature'.[77] A mixed mode is a 'general term' constituted by the relation between distinct entities. We bring these entities together in our mind in such a way that they now come to belong together, in the sense that a conceptual relation is formed of the kind that Locke envisages when using the terms mix, join and annex in the *Two Treatises*. Given this term of epistemological art, we might therefore expect to read about men mixing their labour with objects when he is talking about how a mixed mode – an individual claim-right in objects – comes into being. If this is the right interpretation of his argument, when he refers to mixing, and so on, the words do not function as 'heuristic device[s]',[78] he does not intend them in a literal or material sense,[79] nor are they mere 'metaphor[s]'.[80] When a 'Man' labours on natural objects, a new relationship is constituted: once separate entities become constitutively related. The general term for this relation is 'property'.[81] It is in this conceptual way, as a normatively significant relation of mutual meaning, that a 'Man' mixes his labour with an object. For this reason, it is intelligible to think, as Olivecrona does, that 'Man' can identify with the objects on which he labours in such a way that they are an extension of him, for in relating to objects he understands them as being part of his practical self.

Notwithstanding this explanatory merit of Olivecrona's interpretation of Locke's argument, it has been the subject of various criticisms. For example, if Olivecrona is correct, Tully complains, a child would be the property of their loving parents to use as they think fit.[82] Yet we know from Locke's conception of power that he rejects this possibility. Parental authority must be exercised for a concrete end: raising children to the age of reason. But it is just here that we find an answer to Tully's worry. Recall, we are 'born to' freedom,[83] it is a 'Title' vested in us by natural law.[84] We cannot exercise agency from birth, but we are born with the potential to do so. In a catchy phrase by Waldron, each child has a 'normative destiny'.[85] It is this potential that secures children from their parents' potentially despotic whims. Therefore, the fact that a child cannot exercise agency now, does not expose them to being claimed as property any more than an adult family member, partner or friend whom we love is exposed to this fate when asleep.

Waldron queries Olivecrona's 'idealist' interpretation on a number of grounds. Two warrant especial attention. We can answer the first, but the second is fatal. First, he says that the intimate identification with objects that is required for claim-rights to arise on Olivecrona's interpretation necessarily 'involves' an expectation of continued control over objects. Expectations, though, do not 'arise naturally'. An expectation of this kind only exists if others respect allocations of rights. Thus, even if identification is the proper reading of Locke, it cannot ground an individual claim. The ground of this right will be the reason we already respect the way in which it is allocated.[86] There is an empirical and a conceptual difficulty with this objection. Empirically, we do not only identify with objects when we expect to control them. Disputes about rights often involve people who do not have control, for example, people who say that land that belonged to their ancestors should be returned to them. Indeed, it is the fact that they identify with land but do not have control over it that is one source of the passions that often characterise such disputes. The conceptual issue with the objection is that Locke is aware of the distinction between *de facto* and *de jure* power.[87] It is true that Locke does not draw this distinction in the chapter dealing with property. If a person is motivated by their identification with an object over which they have effective power, however, there is no self-evidently principled reason why identification cannot function as the ethical basis of their claim to the object, with force securing the right's efficacy.

Waldron raises another issue with Olivecrona's interpretation, albeit without developing it.[88] Empirically, we rarely form relations with objects sufficiently intimate to satisfy the requirement of identification, and we almost never do so with the objects that are the subject of Locke's well-known examples.[89] Few would consider that a particular apple they gather when roaming the forest is essential to their identities, that is, forming part of *who* they are. Whilst Waldron's remark is fatal to the interpretation given by Olivecrona, his interpretation does make sense of the idea that people can mix their labour with objects. Can this aspect be rescued? I think that it can: a version of Tully and Sreenivasan's interpretations of Locke, which differs somewhat by emphasising his model of the person, is faithful to Olivecrona's insights, it can avoid Waldron's scope-objection, and it renders coherent a number of other aspects of Locke's theory.

Drawing from the *Essay*, Tully says that Locke believes that individuals, like God, can have exclusive 'makers' rights' in the products of their labour.[90] We find a similar reading of Locke in Sreenivasan's work. Sreenivasan can be distinguished from Tully, though, since he points to the distinction between acts of creation by God and acts of making effected by persons. A benefit of this distinction is that whilst Lockean property is grounded in the act of making, the rights differ from those that arise from God's creative acts.[91] Olivecrona and Waldron object to this 'making' interpretation for similar reasons. Whilst Olivecrona complains that Locke's principal examples do not actually involve making, that is, gathering an apple is not like making an axe,[92] Waldron says that Locke does not use make in the sense of 'production'.[93]

It seems to me that both objections miss the mark, for they are premised on an unduly narrow conception of making.[94] As Hannah Arendt explains, by means of her distinction between *animal laborans* (labour) and *homo faber* (work),[95] Locke's individuals do not produce objects that have concrete, particular identities that endure over time, outlasting the immediate ends for which they are made. The instruments they make do not form part of a world common to but independent of their existing desires or ends.

They make consumables,[96] that is, instruments the concrete functional forms or identities of which are constitutively bound up with their satisfaction and realisation of their user's existing desires and ends. As consumables, Locke tells us, they often only exist for a '*short duration*',[97] for their use is bound up with their essential functions: preserve life and make it more convenient.[98] In the teleological, purpose-oriented idiom used in the *Two Treatises* and *Essay*, when we gather 'Apples',[99] we appropriate them to our ends and thereby transform them. Recall, we live just below the level of the angels, so when we labour on nature, we lift its objects into a higher rational realm, we create human objects: apples become food for 'nourishment'.[100] When we labour, we transform nature's heap of simple substances into concrete objects, defined by our desires or ends. Rather than 'waste',[101] the object *is* food *for* eating.[102] In our labouring on it, we add 'something to [it] more than Nature . . . had done',[103] that is, our reasons for labouring. It is this transformation of nature's 'loose' material by the rationally industrious into immediate,[104] 'truly useful' instruments that defines the making of consumables.[105]

If right, this means Locke's object-relations are constituted by two qualities: instrumentality and immediacy. This is the truth in Olivecrona's interpretation: 'We can have a feeling of things being so intimately connected with ourselves that they are part of ourselves.'[106] This connection exists, however, not because people feel rather attached to the objects that they use, but because of the qualitative structure of the relation, for we *understand* objects in terms of the concepts and categories of instrumentality and immediacy. As a result, their concrete forms and identities – the apple *is* food *for* eating – are bound up with the ends we give them. From this constitutive fact, an important consequence for property follows. Because of the constituting nature of the relation, if the person relating to the object does not *use* it to satisfy their *existing* desires, then their rights in the object will be annulled. For nature's objects only exist as human, purpose-laden objects when used to satisfy present needs or pursue present ends. If the gathered object is later neglected, then it will retake its place in nature, where it will cease to be what it was in the hands of its user, for the object will no longer exist as a consumable. Having retaken its place among nature's heap of unrelated simple substances, it will become available for other people to use for their own ends, thereby constituting a new claim-right. This is exactly what Locke says happens to useful objects when neglected.[107]

Therefore, if we follow Arendt and broaden our concept of making beyond the durable one presumed by Olivecrona and Waldron to one that treats making as a process of giving abstract matter concrete form, then it appears to me that their objections to the interpretations offered by Sreenivasan and Tully cannot be sustained.

This interpretation helps to explain Locke's assertion that our labour 'necessarily introduces *private Possessions*',[108] that is, claim-rights to exclude. In Hohfeld's terms, duty is the correlative of claim: if somebody has a claim, someone else necessarily has a duty. Labour creates claim-rights because others have a duty not to interfere with an individual's efforts to preserve life (AS3), that is, when we create truly useful objects, such as food for nourishment. Only if such claims and duties exist, Locke believes, can individuals realise what actually (AS2) matters: preserving life (AS1). In the absence of this claim, individuals would likely 'starve[d], notwithstanding the Plenty God had given him',[109] Locke argues, and without the duty, other individuals would take from those using nature's objects and thereby do 'injury' to them.[110]

It is worth touching on some other common interpretations of Locke. Apart from those who interpret his talk of mixing labour with objects literally, which we must reject for the reasons we have already given, others read Locke as grounding claims in desert or efficiency.[111] Whilst there is support for these readings, we go astray by reading him as a desert or efficiency theorist. Once we reveal his privileged concern for bare life, and the conceptual and categorical implications of his concern for how we relate to nature – instrumentally and immediately – we also see that these readings misconstrue his talk of industry, effort and value. One reason Locke talks about industry is that purposive action is required for people to transform nature's objects into goods that can be consumed, materially or in the pursuit of chosen ends. Similarly, pain and toil matter because the 'penury' of the human condition means that we all have to struggle simply to stay alive.[112] Man is not rewarded for hard work with claims in objects. After our fall from grace, pain and industry are part of what it means to be human.[113] Similarly, it seems to me that Locke discusses an increase in the value of goods created through labour not to justify individual claim-rights. Rights of this kind are not justified because they facilitate the production of surplus value. Rather, Locke talks about increase for two reasons. First, it reiterates the conceptual claim that objects only become useful ones through human labour. Second, it pre-empts a possible criticism.[114] Since life (AS1) is sacred (AS2), he has to explain why individual claim-rights will not violate it. Pointing to the productive potential of labour,[115] he thinks that he shows that there will be 'enough, and as good, left' for others to preserve their lives,[116] which means that property (AS3) will still serve its real purpose (AS2), which is to preserve life (AS1). Believing that he had shown this, he headed off a likely objection to his justification of individual claim-rights.[117] In fact, Locke adds, we should embrace them, for in doing so we 'make use of' nature's objects not only to 'the best advantage of Life', but 'convenience' and 'enjoy[ment]' too (GP3).[118]

Returning to our anthropological reading of Locke, it assists in making sense of his claim that when 'Man' works on objects, they become 'part of him'.[119] To reveal this, we must draw further on his idea that when we act on nature, we mix our labour with objects. Locke adopts these terms to refer to a conceptual relation between parts. When 'Man' mixes labour with objects, he creates something new: a whole that is constituted by parts. This is what I understand Locke to mean by the claim that labour is the '*beginning of Property*',[120] in the sense of an individual claim-right in objects.[121] When we appropriate nature's objects to our ends,[122] we make consumables. Because labouring men treat objects as instruments of this kind, they exist as such. It is in this conceptual way that an object becomes 'part of him'. It is part of him, an extension of him, not because there is an intimate link with it, but because it *is* an instrument to satisfy *his* desires or ends.

Emphasising the anthropological structure of Locke's theory, which is constitutively bound up with the concepts or categories of instrumentality and immediacy, also helps to make sense of his twin assertions that a Man's 'Labour of his Body, and the Work of his Hands . . . are properly his', and that 'every Man has a *property* in his own *Person*'. These two notorious claims must be read together.[123] For Locke, we only attain freedom by exercising agency.[124] In the *Essay*, Locke says that each 'Person' is constituted by memory of past exercises of agency.[125] In remembering the past exercises of our capacity to 'see, hear, smell, taste, feel, meditate, or will', we constitute our 'personal identity'.[126] We are also responsible for the identities we create, for we are what we do. In this sense, we 'own' our actions,[127] since we are 'accountable' for them,[128] and so they are 'a part of' ourselves.[129] In the *Two Treatises*, he asserts that it is 'by being Master of himself',[130] that is, a responsible subject, with power to author his own life through the 'free Disposal' of his actions,[131] that he is the '*Proprietor of his own Person*'.[132] Just as objects belong to men because, in acting on them, we create instruments, so we have property in ourselves. No longer just a heap of unrelated impulses, through the exercise of agency we create ourselves, for which we become responsible. Because there exists a constitutive conceptual 'unity' between action and identity,[133] self-ownership and having property in one's own actions are related, for to say that an individual has property in his person is just to say that he has property in his actions.

This may seem too easy. For Locke, property *is* a right not to be deprived of objects without consent. What does it mean to be deprived of one's actions or 'Person'? One obvious example is slavery. It deprives individuals of their 'Person', because it reduces them to an object instead of a subject, and it deprives them of their actions, for it extinguishes their freedom to act. But we may better clarify matters if we consider how deprivation can occur through normal forms of theft. To start, recall that according to Locke a 'Person' is constituted in part by their labour. Provided that he is conscious of what he does, he is his action and his action is him.[134] Because we are what we do, we constitute ourselves through and in our actions. So, explaining how we can be deprived of our labour is to explain how we can be deprived of our 'Person'. Further, when a person labours on an object, a relation is established, for he uses the object as an instrument. If we couple these ideas, the route to deprivation reveals itself. To appropriate an object that someone else is using is to deprive them of their capacity to labour on it. To deprive them of this capacity is to frustrate their labour. And since labour in part constitutes personal identity, the thief deprives them of this part of their 'Person', that is, of that 'part *of himself*'.[135] Because the ends towards which you use objects (cooking, cutting) in part fixes who you are (chef, carpenter), to deprive you of an object you are using is to attack your 'Person', for you cannot continue to be a chef or carpenter without the objects needed to cook or cut.

Citing Nozick,[136] Waldron proffers a second objection to the making interpretation.[137] Recall, Locke claims that parents do not have property in their own children. Waldron and Nozick locate this fact on the making interpretation in the fact that parents 'do not know how literally to *make* a child'. Yet, this lack of knowledge is found in, for example, farmers who do not know how seeds become apple trees, yet own the trees. The reply to this point has two parts. First, agential rather than technical knowledge is required for Lockean making.[138] What matters is the farmer's idea or purpose when labouring. If she plants seeds for the sake of growing apple trees, then she 'knows' what she is doing.[139] Second, whilst Locke does talk about bodily creation, when he is discussing men, his emphasis is on God giving man 'being' with the 'Breath of Life', in the sense that God is '*our Maker*' by virtue of the fact that he instils our body with a 'living and rational Soul'.[140] It is because he gives men life as 'corporeal rational creatures' that he is our creator.[141] Parents, on the other hand, are 'occasions of their [child's] being',[142] mere causal and in a sense inadvertent factors of their lives. Parents do not make children in the way that God creates men. Whereas we give natural objects purpose, there is an analogous but more ultimate sense in which God gives us purpose. He is the reason why, as Waldron himself puts it, we have a 'normative destiny',[143] that is, the power to give objects and ourselves purposes at all.[144]

MONEY AND THE DUTY TO WORK

Grasping Locke's vision of the person and her relation to the world is necessary to make sense of his property theory. It is because we ought to be concerned with the preservation of life (AS1) above all else (AS2) that the property rights he prescribes (AS3) are directed towards facilitating this end.

Every man, he says, originally had an exemption to use nature's materials, and human-made objects insofar as they were only used for comfort-facilitating purposes (AS2), to preserve their lives. When we recognise that others also have a duty to preserve life (AS1), we should, on pain of contradiction, also recognise that they too had an exemption to use objects they require to live (AS3). Since we exited the state of nature, we can now obtain claim-rights in objects for the sake of satisfying subsistence and other comforting purposes. Our rights, however, are internally limited: their existence is tied to their use to satisfy desires or ends. Provided these conditions are satisfied, though, whatever complex of rights emerges through and in the passage of time should not in any real sense concern us.

Once we reveal the anthropological structure of Locke's theory, two conclusions follow.[145] First, there is no concern for the rights that emerge after life has been maximally sustained. Yes, the more comfort and convenience, the better; and, as it happens, Locke argues, the introduction of claim-rights and money will enable an increase in these goods. If life is maximally preserved, though, property has functioned as it should. In practice, this means that there is nothing internal to the logic of his model of the person – his concrete formulation of AS1 to AS3 – that can check the accumulation by individuals, families and groups of vast quantities of claim-rights in material objects or money, nor is there anything that can be used to justify their distribution to others. The holders of these rights, in other words, find themselves with immunities-through-no-prescriptive-alternative. On Locke's answer to the anthropological question, therefore, there is scope for the infinite 'accumulation' of what Marx will later refer to as 'the money commodity'.[146] The reason why is that money is not 'perishable' or 'truly useful',[147] it has 'Phantastical imaginary value'.[148] It does not immediately satisfy desires or ends, but rather mediates between them.[149] As such, it is not subject to the due-use and non-spoilage provisos, which means that money can be 'hoarded up' by men.[150] Absent the provisos, though, this useless class of objects, together with objects for which he can pay, like land,[151] is unmoored from ethical structure and social control. This part of Locke's theory is termed and criticised by C.B. Macpherson as 'possessive individualism'.[152] We can now see, though, that it flows not entirely from his individualistic and possessive worldview. Whilst these constitutive qualities of Lockean object-relations matter, this world also arises from his privileging (AS2) of bare life (AS1) and treatment of labour – that is, immediate instrumental relations to nature – as a necessary means for maximally preserving life (AS3).

The second further feature of his theory is the duty to work, which, on the logic of his scheme, is enforceable by others. Through a close reading of the *Two Treatises*, Sreenivasan has revealed that this is the right interpretation.[153] That it is Locke's view emerges even more clearly from his policy proposals for 'methods for setting on work and employing the poor of this kingdom, and making them useful to the public, and thereby easing others of that burden',[154] like his 'labour-rate system';[155] and correspondence: 'I think that everyone, according to what way Providence has placed him in, is bound to labour for the publick good, as far as he is able, or else he has no right to eat.'[156] The Lockean duty to labour is so basic to this picture that this limit on the right to eat applies to children: 'if it be necessary to his Condition', he writes, the father is free 'to make them work when they are able for their own Subsistence'.[157] Thus, the advocacy of forced labour flows from his model. The liberty to use nature's material is an exemption, permitting us to do what Locke thinks we may otherwise not do: use objects at all.[158] Not just exempt, though, we have a duty to exercise the liberty, and we have to exercise it through labour. If we can work, we must, for the 'Publick Good',[159] which is to preserve life, for this is what really matters. If we embrace this first (AS2) law of nature to preserve all life (AS1), its internal logic dictates that we can and should coerce and be coerced (AS3) into fulfilling this duty.

After starting with a shared exemption motivated by the laudable ideal of preserving life, we find ourselves in a world of unconstrained accumulation, workhouses and child labour. Yet at no stage does Locke effect a reversal in his thinking. It was the rigorous application of his concrete formulation of AS1 to AS3 that moved him not only to provide certain answers in theory but to advocate corresponding policies in practice. Not a contradiction, rather consistency, explains this movement from a form of primitive communism to a world that sits precariously on the precipice of coercive consumer capitalism.

NOTES

1. For a survey, see Christopher Pierson, *Just Property: A History in the Latin West Volume One: Wealth, Virtue, and the Law* (2013) 220–31.
2. TTG II § 4.
3. TTG II § 61. On equivalence as the criterion, see Jeremy Waldron, *God, Locke and Equality* (2008) 83–107.
4. For some references to this set of ideas, see TTG I § 30, 51 and 58 and 67 and TTG II § 4–5, 16–24, 54–55, 61–63, 87, 99, 123 and 172.
5. TTG II § 4.
6. TTG II § 63.
7. TTG II § 6.
8. TTG I § 86. See also TTG II § 25.
9. TTG II § 31. See also TTG II § 10, 16, 25 and 57.
10. TTG I § 86.
11. TTG I § 86 and 88.

12. TTG II § 6.
13. Cf. G.A. Cohen, *Self-Ownership, Freedom, and Equality* (1995) 188–94.
14. TTG II §16. See also TTG II § 134–35 and 159.
15. TTG II § 6.
16. On familial duties, see TTG I § 89–90 and TTG II § 36, 48 and 52–76. Matthew H. Kramer, *John Locke and the Origins of Private Property: Philosophical Explorations of Individualism, Community, and Equality* (1997), says the family is the basic 'moral unit' (13).
17. TTG II § 6 and 183.
18. TTG II § 5. On the theological underpinnings of his theory, see James Tully, *A Discourse on Property* (1980) 46–48, Kramer (n 16) 37–89, Waldron (n 3) 76–82, Michael Oakeshott, *Morality and Politics in Modern Europe* (ed. Shirley Robin Letwin, 1993) 47–58, and Charles Taylor, *Sources of the Self: The Making of Modern Identity* (1989) 234–47.
19. TTG II § 6.
20. TTG II § 6.
21. TTG II § 6–12.
22. For references to comfort and convenience, see TTG I § 33, 41, 87, 89–92 and 97 and TTG II § 26, 37, 41, 44, 66, 77 and 95.
23. TTG I § 86 and 88 and TTG II § 11 and 149.
24. TTG II § 13, 16–21 and 123–27.
25. TTG II § 15.
26. TTG II § 95, 99 and 192.
27. TTG II § 145.
28. TTG II § 57.
29. TTG II § 123–24.
30. TTG II § 145.
31. TTG II § 7–8.
32. TTG II § 65.
33. TTG II § 55, 58, 69 and 170.
34. TTG II § 4.
35. TTG II § 71.
36. TTG II § § 95.
37. TTG II § 134, 157 and 212.
38. TTG II § 149.
39. TTG II § 155.
40. TTG II § 221.
41. TTG II § 168 and 196.
42. TTG II § 219–20.
43. TTG II § 87–89 and 129–30.
44. TTG II § 135.
45. TTG II § 22, 142, 149, 171 and 221–22.
46. TTG II § 87, 136–37 and 142.
47. TTG II § 94, 131, 135–36, 140, 171 and 222.

48. TTG I § 25. On this divisive issue, see Tully (n 18) 60–61 and 124–28, Jeremy Waldron, *The Right to Private Property* (1988) 148–57, Kramer (n 16) 99–109 and 113–14, and Gopal Sreenivasan, *The Limits of Lockean Rights in Property* (1995) 24–32 and 141.

49. TTG II § 26.

50. Tully (n 18) 62–63.

51. TTG I § 42.

52. TTG II § 134.

53. TTG I § 42.

54. TTG II § 25–26.

55. TTG II § 32, 138 and 193.

56. TTG II § 138.

57. TTG II § 27.

58. TTG I § 58.

59. Tully (n 18) 105ff and Waldron (n 48) 178–79.

60. For references, see the discussion of personal identity below.

61. Generally, see ECHU II Ch. 27.

62. TTG II § 27.

63. In TTG II § 44, Locke equates labouring with action in general.

64. TTG II § 34.

65. TTG II § 30.

66. TTG II § 26.

67. Karl Olivecrona, 'Locke's Theory of Appropriation' 24(96) *The Philosophical Quarterly* (1974) 220–34.

68. TTG II § 120 and 135.

69. TTG II § 132.

70. TTG II § 65.

71. TTG II § 73 and 116.

72. TTG II § 171.

73. On the importance of the philosophical links between the *Essay* and *Two Treatises*, see the analysis in Tully (n 18) 3–34.

74. These terms litter the *Essay*. For examples in ECHU II, see Ch. 27 § 3, 8, 10, 13, 17–18, 22–23 and 25, and for examples in ECHU III, see Ch. 3 § 9, 12, 14–15 and 17–18 and Ch. 4 § 6.

75. For example, mixed mode and annexed are used together in ECHU II Ch. 28 § 4 and ECHU III Ch. 5 § 1.

76. For a helpful discussion, see Tully (n 18) 8–16.

77. ECHU III Ch. 5 § 12.

78. Waldron (n 48) 194.

79. Ibid., 184–88.

80. Sreenivasan (n 48) 89.

81. See TTG II § 123, where Locke uses 'the general Name, *Property*' to refer to 'Lives, Liberties and Estates' when he says the end of society and government is a '*mutual Preservation*' of this property. See also TTG II § 173.

82. Tully (n 18) 120.

83. TTG II § 55.

84. TTG II § 87. See also TTG II § 190.

85. Waldron (n 3) 141. Further, see Jeremy Waldron, *One Another's Equals: The Basis of Human Equality* (2017) 235–40.

86. Waldron (n48) 195–98.

87. For example, see TTG I § 16, 48 and 160 and TTG II § 76, 103 and 202.

88. Waldron (n 48) 195.

89. TTG II § 28, 30 and 46.

90. Tully (n 18) 35–38 ('God as Maker') and 116–24 ('Man as maker').

91. Sreenivasan (n 48) 59–92.

92. Olivecrona (n 67) 225–26.

93. Waldron (n 48) 199–200.

94. This conception underlies the concerns in Sreenivasan (n 48) 85–88.

95. Hannah Arendt, *The Human Condition* (2ed, 1998) 79–135 (labour) and 136–74 (work).

96. For the word 'consume', see TTG II § 36, 46 and 48, where it is tied to enjoyment, truly useful goods and perishables in contradistinction to money.

97. TTG II § 46.

98. On Lockean value as use-value, see Cohen (n 13) 175–80.

99. TTG II § 28 and 46.

100. TTG II § 28.

101. TTG II § 36–38, 42–43 and 45.

102. If objects only become 'private possessions' when they are made 'truly useful' (TTG II § 46–47), this explains why picking fruit, drinking water or hunting animals creates individual claims, struggled with by Sreenivasan (n 48) 85–88.

103. TTG II § 28.

104. ECHU III Ch. 5 § 6-7.

105. TTG II § 47. Spilling objects into wet cement (Waldron (n 48) 188) or the ocean (Robert Nozick, Anarchy, State and Utopia (1974) 174–75), therefore, would not create a claim-right, for we do not use either.

106. Olivecrona (n 67) 224.

107. TTG II § 31, 37–38 and 46. The 'spoilage' proviso has a due-use and non-spoilage condition (Sreenivasan (n 48) 100–02) on 'truly useful' goods (TTG II § 47).

108. TTG II § 35.

109. TTG II § 28.

110. TTG II § 32.

111. For discussions of these other interpretations, see Waldron (n 48) 201–07, Robert Nozick, Anarchy, State and Utopia (1974) 174–78 and Cohen (n 13) 175–86.

112. TTG II 32.

113. TTG I § 35.

114. In Jeremy Waldron, *The Dignity of Legislation* (1999) 68–70 and 73–75, we are encouraged to read much of Locke's property theory in this way.

115. TTG II § 36–37 and 40–44.

116. TTG II § 27, 33, 34 and 36.

117. Robert Nozick, Anarchy, State and Utopia (1974) 176–77.
118. TTG II § 26 and 31.
119. TTG II § 26.
120. TTG II § 30.
121. TTG II § 45.
122. ECHU III Ch. 5 § 6.
123. For critical analysis, see J.P. Day, 'Locke on Property' 16(64) *The Philosophical Quarterly* (1966) 207–20.
124. TTG II § 61.
125. ECHU II Ch. 27 § 9–10 and 26.
126. ECHU II Ch. 27 § 9.
127. ECHU II Ch. 27 § 17–18 and 26.
128. ECHU II Ch. 27 § 15–16 and 26.
129. ECHU II Ch. 27 § 11, 14, 18 and 25.
130. TTG II § 44.
131. TTG II § 190.
132. TTG II § 44.
133. ECHU II Ch. 27 §, 6, 10–11, 14, 16 and 23–25.
134. For worries about 'mixing one's mixing', which I think my interpretation helps to address, see Waldron (n 48) 185–87.
135. ECHU II Ch. 27 § 11.
136. Robert Nozick, Anarchy, State and Utopia (1974) 288.
137. Waldron (n 48) 199.
138. Sreenivasan (n 48) 81–85.
139. TTG I § 52–53 and ECHU III Ch. 6 § 40.
140. TTG I § 53.
141. ECHU III Ch. 11 § 16: 'We mean nothing by Man, but a corporeal rational Creature.' On this concept, see Waldron (n 3) 66–82.
142. TTG I § 54.
143. Waldron (n 3) 141.
144. On the analogy, see Tully (n 18) 36 and 116–17.
145. For a third strand, see Ellen Meiksins Wood, *Empire of Capital* (2005) 91–101.
146. CVI 162–63 and 230–31.
147. TTG II § 47.
148. TTG II § 184.
149. TTG II § 47.
150. TTG II § 48 and 50.
151. TTG II § 50.
152. C.B. Macpherson, *The Political Theory of Possessive Individualism* (1964) .
153. Sreenivasan (n 48) 41–47.
154. John Locke, *Report to the Board of Trade*, quoted in Sreenivasan (n 48) 42.

155. Karl Polanyi, *The Great Transformation: The Political and Economic Origins of our Times* (2001) 111.
156. Letter to William Molyneux, 19 January 1694, quoted in Tully (n 18) 168.
157. TTG II § 64.
158. TTG II § 26.
159. TTG II § 3.

Chapter 3

Ghosts and Gulags

Critics often group together Bentham and Hayek, pointing to their overlaps and similarities. This is fine as it goes, since there is a family resemblance between their ontologies and ethics, with a nearly straight line capable of being drawn from Benthamite pleasure to Hayekian preference. In analysing them in this way, however, we neglect much that remains philosophically interesting in and practically important about their work on property. What makes continued consideration of their property theories worthwhile is not what they share in common, but what distinguishes and opposes them.

We exist, Bentham says, on the precipice of total war. This war would not be waged between nations or fought by armies; rather, it would take place within and amongst the strangers who aggregately constitute the mass that we feign to call 'the public'. War is near because we are surrounded by individuals who would, but for some risk they judge too great, opportunistically lunge for power or control of resources. This is due not to man's vainglory and greed. We tend towards this state because each person fears these vices in others. Not robust and selfish, but rather timid and alone, we lunge for and grab what we need to maximise pleasure and minimise pain, before others inevitably do. Perhaps others are fearful like us, but perhaps not, so better safe than sorry. Quite perversely, therefore, it is through our discordant efforts to secure ourselves that the danger is made actual. Fear and felt vulnerability become a self-fulfilling prophecy. Man is his own worst enemy. Luckily, he is also rational, potentially perfectly so. If we can identify what each individual in fact desires and disdains, bringing these facts together to form a coherent and directed plan, we can avoid our self-immolation. The first regulative principle of this plan hardly needs saying: security. Only when made to feel safe from all the potential robbers lurking in the shadows can we let loose our capacities to reason, always for the sake of realising what matters most: more pleasure, less pain.

Obviously, Hayek replies, maximising individual preference-satisfaction, what an individual thinks desirable, is the goal of politics and law, and the effective use of information is essential to this project, but in trying to realise it, Bentham, like others, goes wrong right from the start. We are not atomised, isolated and vulnerable to attack from others. True, we are individuals, but we are born into families and social orders that structure or shape us. Whilst upheaval is possible, it is not internal to all social relations, such that we need to plan ourselves out of this ever-present danger. The frustration of our preferences is not due to a lack of planning but its excess. Both as individuals and groups, we are incapable of knowing all that people want, how much they want it, and how to give them what they want. If we knew all of this, we could act on this knowledge as Bentham proposes, but we do not, and so we cannot. For this reason, all efforts to enact overall plans will fail. It is this failure that produces oppression. In striving to overcome their ignorance, planners limit what is beyond their control, first by restricting and extinguishing preferences, and then by restricting and extinguishing their bearers. There is, however, an existing solution to this problem, the market's price mechanism, which aggregates and disseminates the planner's desired information. Rather than controlling and securing individuals and objects through directed plans, therefore, we must unfetter them, allowing for their competitive movement. Only through and in this fragmented, relatively stable but perpetually evolving order, can each individual realise what matters in the last resort: maximal preference-satisfaction.

There are three basic differences between Bentham and Hayek. Each implicates their models of the person, for each goes towards their construction of logically incompatible anthropological visions, which in turn generate incompatible property theories. For Bentham, every individual is atomised and vulnerable but capable of rational perfection. Hayek, contrarily, sees an individual who, despite their constitutional ignorance, navigates more or less successfully within a relatively stable social order. From their two competing visions emerge competing practical priorities. Both think that satisfaction of *de facto* desires (GP1) is exhaustive of the good (GP3, GP5). It is what each thinks is bad, however, that does the normative heavy lifting in their theories. For Bentham, because we must first (AS2) make individuals feel safe from the heaving social mass (AS1), the first duty of those who allocate property rights is to grant a near-absolute immunity (AS3) to all existing right-holders. Hayek's primary (AS2) concern about ignorance (AS1), contrarily, leads him to privilege the power to exchange these rights in markets (AS3).

The anthropological structures of Bentham and Hayek's property theories, therefore, mean that despite them having related ontologies and ethics, their contrasting concerns about what is bad – insecurity and ignorance – moves them to prescribe schemes for the allocation of property rights that are logically incompatible.

THE SIGNIFICANCE OF FICTIONS

Bentham is a true child of the Enlightenment, a mixture of British empiricism and continental rationalism,[1] driven by the idea, messianic in its zeal,[2] that for any proposition to be meaningful it must be axiomatically grounded. Just as mathematics and logic have formal principles and the sciences have empirical ones, so morality must find its own foundation. Axioms matter because we can deduce from them concrete rules, each as valid as the axioms. So, if we could identify a 'fundamental axiom' of morality,[3] we could then construct a 'science of legislation',[4] grounded on neutral language,[5] 'truth and reason'.[6] Armed with an axiomatic foundation, this 'Decalogue-in-one for a new Moses',[7] as one of Bentham's biographers puts it, we could construct rationally justified laws. This is the rationalist-inspired part of Bentham's system.

The foundation of this system is the principle of utility. He arrives at it through two inductive claims. Here, his empiricist side exerts itself. First, drawing on introspection and observation, he says that all individuals experience various types of pleasure and pain.[8] We all desire the former and avoid the latter. Pleasure and pain talk to the individual from within, in a universal language that even the 'stupid or perverse' can understand.[9] Since denying the fact and uniformity of our response to pleasure and pain would mean 'falling into absurdity',[10] this empirical claim 'needs no proof'.[11] It is axiomatic. The second empirical claim is that pleasure and pain govern all our thoughts and actions: 'On the one hand the standard of right and wrong, on the other the chain of causes and effects, are fastened to their throne.'[12] All reasoning, practical and theoretical, begins from forceful drives to maximise pleasure. Every motive, habit, intention, choice and action is a product of pleasure and pain. All ethical ideas are abstract descriptions of pleasure or pain. They are the 'efficient' and the 'final' causes of all.[13] We cannot but judge good that which augments pleasure and bad that which causes pain, from which it follows that we will always act as one or the other directs. This second empirical claim is also axiomatic.

From these twin empirical axioms, Bentham deduces a moral maxim. Given the all-totalising causal power of pleasure and pain, the question 'What should I do?' obviously can only have one answer: maximise pleasure (GP3, GP5). Because all thought and action are governed in this way, all morality and legislation, whatever differences might exist between them conceptually and in practice, must necessarily conform.[14] To do otherwise, Bentham says, would be nothing less than man's 'renouncement of [his] self'.[15] As such, we must sit the drive to maximise pleasure at the heart of practical life. We must employ all our faculties – understanding, reason, willing, and so on – to strive after and realise this single end. The principle of utility 'serves to prove everything else',[16] it is 'the sole and all-sufficient reason for every point of practice whatsoever'.[17] Every institution, goal, action and idea must be 'measured' against it.[18] To adopt the principle in this practical way, therefore, is to grasp reality and the moral duties that it generates.[19]

To implement the principle, a legislator must identify the sources and natures of pleasure and pain, and the degrees or ways in which they affect men.[20] The legislator does not decide what is pleasurable and painful. It observes what experiences people in fact experience as pleasurable or painful – their 'prejudices' not the legislator's,[21] which in fact drive their thoughts and actions.[22] The method of this investigation, which Bentham thinks can be perfected through an adoption of scientific techniques,[23] where legislators are psychologist-sociologist-statisticians, is the essence of legislative action. After observing what individuals find pleasurable and painful, the legislator must 'calculate' what laws are necessary to maximise pleasure relative to pain.[24] In adopting this calculative stance towards men, where the act of making laws 'becomes a matter of arithmetic',[25] the legislator acts as an administrator of 'instruments',[26] relating, as H.L.A. Hart puts it, to men as 'manipulable . . . pleasure and pain machines',[27] balancing all real, existing parcels of pleasure and pain against each other (GP1).[28] Law is required and therefore good if it maximises pleasure relative to pain, meaning that this criterion prescribes what laws to make.[29] When well made, law functions as 'the medicine of the soul'.[30] Shortly, I will explain how anathema all of this is to Hayek, but to understand why, we should bring to the fore the atomistic nature of Bentham's person and identify its relation to this mechanistic, calculating and pleasure-seeking picture.

To say that Bentham's person is atomised is not to say he lacks ties of affection or interests in others. In this sociological sense, 'Man is not a solitary being.'[31] This fact about relations, though, must not distract from the atomising implications of the sovereign force of one's 'own' pleasure and pain.[32] This force manifests in various ways. For example, the 'true' reason that men have in 'maintaining a government' is that it serves our own interests: security, enjoyments, property and industry.[33] Even if we derive these benefits, though, it is not an unalloyed good, for 'dependence' is by nature 'evil'.[34] To pretend that it is not, to behave as if men are driven by forces other than a 'love of self', by the desire to increase the sum of their happiness, is to forsake what is essential to their nature, for it entails the denial of their real self: 'what a ridiculous, what a fatal confusion would be the consequence!'[35] Sociological facts are subordinate to this ontological fact. As such, that we can form relations does not mean we are relational beings. The opposite is true. Rejecting the notion that individual interests should sometimes 'yield to the public interest', he writes:

> But what does that mean? Is not one individual as much a part of the public as another? This public interest, which you introduce as a person, is only an abstract term; it represents nothing but the mass of individual interests . . . Individual interests are the only real interests.[36]

And writing in a different context, Bentham asks rhetorically: 'Now what is the wealth of society, if not the sum of all individual wealth?'[37] A third example:

> Would it be believed that there are men so absurd as to love posterity better than present generations; to prefer the man who is not to the man who is; to torment the living under the pretext of doing good to those who are not born, and who perhaps never will be?[38]

Bentham's ontology is doing all the work here.[39] Social forms and relations are 'fictitious',[40] the 'sum of the interests of the several members' composing them.[41] For Bentham, operating in the epistemological frame of Locke, touched on in chapter 2, the apparent reality of social forms is 'feigned by the imagination . . . for the purpose of discourse', only 'spoken of as if [they were] real' because it is useful.[42] In truth, there are 'discrete' individuals,[43] constituted by 'immediate . . . perception[s]' of pleasure and pain,[44] and the 'things' that give them pleasure or pain, nothing else is 'real'.[45] Because social forms are always products of language and thought,[46] abstractions from real existing substances, 'disguised descriptions' of what is real,[47] as Hart puts it, reasoning that proceeds from them is 'false',[48] resting on nothing but a 'foundation of sand'.[49] Rather than on fictions, the science of legislation should be 'founded' on 'the immovable basis' of pleasures and pains.[50]

With some of this, Hayek agrees. For example, he agrees with Bentham that there is nothing valuable other than what individuals deem important (GP3, GP5). Thus, what matters is that we maximise preference-satisfaction.[51] This is what I meant above when I said that a nearly straight line can be drawn from Benthamite pleasure to Hayekian preference. Their differences are more pragmatic than real.[52] Another overlap is in their ontologies, for Hayek agrees that social wholes are the products of the 'motivating or constitutive opinions', 'attitudes', 'concepts' and 'beliefs' of individuals, which in 'combination' function as 'constitutive . . . elements' of those 'complex phenomena' that we call social 'wholes'.[53] Despite this overlap, his account of how they appear to exist and his response thereto is importantly different to Bentham's. Opposing classical social contract theorists like Locke and rationalist utilitarians like Bentham, he says that it is a mistake to imagine individuals as being originally unencumbered and free, only later coming together to form communities.[54] What we call 'society' might just be the effect of the actions and properties of individuals, but an 'order [still] arises as a result of . . . the relationships between' them.[55] It is correct that what really matters is the satisfaction of individual preferences, but the bearers of the preferences are born in, live in, and are shaped by already-existing,[56] 'coherent wholes, persistent structures of relationships'.[57] So, rather than treat talk about society as 'absurd', like Bentham, he invests a great deal of significance in its apparent reality, expending much effort explaining how it is that these Benthamite 'fictions' in fact come into being.

The explanation that Hayek gives for how social phenomena come into being is rooted in the ontology he partly shares with Bentham. Because social phenomena are constituted through and in the opinions, attitudes, concepts and beliefs of individuals, always interacting within an 'external . . . environment' of some kind,[58] their nature is fixed by this interplay of forces. The what of any social form, in other words, is in part fixed by the why of all the individuals who bring them into being. Working with this 'systematic subjectivism' about the character of social forms,[59] together with, as I explain in the next section, his epistemic pessimism regarding what we can ever know about the world, Hayek the ethical individualist strives to construct 'a *theory* of society' that has as its goal trying to 'understand the forces which determine the social life of man'.[60] The account that he provides is not one of 'detail' but rather one of 'principle',[61] in the sense that he strives to analyse the structured processes through and in which society emerges.

Of course, Hayek focusses on the market. The reason for this essentialism, what he denigrates as the 'Philosopher's Blindness' when criticising others whose concerns lay elsewhere,[62] reveals further structural differences between his and Bentham's models, concerning what each thinks is important (AS1) for our lives. In the next section, we unpack this essential (AS2) difference, with the following section drawing out its implications for their property theories (AS3).

FROM BAD TO GOOD

An ethics of utilitarianism or preference-satisfaction does little to determine the abstract, let alone concrete, form of a property theory.[63] It tells us nothing at the level of theory because its content is essentially empty. It says that what matters is what individuals find pleasurable or prefer. That is all. For this ethics to prescribe anything more concrete than 'Do what will maximise pleasure / preference-satisfaction', more is necessary. To understand why

Bentham and Hayek advocate the property theories that they do, we must look not just to what they think is good, but also to what they think is bad, that is, those facts about or qualities of individuals that frustrate either utility or preference-satisfaction. Thus, whereas Locke, Hegel and Marx prescribe property rights (AS3) to facilitate directly what is good (AS1, AS2), Bentham and Hayek facilitate it indirectly, by fixing (AS2) rights (AS3) for the sake of frustrating what is bad (AS1).

We begin with Bentham. When reading him, we must keep in mind his atomised, essentially anthropocentric model of man, according to which individuals, like isolated particles of matter,[64] are moved by internal or external forces of pleasure or pain. This model functions not only to fix what is good, it also informs what he thinks frustrates it: insecurity. In the context of prescribing how to allocate property, he paints a depressing picture. When force and fraud exist as means for acquiring the objects needed by individuals to enhance their pleasure and diminish their pain, the sad truth is that people are too lazy, impatient, unjust and insolent to resist the temptation to seize that which is held by others. Bentham writes about 'savages', who, absent security, will:

> . . . strive incessantly against famine; which sometimes cuts off entire tribes. Rivalry for subsistence among them produces the most cruel wars; and, like beasts of prey, men pursue men, as a means of sustenance. The fear of this terrible calamity silences the softer sentiments of nature; pity unites with insensibility in putting to death the old men who can hunt no longer.[65]

Bentham's fear of the masses is striking. As I explain in the next section, it provides (AS1) the measure (AS2) that his empty theory of the good cannot. It enables him to prescribe a concrete scheme for allocating property rights (AS3). By way of preview, for Bentham, the allocation of property must always prioritise the individual's sense of security. The results of failing to do so, Bentham says, are almost too terrible to imagine:

> Every instant of its duration is fertile in calamities; at every step which it prints upon the earth, at every movement which it makes, the existing mass of riches, the fund of abundance and of subsistence, decreases and disappears. The cottage is ravaged as well as the palace; and how often the rage, the caprice even of a moment, delivers up to destruction the slow produce of the labours of an age![66]

Without a state enforcing laws to keep men in check, the control of resources is insecure, with the weak always overwhelmed by the 'crowd of indefatigable enemies' surrounding them.[67] Only by threats of pain can the legislator stop men from seizing what they want when they want it. A loss of secure property rights will destroy the nation itself and cast back into a state of chaos, conflict, pain and misery a savage, beastly creature driven solely by 'native ferocity'.[68] If men 'but taste a drop of blood', it inevitably follows that the 'savage instinct of plunder' will destroy civilisation itself,[69] its debris ruled over by a 'monster . . . beasts joined together back to back'.[70] Without the 'vigilance' of a strong state that is directed towards securing men and their property,[71] happiness is but a fleeting thing. On Bentham's model, promoting security (AS1) by allocating Hohfeldian immunities (AS3) is 'the noblest triumph of humanity over itself' (AS2),[72] for the 'beasts of the forests are not so dangerous to man as he is to himself'.[73]

For critics who emphasise Bentham's theory of the good, what he says is obviously wrong or simplistic; or, as Marx, Nietzsche and Oakeshott put it: stupid, boring and unimportant.[74] Even if we agreed with these polemical assaults, though, because they rest on his utilitarianism, they lose at least some of their sting if we emphasise not what Bentham thinks is good, but what he thinks is bad. For if we imagine how his 'real' individuals will interact in modern, crowded cities where resources are scarce and labour is toil, we begin to see why he advocates the property system that he does. In this society of strangers, men lunge for power or control of objects.[75] They do this not because they have what Rousseau calls *amour-propre*. They do not suffer inflated, vainglorious self-esteems. The opposite is, in fact, true, for his men are lazy, they just want to be left alone. It is 'not desire but fear', as Arendt puts it, that drives them.[76] They have no will-to-dominate but fear this desire in others. To protect themselves, they push out their chests, but their chests are hollow. Not robust or confident, rather timid and alone, each desperately tries to shore up their defences or increase their supplies, tragically leading to the social violence that they fear.

Concerns of this kind, Hayek says, are nothing more than 'myth'.[77] The road to serfdom does not emerge through and in social life itself; rather, it is constructed by means of a particular form. The violence Bentham fears is the product of his solution, rooted as it is in his crude and naively optimistic rationalism. The red thread that runs through all of Hayek's political and legal thought is this epistemic pessimism. Nobody, Hayek says, can ever have access to all of the information constitutive of social phenomena and which bear on the satisfaction of individual preferences.[78] He offers both contingent and logical arguments for man's 'inevitable ignorance'.[79]

Practically, nobody could know all the facts relevant to society's effective functioning. The world, partly constituted by diverse preferences (GP1) and the means to satisfy them, is just too complex. As for the means, only the 'man on the spot',[80] the farmer or store manager, has access to the details or technical facts.[81] No office bureaucrat can know how it works on the ground. As for preferences, what individuals value exists 'inside' them,[82] it belongs to a complex diversity of 'subjective worlds'.[83] Only they can ever have 'immediate' access to all of their ideas,[84] beliefs, motives, and so on, that inform the actions that constitute the social whole. Because only the individual himself can know what he wants, unless we extinguish our unique 'differentiation and diversity' (GP1),[85] such that the why that informs our actions is rendered largely uniform, it is both 'naïve and childlike'[86] to think that it could be 'mastered by a single mind'.[87]

The total accumulation of all this information, though, is impossible for a more basic reason, for there are at least four obstacles that render it 'logically untenable'.[88] First, social interaction is always generating new preferences. For example, the advertiser might provoke or create a desire that did not previously exist.[89] Second, whilst individuals have access to their preferences, much of their knowledge is tacit. Whilst this knowledge impacts on what we decide and do, we are not conscious of it. Some preferences are only revealed when we choose and act. For this reason, we cannot articulate its content in advance. Since even the individual cannot consciously identify all their preferences, let alone others,[90] it is not possible to collate as propositional knowledge all the information that is relevant to their satisfaction. Third, the 'particular circumstances' relevant to what goods and services we produce and offer are often 'unarticulated', hardly 'articulable', in the sense that it depends on the 'entrepreneur's hunch' and thus is 'impossible to make . . . public'.[91] And finally, individuals 'never act, and could never act, in full consideration of all the facts of a particular situation', but rather they act by 'singling out as relevant only some aspects of it'. For this reason, we necessarily perceive, evaluate and decide on the basis of incomplete information. It is 'impossible', Hayek says, for us 'fully to understand why we do what we do'.[92] We always 'move' unawares within a 'framework' of this kind.[93] Because these frameworks operate 'supra-consciously', they cannot be articulated as objects of 'explicit knowledge',[94] which means we are constitutively ignorant of facts relevant to the satisfaction of our preferences.

Citing these diverse epistemic limits, Hayek positions himself against all those who think that social problems can always be solved by applying our reason to facts. It does not matter whether they are his mentors like Ludwig von Mises,[95] utilitarians like Bentham,[96] or communalists like Marx.[97] With his 'low opinion of men's wisdom and capacities',[98] he opposes all 'planning'.[99] He is not against reason itself, but rather positions himself against 'constructivism',[100] that 'crude rationalism' which purports to design 'social institutions according to a pattern prescribed by . . . individual reason'.[101] He rejects Bentham and his legislator, who pretend to have the knowledge and capacity to 'construct . . . rules by deduction from explicit premises'.[102]

This premise, that we are constitutively ignorant, produces in Hayek a political scepticism, for whom all theory and politics must be structured by the recognition of our epistemic limits. Only with this 'humility',[103] he says at different times throughout his intellectual life, can we resist the noble but destructive idea that we could be effective social 'engineers'.[104] These epistemic (AS1) worries (AS2) mean that he warns against altering (AS3) existing rules without a clear, positive reason to do so.[105] In this sense, he is a conservative, but tradition is not itself 'sacred' (GP5).[106] Change should be approached cautiously, but only because we usually do not know what we are doing. Existing institutions, contrarily, by 'trial and error',[107] will often embody an 'accumulated cultural knowledge' about what works.[108] If a social form exists, chances are that it is facilitating the 'successful pursuit of our conscious aims' better than anything else we could imagine.[109] For this reason, they deserve our 'reverence'.[110] When we know the facts, though, Hayek is open to the 'radical departure' from,[111] 'radical changes' to,[112] the 'sweeping-away' of,[113] the prevailing order and its presumed fundamentals.[114] Progress, 'experimentation',[115] and even radical change can be good, but only if effected consistently with the principles of 'true individualism'.[116] What are these principles? They are those that best satisfy our individual preferences. To identify them, however, we must centre our 'constitutional ignorance' (AS1),[117] keep it 'constantly in mind',[118] for this is the 'fundamental fact', it is always our 'central problem' (AS2).[119]

To satisfy preferences, we need two forms of knowledge: first, knowledge of what individuals prefer; second, what resources exist to satisfy these preferences. Given our necessary ignorance, we cannot look to a Benthamite legislator to assimilate all the facts. Thus, the central problem of social theory is always: 'what is the best way of utilizing knowledge initially dispersed' amongst individuals?[120] How can we combine the 'fragments of knowledge existing in different minds' in a way that will generate the 'results which, if they were to be brought about deliberately, would require a knowledge on the part of the directing mind which no single person can possess'?[121] In fact, this epistemic worry (AS1) is so fundamental (AS2) to Hayek's social and political thought that how we resolve it must form the basis of all 'political maxims',[122] property included (AS3). Before outlining how he assuages his worry, let me outline his conceptions of liberty, liberalism, democracy and the rule of law, for they further demonstrate the privileged status that he affords to ignorance in his social and political thought.[123]

Hayek's liberty is negative in form: do not interfere with how private persons decide and act. Whilst interference is never right in the private sphere, the boundary of the private is not drawn in the abstract, but is delimited by applying principle to facts. This principle is the mitigation of ignorance, which means that each person should have as much liberty as necessary to apply their 'peculiar knowledge and skill with the aim of furthering the aims for which *he* cares'.[124] Whilst freedom must be upheld against 'expediency' or 'pragmatism', where we act for a 'certain known and tangible gain',[125] its value is instrumental. Protecting liberty is the most effective 'means for the fullest development of the powers of the inter-individual process',[126] that is, the mechanism through which dispersed information is aggregated and used to satisfy preferences. So, liberty is 'supreme',[127] but because no person can know all the facts. Like all concepts, it is 'an adaptation to our ignorance'.[128] Because the 'value of freedom' is rooted in our ignorance,[129] in its absence 'action would have to be judged as a means of bringing about known effects',[130] which is always satisfying preferences. What matters is not that you decide but that you are best placed to decide. This is why freedom is important: 'If we knew how freedom would be used, the case for it would largely disappear',[131] he says, for ultimately it is only 'because we want people to use knowledge which we do not possess that we let them decide for themselves'.[132]

Concern about ignorance also informs Hayek's favoured form of political rule: democracy.[133] As the procedure of majority-rule, democracy 'is not an ultimate or absolute value and must be judged by what it will achieve'.[134] Democracy 'is a means rather than an end'.[135] It is often good since it tends to promote liberty, peace and public education,[136] which matter since they facilitate information-use to satisfy our preferences. Mitigating ignorance is also the end of all state action, with liberalism a policy that adopts 'competition, the market, and prices as its ordering principle and uses the legal framework enforced by the state in order to make competition as effective and beneficial as possible', supplemented 'where, and only where, it cannot be made effective'.[137] In the next section, I unpack the market's role in his theory. Important for now is that he thinks that it mitigates ignorance by aggregating and communicating dispersed information.

Ignorance also underlies his account of the rule of law. The exercise of public power must be:

> bound by rules fixed and announced beforehand – rules which make it possible to foresee with fair certainty how the authority will use its coercive powers in given circumstances, and to plan one's individual affairs on the basis of this knowledge.[138]

So, law has two basic functions. First, it must secure the space in which individuals can pursue their ends. Second, it must promote the certainty of expectations. This matters not for Bentham's reasons – without it, property does not exist – but because we need to know with a degree of confidence how the state will act, either on its own accord or when judging private disputes. Law must not try to realise particular interests, but must embody abstract rules that mediate peaceably conflicting relations (GP1). Only if law is general, negative, public, clear, equal, stable, coherent and prospective, he argues, can we access information relevant to our plans, thereby positioning us to realise our own ends.[139]

If freedom is that space in which individuals use what little they know in the pursuit of their ends, if liberalism is the policy of creating this space, and if democracy and law secure, stabilise and make this space useful, how can we effectively utilise it given our ignorance? To answer, we must turn to Hayek's property theory. In doing so, Bentham will again act as his foil.

SAFE SPACES OR OPEN SOCIETIES

For Bentham, the first duty of the legislator is to provide the security needed to stop individuals lunging for power or control of the resources needed to maximise their pleasure and to minimise their pain. Without it, happiness is always fleeting; with it, humanity can triumph over itself. This privileging (AS2) of security (AS1), for the purpose of making individuals feel safe from all the 'potential robbers' lurking in the shadows,[140] functions to fix the complex of property rights that Bentham prescribes (AS3). To see this, we must sketch his conception of law.

For Bentham, the existence of a sovereign legislator with power to issue various commands, prohibitions, liberties or powers, backed up by the threat of punishment, is of central importance. For only threats of pain can restrain his timid but savage individuals from seizing whatever they want, whenever they want it. Commands, prohibitions, liberties and powers constitute the logical structure of law itself.[141] The substantive content of this logical structure, though, is fixed by his ethics and ontology.[142] Like all that exists, law is reducible to distributions of forces: pleasure and pain.[143] In law, we call them rights, to which correspond obligations.[144] 'Rights are in themselves advantages, benefits, for him who enjoys them. Obligations, on the contrary, are duties, charges, onerous to him who ought to fulfil them.'[145] When the pleasure-maximising legislator is making laws, therefore, it follows that it must only pass a law if the 'evil' obligation is outweighed by the 'good' right.[146] In the context of the rights and obligations that attach to property, Bentham says, four 'subordinate ends' should structure the legislator's weighing up of goods and evils: security, subsistence, abundance and equality.[147] The more perfectly any law fulfils each subordinate end, the more effectively it will maximise what ultimately (GP5) matters: pleasure (GP3). Whilst the subordinate ends can overlap, in the sense that promoting one contributes towards the fulfilment of the others, the overlap is not total. For this reason, Bentham ranks the subordinate ends in their order of relative importance (GP7).[148]

Neither subsistence nor abundance require much direct aid from laws,[149] Bentham argues, for the 'constant and irresistible power' of the pains of 'need' and the 'enjoyment' of its satisfaction, are sufficient 'motives' for individuals to 'labour' to sustain themselves.[150] Moreover, desires are elastic, they 'extend with [the] means' available, and in fact we tend to work harder the more we have, so to the question as to whether law is necessary to promote abundance, Bentham answers: 'No!'[151] But law is necessary for equality and security to be possible. On equality, Bentham says that property rights afford their holders 'a *certain chance of happiness*',[152] for they are means to satisfy their needs. As an observable fact, therefore, those with more rights will have a better chance of increasing their pleasure than individuals with fewer rights.[153] Then relying on a version of the law of diminishing marginal utility, he says that the pleasure of holding and exercising property rights does not increase proportionately with their holding and increase of such rights. Therefore, there is prima facie reason for a greater equality of holdings, albeit a rather qualified one.[154] This reason, however, is gutted by Bentham's analysis of security.

Security, for Bentham, is 'the principal object of law'.[155] Both pleasure and pain pertain not just to the present but also the future, which means that his individuals have to be made secure in their 'expectations'.[156] Moreover, 'there is no such thing as natural property', because property is 'entirely the work of law', and property 'is nothing but a basis of expectation; the expectation of deriving certain advantages from a thing which we are said to possess', in the sense that we stand in a certain relation to it: our expectation of control. 'Property and law are born together, and die together.' Only by securing expectations can the legislator fulfil its end: maximise 'the happiness of society',[157] everyone included, for security will 'contribute as much as to the happiness of the cottage as the security of the palace'.[158]

Like subsistence, this expectation is necessary for life as such, whilst abundance and equality relate only to its quality. Security, however, is more important. This is for two reasons. First, it is concerned with all that is pleasurable or painful in life,[159] not only with the present and fleeting, like hunger and thirst.[160] Second, security is necessary to fulfil our other subordinate ends. The expectation of future control is necessary for the production that enables subsistence, abundance and equality. Without the expectation that we will have this control over the fruits of our painful labour, we will not produce useful objects, thereby frustrating efforts to promote subsistence and abundance.[161] Industry and commerce benefit others,[162] so a diminution in productivity will also diminish their pleasure. Moreover, without security, we fear losing existing stores of objects. This fear is itself a pain, but it also drives individuals to neglect and diminish their stores, yet again to the detriment of others. Finally, loss or fear of loss generates conflict over resources. Not only is the harm caused by conflict bad, but conflict diminishes the means to satisfy wants, for it results in the destruction of existing objects, and it negatively impacts production.[163]

For Bentham, security is non-existent without laws that create and enforce existing control of objects. Without law, we lunge for power and control of objects. Because property is an expectation of future control, it follows that without law property does not exist. And since positive, effective law is needed to ensure our expectations of control, law itself is constitutive of property: property *is* an expectation. Because Bentham's world is formed by atomised pleasure-seekers who will seize what they can when they can (AS1), it follows from his conception of property that property only (AS2) exists when we protect existing rights (AS3). The 'triumph of humanity over itself' is this 'beneficent genius' of security,[164] that is, the enforcement of almost-absolute immunities (AS3). Law's 'first duty' is always to 'maintain' actually 'established' property rights.[165] This is so even if slavery,[166] which Bentham recognises as a pain and opposed in practice, is part of the existing system. Similarly, whilst equality tends to increase pleasure, the insecurity accompanied by most efforts to promote it is so great that when security and equality conflict, the latter must 'yield'.[167] If it does not, all will 'shortly be destroyed'.[168] Only if altering rights is the only way to prevent a worse fate,[169] like starvation or death,[170] can sacrificing expectations through the redistribution to others be justified. If law intrudes further, if it forces equality or aims for abundance by means of threats of pain, then the only 'wise course' for an isolated individual will be 'prodigality',[171] for the sacrifice of security cannot but lead to chaos, slavery and death.[172]

A benefit of contrasting Hayek and Bentham is that we reveal the importance of the concrete forms of models. Despite related ontologies and ethics, because Hayek sits the individual within a social setting instead of seeing him as isolated, and because he emphasises epistemic limits in a way that inversely correlates with Bentham's belief in potential rational perfection, makes all the difference when it comes to their views about property. Rather than making individuals feel safe, Hayek says that the allocation of property (AS3) is ultimately (AS2) 'a problem of how to secure the best use of resources known to any of the members of society, for ends whose relative importance only these individuals know' (AS1).[173] Stated more fully, property always concerns the effective use of classes of information: private information of one's desires or settings; public information pertaining to state action; and information about the preferences and actions of other people insofar as they affect the environment in which an individual acts.

So, apart from conscious and tacit information about what we value, our natural environment and applicable laws, we also need information about what others desire and do. Because this last class of information is dispersed, the basic (AS2) problem when we are deciding how to allocate property (AS3) is to determine how most effectively to communicate all the 'further information' the individual 'needs to fit his decisions into the whole pattern of changes of the larger economic system' (AS1). We need a system that operates to facilitate the aggregation and communication to individuals of information about 'how much more or less urgently wanted are the alternative things he produces or uses'.[174] We do not need information about why the desires of others and conditions change, only the importance to them of the things with which we are concerned. This social knowledge, Hayek tells us, can only be acquired through and in a 'procedure of discovery' that is characteristic of markets, 'the extended order',[175] that has evolved through time and in fact is coterminous with 'civilisation' itself.[176] The argument for this bold proposition, his conception of the theory of 'marginal utility',[177] has five related parts.

First, the value of scarce objects or services is determined by desire, not an inherent property attaching to it.[178] Second, in competitive markets, where individuals can choose between similar rights in goods and services supplied by different producers, the fact that someone with limited resources purchases a right at the price fixed by the market reveals that their having it will satisfy some desire.[179] Third, in the market, rights are allocated to those who desire them the most (GP3), since your decision to purchase the right on offer and my decision not to evidence the relative strengths of our desires (GP1).[180] Fourth, prices capture information about scarcities and diverse and changing desires or actions of 'unknown' others.[181] Lastly, the knowledge of prices provides information, or 'signals',[182] relevant to the desires and actions of consumers or producers.[183] So, Hayek concludes, we most effectively facilitate the satisfaction of preferences through a process that integrates and disseminates dispersed information in the form of prices (AS2). This process can only arise if individuals have Hohfeldian powers to exchange and claim-rights to exclude all other individuals from their use of objects (AS3). This requires laws that demarcate and protect the 'ranges of objects over which only particular individuals are allowed to dispose and from the control of which all others are excluded'.[184] So, rather than prescribing rights to persons directly, we best allocate resources for purposes whose relative value only an individual knows by making their decision to pay (or not to pay) for property – goods and services – the ground for allocating them.[185] And because these allocations occur without conscious direction, the property order that emerges through and in the operation of the market's processes is 'spontaneous'.

With the concept of spontaneous order, he turns Bentham on his head. For both, all politics is essentially concerned with the effective use of information. Contrary to Bentham, though, Hayek directly confronts 'the limits of what individual conscious reason can accomplish'.[186] Therefore, the constructive function of this idea is to retrieve from the rubble of his critique of the naïve and childlike rationalism he condemns, a theory that likewise privileges the prescriptive function of information. As Oakeshott describes Hayek's project: 'A plan to resist all planning may be better than its opposite, but it belongs to the same style of politics.'[187] In place of the crude, centralising plans of rationalists, he constructs a more sophisticated one. Since individuals are constitutively ignorant (AS1), we must necessarily (AS2) decentralise decision-making powers to a system of competitive exchange (AS3), which will thereafter work behind our backs, ordering diverse and conflicting (GP1) desires and actions.[188] It is not enough, however, to understand this fact, since conflict is not always reconciled 'faultlessly' in a competitive form.[189] When not, the system will not efficiently facilitate the satisfaction of preferences (GP3). Therefore, the 'march of individual liberty',[190] he says, demands not just an 'intellectual mastery' of the principles by which markets work,[191] but also their proper use and application. This does not mean *dirigisme*,[192] or conscious direction. We can only apply true individualistic principles, he argues, by cultivating 'conditions favorable to further growth' of competition.[193] Therefore, whilst the state must coordinate all the spontaneous forces of desire that make good possible, as well as correct their defects when they arise, 'encasing' them in rules, as Quinn Slobodian puts it,[194] ultimately society must be ordered by itself. The resulting social whole will not be a final, holistic equilibrium but a fragmented, and for particular individuals sometimes 'painful',[195] systematic whole. This totality, though stable in large part, always evolves and adjusts, as reflected in the changes in market prices, to a 'pattern' of forces that we can describe,[196] but whose 'particular content',[197] some of which will be known to particular individuals, is forever beyond our theoretical grasp and practical control.

So, Hayek concludes in a metaphysical flourish, we must admit our ignorance (AS1), 'bow in recognition' (AS2) to the 'super-individual structures' that make possible progress itself,[198] and by means of created or conventional rules regulate (AS3) these forces in a way that promotes the competition required to mitigate ignorance. In doing this, he says in Marxian spirit, the 'chains' on 'human Reason' will be broken.[199] And with this, we will release a 'self-ordering process',[200] the operation of which distributes property in the most efficient way possible, in the sense that it 'assures a maximization of output',[201] and thereby the opportunities for satisfying the diversity (GP1) of preferences (GP3) held by the elements who constitute this social whole.

If we adopt this model, Hayek's property theory follows close behind. If the content of ethics rests on preferences, we must enable their satisfaction.[202] Given scarcity and ignorance (AS1) of the information relevant to allocating resources to satisfy preferences, we need a system that will efficiently aggregate and communicate this information. In 'fact and logic' (AS2),[203] Hayek says, the system that most efficiently performs this function is one regulated, but not controlled, by the state, in which individuals have the power to exchange rights with others (AS3).

Despite the market's fundamental role, Hayek also believes that the state must ensure that each individual has a 'minimum income' to obtain goods or services like food, water, shelter, education, medicine, and so on, and it must also ensure the provision of insurance against harm and unavoidable unemployment.[204] Often, the market will provide, but if it does not, the state as a 'service agency' must.[205] Absent these rights, Hayek says, we will be exposed to coercion by those with them,[206] treated not as desiring subjects but as another's objects. This treatment is bad not because it violates our autonomy, but because, desperate to stay alive and avoid pain, we will not use our limited knowledge as we know best, but rather will act as others prefer or direct.[207] Once again, we see the intimate link drawn by Hayek between good (GP3) and bad (AS1), where the former is ideally maximised by minimising the latter.

Hayek knows that 'luck'[208] or 'chance'[209] means that individuals will often have unequal rights in the objects needed to participate in markets. Because this will diminish competition, law must try to improve opportunities to participate (AS3). Perfect competition, however, is impossible: efforts to equalise fully participation are incompatible with a competitive market, so imperfect market-allocations of property rights are unavoidable. Whatever those who say they follow Hayek argue, therefore, he does not think that ignorance can be obliterated. What he thinks is that given the perceived 'alternative',[210] that is, centralised power and the resulting loss of competition,[211] residual imperfections are something that must be endured. Relatedly, because competition mitigates ignorance (AS1), rights must (AS2) be fixed in a way that best promotes it (AS3). This is primarily an empirical task. Here there is a critical difference with Bentham, for whom our security is so important that he tolerates slavery. Hayek, however, is less concerned about security and he would never permit slavery. Slavery is bad for the same reason he opposes coercion and trade unions.[212] They are not efficient. Provided that the rule of law is satisfied and just compensation is provided to cater for upset expectations, however, property rights must be swept away if this will advance competition.[213]

Whilst for Bentham, these changes lead to war, Hayek's view that we are socially situated means that he does not think us so vulnerable or insecure. His fatalism is epistemic.[214] A loss of competition by centralising of economic decision-making power, not regime change, will not only 'destroy . . . developed individuals and buildings and art and cities' and thus 'doom a large part of mankind to poverty and death',[215] it puts humanity on the road to serfdom.[216] As Slobodian explains: 'Hayek saw the real danger not in the rule of the jungle but in the rule of the engineers.'[217] To satisfy preferences by way of a centralised plan, those with political power must overcome their lack of information. Engineers only have one way to do this: like 'Spartan' tyrants,[218] they have to strip individuals of the independence and freedom that lie at the root of their heterogeneous (GP1) hidden (AS1) preferences (GP3). Bentham strives for a society with safe spaces, where each individual is secure from the spectral presence of 'ghosts' from which he could never 'wholly' 'free' his 'imagination',[219] of men 'drunken' on evil spirits.[220] Hayek, contrarily, aims to revive the nineteenth century's '*Great* or *Open* society',[221] one without 'walls',[222] before the gates of the gulag slam shut.

Much like Bentham is called stupid, boring and unimportant by some and a genius by others, to his followers Hayek is a polymath to whom we owe our freedom from Stalinist forms of domination, whereas for Hayek's critics he is a principal enabler of neoliberal coercion and hegemony.[223] Like all great systematisers, both devotees and critics, though perhaps guilty of exaggerations, are right. Each does well to emphasise a fragment of the larger picture, which is true and important: often we are vulnerable, often we are ignorant. To paraphrase perhaps the greatest systematiser, Hegel, to whom we turn in chapter 4, this fact means that when we criticise others, approval or disapproval is dependent on whether we look to find 'fault' or to reveal what is 'positive' in their systems.[224] Or as I argue in part II, since the anthropological approach by its nature both illuminates and obscures what matters, philosophers who use this method are necessarily deserving subjects of both esteem and excoriation.

NOTES

1. For background, see Emmanuelle de Champs, *Enlightenment and Utility: Bentham in French, Bentham in France* (2015). See also Ross Harrison, *Bentham* (1999) 7–13, J.H. Burns, 'Jeremy Bentham: From Radical Enlightenment to Philosophic Radicalism' 8 *Bentham Newsletter* (June 1984) 4–13, and Michael Oakeshott, *Rationalism in Politics and Other Essays* (new and expanded ed, 1991) 132–50.
2. James E. Crimmins, *Secular Utilitarianism* (1990) 282–92 and 314–16.
3. FG Preface p. 393. On science as epistemological ideal, Mary P. Mack, *Jeremy Bentham: An Odyssey of Ideas 1748–1792* (1963) 102–17, 129–41 and 262–331, Crimmins (n 2) 21–40 and 273–82, and David John Manning, *The Mind of Jeremy Bentham* (1968) 8–16.
4. PL Ch I p. 1.
5. On paraphrasis, a method indebted to Locke's epistemology in ECHU, by which neutrality and clarity are attained, see FG Ch. V p. 495 para. 6 fn b.
6. PL Ch. XIII p. 74.
7. Mack (n 3) 209.

8. IPML Ch. III pp. 24–28 (sources of pleasure and pain) and Ch. V pp. 33–42 (kinds of pleasure and pain). See also PL Ch. VI pp. 20–27 (kinds of pleasure and pain).

9. IPML Ch. I p. 4.

10. PL Ch. I p. 3.

11. PL Ch. V p. 20.

12. IPML Ch. I p. 1.

13. IPML Ch. III p. 24.

14. PL Ch. XII p. 60.

15. PL Ch. II p. 4, on 'The Ascetic Principle'.

16. PL Ch. V p. 20.

17. FG Ch. 1 p. 446 para. 48.

18. IPML Ch. IV pp. 29–32.

19. For readings against and for that offered here, see Harrison (n 1) 167–94, Manning (n 3) 24, Alasdair MacIntyre, *After Virtue: A Study in Moral Theory* (3ed, 2007) 62–63 and Mack (n 3) 143–44 and 291.

20. For an example of this, see IPML Ch. III pp. 24–28 (sources), Ch. IV pp. 29–32 (measurement), Ch. V pp. 33–42 (kinds), and Ch. VI pp. 43–69 (circumstances influencing sensibility).

21. PL Ch. XIII pp. 76–77.

22. Pleasures like sympathy, friendship and possession, and pains like defamation, fear and loss, along with mixtures of these and other experiences (PL Ch. VI pp. 20–27 and IPML Ch. V pp. 33–42), natural and artificial (PL Ch. XII p. 64).

23. PL Ch. X p. 52: 'This analysis will furnish us a moral *criterion*, a means of decomposing human actions, as we decompose the mixed metals, in order to discover their intrinsic value, and their precise quantity of alloy.'

24. PL Ch. VIII p. 31.

25. PL Ch. VIII p. 32. Law can be direct or indirect, impose sanctions or nudge (Mack (n 3) 291–331). For both, it can conflict with what subjects think best (Harrison (n 1) 228–32).

26. IPML Ch. IV p. 29.

27. H.L.A Hart, *Essays on Bentham: Studies in Jurisprudence and Political Theory* (1982) 51.

28. IPML Ch. IV pp. 29–32.

29. PL Ch. XIII p. 67.

30. PCC Part First Ch. V p. 103.

31. PCC Part Second Ch. III p. 177.

32. IPML Ch. XIII p. 313: 'it cannot but be admitted, that the only interests which a man at all times *adequate* motives for consulting, are his own'.

33. PL Ch. XIII p. 74.

34. PCC Part Third Ch. III p. 212.

35. PCC Part Second Ch. V p. 189.

36. PCC Part First Ch. XV p. 144.

37. PCC Part First Ch. V. p. 101.

38. PCC Part First Ch. XV p. 145. On the 'illusion' of intergenerational identity, see PCC Part Second Ch. II p. 175.

39. For discussion, see Harrison (n 1) 24–105.
40. FO 202–03.
41. IPML Ch. I p. 3.
42. EOL Ch. VI p. 325 and FO 197-98.
43. FO 201.
44. FO 195, 197 and 203.
45. EOL Ch. VI p. 325.
46. FO 198.
47. Hart (n 27) 129.
48. PL Ch. XIII p. 71.
49. PL Ch. XIII p. 74.
50. PCC Part First Ch. V p. 102.
51. What matters is creating conditions for individuals to achieve 'their aims' (LLL 53), so only 'general and abstract rules that one must take into account in individual decisions in accordance with individual aims deserve the name of morals' (FC 65). In FC, ethics is portrayed as a product of evolution, with values being adaptations that enable group survival (11–28). This matters since we prefer life to death – life being a necessary condition (27–28) to 'prosper' (76), that is, to 'obtain *what they want*' (104–05), or have 'a better chance' of doing so (85). From this ideal, it follows that 'capitalists', who 'create or preserve' more life, are 'more important' than workers and those on the 'periphery' (127–33) of the market, who cannot complain, for they owe their lives as a 'surplus' 'population' to 'capitalism' (SPPE 208). For further references, see RS 62–63, CL 35 and SPPE 173–74. For efforts to classify Hayek's ethics, see John Gray, *Hayek on Liberty* (3ed, 1998), Chandran Kukathas, *Hayek and Modern Liberalism* (1989), Roland Kley, *Hayek's Social and Political Thought* (1994), and Richard A. Posner, *The Economics of Justice* (1983).
52. On the move from utility to preference being difficulties with measurement, see Amartya Sen, *Development as Freedom* (1999) 67–70 and Anton Jäger and Daniel Zamora Vargas, *Welfare for Markets: A Global History of Basic Income* (2023) 37–45.
53. CRS 36–43.
54. On this issue, see Kukathas (n 51) 124–29.
55. CRS 39.
56. SPPE 76–78.
57. CRS 80.
58. SPPE 71.
59. CRS 39.
60. IEO 6.
61. CRS 40–43.
62. FC 45–47.
63. This fact is often remarked upon, for example, CVI 758–79 fn 51, Posner (n 51) 33–34 and 42, and Alan Ryan, *Property and Political Theory* (1984) 91–94.
64. De Champs (n 1) 47 quotes a draft letter by Bentham, where he writes: 'Thus, after Descartes, I reduce everything to matter and movement. Matter and movement are, in my opinion, all that exist. Quality, properly speaking, does not exist.'

65. PCC Part First Ch. VII p. 109.
66. PCC Part First Ch. VII pp. 109–10.
67. PCC Part First Ch. VII p. 110.
68. PCC Part First Ch. XV p. 145.
69. PCC Part First Ch. XV p. 145.
70. PCC Part Second Ch. VI p. 195.
71. PCC Part First Ch. VII p. 110.
72. PCC Part First Ch. IX p. 114.
73. PCC Part First Ch. X p. 118.
74. CVI 759 fn 51, Friedrich Nietzsche, *Beyond Good and Evil: Prelude to a Philosophy of the Future* (tr. RJ Hollingdale, 2014) § 228, and Oakeshott (n 1) 150.
75. Affection can drive individuals to act together (Ch. VI IPML 53–55), but the relations are weak and unstable, so must be reinforced by threats: see PCC Ch. III pp. 209–13 (guardian and ward) Ch. IV pp. 213–15 (father and child), and Ch. V pp. 216–36 (marriage).
76. Hannah Arendt, *The Human Condition* (2ed, 1998) 309.
77. FC 12.
78. LLL 10–15.
79. CL 29 and SPPE 115.
80. IEO 84.
81. FC 88.
82. IEO 76.
83. FC 95.
84. CRS 60.
85. FC 126–27.
86. FC 47.
87. CRS 52.
88. FC 8.
89. IEO 96.
90. SPPE 36–37.
91. FC 89.
92. LLL 30.
93. SPPE 87.
94. SPPE 60–63.
95. Stephen Kresge and Leif Wenar (eds), *Hayek on Hayek* (1994) 62.
96. LLL 184–90. For specific references to Bentham, see SPPE 162 and LLL 22.
97. FC 52–53.
98. CL 8.
99. SPPE 82–105.
100. NSP 3–22.
101. CL 406.
102. LLL 21.
103. IEO 8 and 32, CRS 92 and FC 8.
104. CRS 94–102.
105. FC 20–21.

106. LLL 191.
107. FC 20, 36 and 74.
108. FC 58.
109. LLL 12.
110. SPPE 39.
111. LLL 4.
112. LLL 85.
113. CL 399.
114. Critique must be 'immanent' to and change must 'proceed within a given system of [existing] rules' (LLL 190–93).
115. FC 53.
116. IEO 1–32.
117. LLL 176.
118. LLL 13.
119. LLL 176.
120. IEO 78–79.
121. IEO 54.
122. IEO 6.
123. On its relevance to his thought, see discussions in Chris Matthew Sciabarra, *Marx, Hayek and Utopia* (1995), Andrew Gamble, *The Iron Cage of Liberty* (1996), and Adam James Tebble, *F.A. Hayek* (2010).
124. IEO 17.
125. LLL 55.
126. CRS 86.
127. SPPE 142 and CL 68.
128. LLL 205.
129. LLL 55.
130. LLL 205.
131. CL 31.
132. CL 95.
133. LLL 349–52.
134. CL 106.
135. CL 107.
136. CL 107–09.
137. IEO 110.
138. RS 75–76.
139. Generally, see CL 20–21, 148–61 and 205–19.
140. This phrase by Hart (n 27) 68, concerns Bentham's later attitude to rulers, but it appears to me to be even more apt as a description of Bentham's view of the masses.
141. For discussion, see the chapter '*Bentham's Of Law in General*' in Hart (n 27) 105–26.
142. Ibid., 125.
143. FO 206.
144. PCC Part First Ch. I p. 95.
145. PCC Part First Ch. I p. 93.

146. PCC Part First Ch. I pp. 93–94.
147. PCC Part First Ch. II pp. 96–97.
148. PCC Part First Ch. III pp. 97–99.
149. PCC Part First Ch. III p. 98.
150. PCC Part First Ch. IV p. 100.
151. PCC Part First Ch. V pp. 101–02.
152. PCC Part First Ch. VI p. 104.
153. PCC Part First Ch. VI p. 104.
154. PCC Part First Ch. VI pp. 105–09.
155. PCC Part First Ch. VII p. 109.
156. PCC Part First Ch. VII p. 111.
157. PCC Part First Ch. VIII p. 111–13.
158. PCC Part First Ch. IX p. 114.
159. PCC Part First Ch. XI p. 120.
160. PCC Part First Ch. II pp. 96–97.
161. PCC Part First Ch. II pp. 96–97 and Ch. III 97–99.
162. PL Ch. X p. 53 and PCC Part First Ch. IX pp. 113–14 and Ch. X 118–19.
163. PCC Part First Ch. X pp. 115–19.
164. PCC Part First Ch. X p. 119.
165. PCC Part First Ch. XI p. 119.
166. PCC Part First Ch. XII p. 122–23. Slavery, he says, must be gradually removed, rather than by means of 'introducing a new social order'.
167. PCC Part First Ch. XI p. 120.
168. PCC Part First Ch. II p. 99.
169. PCC Part First Ch. XIII pp. 124–26: '*Sacrifice of Security to Security*'.
170. PCC Part First Ch. XIV pp. 132–33.
171. PCC Part First Ch. XI p. 121.
172. PCC Part First Ch. IX pp. 119–22 and 201–09. This is consistent with the fact that he permits succession laws promoting equality (PCC Part First Ch. XII pp. 122–23), and allows for taxes to fund the state, 'useful' religious bodies, arts and sciences (PCC Part First Ch. XIV pp. 133–37), since he distinguishes impermissible loss of security and permissible 'defalcations' (PCC Part First Ch. XIII pp. 124–26), the latter covering changes effected by regularly legislating for the future and so not undermining security. For more on distribution, see PCC Part Second pp. 158–98.
173. IEO 78.
174. IEO 84.
175. FC 19.
176. FC 16.
177. FC 94–100.
178. FC 95–96.
179. IEO 84–86.
180. FC 95–96.
181. FC 72 and 97.
182. FC 31, 46, 59, 74–76, 84, 113 and 123.

183. RS 50–52. For detailed examination, see the three chapters on competition, free enterprise and socialist calculation, in IEO 92–208.

184. LLL 102.

185. IEO 78–79.

186. CRS 203.

187. Oakeshott (n 1) 26. For a similar point, see Quinn Slobodian, *Globalists: The End of Empire and the Birth of Neoliberalism* (2018) 271.

188. On non-intentional but purposive ordering, see CRS 80–86.

189. CRS 97. On spontaneous disorder, see LLL 34–52.

190. RS 16.

191. RS 18–19. The principles concern the impersonal allocative function of competition rather than allocative outcomes (CRS 203).

192. CL 231.

193. CRS 91.

194. Slobodian (n 187) 5–7. Rather than 'directing' individuals, we must 'enforce[e] and improv[e] the rules conducive to the formation of a spontaneous order'. (LLL 49).

195. FC 6.

196. SPPE 34–36.

197. LLL 44.

198. FC 10 and 75.

199. IEO 32. See IEO 15, where he distinguishes his conception of human reason from that of the rationalists.

200. FC 73.

201. SPPE 36.

202. LLL 169–73.

203. LLL 5.

204. RS 124–26 and 131, SPPE 175 and CL 257–60 and 285–26.

205. CL 258.

206. Another reason is the 'desire of individuals to protect themselves against the consequences of the extreme misery of their fellows' (CL 286).

207. CL 134.

208. LLL 234–36, 256–57 and 276.

209. LLL 176–78.

210. FC 63.

211. RS 91–104.

212. FC 131.

213. CL 217–18.

214. Judith N. Shklar, *After Utopia: The Decline of Political Faith* (2020) 235–39.

215. FC 27–28.

216. Until we grasp that concrete allocative principles will, through their 'inherent logic', lead to 'totalitarianism', this will be the 'inevitable outcome' (LLL 60 and 68).

217. Slobodian (n 187) 259.

218. FC 31–32.

219. Bentham, quoted Mack (n 3) 49.

220. Ibid., 44: 'As they [undergraduates at Oxford] roared their drunken songs at midnight, he [a 13-year-old Bentham] cowered under the sheets hiding from ghosts.'

221. SPPE 163–64.

222. On the 'wall' metaphor, see Slobodian (n 187) 27–54.

223. For sustained treatment, see Slobodian (n 187). For a U.S. perspective, see Gary Gerstle, *The Rise and Fall of the Neoliberal Order: America and the World in the Free Market Era* (2022) 73–106. For comments by: a Marxian, see David Harvey, *The New Imperialism* (2005) 157–69 and *A Brief History of Neoliberalism* (2007) 19–38; a conservative social democrat, see Michael Lind, *The New Class War: Saving Democracy from the Metropolitan Elite* (2020) 44–48; and a democratic-socialist, see Grace Blakeley, *Vulture Capitalism: Corporate Crimes, Backdoor Bailouts and the Death of Freedom* (2024).

224. EPR § 268A.

Chapter 4

The Riddle of History

Historians of ideas, in terms sweeping but no less accurate for that, explain that despite all their differences, the great German poets and philosophers of the eighteenth and nineteenth centuries united around a basic theoretical issue.[1] Whilst burdened by the breaking of communal bonds, social chaos and self-estrangement that appeared to be constitutive of modernity,[2] they were equally committed to the ideals responsible for it: individuality, rationality and freedom. Pulled in different directions, many were moved, in 'agreement with the age',[3] to reconcile 'two seemingly indispensable' yet also 'utterly incompatible' 'images of man'.[4]

To make sense of Hegel or Marx, we are then told, we have to situate them within this larger project of reconciliation, which in turn requires understanding them from the inside, identifying these conflicting images, and unpacking their efforts to reconcile them. This was foreshadowed in chapter 1 when grappling with logical incompatibility: constituted by mutually exclusive modes, attitudes, concepts and categories (GP4), the existence of one form excludes others. Both Hegel and Marx grasp this conflict and labour to resolve it, but they offer incompatible answers to this 'riddle of history'.[5] In this chapter, we look to unbundle their theories of property by contrasting these answers.

For Hegel and Marx alike, what matters is free, conscious and expressive activities (GP3, GP5). What is important is externalising and satisfying or realising our inner desires or potential ends. From this premise, it follows that any limit or constraint on activity is the greatest bad since it frustrates what really matters. The problem, though, is that these bads appear to be everywhere. In our relations with nature, others and ourselves, we constantly confront and are confronted by forces intruding upon our efforts to satisfy our desires or realise our ends.

They agree again that to transcend this vale of tears and rise to the level of freedom, we must begin with ontology – that is, our understanding of reality itself. Driven by the dread of the chaos of contingent appearance, and their disbelief in the reality of seeming separateness, they reject all atomising ontologies. They stand against not only empiricists like Locke or Bentham, for whom we are originally and simply individuated and unencumbered from external relations. They also reject more socially situated forms like those in the liberal individualist tradition to which Hayek belongs. Of course, we are born into social settings, but this is not a contingent sociological fact. Drawing on organic metaphors popular at the time,[6] they consider the person to be an essentially relational being. To be a person at all is to exist through and in the unfolding expressive relations we have with ourselves, others and the world, which means that every effort to detach ourselves from these structures entails falling away from our true, actual, real selves.

Applied to social and political issues, this ontology generates results. One is methodological. With our attention directed to expressive relations, we become aware of the qualitatively diverse nature of forms, all the more if we consider historical ones too. Forms are not only contingently different in the sense that we cannot actualise both simultaneously (GP1), they are also logically different (GP4), since they come into being through and in relations constituted by incompatible qualities. Consciousness of this diversity, coupled with the commitment to describing, first, how the internal relations amongst qualities structure logically incompatible forms and, second, how the conflictual interaction within and between forms can generate change, unites Hegel and Marx. It is the essence of their dialectical method.

United around the significance of expressive activity, ontology and method, though, the two come apart, articulating incompatible interpretations of the method, opposing accounts of reality and conflicting solutions to the fact that everywhere we turn we find limit and constraint.

For Hegel, we are essentially rational or spiritual beings, which means the expressive activity that should be free from limit or constraint is at the level of thought. As particular persons, Hegel observes, we are often frustrated. Nature is stingy and threatening, and so are many of the people we meet. Further, the relations that we have with ourselves, as individuals and family members, are often frustrated – since how we act towards those whom we love necessitates an ensemble of modes, attitudes, concepts, and so on that is incompatible with the ensemble necessary for us to exist as individuals living self-determined lives. In reality, though, all these natural and particularistic limits do not actually frustrate our free activity. In fact, we only actualise our conscious, free and expressive selves through and in this multi-form conflict. It is true that being a particular woman conflicts with being a mother or a daughter, and belonging to a family conflicts with operating in markets, and in markets we face people with conflicting desires. If we take a step back, however, casting our intellectual eyes over the field of relations that constitute reality, we will see how its conflicting moments are internal to reality itself. On the surface, it seems that expressive activity is stymied by particular relational conflicts. Actually, through and in this tumultuous movement, our true nature becomes real. When we understand our expressive activities in this way, we free ourselves from the illusion of limit and constraint, since we become reconciled to its constitutive necessity, grasping that it is internal to the logic of all that we feel, think, say and do.

All this is transcendent fantasy, Marx says, the luxury of philosophers sitting in studies whilst the working class exists in a 'mass of misery, oppression, slavery, degradation and exploitation';[7] or as his friend and long-time collaborator, Friedrich Engels, says before him, whilst these 'pale, lank, narrow-chested, hollowed-eyed ghosts',[8] both physically and morally degraded, each made to work, 'eat, drink, and sleep at command',[9] sink ever deeper into the sewerage of modern life, into its 'foul pools of stagnant urine and excrement'.[10] It is not in thought that we should be free, but in the material world itself, in the particular, actual relations that we have with nature, others and ourselves. True reconciliation calls not for an exercise of thought where we abstract from the present and cast our intellectual eyes over the divided products of the past. It requires collective action that restructures these given relations in a way that abolishes, or at least diminishes as far as possible, limits or constraints on existing desires or ends. To do this, we have to break nature's bonds, transform its historically stingy and threatening self into a bounty of opportunities, and also dissolve all inter- and intrapersonal conflict. For the individual to rise to the level of true freedom and obtain real reconciliation, we must assume mastery over nature and eliminate command over each other and ourselves. In fact, each relation – with nature, others and ourselves – rises and falls together, for it is only through and in collective command of nature that each person can liberate themselves from the social strife and self-stifling that comes with having a certain activity forced upon them. Whereas for Hegel we will embrace incompatible (GP4) goods which matter for their own sake (GP3) if we understand them as modes, aspects, constitutive moments of one relational whole that is itself ultimately (GP5) good, Marx sees as unacceptable (GP2) the logical conflicts (GP4) that are constitutive of modernity in its current form.

Hegel and Marx both embrace expressive unity (GP3, GP5), but whereas Hegel answers the riddle of history by reducing all of its conflicting forms (GP1, GP4) to constitutive moments of a single ultimate (GP5) expressive whole, Marx dissolves the riddle by rejecting (GP2) one of the forms (GP4) which produce conflict: markets. As we shall see, their answers (AS2) to this riddle (AS1) generate incompatible schemes when they allocate property rights (AS3). To defend these summaries, we must start with their related but inverse ontologies.

FLOWER POWER

Hegel teases us with his solution to the riddle of history in the Preface to his *Philosophy of Right*, deploying the flower as a symbolic call for intellectual action:

> To recognize reason as the rose in the cross of the present and thereby to delight in the present – this rational insight is the reconciliation with actuality which philosophy grants to those who have received the inner call *to comprehend*, to preserve their subjective freedom in the realm of the substantial, and at the same time to stand with their subjective freedom not in a particular and contingent situation, but in what has being in and for itself.[11]

To make sense of Hegel's solution, we must briefly sketch his ontology, that is, his conception of our reality's essential structure.[12] He rejects traditional 'realist' ontology,[13] by which he means a form of thought that 'consider[s] things as they are, to be in and for themselves . . . absolute',[14] and so treats the object as '*being-in-itself . . . truth*'.[15] Both Locke and Bentham's concepts of 'mixed modes' and 'fictions' embody this view. For Hegel, though, our reality is not as these empiricists imagine it to be. Reality is not a self-subsisting entity that exists externally to us, an alien totality of forces formed independently of us, passively imbibed and combined by our minds into mixed and thus unreal forms.[16] The mind is not a 'wax tablet' onto which a substantial reality leaves its marks,[17] after which we have to carve up our contingent ideas about it, extracting its originally simple substances in an effort to obtain undistorted, final ideas that 'correspond' to what is 'True and Universal . . . and self-identical' about the real world.[18]

For German philosophers of the time, the first step away from this wax tablet empiricism was Kant, who explains that our minds do not, like a 'mirror',[19] reflect nature.[20] We do not passively receive experiences. We come to know and structure our reality – what we judge as normatively significant – through concepts and categories that we bring to our experience of it. Empiricism is right that knowledge comes from experiences of the world, but we are also active participants in the constitution of this knowledge.[21] For a concept to have meaning it must be rooted in sensory experience, but for experience to make sense it must be organised by our concepts or categories. According to Hegel, though, Kant is wrong to think that any part of our reality exists beyond our rational grasp. There is no 'thing-in-itself', the 'truth' of which we cannot 'know',[22] because our necessary involvement alters it.[23] Knowledge of our reality can be absolute, total, complete. So, Hegel argues, just as Kant advanced upon wax tablet empiricism whilst retaining its true insights, we must advance upon Kant whilst holding firm to his true insights, by overcoming his mistaken epistemological dethroning of reason.[24]

Fichte was close to reinstalling reason,[25] Hegel says, with his conception of thought as active, autonomous and willing. Fichte is right that Kant's 'thing-in-itself' is a 'piece of whimsy, a pipe-dream, a non-thought'.[26] For it is through and in our free self-conscious actions that our reality – what is normatively significant – comes or should come into being. Absent this constitutive role, what is left is not 'things-in-themselves' but 'a pure direction or a blank space',[27] which is to say, it is 'for' us 'nothing at all'.[28] Fichte, however, only tells one part of the story,[29] for thought does not constitute reality by itself, with the material world a passive heap lying about waiting for free subjects to impose their wills on it.[30] Reality is not that which is posited by the subject's 'infinite task' of trying to know the world by imposing their norms on it.[31] Reality does not emerge in two 'successive' moments,[32] originally constituted by free subjects, on the one hand, who act on dead objects, on the other. Rather, internal to reality's structure is one perpetual, temporally extended and thus historical relational movement,[33] 'a set of underlying forces', as Charles Taylor puts it, 'which manifest themselves in phenomena'.[34] Thus, not just willing subjects who constitute their reality by striving to control it, but reality itself is 'living Substance', it 'is in truth *Subject*',[35] but which is only made actual when freely expressed and embodied in the material world.[36]

The name of this dizzying speculative narrative, in which our reality, our freedom, by way of a 'momentous transition',[37] unfolds itself from an internal potentiality externally into substantial actuality, is 'spirit'. Later, we see that this idea sits in the heart of Hegel's property theory, for as he explains: 'The basis of right is the *realm of spirit* in general'.[38]

What is important here is the role performed by individuals in this unfolding process. Similar to J.G. Herder's organic expressivist self,[39] to whom we owe some of these ideas, which requires that we recognise as our 'own' the thoughts, beliefs, feelings, and so on, we make concrete in actions, spirit needs its own rational embodiment: '[it] is actual only as that which it knows itself to be'.[40] As noted, this means that spirit must be made concrete by being embodied in the material world. When embodied in merely inorganic and organic nature, for example, non-human animals, spirit exists in a 'petrified',[41] rather than in its actual form. The reason why is that its process of unfolding into the world is 'naturally determined' by 'immediately' given 'drives, desires, and inclinations'.[42] For spirit to unfold into its actual self, it must be embodied in a being that 'is aware of [its own] subjectivity'.[43] This being is man, for our free, conscious and expressive actions provide spirit its 'phenomenal shape, and actuality'.[44] We are its vehicles for 'entering into actuality',[45] for '[o]nly in the will as subjective will can freedom [spirit] . . . be actual'.[46]

This '*purposive activity*',[47] Hegel says, must be structured by three thoughts. First, when we act, we must recognise the necessary role we play, through words or deeds, in constituting spirit. Second, we must grasp the equally essential role played by nature, since it is the material through and in which individuals, by way of their conscious and freely willed actions, constitute the form and shape of spirit.[48] Only after recognising these truths, Hegel argues, can we begin to actualise ourselves as particular individuals: 'A soul without a body would not be a living thing, and vice versa.'[49] Prior to this recognition, we are 'immersed' in immediate sensory experiences,[50] acting not on the basis of what we willingly determine, but according to whatever arbitrarily strikes our fancy. Abstraction from immediate sensory experiences, necessary to the formation of particular individualities, separates us from objects, but it also puts us on the 'path'[51] to us recognising that there is a constitutive relation between spirit, matter and individuality.[52] After we grasp this third truth, revealed by and along with the first two, the apparently radical otherness of objects, arising out of our abstraction from immediate sensory experience, is exposed as a sham. When we grasp the dialectical and thus oppositional structure of reality,[53] we see that spirit – man's true self, his freedom – is constituted through and in the relation between thought and matter.[54]

Therefore, Hegel tells us, of course your subjective willing, what you desire or pursue (GP3), faces limits and constraints (GP1, GP4). This is simply in the nature of things, since to be at all is to be in the world, and to be in the world is to confront and be confronted by oppositions to your willing self: 'actuality is that which is effective and sustains itself in otherness',[55] in 'division',[56] thus 'limitation and restriction are always inherent in finitude'.[57] When we grasp this constitutive necessity, he comforts us, we are 'liberated' from a great 'burden'.[58] In understanding what must be, we are freed from the 'semblance',[59] the false idea, that limits and constraints are external to, and so other than, our free selves. They are not external and other but constitutive (GP3) and thus necessary to be anything at all. After we recognise this truth, with particular losses seen as actual wins and apparent failures viewed as moments of a more ultimate success (GP5), we may lament at some particular 'ill fortune',[60] but we will be lifted infinitely higher into an 'intellectual realm' where we are reconciled to their necessary happening.[61] For in 'comprehending' the object, 'I . . . penetrate' through what seems to exist to what actually exists,[62] to the '*present and the actual*',[63] so that it 'no longer stands opposed to me'.[64] When we see that 'necessity' is 'fate',[65] recognising reason as the rose in the cross of the present and thereby delighting in its constitutive conflict, we heal the ruptures wrought by 'the *modern* age',[66] for we become reconciled to them.

Reconciling ourselves to the constitutive necessity of limit and constraint does not mean that we abandon or still our freely willing selves. Reality is experienced as a limit and constraint only because we always push outwards, striving to satisfy desires and realise ends.[67] Rather than still or abandon our willing selves, Hegel writes, we experience an erotic desire to negate what seems to limit us: 'Personality is that which acts to overcome this limitation and to give itself reality – or, what amounts to the same thing, to posit that existence as its own.'[68]

With natural desire, like hunger, Hegel says in his *Phenomenology of Spirit*,[69] we negate the erotic desire and the object that satisfies it by 'consuming' the object.[70] Through consumption, we overcome the experience of otherness, the appearance of limit or constraint on our expressive selves, because in 'destroy[ing] the independent object' we become subjectively 'certain' that we are free.[71] This form of reconciliation is fleeting. Soon enough hunger returns, forcing us to find more food, and thereby 'produces the object again, and the desire as well'.[72] Whenever desire is for material objects, Hegel says, freedom is frustrated. To realise objective freedom, in the sense of lasting reconciliation, desire must be directed towards objects the 'negation' of which will not destroy the object in the activity of desire-satisfaction. This object is a second subjective willing: '*Self-consciousness achieves its satisfaction only in another self-consciousness*.'[73] Each 'equally independent' person,[74] Hegel continues, must desire to be rationally desired by the other.[75] When we relate in this way, then rather than the natural cycle of desire-negation-replenishment-desire, satisfaction of rational desire will stand and endure. In this process of recognising the freedom of the other,[76] we see ourselves in each other, the result of which is that 'different independent self-consciousnesses . . . in their opposition, enjoy perfect freedom and independence', since 'only in this way does the unity' of any particular subjective willing 'become explicit for it'.[77] When our relations have this structure, where we relate as particular individuals (GP3) and as embodiments of spirit (GP5), each with our own desires and ends, and both capable of evaluating and choosing between them,[78] we are freed from life's natural cycle and become united in our rational relations (GP5). United in this way the subjective self-certainty of each willing that it is free, will, through and in the 'action' of each,[79] be transformed into 'objective' actuality.[80]

Later, we bring these abstract concepts down to earth, explaining how they animate Hegel's account of the 'ethical state', then revealing the property rights essential for the social forms that constitute it. Before we do, however, we must consider Marx's related but inverse ontology. This sets the scene for his correspondingly conflicting theory of property, whilst also clarifying a little the picture of Hegel just sketched.

Like Hegel, the generation that followed struggled with the unhappy consciousness that often accompanies 'separation' and 'dualism',[81] judging that it corrupts man's true life as an integrated whole (GP5). After embracing 'unity' as an ontological premise, having adopted 'totality' as one of the structuring categories of their thinking,[82] many concluded that Hegel's 'spirit' represents speculative philosophy at its best. Ever since Plato's cave parable, philosophers had associated reality with the realm of thought, treating the world of beings, that which appears to the senses, as being ontologically defective or derivative. This idea is even found in Kant,[83] in his distinction between noumena (things-in-themselves) and phenomena (things-for-ourselves). The reason why Hegel is such 'a great' thinker and his theory is a work of 'world-philosophy',[84] is that he strives through speculative means to reconstitute the divide between these two worlds by analysing the thought-relations that structure them. This claim, these 'Young Hegelians' believed,[85] that whilst matter is a vehicle for self-conscious thought, this thought is only real when embodied in matter, is a remarkable attempt to solve the riddle of history: the oppositions between spirit and matter, universal and particular, necessity and freedom, and so on. In this sense, 'The culmination of modern philosophy is the Hegelian philosophy',[86] for he gives it 'its most logical, profound and complete expression'.[87] If philosophy is the speculative journey out of Plato's cave, from the contingencies of appearance to the sky of universal ideas, Hegel finished it, showing that true understanding of reality involves following the back-and-forth movement between these two worlds.[88]

Yet Marx, like others,[89] came to believe that Hegel did not solve the riddle. The unity that he describes may allow the philosopher to delight (GP5) in conflict (GP4), but it does not help those on the ground, who, poor or weak, are dominated by nature and men. Hegel may have felt at home in thought, reconciling himself to external constraints by calling it all mere semblance, but this is subjective not objective unity.[90] In a situation where 'combating the real existing world' is called for,[91] his dialectic just 'confirms' the individual's alienation and 'passes it off as his true mode of being – re-establishes it, and pretends to be at home in his other-being as such'.[92] As Marx writes about money, Hegel's speculative dialectic can only do this by making 'contradictions embrace' (GP5).[93] What lies at the heart of the difficulty, therefore, is the 'unresolved antinomy' (GP4),[94] the very riddle Hegel set out to solve. Despite philosophy culminating in Hegel, the constitutive ruptures wrought by modernity persist. Owing to Hegel's 'mystical speculation', 'the individual arrives nowhere at his true universality' (GP5).[95] Still dominated by material and alien powers or forces, we remain alienated from ourselves, others and the world.

One principal source of Marx's dissatisfaction with Hegel is the 'theoretical revolution',[96] as he describes it, effected by Ludwig Feuerbach. A contemporary of Marx, Feuerbach reverses the premise shared by most philosophers since Plato: the privileging of thought. Reality, Feuerbach says, is not found in Plato's forms or Hegel's spirit, it exists in the sensuous and material world. With this reversal, Marx announces, Feuerbach 'has in principle overthrown the old dialectic and philosophy'.[97] Because reality is essentially material, 'Hegel's chief mistake consists in the fact that he conceives of the contradiction in appearance as being a unity in essence', when his logic, in truth, is constituted by 'an essential contradiction'.[98] In the next two sections, we shall see that Marx's embrace of Feuerbach,[99] his turning away from the old philosophy, is an original spring for the later development of his radical proposals for property.[100]

Like Hegel, Marx forms part of the tradition inspired by an organic metaphor, for which our personhood is realised after a process of unfolding, following a period of self-development that involves the expression of thoughts, feelings, emotions, and so on, experienced by each person as their own. This ontological premise serves as the ground for Marx's criticism of Feuerbach's merely 'contemplative materialism',[101] and his talk of 'revolutionary practice'.[102] Only in actualising our inner potentiality (GP3) through word or deed do we produce our particular selves (GP5).[103] His materialism, though, sees him draw from the expressivist image conclusions opposite to Hegel's. Hegel says we are essentially spiritual, to which Marx replies: 'Man is directly a natural being.'[104] We are rooted in, and emerge from, the material world. Hegel begins with abstract 'I', Marx says,[105] a subjectively free being that can withdraw from the world of immediate appearances, and will a particular action that it judges best, positing it as their own. For Marx, this starting point is due to Plato's lordship over philosophy: the idea that thought has priority over being. In truth, however, man is anchored to the material world, it is our basis and ground. So, we must reorient ourselves. Rather than conceiving of man abstractly as rational, free and self-determining, we must see him as a concrete being that is always-already in the material world: 'He creates and establishes only objects, because he is established by objects – because at bottom he is nature.'[106] So, Marx says, with his concept of spirit, Hegel got reality 'upside down'.[107]

Whilst Marx, like Hegel, emphasises expression originating in desire, the desires each think basic diverge. Starting with the abstract 'I', Hegel prioritises the need for the objective, external actualisation of subjective freedom. This is not effected through and in the satisfaction of material desires, like hunger, but requires a standing negation – the recognition of our own and the other's rational freedom. For Hegel, in seeing each other as particulars and universals, we recognise that whilst our desires and actions conflict, unity is constituted through and in this conflict. For Marx, because we are expressive but material beings, there is no reason to privilege rational over natural desire. He instead starts by privileging our sensuous needs, like eating, drinking and shelter.[108] Thus, a mere rather than a standing negation of need is sufficient for freedom to be real. If a need is satisfied, that is enough. By satisfying natural need, in the conscious and social way I touch on below and develop in the last section, we actualise our true selves.

Marx's picture of man as a material rather than abstractly rational being, with his consequent privileging of a mere rather than a standing negation, produces a conception of unity and attitude to limit that conflicts with Hegel's. As noted, Marx embraces the metaphysics of relational unity. Central to Marx's thought is the idea that man is a 'species-being'.[109] We each exist as particular individuals, with discrete lives and personalities, but only insofar as we form concrete moments of a 'differentiated' whole, for whilst we differ in our 'existence' (GP3), we share one 'essence' (GP5),[110] as aspects of an 'ensemble of . . . social relations'.[111] When in contrast to an abstract 'I' Marx refers to real persons, he is talking about a creature living in the world with others, striving to satisfy its empirical needs. This is not unlike Locke's equality, which grounds his fundamental duty to preserve life. It also resembles Hegel's master-slave relation,[112] a heuristic device he uses to articulate the structures of self-consciousness and civil society, and, we see later, to advocate a particular form of the welfare state. Because Marx privileges expressive relational unity, though, he advocates radical conclusions not available to Lockean liberals, who fixate on an animal form of the 'desire to exist and procreate'.[113] And since Marx, in Feuerbach's wake, privileges matter over thought, he wants to overthrow the social forms described by the more sophisticated but still bourgeois Hegel.

The unity that Hegel imagines as arising through and in material conflicts, Marx tells us, is a 'logical, pantheistic mysticism',[114] it is the 'uncritical mysticism' that constitutes the 'mystery of Hegelian philosophy',[115] which in turn elevates Hegel into one of the many German 'mystics of sovereign private property'.[116] To be real, unity must exist in the empirical world, in our material social relations. So, when Marx criticises the philosopher for only trying to understand the world but not changing it,[117] he has in mind a society the form of which is structured in such a way that competition over objects that serve our needs is necessary. It is only if this atomising conflict – Bentham's war, Hegel's civil society, Hayek's extended order – is abolished that we can realise the material reconciliation that we all ultimately (GP5) need for its own sake (GP3).

Marx's materialism also shapes his attitude to limits on self-expression. Like Hegel, he says that free and conscious expression of desire is essential to being human. The term that he uses in this context is translated as 'production'. When Marx employs this word, he often has in mind an activity like creating commodities or tools,[118] but its meaning is far broader, for we also produce ourselves, ideas and social forms,[119] history, classes,[120] and so on.[121] All expressive activity (GP3), all words and deeds, not just narrow economic activity, is productive. And only if all production unfolds from the conscious, willing expression of our particular desires or ends, do we constitute ourselves in our true particular forms (GP5).

Marx refuses to reconcile himself to the presence of limits. He does not imagine us free when we live in chains. Instead of having a 'definite activity forced' on us at the expense of others,[122] thereby dividing our potential activities, splitting us into fulfilled and unfulfilled parts, we must rather all be free 'to do one thing today and another tomorrow, to hunt in the morning, fish in the afternoon, rear cattle in the evening, criticise after dinner'.[123] To make this world a possibility, he says, we must bend nature to our will, freeing ourselves from its bonds. Producing the possibility was the historical mission of capitalism. Rather than competing over objects, however, we must now direct nature's bounty collectively. Only by controlling nature in this manner can we freely fulfil needs that are truly our own.

After we rise to this realm of 'full freedom',[124] where nature itself is tamed and social strife is stilled, the ideal of 'human emancipation' will become real.[125] Here, our lives will be constituted by a new relation amongst individuals and with nature.[126] In this 'true realm of freedom',[127] our needs (GP3) will not conflict (GP4). Instead of the 'free-trade dogma' that 'mutually antagonistic interests' further 'the common welfare',[128] we will relate for the sake of actualising the potential of all individuals. Nor will objects appear as obstacles or be treated as mere tools with which to tackle threats or abate desires. Having tamed nature, its objects will belong to us, they will be us and embody us since they will be produced and reproduced by us. Having humanised nature, its objects will lose their alien, crudely instrumental dress.[129] Free to relate to nature how we judge best,[130] need will be experienced as opportunity. Hunger will not remind us of how precariously we move between starvation and toil,[131] but will be experienced as the prompt to act, consciously and without artificial constraint (GP4), to fulfil our needs. No longer subjected to hunger, having humanised it, choosing it as something good, with labour now not 'a means of keeping alive' but itself 'a vital need',[132] we will no longer feed like animals but instead dine like men (GP5).[133]

When Hegel tells us to 'recognise reason as the rose in the cross of the present', to see unity in this-worldly conflict, Marx argues, all that he does is decorate our chains with flowers: '*Here* is the rose, dance *here*.'[134] Rather, we have to 'cast off the chain and gather the living flower'.[135] By doing this, by breathing in nature's scent, internalising its essence, collectively subordinating its material to our particular needs, we will give birth to real individuals to replace all the limited, divided and suffering ones who wander alone the plains of this 'vale of tears'.[136]

MASTER-WORKERS; NO, MASTERS-OF-WORKERS

Hegel's compelling theodicy, where conflict and limit (GP4) are internal to the logic of unity and as such must be embraced in its diverse particular moments (GP3) without ethical residue (GP5), was sketched above in the abstract, demanding idiom of ontology. Hegel's speculative dialectic, though, is made more 'concrete' and digestible in his *Philosophy of Right*,[137] where he articulates his property theory. The central message of that book is that the subjective willing, the individual possessed with the self-certainty that it is free,[138] must strive to actualise this freedom objectively in the world: the ideal is '*the free will which wills the free will*'.[139] The book articulates how it is that the abstract 'I', a subjectively free willing, progressively unfolds towards this ideal. Hegel's 'architectonic edifice',[140] as he puts it, has three related parts: abstract right, morality and ethical life. Each articulates a stage of the subjective willing's unfolding towards its objective and actual freedom. To make sense of Hegel's property theory, rooted as it is in his conception of spirit, it is necessary for us to follow this movement.

Having abstracted from its immediate sensory experiences, the subjective willing strives to determine and impose its purpose on the world. Essential to this subjective, purposive striving is our control of objects that we use in the pursuit of chosen ends, for example, eating an apple or making a table. We first obtain this control by taking possession of objects we find in nature,[141] using them,[142] or alienating them.[143] This is how subjective freedom starts to externalise itself and thereby become objective and actual.[144] Possession, use and alienation, however, are inadequate for this freedom to become actual. As noted above, recognition by other people is necessary if our subjective self-certainty that we are free is to become objective. A first step towards this freedom is taken when individuals conclude contracts in which they exchange rights in objects.[145] A contract serves this function because the act of exchange implicitly entails recognising another's freedom.[146] To stop here, thinking that this is the core of Hegel's property theory, as some do, is a mistake. Not only does it mistake the part (the initial unfolding of subjective freedom) for the whole (a theory that is concerned with actual freedom), if 'this were all that Hegel had to say about property', writes Christopher Pierson, 'it would be interesting but perhaps unremarkable'.[147]

To see why, we must sketch the distinctions that Hegel draws among different ways of using objects: arbitrary, moral and ethical. First, when action is determined by whatever our desires or ends happen to be, the use of objects is arbitrary. Arbitrariness is a problem for Hegel because its radical contingency is incompatible with his actualised freedom. We remain 'dependent on [the] content' of what seems to be attractive to us in any particular moment,[148] in circumstances where 'what matters is to recognize in the semblance of the temporal and transient the substance which is immanent and the eternal which is present'.[149] For Hegel, we saw above, this arbitrariness can be mitigated by the rights and duties in contracts.[150] A contract can mitigate arbitrariness because it is formed by the 'common will' of the parties,[151] breach of which constitutes a wrong that can be remedied by legal means.[152] Contracts, though, remain contingent, since the rights and duties that they embody can be whatever the parties decide them to be.[153]

At an impasse, Hegel turns to the second use-form. The arbitrariness of a subjective willing's choice, he says, can be mitigated further, thereby further actualising freedom, when we adopt the 'moral point of view'.[154] Moral use is still structured by 'subjectivity and particularity',[155] but we affirm the particular content of our desires or ends only after reflecting upon them in two related ways. First, rather than acting on the basis of a contingent whim,[156] we form 'intentions', assume 'responsibility' for what we do, and become 'accountable' for actions we will,[157] by reflecting on what we think is good, what promotes our '*welfare* or *happiness*',[158] and deciding on the basis of particular judgement.[159] Second, our particular judgements are 'raised to a *universal* end',[160] in that we think them objectively good.[161] Whilst reflection mitigates radical contingency, it does this in a purely 'formal' way,[162] for it does not articulate a concrete end towards which we should act.[163] All that it demands is 'abstract universality'.[164] It says that our value-judgements must be capable of being willed universally and so without contradiction, which we do by considering 'the will of others',[165] their 'welfare',[166] and 'duty'.[167] As individuals, though, we make judgements '*relative*' to our circumstances,[168] which means that moral judgement is 'capable of being *true* and of being mere *opinion* and *error*',[169] and therefore it remains dependent on contingency.[170]

To obtain a concrete end, missing in moral use, we must use objects ethically.[171] With ethical use, rather than relating to ourselves and others as isolated, formally equal parts of some abstract 'aggregation' of individuals,[172] like with moral use, we understand ourselves as existing through and in the community, living as 'a member of a whole'.[173] We continue to further our particular desires or ends (GP1, GP3), but we 'subordinate' them to 'the ethical whole' (GP5),[174] adopting the 'good as an end in itself',[175] as '*the absolute and ultimate end of the world*'.[176] Only if use is ethical, when we will not as a 'particular' individual but according to 'ethics in general',[177] does subjective freedom become objective, since only in ethical life does the free will actually will the free will.[178] With property, what is important is the structure of ethical life. We must explain how ethical life is constituted by two logically incompatible (GP4) social forms – the family and civil society – each important for its own sake (GP3) but neither of which is ultimately good, which in their opposition constitute a unified whole: the ethical state (GP5).[179]

The essence of Hegel's family life is love. When in love, individuals experience a subjective and '*immediate*' '*unity*' constituted by their mutual '*feeling*' that their particular self is bound up with another particular self.[180] Rather than being 'isolated on my own', when in love, I 'gain my self-consciousness . . . through the renunciation of my independent existence', which you do too, the product of which is that we 'gain recognition' in each other.[181] Renunciation does not abolish the existence of individual particularities, for lovers embrace as particulars and therefore remain 'infinitely unique to themselves'.[182] Like all that is subjective, lovers desire to express their love and thereby make it objective. This is the function of marriage,[183] for in marriage the individuals renounce their isolated existences, forming a '*single person*'.[184] Rather than using each other, like in contract,[185] they share 'a *common* point of view',[186] as Terry Pinkard puts it, internalising each other's desires and ends.

The necessity of marriage is rooted in its more permanent nature. In the 'solemn declaration of consent' to the marriage,[187] individuals tie down the 'transient' and thus contingent nature of feelings, 'a shape which the ethical may not assume'.[188] Whilst marriage 'should be regarded as indissoluble *in itself*', it is 'not absolute but unstable',[189] so divorce must be allowed if 'partners are totally estranged'.[190] This threatened loss of unity is mitigated, though, by having a child, for in their child partners see 'their union' and 'love before them',[191] embodied and therefore actual. Even having children, however, does not fully actualise the immediate ethical unity of love. For as children develop and become 'independent',[192] parental authority is experienced as an external limit. As a particular subjective willing, children eventually experience a desire to actualise their own freedom. When they act on this desire, identifying now as individuals not children, a family is 'fragmented and its members behave towards each other as self-sufficient individuals',[193] with familial interests subordinated to particular ones.

Through and in the division arising out of the child's newly developed sense of individuality, Hegel argues, familial life passes over into civil society,[194] a social form the structure of which is incompatible (GP4) with the loving family. When in civil society, individuals work, produce and exchange rights that they have in objects,[195] for the sake of promoting their welfare.[196] In doing so, their relation constitutes a 'system of needs',[197] that is, a competitive exchange economy. Whilst the system's instrumental individualism can produce a 'spectacle of extravagance and misery',[198] it works because although other individuals exist as a 'means to the end of the particular person', each only 'gains satisfaction by simultaneously satisfying the welfare of others'.[199] In this form, '*universality* asserts itself'[200] through the 'laws' of 'political economy'.[201] Universality is further present in the fact that 'needs' and 'means' for satisfying them are 'mutually conditioned' by the interdependence of individuals who work within this system, the result of which is that they take on a '*social*' character.[202] To function as promised, the powers to acquire, produce and exchange rights must be made objective by making laws that fix the concrete content of property rights.[203] This system also requires institutions to apply[204] and enforce rights.[205] This is not for the reasons provided by Bentham, for whom this protection is coextensive with property. Rather, it is because for Hegel embodiment is necessary for anything to be real at all.

Despite civil society's particularistic, self-interested nature, internal to this relational form are three relative-universal features. First, as noted, the system of needs only works because internal to its logic is the promise that it will increase the available wealth in respect of which individuals have an 'opportunity to share'.[206] Second, ways of working in civil society 'converge', assuming a communal form in 'estates', each with its own 'corresponding means, varieties of work, modes of satisfaction, and theoretical and practical education'.[207] Hegel classifies the estates into three main forms: agricultural,[208] trade and industry,[209] and universal or government service.[210] Third, and relatedly, the interests of estate members, especially those in trading and industrial sectors,[211] often overlap, with individuals forming associations that function to serve these interests, thereby promoting 'the less selfish end' of their associations.[212] When associations are legally recognised, they are called 'corporations'.[213] As members of estates that share a way of life, individuals 'gain *recognition* in [their] own eyes and in the eyes of others',[214] and thereby they develop a concrete communal identity.[215] When they then also recognise that the framework and powers of the state are what supports and sustains their associations,[216] they internalise not only the interests of their own associations but the ends of the community itself. In doing so, by taking a dialectical leap in thought and feeling from the relative-universal ends (GP3) of their communal association to 'the *end which is universal* in and for itself' (GP5), an individual 'passes over' from civil society into a new social form: the ethical state.[217]

In the ethical state, we exist as citizens. Political and legal power is separated between,[218] and is mediated through,[219] an executive filled by those with 'knowledge and proof of ability',[220] and a legislature filled with '*expert*' deputies.[221] The citizen's '*highest duty*' (GP5) is to actualise the concrete (GP3) but incompatible (GP4) forms that constitute reality.[222] That we see ourselves in this way does not mean that the family or civil society is annulled: 'The *family* is the first *ethical* root of the state; the *corporation* is the second, and it is based in civil society.'[223] Whilst both the family and civil society are subsumed within the state, neither is extinguished. Rather, they exist 'as an *organic* totality in *laws* and *institutions*'.[224] It is essential (GP3) that families have control over resources, and it is essential (GP3) that civil society is free. Something, however, important about their essence changes: the absoluteness of each is overcome. Their ultimate justification is now derived from their contribution towards the '*constitution of the state*' (GP5).[225] Although the state 'is alive only in so far as both moments . . . are developed within it', the moments have their 'ground and ultimate truth . . . [in] spirit'.[226] Therefore, whilst freely willed, every action – by every individual, family, estate, association, and so on – must be directed towards, in the sense that it must fit within the concrete limits of, this ultimate end.[227]

The ethical state, therefore, is constituted by negative and positive liberty. Whilst the latter, concerned with expressive relational unity, is ultimate, it does not extinguish the former. For the 'objective origin [of marriage] is the free consent' of individuals,[228] and if it 'is supported by the objective order, conforming to the latter and at the same time retaining its rights . . . particularity becomes the sole animating principle of civil society'.[229] Constituted by particularity, individuals in their unique circumstances are free to judge how to live best in spirit's light, free to determine how best to actualise their subjective freedom in accordance with ethics in general. When we act in this way, our particular desires and ends will sometimes conflict. When they do, we exist as obstacles to each other, but these obstacles will not be experienced as '*alien*', since in ethical life 'the subject bears *spiritual witness* to them as to its *own essence*',[230] recognising that civil society as a constitutive moment (GP3) of the ethical state (GP5) emerges through and in conflict (GP4), within itself and in opposition to families. Because conflict is due to our subjectivity, even when a competitor frustrates your own goals (GP3) or your child leaves home to chart her own destiny (GP3), your ultimate goal (GP5) is still actualised.[231] This is Hegel's speculative dialectic. For if 'necessity is elevated to a work of freedom',[232] it follows that we will become reconciled to conflict and its resulting 'loss', 'infinite pain' and 'suffer[ing]'.[233]

If Hegel articulates a theodicy, Marx provides an eschatology. Marx rails against misery and exploitation, advocating for the abolition of what he considers is its cause and symptom: private property. This revolutionary call can mislead. For example, it is not right that Marx opposes 'all property relations as such'.[234] After all, when the 'expropriators are expropriated', Marx tells us, there will be 'individual property' not 'private property',[235] say, liberties to use fishing rods. It is also wrong that Marx opposes all 'individualistic possession that may imply exclusion'.[236] He says we must share in the production process: the creation of useful things must be organised in a cooperative way, not anarchically fragmented. However, what any individual then does with her 'divided' share of this 'social' wealth, how to 'consume' it,[237] is up to them. The reason why is that if you do not have a claim-right against others frustrating your use of the fishing rod, if you are disabled from giving it to your son, or if I can annul your liberty to do either, then the goods realised through and in this consumption – play and love – would be imperilled.

Because individual liberties, claims, powers and immunities will exist in Marx's future ideal world, his call to abolish private property must be read carefully. His criticism is directed against rights that conflict with his model of the person. Private property is bad, Marx writes, because it embodies 'the material, summary expression of alienated labour',[238] it 'rests on the exploitation of alien, but formally free labour'.[239] Recall his conception of unity. On this model, unity's twin nemeses are scarcity and strife, 'penury and antithesis',[240] with the former in modern life a result of the latter. Thus, it is Hegel's civil society,[241] in particular the market power to exchange rights, together with the wage-relation and production of the 'disposable industrial reserve army' that is constitutively bound up with it,[242] that is the principal target of his critique.[243]

The market's constitutive 'principle' is 'rupture' (GP4).[244] Divisions have always existed,[245] but when the capitalist mode of production is dominant, conflict over material objects is total, for 'only capitalist commodity production is an epoch-making mode of exploitation'.[246] In this world, individuals have the power to exchange property rights, which they exercise to satisfy desires or realise purposes that are private and external to the exchange itself.[247] The rise of this system of competitive exchange was essential to the development of true humanity (GP5),[248] for only with the productive powers it made possible, its 'gigantic extension of technique',[249] can we afford to every individual the means that they require to fulfil their needs (GP3).[250] Now that we have the means, if a system frustrates this end, like civil society does, it is unacceptable (GP2).

There is a more basic problem than the market's results,[251] namely, the market's logic, which presupposes conflict (GP4) over needs. Like Hegel,[252] Marx understands that competition entails conflict. This 'antagonism of interests, the struggle, the war',[253] is internal to the logic of Hegel's civil society, a constitutive moment of the unfolding of spirit into the form of the ethical state. For Hegel, if you recognise this necessity you will delight in its spiritual reality. For Marx, this is the apogee of man's material alienation.

With workers, the alienation is clear. Forced to compete to 'keep alive',[254] their labour and its products do not express their desires and ends.[255] Rather, through a contingent 'social relation of production', the objects they use when working and produce when doing so are 'autonomous', in the sense that they exist as 'independent powers' over the 'living' individual.[256] In following the commands of the capitalist, therefore, the worker actualises only a naked instinct to keep alive.[257] All his 'eating, drinking, procreating, etc.' do not embody a 'human activity', but rather 'animal' ones.[258] Non-workers, like philosophers and capitalists, are also alienated. A philosopher ascends into the world of ideas, and so no longer lives in the real one.[259] The capitalist is alienated in two related ways. First, in exploiting others, he betrays his relational nature. Like Hegel's speculative dialectic, where the master, despite having a semblance of power, cannot realise his actual self if he relates to others as slaves, a capitalist cannot realise his relational self if he deprives a worker of the products of their labour. Second, a capitalist also cannot express himself,[260] because the 'laws of capitalist production' and 'competition' continuously confront him as 'coercive force[s] external to him',[261] they 'enter into [his] consciousness',[262] they compel him 'to keep extending his capital',[263] rather than using objects to develop his own potential. Within the capitalist mode of production, there is no escape.

In markets, we act self-interestedly and, at least in the early stages of the rise of capitalism in its industrial form,[264] deceitfully, fraudulently, violently. The idea that markets are compatible with '*respect [for] others as persons*',[265] is the dream of speculative thinkers who ignore reality. In the market, individuals do not just want to succeed, but to dominate: not to be master-workers, but masters-of-workers. In this world, there is a 'mutual swindling and mutual plundering',[266] we become 'fragment[s]' of ourselves,[267] we exist as 'living appendages' of machines,[268] and all the while we humiliate nature to satisfy crude, imaginary or inhuman needs. Agnes Heller articulates this final point well: 'Capitalism is the pimp that by constantly producing new objects creates an unending stream of new needs which make people prostitute themselves.'[269]

Bentham's society of strangers who lunge for power and therefore above all stand in need of security is not a mere quirk, a contingent psychological fact to be overcome by 'good . . . will'[270] or by good 'regulations'[271] whilst retaining the social form. It is internal to the market's logic, its 'subjective essence',[272] the form of life that arises whenever individuals, motivated by their private needs, structure social relations according to the power to exchange rights in markets.[273] For the market relation to form, each individual must equally have a space in which they can use their property as they choose. This 'Eden of the innate rights of man . . . is the exclusive realm of Freedom, Equality, Property and Bentham.'[274] So isolated, their equal formal freedoms and their property secure, the individual turns within. He comes to see himself, his needs and his relations with others and nature not through the lens of material self-expressing unity, but through the lens of mere instrumentality and material conflict. So, rather than social relations amongst particular self-expressing individuals relating to one another as parts of themselves, there is a 'relationship of reciprocal isolation and foreignness'.[275]

In this atomised yet suffocating world, constituted by an inter- and intra-class war, we relate to nature as a stock of alien objects. Of course, we can try to utilise its standing reserve, but with market anarchy rather than a shared control of nature being society's regulating principle, nature often frustrates us. And even when we are effective in using its materials, this is mostly luck. In markets, we are degraded, fragmented, the 'plaything of alien powers'.[276] For this reason, Marx explains, the outcome of our expressive but exploited efforts necessarily depends on 'chance',[277] that is, on a rather mundane form of fate: the 'invisible hand' of the market.[278]

THE ETHICAL STATE; OR AN ASSOCIATION OF FREE MEN

Whilst Hegel's ideal of a '*free will which wills the free will*',[279] resembles Marx's ideal of 'From each according to his abilities, to each according to his needs',[280] they prescribe property systems that are logically incompatible. The root of this systemic incompatibility is their models of man. Despite having formally related ontologies, the form it takes – either speculative or materialist – produces incompatible solutions to the riddle of history. Whilst Hegel reconciles incompatibility (GP4) between forms (GP3) by reducing them to modes of a single ultimate good (GP5), Marx denies the acceptability (GP2) of one of these forms, markets, thereby dissolving the riddle itself. Their conflicting ideas about what relational forms (AS1) matter for their own sake (AS2) result in them advocating incompatible allocative property schemes (AS3).

Let us start with Hegel's property theory, which is structured by three categories of property, embodied in the social forms outlined: family, civil society and the state. Each is comprehensible when viewed through the lens of his model of the person as a vehicle of spirit.

Familial life, Hegel says, is constituted by a felt or immediate unity, where family members internalise or share each other's desires and ends. When individuals marry, they 'surrender' their 'personality',[281] subordinating their own desires or ends to the familial whole. In doing this, they form a single person, with a shared purpose. This logic of familial life, which legal and political authorities must respect, generates numerous prescriptive consequences (AS3). The family, 'as a person', obtains 'its external reality in *property* . . . in the shape of *resources*',[282] which must be '*permanent* and *secure*'.[283] Because Hegelian property is constituted through possession and use, that is, the instilling of a subjective willing in an object, ownership for Hegel is 'essentially *free* and *complete*',[284] both as regards its use- and exchange-value.[285] Because family is an immediate ethical unity, though, property is held in common. Its members do not relate as individual rights-bearers but as aspects of the felt whole,[286] with property acquired for the sake of 'caring for the family's needs'.[287] It is the duty of parents to promote the welfare of family members.[288] Whilst they can participate in civil society by using or exchanging objects in markets,[289] this freedom is conditional on first satisfying their family's needs. Parents must give resources to, feed, educate, and so on, their children,[290] raising them to a level at which they can live as free citizens.[291] Only after this first duty is fulfilled (GP7), do the rights that constitute civil society take full effect. Similar limits (GP7) attach to the distribution of property as inheritance and after divorce.[292]

A second component of Hegel's theory concerns the other constitutive moment of the ethical state (GP5), civil society, which is logically incompatible (GP4) with family life but is also good for its own sake (GP3). Each individual, he says, must have a liberty to use objects as they think best, for 'free ownership is a fundamental condition of [civil society's] success',[293] as well as the power to transfer their rights through contract, donation, gift, and so on.[294] This liberty and power must be coupled with a claim-right against others frustrating their exercise,[295] and an immunity against their being annulled arbitrarily.[296] Only with this complex of rights can the individual externalise their desires and ends, and so actualise their freedom. For example, if you want to be a carpenter, you can only make tables if you have a liberty to use objects as 'raw materials' and tools;[297] only if this liberty is exclusive and secure will your way of life not be frustrated; and only if you have the power to exchange your rights in the table that you make can you realise your particular goal of continuing the family's furniture store.

This ensemble of rights is constitutive of a market economy. Thus, it is not correct to say that Hegel can be read as offering the 'seeds' for an argument to abolish 'private property'.[298] Absent rights to act freely as a subjective willing, civil society cannot exist, which is why Hegel refers to the 'permissible arbitrariness of inherently rightful actions and of the private use of property'.[299] This social form matters for its own sake (GP3), it is necessary to the unfolding development of the subjective willing,[300] a constitutive moment of the ethical state (GP5).

We must not, however, make the opposite error. In no sense is private property 'absolute' in Hegel's ethical state.[301] Yes, for Hegel 'a community does not ultimately have the same right to property as a person does'.[302] The reason why, though, is that individuals must have rights if they are to actualise their true, particular selves. This precludes, as Michael Hardimon notes, 'Marxist proposals for the elimination of private ownership of the means of production',[303] and abolition of the market power to exchange goods and services. He does not, though, privilege such rights: 'one of the commonest errors of abstraction is to insist on private rights and private welfare *as valid in and for themselves* in opposition to the universality of the state'.[304] As he explains, these rights have 'validity only in so far as [they are] in conformity with . . . and subordinate to' what is ultimately important (GP5).[305] And that ideal is the unity that is constituted through and in the conflicts (GP4) between family and civil society and also within civil society (GP3). If this ideal (AS1, AS2) is facilitated by allocating property to a group,[306] or to religious communities,[307] or to the public itself,[308] this is permissible (AS3).

As such, Marx errs in describing Hegel as a 'mystic[] of sovereign private property',[309] as do commentators who think that his property theory is 'possessive individualist' in structure.[310] Yes, he does contemplate individuals who are free to buy and sell their labour-power.[311] Moreover, he writes about the need for law to embody individual rights, thereby affording it 'security, stability, and objectivity',[312] so that '*undisturbed security* of *persons* and *property* [is] guaranteed'.[313] It is important, though, to locate these ideas within the structure of his conception of the ethical state. After individuals '*pass over* of their own accord into' this state, we remain free to exercise rights as we judge best, but their exercise must always be consistent with our '*ultimate end*'.[314] This is not the negative freedom of possessive individualism, in which the limits on actions are fixed by what empowers equivalent free action by others. There are limits on state interference, we 'must retain [our] rights',[315] but rights are for the sake of unity. Therefore, the state must alter positive laws embodying rights when their form or exercise conflicts with this end (GP5).[316]

Turning now to the third feature of Hegel's theory. When individuals, for either systematic or natural reasons, suffer material deprivation,[317] they have rights and civil society or the state have duties to provide (AS3). We can sit these rights and duties into four categories. First, the individual has 'a *right of necessity*',[318] that is, an exemption to take objects in which people who are secure have rights when required to preserve their lives. Second, individuals have immunities against certain classes of rights-deprivations, for example, when indebted to another, which extends to whatever they require 'to support [them] in [their] accustomed state in society'.[319] Third, civil society itself has general welfare duties, including providing food, work training, education, healthcare, and so on.[320] These duties are mediated through estates, especially the corporations emerging within trade and industry.[321] The reason why these duties exist, Hegel tells us, is that poverty only exists because civil society fragments the families that used to care for their members.[322] Whilst Hegel couples this claim-right with the obligation to work,[323] this right extends to individuals who 'destroy the security of their own and their family's livelihood by their extravagance'.[324]

Fourth, as for 'poor' individuals not cared for by their families and who are not members of any corporation, the state has a duty to 'take[s] over the role of the family with regard not only to their immediate deficiencies, but also the disposition of laziness, viciousness, and other vices to which their predicament and sense of wrong give rise'.[325] These positive duties exist, Hegel says, because the inherently contingent nature of charity renders it inadequate as a means to do justice to the freedom of individuals.[326] However, because exercising agency is part of being human, the poor having to rely on the state to provide goods or services is inadequate. In this condition, they are without that 'feeling of self-sufficiency and honour' that comes with working for a living.[327] A consequence of this is that the poor over time devolve into a 'rabble', that is, individuals who are not just poor, but are possessed with an 'inward rebellion against the rich, against society, the government, etc'.[328] To overcome this problem, Hegel imposes on the ethical state a duty to find more consumers for the excess of goods produced by civil society by establishing trade relations with other states and thereby increase employment at home,[329] and, notoriously, a duty to create new markets by means of colonisation.[330] And until international trade and colonialism generate demand to increase productive employment at home, Hegel says, if the poor want anything more than the immediate provisions that the ethical state is duty-bound to provide, the state must leave them 'to their fate and direct them to beg from the public'.[331]

Each right and duty is comprehensible when regard is had to Hegel's model of the person. By way of contrast, Hayek's advocacy of a basic income is rooted in information efficiency worries. If the poor are coerced by the rich, they will not act according to what they know, and if they are not participating in markets, the price mechanism will not function as efficiently as it should. For Hegel, contrarily, objects are the 'raw material of self-determination',[332] as Dudley Knowles puts it, which means that poverty deprives the subjective willing of the means that it needs to embody its freedom in the world. Therefore, more than a Hayekian basic income is necessary. The ethical state's institutions must, through a mixture of direct and indirect means funded by tax,[333] take all necessary steps – consistent with the structures of the family and civil society, hence colonialism and begging – to enable individuals to make their freedom real.

Can we not offer more detail than this general structure? In two respects, yes, and we shortly touch on these, but in a more important respect, no, we cannot. Despite Hegel's grand ambitions, he is acutely conscious of philosophy's limits. The function of the philosopher is not to engage in mundane policy work. Rather, it is to describe the expressive relational whole that he calls spirit: 'To comprehend *what is* is the task of philosophy, for *what is* is reason.'[334] This understanding is able to generate prescriptive results, but only immanently and in outline.[335] Therefore, whenever philosophers strive for more, they misunderstand not only their function but the nature of reality.

To be actual spirit must be embodied, but when we enter the material world spirit 'emerges in an infinite wealth of forms, appearances and shapes'. We can discover unity here, 'the inner pulse', the dialectical and therefore necessary structures of the family and civil society, but the particular forms that the structures take are contingent.[336] Contingency produces the conflict through and in which spirit is actualised and therefore it must be embraced. All this fleetingness, though, means we cannot say anything detailed and final about this world. Hegel's relative prescriptive humility extends to what he can say about property. All that actually exists is embodied, which is done by positing laws,[337] property included.[338] Whilst property law must conform to ethics in general, the necessity of particularity and its resulting contingencies limits the power of theoretical reason to prescribe. For not only are particular laws made and applied by particular persons,[339] the context in which we make and apply law is always changing.[340]

That said, Hegel does offer more than the basic structures of a family-centred, market-based and welfare-backed society articulated above. Two aspects warrant special mention. First, Hegel comments on: what objects can be property;[341] intellectual property;[342] use and transfer;[343] state intervention and regulation of property;[344] tax-funded bureaucracy;[345] property held by religious institutions;[346] primogeniture;[347] and the duty to sacrifice property in times of war.[348] His model of the person animates all of these prescriptions: property must (AS2) be allocated (AS3) for the sake of enabling the expressive activity of the ethical state's citizens (AS1). The second relevant additional aspect is that whilst Hegel writes about our being 'at home' in the world,[349] and refers to the master-slave relation and mutual recognition,[350] he says little about these issues when he is describing how his ideal of unity-in-conflict (GP5) will unfold in actual life. Whilst the potential for civil society to divide is prominent in early works, Shlomo Avineri writes,[351] it is 'marginal' in *Philosophy of Right*. He refers to 'mechanical' labour,[352] says that the division of labour 'leads to an inability to feel and enjoy the wider freedoms, and particularly the spiritual advantages of, civil society',[353] hints at the problem of the 'rabble',[354] observes that citizens can be '*alienated*' from positive law when lawyers make the law into their own 'property' by using 'language' that is 'foreign' to laymen,[355] and alludes to familial alienation.[356] There is little else, though, and he says almost nothing by way of exposition. Rather than attempting to develop his property theory on his behalf, however, this offers a good transition to Marx, for whom these issues served as his motivation for repudiating the entirety of Hegel's system.

Shortly after Hegel carefully prescribed the features of the ethical state, Marx agitated for its abolition. For Marx, the state is just the secularised, embodied form of the old religious desire for an external legislator. As with religion, the state is 'the illusory sun about which man revolves so long as he does not revolve about himself'.[357] Rather than being the subjects of 'state aid',[358] we must together provide for ourselves, by collectively exerting productive power over the free gifts of nature. On Marx's ontology, reality as a whole must (AS2) be structured around the needs of living individuals (AS1), in a form that will abolish constitutive (GP4) conflict between them (AS3). Marx does not avoid the conflicts that Hegel thinks are bound up with our particularity by subordinating particularity to the whole. He rejects the reality of the distinction itself, for he says that when we break nature's bonds and exert collective productive power over its materials, then the possibility of constitutive conflict will be 'annulled'.[359] If we exert this power, the structure of our relations will be transformed. Instead of competing (GP4) as particular (GP1) individuals, we will relate in a way that is more characteristic of love.

This is revealed in what Marx says about the power to exchange objects. Marx is not against all forms of exchange, just those that divide rather than unify us. Our unity must be direct, in the sense that we must relate as concrete individuals who, through our freely willed words and deeds, actualise ourselves together. So, for an exchange to be valid, it must be constituted by immediate relations. There must be no external mediations between needs,[360] and it must express the needs of the exchanging parties as species-beings. Only when (AS2) these exchanges conform to your 'species-bonds',[361] when a transfer of rights (AS3) is a 'specific expression, corresponding to the object of your will, of your real individual life' (AS1),[362] is it permissible.

Unpacking this further, individuals may only exchange concrete objects for concrete objects, each of which is produced not because they are striving to satisfy their private needs, but because exchange is how they express their particular selves as species-beings. For the exchange of rights in the products of individuals who rear cattle and catch fish to be permissible, it is necessary that their relation be defined by three qualities.[363] First, they must rear cattle and catch fish because it is an expression of their particular needs. Second, the exchange must not be the 'means' for each to fulfil another need.[364] Their transfers of the objects must not be understood as a compromise, with the objects merely standing in for each other as 'substitutes',[365] in the sense that I give you something for the sake of you giving me another thing in return. The exchange must be direct, it must fulfil immediately an existing need, namely, what is expressed in the act of exchange itself. Third, the two parties must act with 'regard for' each other,[366] internalising each other's needs as their own, recognising that every particular need is essentially social in nature. For any exchange to be permissible (AS3), it must (AS2) be structured by these qualities (AS1). Only then will it conform to Marx's model of the person, in terms of which we are particular expressions (GP3) of a single material, expressive and relational whole (GP5).

If you struggle to imagine these exchanges, Marx will tell you, you should not be surprised. Moving inside our 'bourgeois horizon . . . where business deals fill the whole of [our] minds',[367] 'caught up in the relations of commodity production',[368] each victims of capitalism's 'ideological word-spinners',[369] we often see reality 'upside-down',[370] in 'superficial and distorted' ways,[371] or suffer from a 'stupid and one-sided' understanding,[372] which blinds us to what it means to relate to others in a truly human way. Perhaps. There is still hope, though, for making sense of what we must do if we are to be true to our real selves. Marx does not provide much detail about his ideal property relations. When he does talk about legitimate exchanges, though, one example he offers is exchanges of 'love . . . for love'.[373] This is expected, given his conception of unity. Like unity, a constitutive quality of loving relations is the sharing by individuals of one another's desires and ends. What exchanges take place between people in love? One familiar form is gift-giving. When an object is produced for people that we love, it exists as the 'living expression' of our love,[374] as something that appears to us as the 'direct embodiment' of our love.[375] If the objects are later exchanged on, say, an anniversary, there will be an exchange of 'love for love', because each of the three constitutive qualities listed above will be present: these objects will have been produced as expressions of their love, the exchange will express this love, and each will give the object to the other because doing so will satisfy the recipient's need – to be loved.

Marxian self-expression requires not just an absence of material strife, nor is his ideal society constituted only by loving exchanges. If that were so, then there would be little to separate Marx from the 'True Socialists',[376] upon whom, as Sidney Hook puts it, he 'poured out the vials of his wrath'.[377] Man is a species-being, but he is more than that, he is also a particular individual. Thus, Marx's ideal property system demands that every individual be free to fulfil their own particular needs: to fish, hunt, criticise, and so on. We must not only be free to exchange love for love and be free from action that will frustrate expression (AS1), such as competition. We each must (AS2) have liberties to use objects for the sake of expressing ourselves (AS3). This is why we must not bow to the market's super-individual powers: it is just the illusory sun about which man revolves for so long as he does not revolve about himself. Instead of production being directed by markets, we must collectively direct it. Only (AS2) if we share power (AS3) over the means that we utilise to produce those objects that we each need to express ourselves can the 'natural, spiritual and social variety' of our species-being actualise itself in our particular words or deeds (AS1).[378] Therefore, it is Marx's materialist version of the concept that he shares with Hegel, expressive activity, that informs his most famous prescription: 'From each according to his abilities, to each according to his needs.'[379] Interpreted through his model, we can give it a two-part meaning.

First, each individual must have a liberty to use objects that will enable them to satisfy their 'strictest bodily needs,' thereby humanising these otherwise 'animal' functions.[380] Marx, though, is concerned with far more than mere survival. So, we must also have a liberty to use objects for the sake of fulfilling other 'physical and mental' needs.[381] Need in Marx has a thick meaning.[382] Subsistence needs matter, but so do all others that we deem important. All of our needs must be fulfilled, all desires satisfied and ends realised, if we are each to constitute ourselves as real, true individuals. The origin of our needs, be it willing, knowing, judging, 'seeing, hearing, smelling, tasting, feeling, thinking, being aware, sensing, wanting, acting, loving',[383] is never important.[384] The 'need of a thing,' Marx says, 'is the most evident and irrefutable proof that the thing belongs to my essence',[385] for all our material and spiritual needs are equally 'ontological affirmations of essential being',[386] each only fulfilled when expressed in the world. As such, it does not matter if the need is to 'eat, drink and read books', or 'go to the theater, the dance hall, the public-house', or 'think, love, theorize, sing, paint, fence'.[387] We must be free to act by ourselves or with others however we like and whenever we like.[388] Consequently, Marx's ideal object-relations are, like Locke's, structured by instrumentality and immediacy,[389] not production of independent objects, that is, objects essentially exist for the sake of satisfying the existing needs of living subjects. But whilst Locke only guarantees subsistence, Marx provides no need priority. This difference (AS3) is rooted in their models: Locke's belief that we must first (AS2) preserve life (AS1), and Marx's that the individual is a species-being concerned (AS2) with expression as such (AS1).

The other part of Marx's imperative, the injunction that we must all contribute according to our abilities, is a practical implication (AS3) of his model (AS2) of the person as a species-being (AS1). Whilst the contributions by individuals must never be coerced, as particular aspects of the ensemble of relations that constitute the social whole, we must all contribute towards producing useful objects as best as our particular abilities allow. When individuals act in this way, they will actualise their own selves and the selves of others. In this social relation, we will 'complete each other',[390] produce each other, since to say that I realise my real self is to say that you realise your real self too: 'the free development of each is the condition for the free development of all'.[391] As constitutive aspects of the social whole, there is no essential (GP4) difference between us. We all are distinct, each living our own lives (GP1, GP3), but as aspects of an expressive material whole (GP5). Thus, we can only exist as real individuals when we exist as particular expressions of this social being, each individual exercising the liberties that they hold in the divided social product to produce themselves, and fulfilling their duties to produce each other.

Unlike Locke's duty to labour, Marx's ethical duty to produce will not be experienced as an external imposition.[392] As socialised individuals who are free from artificial limits, we each will contribute freely. When we recognise our species-being nature, we will not, as Hegel thinks, see each other as competitors (GP4). Rather than relating as means or as obstacles, recognition of the ensemble of social relations of which we are constitutive aspects will move us to strive to fulfil the needs of others, just because they need it. Rather than on profit, production will be based on 'the needs of socially developed human beings'.[393] As G. A. Cohen puts it, we 'will work for one another',[394] each labour as best as our abilities allow,[395] to produce enough useful objects to provide each individual the liberties in objects they require to fulfil their own particular needs – always structured, though, by our internalisation of the needs of others.

By coming to grips with these truths (AS1, AS2) and then allocating property in a form that is consistent with them (AS3),[396] modernity's 'theoretical riddles' will be solved.[397] This radical change in property rights, this 'top to bottom' revolution in relations,[398] will give birth to a new world: a world with 'social evolutions' (GP1) not 'antagonisms' (GP4),[399] a world with the need for administration but not 'politic[s]'.[400] In bringing this world into being, not imagined but one that already passes 'before [our] eyes',[401] albeit only in an embryonic form, in abolishing Hegel's civil society, we will resolve modernity's constitutive conflicts.[402] Structurally, the outcome will be the 'systematic restoration' of much that capitalism has 'destroyed', but in a 'new and higher synthesis',[403] along with other unknown changes, as the Marxian scholar David Harvey puts it, in our 'technologies, the relation to nature, social relations, mode of material production, daily life, mental conceptions and institutional frameworks'.[404] Ontologically, with the 'original connection between means of production and labour-power' reconstituted,[405] there will burst forth from the embryo of capitalism the longed-for 'resurrect[ed]', 'consummated oneness' of all.[406]

As sweeping as Marx's eschatological vision might be, he offers little detail on how property should be allocated.[407] Despite the ink spilt over his refusal to 'writ[e] recipes . . . for the cook-shops of the future',[408] there is a logically coherent reason why Marx, in contrast to his acute and rigorous criticism, offers prescriptive generalities. For Marx, what ultimately matters is free, conscious and willed expression. To facilitate it, we must tame nature and eliminate social strife. This follows from his vision of man. To prescribe more than this structure, though, would violate this vision. For the future to be composed of his ideal individuals, each generation should be free to fix the concrete forms of the social world as they judge best.

Apart from calling for revolution in theory and practice, therefore, there was little else Marx could say. Marx could say that in a 'communist society

. . . money capital would immediately be done away with, and so too the disguises that transactions acquire through it'.[409] He could further say that in place of the market's anarchic 'reckless squandering of labour-powers',[410] and 'waste' of potentially useful objects,[411] we must adopt a 'collective' form of production.[412] And he could say that this society will 'distribute[] labour-power and means of production between the various branches of industry',[413] according to plans which we 'reckon' will best serve each person's self-determined needs.[414] He could further say that the procedures for reckoning and for distributing wealth should stand under the 'conscious and planned control' of an 'association of free men'.[415] And finally, Marx could say that this association will be inspired by a vision in which 'the social relations of the individual producers, both towards their labour and the products of their labour', are in their essence 'transparent in their simplicity, in production as well as in distribution',[416] not as they exist today under the capitalist mode of production, namely, 'bewitched and distorted'.[417] Beyond these and similarly abstract prescriptions, however, the more concrete forms (AS1) that will emerge in his ideal world must necessarily (AS2) remain indeterminate (AS3).

Only once free from the 'dominion of past, accumulated, materialized labor', replaced with a system in which 'living labor' serves the needs of the present,[418] where the collective stock of objects useful to our needs has accumulated to levels that our society can 'control' the 'means of its own reproduction',[419] will our 'time' really be 'free'.[420] Only when we all share this freedom, when 'socialized man, the associated producers, govern the human metabolism with nature in a rational way, bringing it under their collective control instead of being dominated by it as a blind power',[421] can we give a concrete answer to the question: What is to be done?

NOTES

1. Generally, see Karl Löwith, *From Hegel to Nietzsche: The Revolution in Nineteenth Century Thought* (1991), Herbert Marcuse, *Reason and Revolution* (2ed, 1955), Raymond Plant, *Hegel* (1973), Charles Taylor, *Hegel* (1977), Marshall Berman, *All That Is Solid Melts Into Air, The Experience of Modernity* (1983), David Harvey, *The Condition of Postmodernity* (1990), David Leopold, *The Young Karl Marx: German Philosophy, Modern Politics and Human Flourishing* (2007), Lee Braver, *A Thing of This World: A History of Continental Anti-Realism* (2007), and Hartmut Rosa, *Social Acceleration: A New Theory of Modernity* (tr. Jonathan Trejo-Mathys, 2013).
2. Plant (n 1) 15–40.
3. Löwith (n 1) 162, quoting Hegel.
4. Taylor (n 1) 3.
5. EPM 72.

6. Eliza Marian Butler, *The Tyranny of Greece over Germany* (1958) and Michael Beresford Foster, *The Political Philosophies of Plato and Hegel* (1965).

7. CVI 929.

8. Friedrich Engels, *The Condition of the Working Class in England* (ed. David McLellan, 1993) 109. Marx relies on Engel's description of the working class in CVI 522–23.

9. Engels (n 8) 187.

10. Ibid., 61.

11. EPR 22.

12. EPR 9–20 and § 9. On the need to situate his political philosophy within his system, see Thom Brooks, *Hegel's Political Philosophy: A Systematic Reading of the* Philosophy of Right (2007) 1–12.

13. Braver (n 1) provides a clear 'matrix' of the six central 'theses' of realism (13–23 and 49–58), which he employs in an equally clear analysis of Hegel's partial rejection thereof (59–113).

14. EPR § 44A.

15. PhS § 82.

16. PhS § 90.

17. Braver (n 1) 22 and 498.

18. PhS § 84–85 and 116.

19. Richard Rorty, *Philosophy and the Mirror of Nature* (1979).

20. On Kant's ontology, see Braver (n 1) 33–58 and Terry Pinkard, *German Philosophy 1760–1860: The Legacy of German Idealism* (2002) 19–44.

21. PhS § 86–87 and 132.

22. EPR § 44R.

23. PhS § 73–74.

24. PhS § 231–39.

25. On Fichte's ontology, see Frederick C. Beiser, *Enlightenment, Revolution and Romanticism: The Genesis of Modern German Political Thought, 1790–1800* (1992) 57–83 and Pinkard (n 21) 105–30.

26. Fichte, quoted in Pinkard (n 21) 107.

27. PhS § 73.

28. PhS § 249.

29. EPR § 6R.

30. EPR § 140A.

31. Fichte, quoted in Pinkard (n 21) 115–16.

32. This is from a comment in the editorial notes (EPR 398).

33. On Hegel's historicism, see Braver (n 1) 72–76.

34. Taylor (n 1) 39.

35. PhS § 18.

36. EPR 20.

37. EPR § 270R.

38. EPR § 4.

39. On Herder's ideas, see Isaiah Berlin, *The Proper Study of Mankind: An Anthology of Essays* (ed. Henry Hardy, 2013) 359–435.

40. EPR § 274.
41. Plant (n 1) 131.
42. EPR § 11 and 11A.
43. EPR § 35A.
44. EPR § 145.
45. EPR § 131.
46. EPR § 106.
47. PhS § 22.
48. EPR § 47–48.
49. EPR § 1A.
50. EPR § 106R.
51. PhS § 233–34.
52. EPR 20–21.
53. For Hegel's own succinct definition of his dialectic, see PhS § 65–66 and EPR § 31R.
54. EPR § 360.
55. EPR § 82A.
56. EPR § 187R.
57. EPR § 117A.
58. EPR § 149.
59. EPR 20, § 32A, 181A, 302R and 324R.
60. EPR § 119A.
61. EPR 23.
62. EPR § 4A.
63. EPR 20.
64. EPR § 4A.
65. EPR § 324R.
66. EPR § 124R.
67. EPR § 28.
68. EPR § 39.
69. Hegel refers to this account in EPR § 57R and 349R.
70. PhS § 171. See also EPR § 52R.
71. PhS § 174.
72. PhS § 175.
73. PhS § 175.
74. PhS § 176.
75. PhS § 177.
76. PhS § 178.
77. PhS § 177.
78. PhS § 182.
79. PhS § 186.
80. PhS § 196.
81. OJQ 99.

82. EPM 74, 79 and 107 and GI 58 and 92-93. On this concept, see Georg Lukács, *History and Class Consciousness* (1971) 8–15 and David Harvey, *A Companion to Marx's Capital* (2018) 26 and 198.

83. As explained by Braver (n 1) 38–42, this interpretation of Kant is controversial.

84. ET 20.

85. David McLellan, *The Young Hegelians and Karl Marx* (1969).

86. Ludwig Feuerbach, *Principles of the Philosophy of the Future* (2012) § 19.

87. CCHPR 136.

88. For example, see EPR § 360 and PhS § 42.

89. For the origins of this dissatisfaction and some of the responses it generated, see Löwith (n 1) 307–25.

90. EPM 87–88.

91. GI 41.

92. EPM 113.

93. EPM 100.

94. CHPR 6.

95. CHPR 39–40.

96. EPM 9.

97. EPM 102.

98. CHPR 91.

99. On Marx's relationship with Feuerbach, see Sidney Hook, *From Hegel to Marx: Studies in the Intellectual Development of Karl Marx* (1962) 220–307.

100. For some of Marx's own acknowledgement of his debt, see ET 184 and EPM 8-10, 78 and 102-104.

101. Theses I and IX (TF 123) and GI 60-64.

102. Thesis III (TF 121).

103. This idea is everywhere in early Marx. One example: 'Only through the objectively unfolded richness of man's essential being is the richness of subjective human sensibility . . . cultivated or brought into being.' (EPM 76) They are also prevalent in later works, for example, GFCPE 487–48, 541–42, and 705–08, CVI 548–50, 618, 637–38, 739 and 798–79, and CVIII 958–59. Given the latter, plainly I reject the idea, for example, Louis Althusser, *For Marx* (tr. B Brewster, 2005), that there is a normative 'break' between his 'humanist' and 'scientific' periods.

104. EPM 110. Generally, see GI 39-48.

105. Generally, see CHPR, CCHPR and EPM 102-120.

106. EPM 110.

107. CHPR 40.

108. For a list of these 'physical' needs, see Leopold (n 1) 228–29.

109. OJQ 99 and 108 and EPM 53-55, 72, 91, 107 and 111. For an allusion in his later work, see CVI 447. On the roots of the concept, see Luca Basso, *Marx and Singularity: From the Early Writings to the Grundrisse* (tr. Arianna Bove, 2012).

110. CHPR 89.

111. Thesis VI (TF 122).

112. PhS § 178–96.

113. ET 75.
114. CHPR 7.
115. CHPR 83.
116. CHPR 108.
117. Thesis XI (TF 123).
118. CVI 285–92.
119. GI 47, PP 119 and CVI 493–94 fn 4.
120. CVI 716–24 and CVII 117–18.
121. On its different usage by Marx, see Raymond Geuss, *A World Without Why* (2014) 56–62. See also Erich Fromm, *Marx's Concept of Man* (2004) 24–34, Allen W. Wood, *Karl Marx* (2004) 27–30, and Martin Hägglund, *This Life: Why Mortality Makes Us Free* (2020) 212–14.
122. GI 69.
123. GI 54. This is not to say free action is easy, that we will always achieve everything that we set out to do, that we will never be confronted with difficult decisions (GP1), or that labour will ever become 'play' (GFCPE 712). It just means that whatever we decide to do, we will do it because we freely choose it, rather than because we have to by virtue of the fact that social relations are riven by internal contradictions (GP4). See Shlomo Avineri, *The Social and Political Thought of Karl Marx* (1968) 103–04, Bertell Ollman, *Alienation: Marx's conception of man in capitalist society* (2ed, 1971) 118–19, Wood (n 125) 24–26 and Harvey (n 83) 114–18.
124. CCHPR 141. Marx distinguishes 'necessary' labour and 'free intellectual and social activity' (CVI 667), with the 'realm of freedom' existing 'beyond' but always on the 'basis' (CVIII 958–59) of labour as an 'eternal' (CVI 133) 'natural necessity' (CVIII 959).
125. OJQ 108.
126. GFCPE 541–42 and CVI 618.
127. CVIII 959.
128. CVI 611.
129. EPM 75–76.
130. Whilst man is the 'root' (CCHPR 137) of meaning, we exist in a material reality. There is always a 'material substratum' (CVI 293), which means that whilst 'labour is the father of material wealth, the earth is its mother' (CVI 134).
131. EPM 83.
132. CGP 1031.
133. EPM 77.
134. This is Hegel's version of Aesop's 'Hic Rhodus, hic saltus' (EPR 22). Near the start of the discussion of surplus value, Marx critically references Aesop (CVI 269).
135. CCHPR 132.
136. CCHPR 131. On regression, see István Mészáros, *Marx's Theory of Alienation* (4ed, 1975) 241–53 and Marshall Berman, *Adventures in Marxism* (1999) 117–19.
137. EPR 10.
138. EPR § 35.
139. EPR § 27.

140. EPR § 279A.
141. EPR § 54–58.
142. EPR § 59–64.
143. EPR § 65–70.
144. EPR § 41 and 45.
145. EPR § 76.
146. EPR § 71R.
147. Christopher Pierson, *Just Property: Volume Two: Enlightenment, Revolution, and History* (2016) 93.
148. EPR § 15A.
149. EPR 20.
150. EPR § 79.
151. EPR § 71A and 75.
152. EPR § 82–103 and 230.
153. EPR § 81 and 113R.
154. EPR § 104R and 105.
155. EPR § 213.
156. EPR § 107A.
157. EPR § 115–18.
158. EPR § 123.
159. EPR § 119–28.
160. EPR § 123R.
161. EPR § 107R, 114 and 129–34.
162. EPR § 111.
163. EPR § 134.
164. EPR § 135. Hegel is criticising Kant. On this and related issues, see the discussions in W.H. Walsh, *Hegelian Ethics* (1969) 6–34, Allen W. Wood, *Hegel's Ethical Thought* (1990) 127–73, and Brooks (n 12) 52–61.
165. EPR § 113.
166. EPR § 125 and 134.
167. EPR § 133–35.
168. EPR § 112R and 128.
169. EPR § 132R.
170. EPR § 125.
171. EPR § 153.
172. EPR § 156A.
173. EPR § 261R.
174. EPR § 70A.
175. EPR § 123A.
176. EPR § 129.
177. EPR § 15A.
178. EPR § 142–43, 151 and 156.
179. EPR § 157.
180. EPR § 158.
181. EPR § 158A.

182. EPR § 168.
183. EPR § 161.
184. EPR § 163R.
185. EPR § 161A.
186. Terry Pinkard, *Hegel: A Biography* (2000) 191.
187. EPR § 164.
188. EPR § 161A.
189. EPR 163A.
190. EPR 176.
191. EPR § 173A.
192. EPR § 175A.
193. EPR § 33A.
194. EPR § 181.
195. EPR § 80, 196, 201 and 203–04.
196. EPR § 182.
197. EPR § 189–208. On his debt to political economists, see Raymond Plant, 'Hegel and Political Economy – I' New Left Review I/103, 1977, 79–92 and 'Hegel and Political Economy – II' New Left Review I/103, 1977, 103–13.
198. EPR § 185.
199. EPR § 182A.
200. EPR § 189.
201. EPR § 189A.
202. EPR § 192.
203. EPR § 208 and 211–18.
204. EPR § 219–29 and 287–97.
205. EPR § 231–49.
206. EPR § 199.
207. EPR § 201.
208. EPR § 203.
209. EPR § 204.
210. EPR § 205 and 303.
211. EPR § 250.
212. EPR § 253.
213. EPR § 251–52, 288 and 289R.
214. EPR § 207.
215. EPR § 207A and 253.
216. EPR § 289R.
217. EPR § 256.
218. EPR § 272–320.
219. EPR § 290A and 300–03 (mediation), with agriculture (EPR § 305–07) and civil society (EPR § 308–11) existing as two houses of the legislature (EPR § 312).
220. EPR § 291.
221. EPR § 308R. A third element of the ethical state is a constitutional monarchy (EPR § 275–86), but it has no bearing on the account being provided here.
222. EPR § 258.

223. EPR § 255. Cf. Karl Popper, *The Open Society and Its Enemies, Vol. II* (2002) 3–88. On the distance between Plato and Hegel, which Popper misses, see Foster (n 6) 72–109.

224. EPR § 256R.

225. EPR § 157.

226. EPR § 263A.

227. EPR § 153–54, 185–87 and 257–70.

228. EPR § 162.

229. EPR § 206R.

230. EPR § 147.

231. EPR § 268.

232. EPR § 324R.

233. EPR § 358.

234. Avineri (n 127) 109.

235. CVI 929. See also GFCPE 87–88.

236. Mészáros (n 140) 136.

237. CVI 171–72.

238. EPM 58.

239. CVI 928.

240. GFCPE 706.

241. For Marx's critiques of Hegel's civil society, see CHPR, CCHPR, OJQ 93–114, EPM 102-120 and GI 57-60.

242. CVI 784.

243. For example, see CVI 715–16 (exchange-relation), CVI 270–80 (the sale of labour power), CVI 675–706 (analysis of the wage-form) and CVII 196 (labour as commodity).

244. EPM 67.

245. CM 61.

246. CVII 120.

247. The desire can be for the use-value of what is bought (CVI 200), for value as with the miser, or for surplus value (CVI 254–57).

248. CVI 617–19.

249. CVII 120.

250. GFCPE 541–42 and CVI 173 and 739. For this idea in his early work, see EPM 16 and 78, GI 55–56 and 107.

251. WLC 217–18.

252. EPR § 289R.

253. EPM 38.

254. WLC 202.

255. GFCPE 541.

256. CVIII 953-54.

257. CVI 723.

258. EPM 53.

259. ET 19–20 and PP 112–20.

260. CVI 342.

261. CVI 381.
262. CVI 433.
263. CVI 739.
264. Engels (n 8) 312ff.
265. EPR § 36.
266. EPM 82
267. CVI 799.
268. CVI 548.
269. Agnes Heller, *The Theory of Need in Marx* (2018) 50. On needs free form alienated existence, see Mészáros (n 140) 173–80.
270. CVI 381.
271. Engels (n 8) 315.
272. EPM 66-69.
273. EPM 49. Commitment to 'an honest price', the idea of just exchange, is the 'innocent vow' of 'good bourgeois and philanthropist economists' (PP 72). There is 'no individual exchange without the antagonism of classes' (PP 84).
274. CVI 280.
275. CVI 182.
276. OJQ 94.
277. GI 117.
278. GI 55 and 85–86.
279. EPR § 27. See also EPR § 258.
280. CGP 1031.
281. EPR § 167.
282. EPR § 169.
283. EPR § 170.
284. EPR § 62.
285. EPR § 63.
286. Love 'excludes all oppositions [and] is indignant if part of the individual is severed and held back as private property', albeit that those in love stand in 'multiplex opposition in the course of their multiplex acquisition and possession of property and rights' (ETW 302–08).
287. EPR § 171.
288. EPR § 174.
289. For Hegel only the father has this freedom (EPR § 166 and 171).
290. EPR § 159.
291. EPR § 174.
292. EPR § 172R, 178 and 180.
293. EPR § 229A.
294. EPR § 80, 206, 217A and 235.
295. EPR § 82–103.
296. EPR § 230.
297. EPR § 203A.
298. Margaret Jane Radin, *Reinterpreting Property* (1993) 46–47.
299. EPR § 232.

300. EPR § 46.
301. Renato Cristi, 'Hegel on Property and Recognition' 51(2) *Laval Théologique et Philosophique* (1995) 342.
302. EPR § 46A.
303. Michael O. Hardimon, *Hegel's Social Philosophy: The Project of Reconciliation* (1994) 80.
304. EPR § 126R.
305. EPR § 130.
306. EPR § 46A.
307. EPR § 270R.
308. EPR § 64R.
309. CHPR 108.
310. Cristi (n 311) 343.
311. EPR § 80 and 199.
312. EPR § 217A.
313. EPR § 230.
314. EPR § 260.
315. EPR § 260A.
316. EPR § 230–42.
317. EPR § 237 and 241.
318. EPR § 127.
319. EPR § 127R.
320. EPR § 239–41 and 252.
321. EPR § 249–50.
322. EPR § 238 and 241.
323. EPR § 255A.
324. EPR § 240.
325. EPR § 241.
326. EPR § 242.
327. EPR § 245.
328. EPR § 244A.
329. EPR § 245–46.
330. EPR § 248.
331. EPR § 245R.
332. Dudley Knowles, 'Hegel on Property and Personality' 33(130) *The Philosophical Quarterly* (1983) 45–62, 55.
333. On taxes, see EPR § 184A, 299, 301A and 302A.
334. EPR 21.
335. On Hegel's theory of law, see Brooks (n 12) 82–95.
336. EPR 21.
337. EPR § 211.
338. EPR § 217 and 324R.
339. EPR § 55A, 96A, 211A, 214 and 227.
340. EPR § 3, 216, 218R, 234 and 274.
341. EPR § 42 and 44.

342. EPR § 43.
343. EPR § 59–70.
344. EPR § 235–36.
345. EPR § 205 and 294.
346. EPR § 270.
347. EPR § 306.
348. EPR § 324.
349. EPR § 4A, 187R and 353.
350. EPR § 57R.
351. Shlomo Avineri, *Hegel's Theory of the Modern State* (1974) 98.
352. EPR § 198 and 253R.
353. EPR § 243.
354. EPR § 244.
355. EPR § 228R.
356. EPR § 238.
357. CCHPR 132.
358. CGP 1037–38.
359. EPM 73.
360. OJM 189–90. On the nature of external or second-order mediation, opposed by Marx, see the discussion in Mészáros (n 140) 78–92.
361. OJQ 113.
362. EPM 101.
363. OJM 202.
364. OJM 201–02.
365. OJM 196.
366. OJQ 103.
367. CVII 196.
368. CVI 167.
369. CVI 757.
370. CVIII 969.
371. CVIII 428.
372. EPM 75.
373. EPM 100.
374. EPM 101.
375. EPM 73.
376. CM 84–87 and GI 119–120.
377. Hook (n 100) 201.
378. EPM 13.
379. CGP 1031.
380. EPM 18. See also GI 48 and 116, for references to need in the sense of subsistence.
381. EPM 52.
382. For extended analyses of Marx's conception of need, see Heller (n 277) and Ian Fraser, *Hegel and Marx: The Concept of Need* (1998) 123–64. For briefer

accounts, see Lawrence Hamilton, *The Political Philosophy of Needs* (2003) 53–59 and Leopold (n 1) 223–34.

383. EPM 75.
384. For the same reading, see Heller (n 277) 67–73.
385. OJM 195.
386. EPM 97.
387. EPM 84.
388. GI 54.
389. On the constitutive relation between consumption and production, each 'immediately' bound up with the other, see GFCPE 90–94.
390. OJM 189.
391. CM 81.
392. With 'must-ought' reconciled (Heller (n 277) 120), law will cease to be a coercive instrument (125–26). For Locke, lazy people can be made to work, but for Marx, we will experience work as a 'vital need' (CGP 1031). See Mészáros (n 140) 185–86.
393. CVIII 367.
394. G.A. Cohen, *Karl Marx's Theory of History: A Defence* (expanded ed, 2001) 130.
395. CVI 618.
396. For examples of the unity being tied to private property's abolition, see EPM 57–58, 73–74 and 115, OJM 193–94, and GI 55, 83 and 117–18.
397. EPM 87.
398. PP 160. On the transition to socialism, see remarks in CGP 1029–31. For a Marxist analysis, see Ernest Mandel, *The Formation of the Economic Thought of Karl Marx: 1843 to Capital* (tr. Brian Pearce, 2015) 187–210.
399. PP 190.
400. PP 190 and CM 81.
401. PP 136.
402. EPM 72, GI 105 and Thesis X (TF 123).
403. CVI 636–38.
404. David Harvey, *Marx, Capital and the Madness of Economic Reason* (2019) 113.
405. CVII 116.
406. EPM 73–74.
407. For remarks on this point, see Harvey (n 83) 433–40 and Leopold (n 1) 293–95.
408. CVI 99.
409. CVII 390.
410. CVI 618.
411. CVII 252.
412. CVII 527.
413. CVII 434.
414. CVII 390.
415. CVI 171 and 173.

416. CVI 172.
417. CVIII 966.
418. WLC 211.
419. CVII 544–45.
420. GFCPE 708.
421. CVIII 959.

Part II

THREE QUESTIONS, NOT ONE

In part I, we unbundled the ideas of five philosophers, whose property theories, probably more than all others, but certainly as much as any other, still structure our thinking on this issue. This continued organising power of their ideas makes it essential for any adequate property theory to start with them. This fact, though, also makes it necessary for theory to free itself from them. For Locke, Bentham, Hayek, Hegel and Marx belong to the same tradition. Despite all their efforts to overcome, reverse or correct each other and the schools of thought to which they belonged, they always found themselves bound back once more to the same question: What is Man? Whilst their answers to this question diverge in almost all of their concrete details, they converge in offering answers at all – and that is the problem.

We began with Locke, whose model embodies the biblical image of fallen man, compelled to subsist through sweat and toil, and sometimes obtain just a measure of comfort. Whilst religious in inspiration, it has a rather mundane basis. The relation between labour and life is borne out of the experience or the witnessing of people struggling just to feed, clothe and shelter themselves and others. This primitive struggle underlies Locke's fundamental law of nature: to preserve life. For present purposes, it does not matter if the origin of this duty is God, Reason, Desire or Sense. Nor does it matter whether it is derived from the affirmation of life or from the belief that when we are hungry, cold or wet we will always privilege survival. What is important is that for Locke, the concern for bare biological life animates all.

Bentham is similarly concerned with survival, but for him the problem is not so much a harsh, unforgiving nature but rather the threats posed by others. Wary of the shadows populating nineteenth-century London's dirty and dimly lit streets, they shoot first and ask questions later. In a modern crowded city where the resources we need to be happy are scarce, they take what they can when they can. This results in total social war, but in this society of strangers, they feel that they have no choice: vulnerable and alone, what would you do? The primitive experience driving Bentham is disorder and fear, with the promotion of security being the way to overcome it. Hayek is less worried. Social order precedes our births, he says, so our natural state is not atomistic or violent. He instead wants to explain the reality that despite our conflicting preferences and a near-global ignorance of the facts required for their satisfaction, a system exists that manages both problems: markets. His awe of its spontaneous ordering of preferences, together with the link that he draws between their satisfaction and the use of facts, moves him to situate in the heart of his system of thought the power of markets to accumulate and disperse information.

Hegel and Marx are equally struck by limit and conflict, but according to their ontologies, we are not just contingently and sociologically related. It is not as though we are born into a social setting but might instead have been isolated Robinson Crusoes. The idea otherwise, Marx says, is 'twaddle',[1] not just historically but ontologically, since to be human is necessarily to live through and in our relations. So, for Hegel and Marx, we require a true or real reconciliation: a rational or material healing of the divide that constitutes this vale of tears. It is not enough just to loosen and push back the limits that mark our diverse relations. A cultivation of forces, in Hayek's idiom, is incomplete. Rather, external alien powers impinging on the will's conscious, purposive striving to express itself in reality, all the forces pushing us hither and thither, must be brought under our comprehensive control. Only by overcoming that which opposes our willing selves do we meet what is most urgent: division. It is only by transcending real limits and conflicts that we can ever escape the frustration, malaise or loneliness that often overwhelms us when we perceive a chasm between our sense of self and a hostile or an indifferent external world. This primitive experience underlies Hegel and Marx: alienation. It moves them to sit in the heart of their great systems the ideals of rational unity and non-antagonistic expression.

Stripped of all their jargon, we grasp better the root and cause of their fierce disagreements about property. Each provides theories that are functionalist and essentialist in form. In building their theories of property, our model philosophers proceed in three stages: AS1, AS2, AS3. First, they identify particular qualities of, or facts about, the person that they judge worthy of practical concern (AS1). When prescribing property, they all start by fixing what is good, for its own sake and/or instrumentally: life, security, information, rational unity and non-antagonistic expression. After fixing what matters, each then abstracts from and essentialises them (AS2). They do this in different ways. Locke lexically orders goods: first preserve your family's lives, then the lives of others, and then look for some comfort. Marx sees the logical conflict between markets and non-antagonistic expression, so he repudiates the former. Hegel recognises a similar conflict between the immediate unity of family life and the separateness of individual freedom, but, not willing to give up either, he reduces them to modes of one ultimate good: spirit. And Bentham and Hayek, after observing the diverse ways that individuals live, manage this reality by reducing the good to one internally coherent thing, pleasure or preference, with security or the impersonal aggregation and dissemination of dispersed information being the best way to maximise it.

Having lexically ordered conflicting forms, repudiating or designating one form ultimate, or making multiple forms internally coherent, each takes a third step in their theory building. Each prescribes rights (AS3), the function of which is to facilitate the realisation of their privileged (AS2) concerns (AS1). In privileging life, Locke initially affords individuals exemptions to use objects to preserve themselves, and then for the same reason affords exclusive claim-rights and duties to work. Bentham fixates on the security of existing property rights to the point that, whilst he was an abolitionist in practice, he cannot bear the thought of annulling slaveholding in theory. Hayek, stunned by epistemic pessimism, says that our options are stark: an individual power to exchange rights in markets or the inevitable winding road to the gulag. And to transcend alienation, Hegel and Marx call for reconciliation. Whereas Hegel's privileging of thought moves him to prescribe the balanced tension of rights that we find in a family-centred, market-based and welfare-backed state, supplemented where needed by colonial expansion and begging, Marx's inversion of Hegel and privileging of matter moves him to prescribe a collective non-discretionary power to produce useful objects and an individually held discretion to consume them. Despite deep disagreements about what matters and contrasting methods for dealing with diversity (GP1, GP4), therefore, our model philosophers all belong to the same anthropological tradition – one that still dominates the liberal, neoliberal, progressive and socialist theories of the present.

Whilst criticism, like that performed in part I, clarifies the nature of theoretical disagreement, it points towards a new problem. When disagreement is at the level of models, there can be hope for resolution. No matter how it is proved, one model might be right: this is what we *really* are. If disagreements are rooted in conflict (GP1, GP4) between forms, though, this hope can diminish. For when allocating property rights, apart from theorists somehow sensibly telling us to select as ultimately (GP5) worthwhile (GP2) for its own sake (GP3) just the experience of being your own person that informs individualism, or just the experience of being part of a relational whole that is communalism's basis, how can they tell us to select struggle, vulnerability, ignorance, alienation, and so on, as our essential practical concern? Likewise, is it not unduly limiting for theory to prescribe only security, expression, and so on, as the one true form of being-in and relation to the world? Even if our horizons were not so 'artificially and dogmatically curtailed', as Heidegger describes people who argue for their preferred 'ethic' in this way,[2] and we prescribed some mixture of them, how could we rank them universally (GP7) or for each person or group or situation (GP6) in advance and devoid of concrete context, given the radical incommensurability arising from their ultimate (GP5) and logically incompatible (GP4) natures?

Such are the problems that plague our tradition. In chapter 5 we consider four traditional but still operative responses: linguistic reduction, modal reduction, rejection and ranking. In the end, though, these efforts fail to grasp the root of the problem: the use of prescriptive models, that is, the structuring of thinking about property with an abstraction or set of abstractions that internally cohere or can be ranked. Any solution to these problems must be more radical, focussing on the anthropological structure itself. What we must grasp is that the problems are pseudo-problems – they only appear *as* problems because we aim to answer the anthropological question. If there is no need to answer it, though, if we gently declined to say what we in fact are, in the ontological and prescriptive sense, then many of the obdurate obstacles that have emerged over the years in the wake of our conflicting interpretations of man would in time simply drift away.

In large part, this book is one long attempt not so much to have all prescriptive anthropology 'reduced to ashes',[3] or to reveal and 'destroy' its 'ontological' presuppositions,[4] or to 'throw off the last anthropological constraints' on property theory,[5] or to strive for a result in which some or other 'arbitrary . . . anthropological postulate' is 'exploded'.[6] Nothing this dramatic. Rather, it is an effort to persuade you to adopt a therapeutic attitude towards the ambitions of all prescriptive anthropologists, in the sense of letting go of the felt need to prescribe by theory, even in outline, what should be done about property. The effort is rooted in the definitions articulated in chapter 1 and criticism in part I, which were intended to 'de-stabilize' the 'closed universe',[7] as Herbert Marcuse calls analysis of this kind, that is created by the anthropological structure. In part II, we outline a positive argument for letting go of the belief that anthropology is essential for property theory. Here, we sketch an alternative, where rather than an ultimate prescriptive question about man, we begin with three deflated and descriptively orientated questions, which direct attention to forms, relations and rights. In chapter 5, we formalise the questions as DA1, DA2 and DA3, and we illustrate them concretely in chapters 6 and 7, by way of a series of qualitative descriptions of diverse relational (DA2) forms (DA1) and the property rights (DA3) that are required to facilitate or frustrate them.

In philosophy, however, solutions to important problems never bring matters to a close. They always generate or reveal new problems. In chapter 8, we confront the problem that will always arise when we endorse a deflated alternative: the tragic conflict internal to property relations. In some ways, this problem is more difficult than the theoretical problems just sketched. Cloistered away in seminars or studies or salons, nothing exhilarates philosophers quite like the confusions wrought by thought. As Nietzsche observes: 'This is why Lessing, the most honest of theoretical men, dared to state openly that searching for the truth meant more to him than the truth itself.'[8] This isolated, navel-gazing pleasure is not available when faced with tragedy. As Chantal Delsol puts it, 'we have immense difficulty admitting the reality of the limit-situation, that is, the limits imposed by what is fundamental or essential'.[9] This might contribute to the resistance to tragedy displayed by our tradition's greatest philosophers. That many of those who have taught us most resist the tragic implications of the deflated alternative should make us pause, for humility is the highest philosophical virtue. If after this modest pause tragedy still seems to be the most realistic of our possible descriptions of reality, though, then we must embrace it no matter what our greats have done. The failure to do so in these circumstances would not be an act of homage paid to our betters. Rather than displaying natural piety, to follow them would be to dishonour them.

In these chapters, I try to persuade you that with property we best pay tribute to those whom we seek to displace through and in an attentive facing up to tragedy – with humility and courage. Not only is doing so necessary to make more meaningful sense of our reality, the 'entire world of goods' that is the subject of 'distributive justice',[10] and thereby do our duty to it, but doing so is also a precondition for making it a more liveable one.

NOTES

1. GFCPE 84.
2. Martin Heidegger, *Being and Time* (tr. J Macquarrie and E Robinson, 1962) 363–64.
3. Louis Althusser, *For Marx* (tr. B Brewster, 2005) 229–30.
4. Heidegger (n 2) 41–49.
5. Michel Foucault, *Archaeology of Knowledge* (2ed, tr. AM Sheridan Smith, 2002) 16.
6. Jean Baudrillard, *The Mirror of Production* (tr. Mark Poster, 1975) 31–32, 58 and 60.
7. Herbert Marcuse, *One-Dimensional Man: Studies in the Ideology of Advanced Industrial Society* (2nd ed., 1991) 103.
8. Friedrich Nietzsche, *The Birth of Tragedy and Other Writings* (ed. R. Geuss and R. Speirs, 1999) 73.
9. Chantal Delsol, *Icarus Fallen: The Search for Meaning in an Uncertain World* (tr. R Dick, 2003) 209.
10. Michael Walzer, *Spheres of Justice: A Defense of Pluralism and Equality* (1983) 3.

Chapter 5

Deflating the Structure

This chapter transitions the book from the anthropological structure to a deflated and descriptive alternative. The formal features of this alternative are delineated in the last section of this chapter, and some concrete content is offered in chapters 6 and 7. First, though, we must proceed through a transitional theorist: Michael Walzer.

Walzer offers us a real alternative to the anthropological approach. We must look to Marx's reversal of Hegel to find a property theorist who departs so radically from his predecessors and thereby alters and improves our thinking on this issue. In fact, he is more radical than Marx. He does not just turn anthropology 'right side up', he rips it up by the roots. In *Spheres of Justice*, he offers a theory that in key respects is strongly plural in form. Having ripped the anthropological structure up by its roots, though, he immediately became entangled in its fraying ends. He shares with it the failure to engage adequately the conflict that is inevitable in our strongly plural world. This failure diminishes his theory, not in its details, but in its basic structure. Before we consider his theory, however, we must touch on four traditional conflict-avoidance strategies, for they are the context in which he offers us his radical, albeit inadequately so, approach to property.

MAKING SENSE

To say that advocates of the anthropological structure fail to engage properly with conflict is not to say that they do not deal with it at all. In a sense, it is all that they do. It is to criticise how they do it. Faced with conflict between, say, relations like individuality and community, or forms like life, security, markets and unity, or concerns like survival, disorder, ignorance and alienation, the theoretical solutions of the philosophers in this tradition diverge in form. Whilst they diverge in form, they converge in their goal: avoid or manage artificially conflict. Their strategies take one of four forms: linguistic reduction, modal reduction, rejection and ranking. I recognise that what is said below is little more than a sketch, but I am comforted by the fact that all of the points that I make have been made by others. Like much of this book, all that I mean to do is bring together what many others have said, explaining how they support the case for SGP.

Theorists in the utilitarian and preference-satisfaction tradition, like Bentham and Hayek,[1] realise that the good is diverse: friendship, memory, possession, and so on. This diversity, though, is in the end always spatio-temporal (GP1) in nature. For some in this tradition, the possibility that the nature of the good may run deeper than platitudes about forms of pleasure or preference never engages their theoretical attention. More sophisticated theorists recognise logical conflict (GP4) but resist its theoretical and practical import. They do this by flattening out the qualitative structures of the conflicting forms, translating their constitutive modes, attitudes, concepts, and so on to a single metric: pleasure or preference. In doing this, by rendering them transparent, they empower themselves to manage practical conflict. They can do this because with qualitative diversity now flattened out, the only important category when deciding what to do is quantity. This is because the ideal of all action will always, because it can only ever, be to ideally maximise, directly or indirectly and by way of whatever complex of sophisticated qualifications, the now uniformly defined good. They might still analyse qualities, but only ever for instrumental reasons. As good scientist-legislators, the aim will be to acquire the facts, the inputs or outputs, needed to make laws – Bentham's Civil Codes, Hayek's Constitution of Liberty, and so on – that effectively manage the movements of subjects and objects to increase the quantum of good.

This isolated analysis of qualities, though, which carves reality up by its joints, is antithetical to one that describes how they constitute relational forms. In reply to these agents of order, these calculating managers of the good, we can only point them to the qualitative richness obliterated and the conflict obscured by their linguistic reductions. This is one goal of chapters 6 to 8. If the descriptions in fact persuade them, this will, as Raz explains, 'put paid to the hope of developing a general system or technology of calculation for practical reasoning'.[2] As Charles Taylor notes, however, whether this pointing method works, 'depends in part on what you feel about reductive explanations'. If reductions seem fine to you, then the occlusion of richness or conflict 'may not seem such a big deal'.[3] Later we confront the limits of reason when arguing with weak pluralists, but let us first sketch three other strategies for dealing with conflict.

As we saw in chapter 4, whilst Hegel recognises logical conflict, he strives to avoid its force in theory and practice by reducing conflicting (GP4) goods (GP3) to moments of an ultimate one (GP5). Whilst being a particular person conflicts with being a parent, and families conflict with markets, and the market is constituted by interpersonal conflict, if we take a step back from these conflicts and cast our reflective eyes over the world's field of relations, we recognise that all its conflicting moments are necessary to constitute reality itself. It may seem on the surface that our expressive activity is stymied by conflicts, but actually it is through and in the hurly-burly of life that we realise our true selves. So understood, we see that all particular conflict is semblance, an appearance that does not reflect the ultimate relational unity of all that really exists.

This modal reduction, which in less fantastic form is adopted by liberals or progressives who strive to make apparently conflicting goods 'complementary',[4] is the second strategy to avoid or manage conflict. It may be the most sophisticated, but its ambition is the same. Like the others, it is rooted in an old philosophical prejudice: refusal to live in the conflictual world of appearances. For this reason, it rests on stipulation; or, more generously put, on a contingent attitude towards conflict. Grasping this attitudinal basis of Hegel's speculative dialectic is one of young Marx's great achievements. The unity that this dialectic reveals, he recognises, might allow philosophers to find peace in this-worldly conflict, but it does not help those on the ground who are dominated by material powers. We need not accept Marx's strategy to avoid conflict to recognise the truth informing his critique. This third strategy, echoed by liberals who 'blind'[5] themselves to relevant reasons for action when designing 'basic structures',[6] or simply define conflict away,[7] is to reject the acceptability (GP2) of one conflicting (GP4) part: markets. Unless we endorse Marx's model of the person, though, this strategy is stipulation, as it is with his heirs who talk about 'true' and 'false' interests.[8] His claim, though, that Hegel pretends to realise unity by forcing contradictions (GP4) to embrace is rooted in a critical insight: whether the narrative perspective will function to reconcile conflict depends on the temperament of those confronted by it. As is well illustrated by the work of the early Frankfurt School,[9] for those who are more affected by the experience of the moment, who feel the loss occasioned by existing and present conflict as ultimate (GP5), Hegel's strategy might strike them as it did Marx: a fantastical fraud.

The fourth conflict-avoidance strategy is to rank theoretically conflicting forms. This aims to do what GP6 and GP7 say is incoherent. It assigns significance in the abstract, devoid of context. We came across a version of this fourth strategy in Locke, who prescribes the nested ordering of goods: first life (and within this: my life, my family, others), and then aim for comfort. This is an impersonal ranking that is applicable to all (GP7), but others, like advocates of a so-called 'ethics of authenticity',[10] prescribe orderings for each person or group (GP6). It is worth touching here on a well-known proponent of universal rankings: J.S. Mill. Whilst ostensibly a utilitarian, Mill grapples with pleasure's qualitative diversity (GP4),[11] citing opposition between its intellectual and sensual forms. Mill, however, refuses to accept the anti-prescriptive implications of conflict. Whilst pleasure is diverse, we are told, it is obvious to anyone who has experienced both that it is 'better to be a human being dissatisfied than a pig satisfied; better to be Socrates dissatisfied than a fool satisfied'.[12] The notoriety of Mill's claim does not come from its structure or ambition, but rather from his honesty. He does not dress up prejudice in definitions or hide it behind epistemic veils. Rather, he states openly what all philosophers do whenever they offer to their readers a list of abstractly ordered ultimate goods (GP3, GP5). No matter their bona fides or the purity of their conviction, whenever a philosopher gives an abstract ranking of ultimate but incompatible (GP4) goods, they move in Mill's shadow.[13] As Michael Sandel says about one such effort, they are just stipulating their 'desired priority with a vengeance',[14] disguising a concrete, contingent judgement as a theoretical and universal one. In doing this, John Gray rightly observes, they embody a form of 'fundamentalism'.[15]

In each of these four strategies reacting to diversity, the goal is the same: avoid or artificially manage forms of conflict that frustrate the construction of models that permit users to prescribe, actually or structurally, the allocation of property rights. Always, though, the strategy never rises higher than empty reduction or contingent stipulation. Of course, for Locke and others, they are not emptying and stipulating anything. For them, they are articulating theoretically what is clear, or at least seems so after reflectively considering and balancing diverse, apparently conflicting, concerns. Their responses to this conflict appear true to them because it explains psychological, economic, and so on, facts, or can be derived from indubitable metaphysical notions. For me, though, the responses fail to make intelligible 'inescapable' features of my experience.[16] Just as it seems to me that the project of preserving life itself is acceptable (GP2) and worth pursuing for its own sake (GP3), this applies equally to many other forms: pleasure, expression, love, and so on (GP1). And just as strategies that reduce all to pleasure/preference seem to distort or obscure the pageantry of this world's qualitative richness, so strategies that diminish the impact of conflict (GP4) between forms by reducing them to constitutive moments of one ultimate good (GP5) appear to endarken-through-numbing what is real. Lastly, it asks too much of theory to rank forms (GP6, GP7). Mill thinks intellectual life trumps sensual life, but from my experience, judgements of this kind cannot be made in the abstract. Different contexts urge upon me different, often conflicting, judgements: sometimes dialectic with friends, sometimes wallowing in mud.

Because all four strategies seem implausible, SGP follows. Yet, I have not demonstrated the truth of SGP. This is for at least two reasons. First, foundations might in fact exist. We may not be happy with Hegel or Marx's ontological demonstrations, Bentham and Hayek's reductions or Locke's intuitions, but we should always remain open to the possibility that some or other proof of the ultimate rightness of a particular model could be constructed or found. To close ourselves off from this possibility would reverse the old prejudice in favour of models, but it would remain prejudice. We might not know how the model will be proved or what a proof might look like, but we should not dogmatically stipulate its impossibility. Second, even if foundations do not exist, I have only pointed to what seems true to me. Revealing the triadic anthropological structure that is shared by Locke et al, and articulating their conflicting theories in the qualitative way we have done, I think, points clearly in the direction of SGP. Yet, in saying this, I am only articulating my own convictions: Locke's rankings are capricious; Bentham and Hayek's reductions are shallow; Marx's vision was constrained by his fixation with the 'single alternative' of use- and exchange-value;[17] and Hegel, in his refusal to take seriously the forms that he reduced to modes, exemplifies an insensitivity common to philosophers.

So, if a weak pluralist is unconvinced, this need not be due to an inductive or deductive error. Often, disagreement about primordial ethical issues arises, as Hannah Arendt explains in a related context, not from individuals being 'just a bit too stupid to discover the elementary flaws in their arguments'.[18] Rather, judgements about good and plausibility rest, to a large extent, on what best 'makes sense' of our experiences,[19] on what seems to explain most convincingly or persuasively, which is not to say coherently or finally, existing views about what really matters.

I can always try to convince you to embrace my perspective. Here, the faculty of imagination and the capacities to empathise and sympathise will be essential. To activate and exercise them, the primary mode of argument will be persuasion supported by deduction and induction, its style being closer to rhetorical flourish than analytical reason and its mode of presentation resembling storytelling and conversation more than a formal treatise. These stories will be structured around questions such as: What is it like to be vulnerable and alone, instead of comfortable and amongst friends? How do we feel when ignorant of facts relevant to satisfying our desires or realising our ends? Is being the origin of our movement important? Does our answer depend on the efficacy of the movement? What do we think about the fact that this freedom often seems to be accompanied by oppression and exclusion? Even if it were not, would it still be better for social life to be more like love or friendship? Or would such a world, though apparently infinitely attractive, be at best insipid, or worse, more suffocating than homely, or worse still, a tyranny without escape?

In telling stories – and indeed, this is one purpose of this book – we must be sensitive to our audience. For sometimes we must tell stories that reveal the depth or complexity, the qualitative distinctiveness, of diverse forms (GP1, GP4). Other times, we must try to persuade people of the acceptability of a relation (GP2) about which they hold a prejudice. On other occasions, the goal will be to get them to take on the idea that a form not only matters for its own sake (GP3) but is ultimately good (GP5) by getting them to feel the impact of its loss, illustrating that often a bad cannot be made good by 'the bigger picture'. And for those who grasp all this, we may still need to weave a narrative to remind them of what they already know: without first situating ourselves, in fact or imagination or both, in the actual moment of decision or action, judgements of relative worth (GP6, GP7) are worthless. Because stories cannot have the force of formal and empirical demonstration, however, if efforts to persuade do not effect a turning, if weak pluralists remain fixed in their reductions or rejections or rankings, there is no deeper theoretical ground to which we can excavate. For there is nothing more than further, often frustrating, efforts to persuade by describing forms; nothing apart from more, often futile, efforts to get them to see the significance of diverse forms, or the truth that their relative importance is always contextual. It is 'difficult to acknowledge', Stuart Hampshire writes, 'bare contingency of feeling as the final stopping point' when arguing about the 'ultimate requirements' of justice,[20] but if strong goods pluralism is true, then it is a difficulty that must be endured.

Because what seems to explain my existing reality best, what I think common sense and what my immediate and considered intuitions suggest, will not necessarily appear this way to you, this is usually where our theoretical debates bottom out. That our spades turn, though, does not mean we can throw up our hands and say 'to each her own'. Tolerance, not just of what one judges as bad but more essentially of what one recognises as good, albeit a good incompatible with a good that one considers more important,[21] is a virtue we all should cultivate, but tolerance is not sufficient. The existence of ultimate (GP5) but incompatible (GP1, GP4) goods means that it is an empirical truth that we will often disagree about how best to organise our communities. A tolerant attitude can structure deep conflicts of this nature, but it cannot avoid it. It is in this spirit that I offer the deflated alternative articulated in chapters 6 to 8.

Before I sketch its formal features, however, we have to consider one final failure to grapple adequately with conflict: Michael Walzer's.

WALZER: THE LIMITS OF SPHERES

Walzer articulates a way of thinking about property that is inspired by the attempt to set aside the anthropological structure. Its problem, he says, is that it obscures the strongly plural nature of the goods that form our reality. In this respect, the deflated theory offered in this book overlaps with and is deeply indebted to Walzer. Yet, as we shall see, it essentially differs from him. Therefore, I focus below not on the subtle, impressive and positive content of his theory, but on his method; and my purpose is not to laud its many merits, but to identify its basic flaw: the failure to engage properly the conflict internal to any strongly plural world.

Walzer's theory is 'radically particularist'.[22] He describes the shared 'deeper understandings' of the relational forms that constitute his community,[23] its conceptions of its conditions, activities or ways of life: 'our actual, concrete, positive, and particular understanding'.[24] Whilst his method is particularistic, he argues, the community he describes is sufficiently homogenous to allow for descriptions that are sufficiently concrete to assist when allocating property. Yes, we often do not agree about the meanings of forms and we often fail to do justice to them even when we do. At a sufficiently high level of abstraction, though, we share conceptions about them, and these should perform a prescriptive role when we allocate property.[25] Pointing to the diversity of modern life, some critics object to this claim.[26] Whilst the critics are onto something, I argue later, the issue is less in his claim about shared understandings, which I think is plausible for the reasons given by Raz in a related context,[27] than in his failure to confront head on the conflict between forms even when our conceptions of them are shared.

Given Walzer's particularism, his concern is with forms he thinks are constitutive of twentieth-century democratic welfare states. These include membership, security, welfare, offices, free time, hard work, education, love, recognition, grace, and political power. This list is not exhaustive or final. Because our self-understanding is partly constitutive of what forms exist, new forms can emerge and old ones fall away or change their meaning.[28] The meaning of 'need', for example, is always in flux,[29] which means 'no *a priori* stipulation of what needs ought to be recognised is possible; nor is there any *a priori* way of determining appropriate levels of provision'.[30] Having identified the forms, he then describes them in an 'imminent and phenomenological' way,[31] articulating the 'principles internal' to each.[32] To do this, he analyses them 'from the inside',[33] explicating their own self-understandings. In describing these self-understandings, he argues, we reveal the 'what' of each particular form.[34] What this approach calls for, therefore, are the qualitative descriptions introduced in chapter 1, where we identify those modes, attitudes, concepts, and so on that 'constitute' a particular form.[35] To see this, let us sketch Walzer's conception of community, explaining how it relates to his qualitative descriptions of security, welfare and need.

For Walzer, understanding the nature of group membership – say, a state, neighbourhood or friendship – is essential to property theory, since membership 'determines with whom we make' allocative decisions and 'to whom we allocate goods and services'.[36] Like every relational form, the essential function of any particular group is fixed primarily by the self-understanding of that group. Our self-understanding of a 'state' is such that its citizens owe each other duties. We may not say 'brother' or 'comrade', but we do conceive, deep down at least, of our relationship in this way. Thus, the 'first' duty of citizenship is 'communal provision of security and welfare'.[37] It is required by the nature of our self-understanding of citizenship. Internal to the state's logic is that it exists for the sake of providing security and welfare to members who need it.[38] A distributive principle flows from this self-understanding. If the state exists to provide security and welfare to the members who need it, the principle according to which we should allocate the property rights that people require to be secure and be well is need.[39] As always, what we think necessary is not fixed, so what we allocate can change,[40] but if we think that healthcare or leisure,[41] for example, is needed to be secure or well, then each citizen must have rights that will enable them to access or experience them. The necessary distributive principle, in other words, must correspond to the form itself, which in this case is need, as understood by us.[42] The correspondence between form and distribution is what Walzer means by internal principles: the function of a particular good or bad, its 'inner logic', he argues, by necessary implication generates a 'moral logic' to distribute it in a particular way.[43]

Walzer's method, where we can identify the required distribution by looking at the structure of the form, is replicated in the book's chapters: commodities must be allocated according to the vagaries of the free market; offices to the qualified; basic education to citizens equally; romantic love to persons who freely evoke and attract it; honour to individuals who distinguish themselves through words or deeds; political power to those who persuade their fellows; and so on.

Walzer's approach has deep implications for how we conceive of distributive justice. If right, then our primary concern should not be about the inequality of particular holdings: justice is not violated if someone's rhetorical ability enables them to obtain political power over me,[44] or their natural talent makes possible for them public recognition inaccessible to me,[45] or because of luck or skill they have shares in Netflix but I invested my money in Blockbuster.[46] What should keep us up at night, Walzer says,[47] is those politicians who use their authority to acquire wealth, or the movie star who relies on their fame to launch their political career, or the real-estate tycoon who lobbies legislators to erect regulatory hurdles to building social housing. Not a 'simple equality' focussed on flat distributions of particular goods,[48] our focus must be on a 'complex equality',[49] such that we criticise relations where access to or control of one good is 'converted' into access to or control of others.[50] When this happens, there is injustice because people use their success in one 'sphere' of life to succeed in some other sphere. Success that is obtained in this way, which is a hallmark of dominant 'ideologies',[51] is 'illegitimate',[52] since the qualities that constitute one form will have been used to obtain access to or control of another.

These conversions occur when particular qualitative ensembles refuse to be 'limited by their intrinsic meanings' and 'shape' other 'meanings' in their 'own image',[53] that is, when one particular set of qualities is adopted when thinking about or striving to actualise a form constituted by some other qualitative set. This is what happens, for example, when the rich 'buy access', since instead of politicians acting in the community's interests, their actions are structured by their concern for a good extrinsic to the political sphere: money. This conversion also takes place when people are awarded honours not because they have distinguished themselves in some manner but because of their 'name recognition', or a Minister 'wins' a state contract to provide goods to the community. Injustice arises in these cases because one form (politics, honour, markets) is related to according to the qualities that belong only to another form (markets, fame, authority).

Acts of conversion, Walzer says, are tyrannous.[54] By leaving its proper domain, invading and colonising another,[55] the form illegitimately extends itself. It does this by altering the qualitative structures – modes, attitudes, concepts, and so on – that we must apply when we think about and strive to actualise forms. When forms 'outgrow their proper place',[56] when they reconceptualise some other distinct form, they exert dominance over them. The opposite of justice is not inequality of holdings, therefore, but tyranny. If the tyranny is total, if a particular form is hegemonic such that we relate to all experience through one qualitative ensemble,[57] then a society is 'totalitarian'.[58] If the boundaries between forms are secure, however, if goods are distributed in ways that conform to their own internal logics, there is no reason to complain, for there is no injustice. If an existing distribution of goods conforms to this 'diversity' of logics,[59] according to Walzer's conception of things, then the only job left for property theory will be to police, through descriptive reminders, the borders between spheres.[60]

Given the structural nature of Walzer's pluralism, it might be expected that he will have a lot to say about logical conflict between forms. Whilst he warns about conversions, the inevitability of conflict even in the absence of a form illegitimately extending itself is, relatively speaking,[61] not engaged. This calls for an explanation. One may proceed as follows. Whilst Walzer neglects this conflict, this does not reveal a problem with his theory. It is a question of emphasis rooted in two ideas. First, for him, egalitarianism pertains to freedom from domination.[62] Second, property theory is the 'art of differentiation',[63] because justice is 'the doctrine that distinguishes' different goods or bads.[64] If theory strives after justice and justice is the art of distinguishing forms, then it follows that theory must strive to differentiate forms. These ideas are related because domination is furthered or frustrated through relations between forms, that is, by whether one form imposes on another their constitutive qualities or whether they let each other be. Thus, if theory concerns justice, and justice is driven by efforts to avoid domination, this means that we must try to avoid conversions. The logic of these ideas, in other words, produces a narrow account. Walzer focusses on the boundaries between forms because this is how best to avoid domination. That he does not spend equivalent time considering other possible sources of conflict, our imagined apology will then conclude, does not reveal any problem with his theory of property. Rather, it speaks to the narrowness of his initial concerns.

I would have sympathy for this apology, but Walzer's failure to interrogate conflict between forms is rooted in a deeper problem with his method. In the final pages of his book, he compares his own theory of justice to the 'classic' conception of justice as 'giving each person his due'.[65] Of course, we must ask what each person is due. For Walzer, we are due that which is specified by the internal moral logics of the forms that constitute social life. If existing allocations conform to every existing social form, if we secure the 'separation' between their qualitative 'boundaries', there is nothing left to ask: 'Good fences make for just societies.'[66] So, it is not only that he does not emphasise conflict between forms. His method and metaphor – justice as his basic analytical category and the language of spheres, boundaries, spaces, enclosures and containment – obscure the conflict that is inevitable in, because it is internal to, all strongly plural societies.

Conflict is internal to these societies because even if social forms contain their own allocative principles and even if we conform to their internal logics, there will still be conflict whenever we decide how to allocate the rights needed to actualise them. The pervasive nature of this conflict is demonstrated in chapters 6 and 7. For now, it is enough to recall the reason for it. In chapter 1, we explained that the qualities of diverse goods can be mutually exclusive. Our examples were love and markets: each form is constituted by incompatible modes (subjective/objective), displays an incompatible attitude (sharing/competitive), and is also understood through and in incompatible concepts or categories (non-instrumental/instrumental). Thus, to say that the qualities of different goods exclude each other is to say that the mere existence of one qualitative ensemble precludes the existence of another. In these cases, it is not that we do not have enough time or space: when in love, I cannot be a market actor. This incompatibility means that the allocation of the property rights needed to facilitate one form will always be at the expense of the rights that are needed for another. This will be so even if neither form illegitimately seeks to breach their internally defined boundaries. To use an example that might appeal to Walzer, even if we chased all money lenders and merchants out of our sacred spaces,[67] we would nonetheless have to decide whether we want more temples or more markets, more love or more capital.

Avoiding dominance by policing boundaries is not enough. Good fences are critical, but they cannot settle matters. After locating the boundaries of each form – delimiting them by describing their qualitative structures – it is not just a matter of giving each form its due. Because what each form is due is logically incompatible, we must face the conflict that arises from all our allocative actions. Before we police the fences, we have to decide where to build them, that is, decide what liberties, claims, powers and/or immunities to allocate and to whom; or if they have already been built, whether we approve of their location. And all the while, we must be sensitive to the reality that no matter what we decide or do, the result will always be the loss of something that is good. Walzer's conception of 'harmony', where qualitatively distinct forms 'fit together' by relating to each other with mutual respect,[68] obscures this fact.

Despite rejecting anthropology, Walzer does not adequately face up to the inevitability of this conflict or the empirical certainty that we will disagree about what to do when we are faced with it. This undermines his theory, not in its details but in its basic structure.

FORMS, RELATIONS AND RIGHTS

Despite this difficulty with Walzer's theory, it possesses features that we must incorporate as part of any adequately strong plural theory of property. Like him, we should persist in our rejection of models when thinking about property. In their place, we should follow him in adopting a form of particularism, where we identify the qualitative structures of diverse relational forms. Lastly, and again like Walzer, we must describe these structures in detail, for doing so is necessary if we are to be effective in facilitating or frustrating goods or bads – recalling here what I said in chapter 1, that good carries a broad meaning, referring to anything that is valuable, worthy or admirable, of whatever kind or category, with the term bad afforded an equal breadth of meaning.

Let us formalise these Walzerian features. To think non-anthropologically, we must set aside questions about man and instead start with the following questions:

> DA1: What forms of being, either good or bad, are relevant to the allocation of the rights that can attach to or obtain in objects?

> DA2: How must we relate to other people or objects – that is, in what modes, with what attitudes, by way of what concepts or categories, etc. – to actualise or frustrate these good or bad forms?

These are the first two questions of the deflated alternative to prescriptive anthropology. These questions can be derived from Walzer's radically particularist (DA1) method, in terms of which we describe imminently and phenomenologically (DA2) diverse relational forms. We could also derive them, however, from the anthropological tradition criticised in part I. As we saw in chapters 2 to 4, Locke, Bentham, Hayek, Hegel and Marx were concerned with certain forms (DA1), and each instructed us on what relations are needed to facilitate or frustrate them (DA2). Therefore, a theory that emerges from DA1 and DA2 will be functionalist, like anthropological theories, but only in the sense that it will offer practical routes or responses to diverse goods and bads. Unlike them, however, it will not privilege (AS2) identified forms (AS1) for the purpose of creating a model that prescribes property rights (AS3). For a theory structured by DA1 and DA2, qualitative descriptions of the existing or possible worlds are the most that it can offer.

As Walzer's oversights illustrate, asking DA1 and DA2 will not be enough if we mean to do justice to the strongly plural nature of our world. They help to avoid the more obvious trappings and failings of the anthropological structure, but they do not make patent the conflict that flows from the incompatible natures of our relational forms. It is ultimately this failure to grapple with practical conflict that disconcerts Walzer's critics. His critics are right to worry, but not because we potentially disagree about the meanings of forms; or if we do, then this fact is not the deepest difficulty. That difficulty is that even when we do agree about their meanings, we often disagree about what to do in the face of the logical conflict between them. Because conflicts are inevitable and because differently situated persons sometimes concretely rank conflicting forms differently, the scope for political domination, where a group imposes its contingent ranking of forms totally on others, is latent in any strongly plural society. This is not only because particular forms might illegitimately extend themselves, as Walzer explains so well, but because our forms, even if well behaved, cannot but come into conflict with each other – and thus necessarily have a tendency to claim, in the domain of action, all for themselves at the expense of all others.

Despite its deep and enduring insights, Walzer's property theory obscures this possibility. It suffers from what many argue has been characteristic of philosophy since Plato pointed his city's rulers to the cave's exit. Because of the 'infinite urge . . . to systematize', as Hegel puts it, the felt need 'to raise to the universal' and thereby 'reduce the infinite mass of [seeming contingencies] to a coherent system',[69] it suffers from a theoretical neglect of the conflictual since plural nature of the human condition. In part III, we see what this entails for law's function in settling conflict. What matters here, though, is that the root of Walzer's neglect of conflict is not his particularism, imminent and phenomenological method, or claim that we often share conceptions of forms. It is rather due to his failure to carry his method all the way through. If he had done so, he might have agreed that conflict will almost always arise even when our conceptions are shared. To carry his theory of property to where it had the potential to go on its own accord, we must add to DA1 and DA2 a third question:

> DA3: To either facilitate or frustrate the actualisation of the forms in DA1 and relations in DA2, how must we allocate the rights that attach to or obtain in objects?

In the next two chapters, we see that when we answer DA3 using Hohfeld's concept of right, all those conflicts that lie coiled in the heart of every allocative choice and action cannot be ignored. Once we clear away the 'mystification' created by asking the wrong questions,[70] as Marx puts it, stepping outside the 'shadows' cast by models,[71] as Baudrillard writes after him, we see that not every form can receive its due. Berlin explains: 'That we cannot have everything is a necessary, not a contingent, truth.'[72]

There are good empirical reasons to doubt Marx's optimistic claim that 'humanity sets itself only such tasks as it is able to solve'.[73] Even if it is correct, however, it seems self-evident that not all of our tasks are self-given. Not only are we compelled to act in conditions that are not of our own choosing,[74] we are also thrown into a world constituted by ultimate but incompatible goods. This reality means that we are fated to live in conflict – our unchosen destiny being to endure the truth that there is no solution to the riddle of history, no ultimate reconciliation of all those constitutive divides that impressed themselves so forcefully on philosophy at the onset of modernity. And it is only 'the dogmatism of assertion',[75] to deploy the idiom of Enlightenment philosophy against it, that could compel one to think that this is ultimately a bad thing.

If philosophers, despite their inability to resolve or rank conflicting forms, are ever to arrive at a property theory that does justice to this tragic fact – as opposed to enabling and legitimating political farce – it is necessary for them not only to understand but also to embrace this shared fate, namely, that because of the diversity of goodness, it is only through conflict and in loss that we can ever achieve anything worthwhile.

NOTES

1. For more recent examples, see Harold Demsetz, 'Toward a Theory of Property Rights' 57(2) *The American Economic Review* (May 1967) 347–59, Richard A. Posner, *The Economics of Justice* (1983) and Thomas Merrill, 'Property and the Right to Exclude' 77 *Nebraska Law Review* (1998) 730, Thomas Merrill and Henry Smith, 'Optimal Standardization in the Law of Property: The Numerus Clausus Principle' 110 *Yale Law Journal* (2000) 1–70 and Thomas Merrill and Henry Smith, 'What Happened to Property in Law and Economics?' 111 *Yale Law Journal* (2001) 357.
2. Joseph Raz, *The Morality of Freedom* (1986) 358.
3. Charles Taylor, *The Language Animal: The Full Shape of the Human Linguistic Capacity* (2016) 85.
4. See discussion of Gregory Alexander in chapter 10.
5. Raz (n 2) 136.
6. See the discussion of Nussbaum in chapter 8, who is indebted for this strategy to John Rawls, *A Theory of Justice* (rev. ed, 1999).
7. For example, see Ronald Dworkin, *Sovereign Virtue* (2000).
8. For examples, see Herbert Marcuse, *Eros and Civilisation: A Philosophical Inquiry into Freud* (2ed, 1969) 180–81, *One-Dimensional Man: Studies in the Ideology of Advanced Industrial Society* (2ed, 1991) 7–10 and *An Essay on Liberation* (1927) 17–30, and Guy Debord, *The Society of the Spectacle* (tr. Fredy Perlman, 2021) 6, 19 and 29–31.
9. For examples, see Walter Benjamin, *Illuminations* (ed. Hannah Arendt, tr. Harry Zohn, 1969) 253–64 and Theodor Adorno and Max Horkheimer, *Dialectic of Enlightenment* (tr. John Cumming, 2016) 78–80.
10. For helpful overview and immanent critique, see Charles Taylor, *The Ethics of Authenticity* (1991).
11. For a useful overview, see MAB 170–83.
12. J.S. Mill, 'Utilitarianism' in *On Liberty and Other Essays* (1998) 140.
13. For a version of the strategy by a property theorist, see Stephen Munzer, *A Theory of Property* (1990).
14. Michael Sandel, *Liberalism and the Limits of Justice* (1982) 21.
15. John Gray, *Two Faces of Liberalism* (2000), describing Enlightenment efforts, like Mill's (60–62), to evade conflict (20–22).
16. Charles Taylor, *Philosophical Arguments* (1995) 37, on 'Strong Evaluation'.
17. Jean Baudrillard, *The Mirror of Production* (tr. Mark Poster, 1975) 45.
18. Hannah Arendt, 'Thinking' in *The Life of the Mind* (One-Volume ed, 1978) 45.
19. On this notion, see Bernard Williams, *Truth and Truthfulness* (2002) 233–69, Charles Taylor, *Philosophical Papers: Volume 2, Philosophy and the Human Sciences* (1985) 15–57, Gray (n 15) 47–68, and Jeremy Waldron, *One Another's Equals: The Basis of Human Equality* (2017) 135–37.
20. Stuart Hampshire, *Justice is Conflict* (2000) xiii.
21. Raz (n 2) 401–07.

22. Michael Walzer, *Spheres of Justice: A Defense of Pluralism and Equality* (1983) xiv.
23. Ibid., 26.
24. Ibid., 18.
25. Ibid., 28–30.
26. Ronald Dworkin, *A Matter of Principle* (1985) 214–20, Gray (n 15) 93, and Steven Lukes, *Liberals and Cannibals, The Implications of Diversity* (2017) 34.
27. Raz (n 2) 307–13.
28. Walzer (n 22) 6–10.
29. Ibid., 64–67 and 78–83.
30. Ibid., 91.
31. Ibid., 26.
32. Ibid., 19.
33. Ibid., 20.
34. Ibid., 9.
35. Ibid., 10. That this is his meaning appears from his reference to 'wanting, making, owning and exchanging' as 'modes' of commodities (105), his distinctions between family and market norms (232) and 'incompatible' forms that constitute 'different social worlds' (276–77).
36. Ibid., 31.
37. Ibid., 64.
38. Ibid., 68–69, 78 and 82–83.
39. Ibid., 64–65.
40. Ibid., 78–83.
41. Ibid., 86–91.
42. Ibid., 74 and 84.
43. Ibid., 75.
44. Ibid., 303–04 and 309–10.
45. Ibid., 267–68.
46. Ibid., 106–07.
47. Ibid., 20.
48. Ibid., 13–17.
49. Ibid., 17–20.
50. Ibid., 11–12.
51. Ibid., 12.
52. Ibid., 19.
53. Ibid., 11.
54. Ibid., 19 and 28.
55. Ibid., 10, 19 and 119.
56. Ibid., 105.
57. Ibid., 279–80, 282 and 290.
58. Ibid., 119 and 315–16.
59. Ibid., 18.
60. Ibid., 20 and 311.

61. There is recognition of this in references to arguments about building more museums (Ibid., 24), healthcare and the good life (83), forms of consumption (114–15), funding further education (209), drawing of boundaries (121–22, 226 and 294), and politics (285–87 and 311). His focus, however, is on disagreement about what forms require, for example, what is our self-understanding of need (66–67 and 79–82), and struggles to enforce them (89, 182–83, 191, 210, 281 and 310–11), for this is the 'chief purpose' (127) of justice.
62. Ibid., xii–xiii and 17.
63. Ibid., xv.
64. Ibid., 319.
65. Ibid., 312–13.
66. Ibid., 319.
67. Ibid., 109.
68. Ibid., 318–19.
69. EPR § 211A.
70. GI 40.
71. Baudrillard (n 17) 87.
72. Isaiah Berlin, *Liberty* (ed. Henry Hardy, 2002) 215.
73. Quoted in John Gray, *Gray's Anatomy: Selected Writings* (new ed, 2016) 71.
74. EB 480.
75. PhS § 54.

Chapter 6

World as Instrument

The next two chapters offer some answers to DA1 to DA3 and thereby give this formal structure concrete content. In doing so, we start to articulate more meaningfully the deflated alternative to the anthropological approach to property.

To argue that we should oppose Locke, Bentham, Hayek, Hegel and Marx's anthropological property systems does not necessarily entail passing negative judgement on all that is positive in these systems. If we follow John Gardner in 'separating out disparate thoughts' they regarded 'as part of some package deal',[1] we may agree with Aristotle that more reasonable than thinking that each of them was 'entirely mistaken' in their arguments about what is good, is to admit that each was 'right in at least one respect, or even in most respects'.[2] Much in our philosophers' models is worth keeping. In fact, so much so that as regards its positive content, this book provides nothing at all like a novel property theory. A great deal of what I say in the next two chapters is gleefully snatched from others. For my purpose here is not to replace old thoughts with new thoughts. It is to understand what theory might look like after 'wearing every thought down to its rightful little size and then keeping it in its rightful little place'.[3] For this reason, the descriptions in chapters 6 and 7 may be familiar to you, for all that I describe are the relational forms that, because they are our own, we already know, but about which we sometimes need a little reminding.

This is apparent from the initial answers provided to DA1: What forms, good or bad, matter when we allocate property? In answering the question, it is reasonable to start with those answers that inform (AS1) our tradition. After all, to say that life, security, information and forms of unity are important, is to say what for many is obvious. This is not to make any claim about their status as goods, for example, that they are objective. It is only to say that most people from my experience think that these forms are good rather than bad or something about which they are merely indifferent. In the last section of this chapter, we identify another good, choice, made possible by mixing the relations described in the first two sections. And in chapter 7 we describe relations other than the ones that structure Locke, Bentham, Hayek, Hegel and Marx's theories. In this limited way, our answers to DA1 depart from tradition. Theory, though, must go well beyond these forms. It must distinguish more concrete forms of the general object-relations I describe, it must describe other object-relations, and it must describe interpersonal relations, like those provided by Walzer, such as offices, education and free time, insofar as they require property to be made real.

For, as Walzer writes: 'Distributive justice is a large idea. It draws the entire world of goods within the reach of philosophical reflection.'[4] This fact, together with the limits of theory when it comes to judgements of significance, means that theorists should not draw up a list of forms to be described, or at least any list which imagines itself to be complete. Strong goods pluralism means theory is less important than many of its practitioners believe. Often, our time will be better spent supporting institutions that empower people to identify, construct, express and evaluate goods. Despite this humbling truth, description remains key. For theory, 'the craftsmen's contemplative glance',[5] is necessary to effect deliberate change at all. Given all this, it may be best just to admit the limits of these chapters and to get on with the descriptive task at hand.

The relational forms described in these chapters can be sat in two categories: instrumentality and directness. This chapter describes instrumentality, the next directness. Within each category, we can draw distinctions. Within instrumentality, we can distinguish between relations where we treat objects as consumables and those where we treat them as reifications; and within directness, we can distinguish between objects we relate to as expressions, and relations that exist as living spirit. In making the distinctions, we point to: the diverse forms that our relations constitute; the modes, attitudes, concepts and categories that constitute each relation; and the rights necessary to facilitate each relational form. Doing so reveals that forms, relations and rights are incompatible, not just spatio-temporally (GP1) but also logically (GP4). This incompatibility is one reason why the deflated alternative is more plausible than any anthropological, prescriptive one. Through our descriptions, we can make sense of more regions of thought and experience than approaches that are structured by the denial or neglect of strong goods pluralism.

Let us unpack and stipulate more concretely this chapter's results. Here, we distinguish two instrumental relations to objects: consumptive and reified. For both, objects serve our desires or ends. They are constituted through and in concepts or categories like utility, means and ends. As Martin Heidegger explains, instrumental object-relations are formed 'by various ways of the "in-order-to," such as serviceability, conduciveness, usability, manipulability'.[6] These two relations are distinguished, though, by the attitudes we have towards the objects. These attitudes structure our understanding of an object's concrete functional form. By concrete functional form, I mean the object's defining purpose, its identity. If this concrete form is dependent on the object being used to satisfy or realise immediately existing desires or ends, the object is a consumable. With these objects, instrumental concepts or categories are accompanied by two constitutive attitudes: eros and indifference. If the concrete form is not dependent on the object satisfying or realising immediately existing desires or ends, we relate to the object as a reification. And this relation is constituted by the attitudes of caution and self-control.

This distinction between consumables and reified instruments, described phenomenologically by Arendt in her distinction between labour and work, that is, *animal laborans* and *homo faber*,[7] is important. Consumables and reifications make possible diverse goods. Consumables are required for forms like life and expression as prescribed by Locke and Marx, whereas reified instruments make possible Benthamite security and Hegelian or Hayekian markets. When the rights required to constitute each form are considered, though, we find incompatibilities. The rights necessary to consume and those needed to relate to objects as reified instruments are mutually exclusive. And within the consumer relation, depending on whether we prioritise life or expression, incompatible rights are needed. Likewise, within reified relations, depending on whether we privilege security, rational unity, or efficient information,[8] the incompatibilities accumulate further. This means that if it is important to actualise all these forms, conflict is inevitable.

I recognise that these distinctions are abstract, but their practical significance is revealed in chapter 10, where we consider South African legislation that employed them to transform property relations to minerals.

THE CONSUMER IS ALWAYS RIGHT

The relation described in this section is required to actualise the forms that structure Locke and Marx's theories: life and expression (DA1). Whilst their theories diverge on countless fronts, the goods that each privileges can only be realised by treating objects as consumables. Because life and expression are constituted by the consumer relation (DA2), they require similar rights (DA3). When the content of the rights is articulated in the detail that corresponds to their forms, though, incompatibilities emerge. To reveal all this, we must move from our answers to DA1 to DA2: the consumptive relation required to actualise these goods.

Eros and Indifference

We start by stipulating three formal conditions that must be met for any object-relation to be consumptive in form, then unpacking and defending them as we proceed.

We use up or discard a consumable after its function, as is given to it by our existing desires or ends, is either satisfied or abandoned, for consumables exist only insofar as they immediately satisfy or realise our existing desires or ends. For any object to be a consumable, therefore, three conditions must be met:

C1: The object must be used by a subject.

C2: The use of this object must satisfy or realise immediately this subject's existing, i.e., present, desires or ends.

C3: The object's identity, its concrete functional form, must be dependent upon, i.e., tied to and determined by, the particular characteristics of C1 and C2.

An example of a consumer relation is one that we often have with food. You experience a desire, hunger, that can only be satisfied by using an object in a particular way: by eating it. When your stomach calls out, you get off the couch and go to the fridge. When you look in the fridge, what greets you is not some heap of matter but options: apples for eating, biltong for eating, cheese for eating. These objects exist for you as food. And they will exist as food until your hunger is sated, but thereafter will cease to exist in this form. Central to the distinction between consumables and reified instruments is the reason why their concrete forms – what they exist for, their being food, not some other object, or a disarticulated heap of matter – undergo this change.

It is tempting to think that its concrete form changes only because it no longer can function as originally meant, for when the apple is 'eaten up' no material object remains that is capable of satisfying your hunger. This is true and captures the folk meaning of consumption: absorption of an object by a subject. There is another way, however, in which the object can cease to be food: when your stance towards it changes.[9] For example, consider a half-eaten sandwich. If you have had your fill and you answer 'I am done' in reply to the waiter's gesture, you communicate that you no longer want to eat it. With this, the object is transformed, not materially but as a concrete object. For the waiter and customer, it ceases to be food: it now *is* waste. Though still edible, in your eyes it is no longer what it was when you were hungry and put in your food order. It ceases to be food by virtue of the fact that you no longer want to eat it. With this change in desire, there is a corresponding change in the object's concrete form. It is this fact you communicate to the waiter, whose recognition of it moves him to clear the table. True, the object need not change in this way when you are full. You may ask for a doggy bag. If you do, it remains food rather than becoming waste. Rather than speaking against my point, however, it reinforces it. What stops the half-eaten sandwich from becoming waste and instead transforms it into leftovers is that your desire to eat it endures. All that has changed is when you want to eat it: later, not now. What sustains its identity, prevents its form altering into something other than food, is that you still treat it in a certain way: your stance towards it remains essentially unchanged.

What the above illustrates is that an object's concrete form, that is, its identity, can be tied to the function we attribute to it. Its existence as a particular object – lunch, waste, leftovers – depends on the end that a subject gives to it. This formative fact must be grasped in full since the nature of this dependency is basic to consumer relations. This requires unpacking the attitudinal content of the stance referred to above. This stance is constituted by two attitudes: eros and indifference. Eros refers to the fact that consumers 'unite' the object's concrete form with their existing desire or end.[10] Indifference refers to their ultimate[11] lack of concern for the object's form before their desire or end appears to them, or after it is satisfied, realised or abandoned.[12]

We came across the erotic attitude when we considered the nature of Hegel's spirit. Hegel's eros is Platonic or negating in form: it is a desire not to desire. Phenomenologically, it refers to a subject's desire to complete a 'lack',[13] fill an 'inner emptiness', materialise its 'void'.[14] Negating desire, Hegel explains, can be effected by way of a standing negation: an enduring recognition of the rationality of another. Another form of negation, which is constitutive of consumer relations, entails a subject absorbing an object. The consumptive form of negating desire can be realised in two ways: materially or spiritually. To reveal this, let us follow phenomenologically the process of material consumption from beginning to end.

Your stomach rumbles: feeling empty, you desire to fill it. You see an object that can satisfy this desire and so you identify it with this desire. By this, I mean that its purpose or being is fixed by your desire, in your mind it now exists to fill your stomach: it is food. To actualise its purpose as food, you are moved to bring it within you, taking the steps necessary to eat it. In reaching out for the object, you transform the object and yourself. Marx writes that:

> Through this movement he acts upon external nature and changes it, and in this way he simultaneously changes his own nature. He develops the potentialities slumbering within nature, and subjects the play of its forces to his own sovereign power.[15]

You transform yourself since in reaching out you become active, you start to actualise your desires or ends. In this process, you become a consumer, say, a grocery shopper. If effective in reaching out, if you find, buy and eat the food, you will be complete. You are complete since your desire will be sated. The object is transformed since in reaching out you move to actualise its end – it is food, it exists to be eaten – as given to it by you. And by eating it, you actualise this end, with its purpose fulfilled. The transformations are immediate. The object's is immediate because you start to fulfil its end as soon as you reach out, with it completed when you eat it. Yours is immediate because desire and its externalisation through and in your reaching out is how you start the process of filling the void within. Immediately becoming a consumer, by eating it, you transform yourself: once a hungry woman, now a satisfied consumer.

Analytically put, the dual and immediate nature of the transformation means that the object's concrete form, its purpose, is dependent (C3) on existing (C2) use (C1). Apart from its perceived serviceability or conduciveness towards satisfying or realising existing desires or ends, it has no purpose. Its identity as a particular thing, not a heap of matter, is constitutively bound up with its being manipulated in a directed way. This dual immediate transformation structures all consumer relations. In this relation, subject and object are always united and integrated in this way, for the subject's stance towards the object means that it is brought wholly within and under their control through and in a process of absorption.

Hunger is negated through and in a material absorption: chewing, swallowing, digesting. As Hegel's master-slave relation and Marx's concept of wage-labour illustrate, erotic absorption can be effected spiritually. Neither Hegel's slave nor Marx's wage-labourer have concrete forms, any desire or end, apart from their master or employer's. Whilst not materially absorbed, the master or employer relates to them as mere extensions of his willing self, that is, they are brought within his control and they are thereby consumed. Eros is realised spiritually because the slave or wage-labourer is left with no personal identity, no original desires and ends. As Hegel says about the slave, his 'personality itself' is 'someone else's property', since the 'entire scope of his activity' exists only through and in the master's desires and ends.[16] The master is his 'essential reality'.[17] And as Marx says about the wage-labourer: subject to the capitalist's 'autocratic power', he lives purely as an extension of the capitalist's 'own will'.[18]

This reveals how non-human objects, material or otherwise,[19] not absorbed materially by use can be consumables,[20] and it also reveals the second attitude constitutive of consumer relations: indifference. Let us unpack the idea in three stages. First, an object's concrete form can change as the ends towards which we put it changes: moving boxes can become storage boxes; walking sticks can become weapons. Second, the desire for these objects can be erotic in form: many will have experienced the longing for, say, a new phone, as a feeling of inner emptiness like hunger. Third, as critics of modern consumption patterns point out, we often discard objects without any regard for their functional capacity. We need not attribute this feature to the 'modern propaganda of commodities',[21] or the 'fallenness' of *Dasein* revealed in 'curiosity',[22] or the 'built in demand to be discarded' inherent in modern culture,[23] or the relation between capitalism and the 'society of the spectacle',[24] or a 'system' that arises out of our 'disappointed demand for totality' and thus 'works to destroy' what it produces,[25] or the systemic logic of 'the growth society'.[26] Nor do we have to speculate that the modern individual is 'addicted' to 'novelty',[27] or is bored and is trying to stay 'sane',[28] or has 'set a discount on the past',[29] or meets the alternative, durable objects, as a 'dead residue of' his 'ambition, hope, effort', that is, recognition that his life is not 'qualitatively transformed' by his 'possessions'.[30] Nothing this all-consuming. Here, it is enough to recognise that we are sometimes indifferent to objects that do not satisfy existing desires or ends.

More concretely, think of a friend who says: 'Yes, it can receive and make calls, take photos, access the internet. But I don't want it, it is rubbish, I want the new model.' Whenever a relation is formed in this way, by a framework in terms of which an object's concrete functional form, 'It is a phone', is fixed by its capacity to satisfy immediately existing desires, 'I want this phone', or realise existing ends, 'I want to fit in' or 'I want to stand out',[31] whenever eros and indifference are constitutive of our being-in-the-world,[32] we relate to objects as consumables.

Let us finish this section by relating these three conditions – C1, C2, C3 – back to Locke and Marx. In chapter 2, we saw that Locke conceives of objects through the lenses of life and labour. In gathering apples, he says, we appropriate natural objects to our ends. By acting on nature, we transform its simple substances into concrete objects, defined now by our desires or ends. Rather than waste, it is now something useful: food. For this reason, natural objects exist as human ones only if used to satisfy existing desires or ends. When not, they lose their concrete forms, returning to nature, ceasing to be what they were when in our hands. In chapter 4, we revealed that not only does Marx tell a similar story to Locke, where the rights in objects must be tied to their use-value, he adopts strikingly similar imagery. Whilst Locke talks of 'mixing' labour with nature,[33] Marx talks of 'raw material [being] bound up with labour',[34] and tells us by way of labour to transform 'natural material . . . into organs of the human will over nature'.[35] Informing both these images is a conceptual link that each draws between utility, desire and form. Just as Locke first conditions rights in objects on their being used to satisfy existing desires or ends, so Marx prescribes rights that serve living subjects' needs. For both, the identity of objects must ideally be tied to their use-value.[36] Their allocative schemes share this structure because they are rooted in their models of man as a labouring consumer: a creature who relates to objects instrumentally, erotically and indifferently. In Arendt's idiom, they conceive of man as *animal laborans*,[37] that is, their ideal object-relations are structured by use (C1), immediacy (C2) and dependency (C3).

All That Is Solid Melts into Air

So far, we have identified the constitutive link between life and expression, on the one hand, and relations to objects as consumables, on the other. Only when we absorb objects materially or spiritually can either form be realised: unless we eat, our bodies will perish; unless we exert free, conscious and purposeful control over objects, so does Marxian spirit. So, if we think them good, we must enable consumption by structuring our world consistently with the relation (DA2), and to do this, we require rights that reflect the attitudes (eros, indifference), concepts or categories (instrumentality, immediacy) that structure all consumption (DA3), that is, rights that are consistent with the conditions identified above: C1, C2 and C3.

To facilitate consumer relations (DA2), each Hohfeldian incident is needed: liberty, claim, power and immunity (DA3). Let us articulate their content and necessity in order:

I. A liberty to use objects, for the sake of satisfying or realising immediately an existing desire or end.

Only with this liberty can Lockeans preserve life, and Marxians can hunt, criticise Hegel, and so on. If Lockeans cannot reply to men who object to their taking the surplus food or drink that they need to eat or quench their thirst, or complain about them using an empty room in the peak of winter, and Marxians cannot say to people who tell them not to fire their rifle, read Hegel, and so on, 'That is no-claim you can make on me', then Lockeans will go hungry, thirsty or become cold, whilst Marxians will become frustrated with the stymying of their material or spiritual desires and ends.

For contingent reasons, consuming either food or drink can only be effected individually, but nothing internal to consumptive logic makes the relation necessarily individualistic. The Lockean can shelter with his family, and Marxians can fish with friends. This fact means that the identities of the right-holder will often vary depending on the nature of the good (DA1), for example, public beach, family house, and individual food and water (DA3). Apart from individually or collectively, the liberty can be exercised simultaneously with but separately from others. Typical forms of this use include public goods, like national highways or parks. With these, right-holders can access highways or parks for the sake of driving or walking, but others also have this right. Whilst each user's purpose is her own, multiple users can exercise the same right over the same object, and each can do this in the company of others. This form of use is not excluded by the logic of consumption. Rather, use-limits are contingent. For example, if a road or park become over-crowded, the relevant goods will become frustrated since traffic slows travel and crowds hinder play. For Marx, here lies the originally revolutionary function of capitalism, namely, to empower man, through our collective organisation and technology, to try to transcend these limits: 'only under the rule of the bourgeoisie does [the proletariat] create the modern means of production, which also become the means of its revolutionary liberation'.[38] For if we can choose to build more roads or parks, there is no necessary reason for traffic or crowds. We instead just make do with tolls or capacity limits. The existence of these laws, though, which target 'overuse', reflects awareness of the contingent limits that attach to consumables.

Not every limit on the exercise of the liberty is contingent. Some are internal to the logic of the liberty. This limit is reflected in the qualifying clause in (I): 'for the sake of satisfying or realising immediately an existing desire or end'. This aspect of the right limits the exercise of the liberty to forms of use that satisfy or realise immediately the right-holder's desires and ends. This qualification reflects C1 and C2, for the liberty is granted on the condition that the object is used in a certain way. Its holder must use it as a consumable, as something that exists to be absorbed, materially or spiritually, for the sake of satisfying or realising her existing desires or ends. Thus, the liberty does not include other forms of use, one being the mediated use that we interrogate in the next section, like when objects function as capital.

If what matters is Lockean life and Marxian expression, those in whom we vest this qualified liberty must not be frustrated in exercising it, they require protection:

II. A claim against others frustrating the exercise of (I), in circumstances when (I) is being exercised.

This claim prevents others from interfering with use, for the correlative of any claim is duty. By vesting in the holder of the liberty a claim, Locke can say to those who try to take the bread off his table, and Marx can say to those who would have him not fire his gun, 'No, the object is mine to use, let me be.' Again, the claim is qualified, for it is subject to the object being used to satisfy or realise the right-holder's desires or ends: hunger, hunting, and so on. The reason for this qualification is the same as the reason for the qualified liberty. The conditional nature of the claim reflects the goods that the right is intended to facilitate: life and expression. The qualification reflects C1 and C2. If the user breaches either condition, she has no-claim against someone using the object in or to which the liberty is attached. In Locke's idiom, if use violates the law of nature, if the object is neglected or wasted, it returns to nature; in Marx's idiom, the failure to exercise the liberty in his prescribed way, according to need, will result in the claim melting into air.

Even those who do not privilege consumption grant rights like (I) and (II). We saw this with Bentham, Hegel and Hayek's theories. Each grants consumer rights. Bentham admits that death and starvation are worse than the harm that is caused by unexpected alterations of rights. Hegel prescribes a right of necessity. And Hayek says that we have basic income rights. They all grant these rights, though, a little reluctantly, for these liberties and claims, if unlimited, will frustrate or diminish their motivating concerns: security, rational unity or efficiency. Without these rights, though, we cannot ideally facilitate what each thinks best because all that many would do before dying anyway, they understand, is struggle just to stay alive.

This reveals important allocative differences between these men (AS3), which differences are rooted in their different privileged (AS2) concerns (AS1). These differences are played out in the more particular content we give to the claim in (II). Because what matters in Marx's conception of things is the expression of all desires or ends, the claim can be left in its general form. We must be free to use all objects to satisfy all existing desires and ends: each is an ontological affirmation of our essential being. Only when we are free in this way will we not be divided against ourselves, others and the world. Therefore, only if the liberty (I) is protected by the claim (II) can we realise ourselves as socialised men. If we privileged life, though, or for pragmatic reasons seek to avoid starvation or death, coercion or necessity, the claim (II) must reflect this fact. We must narrow it so that it corresponds (DA3) to our concern (DA1). We must formulate the right, in other words, to enable the good. Whether for reasons of principle or pragmatism, absent a world of unlimited distribution of material resources, we must modify the claim:

> II.a. A claim against others frustrating the exercise of (I) in circumstances where (I) is being exercised, save when [. . .].

For Lockeans and pragmatists, whilst non-subsistence desires and ends matter, there is no point in talking about them when the people meant to actualise them either cannot survive the night or act in essential ways. We should get our priorities right: food, drink, healthcare, and so on, come first, after which we can then strive to realise other goods, be they lexically subordinate ones (GP7), such as comfort, or ultimately important ones (GP3, GP5), like unity, pleasure or preference.

A third Hohfeldian right is necessary: a power to alter the liberty and the claim in (I) and (II or II.a). The necessity, however, differs from the necessity of the liberty and claim. The latter are absolutely necessary: we need them for life or expression to be possible at all. Without them, we die, materially or spiritually. The power, contrarily, is conditionally necessary. We only need it if the power to alter rights is understood as a way of satisfying or realising immediately a desire or end. If this self-understanding does not exist, there is no need for the power.

We can make this more concrete by returning to Marx. For Marx, not every transfer of rights is for the sake of ends external to the transfer. There are transfers that exist outside of markets; in fact, to be transfers of this nature, they must exist outside it. Marx's ideal exchanges include love for love, as can be the case with gift-giving. These exchanges are good because they immediately satisfy or realise desires or ends. When a gift is produced as an expression of love, the object will embody their love, the exchange will express their love, and each person will give the object because in doing this, they will satisfy the recipient's desire – to be loved. In these cases, there is use (C1), immediacy (C2) and dependency (C3). Thus, to say that the need for the power to alter rights is conditional, is to say it depends on, for example, love being a desired relation and giving of gifts being a recognised way of expressing love. If so, then the power must be granted to alter the liberty (I) and the claim (II or II.a). Put formally, the following right is needed:

III. A power to alter the liberty in (I) or claim in (II) or (II.a), if doing so would constitute an exercise of (I).

The logic of this power is not limited to exchanges. Alterations may be in the form of annulment, creation or waiver of rights. Apart from exchanging gifts, Marx was free under his consumptive logic to: annul his rights by non-reciprocally giving a gift to Friedrich; or create a community of property by marrying Jenny; or forgive either for the occasional breach of his rights and thereby waiving any claims he has against them.

Lastly, we must allocate to the holder of the liberty, claim and power in (I), (II) or (II.a) and (III), the following right:

IV. An immunity against others altering the content of (I), (II) or (II.a) or (III).

This immunity is not required by the unique logic of consumer relations, but rather by a concern for the relation itself. Immunities limit the power of others to alter rights. They serve a protective function against authority. If we want to protect the goods constituted through and in consumer relations, we must disable others from altering the rights that we need to realise this relation and these goods. In South Africa, this is one function of the right not to be evicted from one's home without an order of court,[39] and the right not to be deprived of property arbitrarily and otherwise than in terms of a law of general application.[40]

If only expression or life is important, then the immunity would be absolute. But if both exert rational force over what we decide and do, then the rights needed to actualise one will sometimes conflict with those needed to actualise the other. They will conflict because the claims in (II) and (II.a) and therefore the power in (III) cannot be reconciled. Whilst logically incompatible (GP4), in practice conflict is contingent (GP1). It is only nature's limits that force us to choose between life-preservation and expressive activity. If we transcended nature, these choices would not arise. When we extend our range of goods beyond life and expression, however, we encounter logical conflicts (GP4) that necessarily not contingently force us to choose.

THE CALL OF THE FUTURE

Not all our instrumental relations are consumptive. Sometimes, when C2 is not met, this will not affect the concrete form of the object, as contemplated by C3. Here, the object's identity – it is a phone – is not dependent on any subject using it to satisfy or realise immediately their desires or ends. In such cases, we treat the object as being independent, not just materially or as some heap of matter, but as a particular object with a purpose of its own that stands apart from the existing desires or ends of subjects. The relation remains instrumental (C1). It shares this quality with all consumer relations. The relations differ, though, for reified instruments have identities that stand apart from what we desire or pursue in the present.

This difference between consumables and reified instruments means that their structures are incompatible (GP4). Because these relations constitute (DA2) diverse forms (DA1), to facilitate each relation we must allocate property rights in ways (DA3) that are incompatible. Whereas the consumer relation constitutes forms like life or expression, reified relations constitute the forms that motivate Hegel, Hayek and Bentham: rational unity, informational efficiency and security. What unites their respective concerns is that each is constituted by the same structural relation to objects: reified ones. For this reason, their property theories call for similar rights. However, like the consumer relation, when we structure allocations according to their distinct privileged goods, incompatible (GP4) differences emerge.

Caution and Self-Control

Consumables and reified instruments are distinguished by the attitudes we have towards the objects with which we relate: consumption is formed by eros and indifference; reified relations are constituted by caution and self-control. To see this, recall Marx's critique of his archetypal reified relation: markets. For markets to exist, we must believe that objects have concrete forms the identities of which do not depend on their role in satisfying or realising immediately desires or ends. Unless we consciously separate these identities from what we now desire or pursue, and thereby separate an object's function from the will of self-determining subjects, a market cannot form. This separation, Marx tells us, is what makes the market form bad. Since man is the root of all, corresponding to this object-relation is objective alienation, for when we relate to objects in this way, we attribute subjectivity or purpose and therefore power to something other than ourselves. It is this attribution of subjectivity to objects – not just instrumentality or objectification, that is, the mere attribution of functions to objects – that Marx opposes.

Like Marx, Locke privileges consumer relations: objects must ultimately function to satisfy or realise immediately existing desires or ends. They also agree that when we do not use objects consumptively, one of two things happen: they will return to the undifferentiated bundle for us to allocate again, or they will assume an abstract mediating function where they do not immediately satisfy or realise existing desires or ends. And lastly, they agree that money serves this mediating function. Rather than having a use-value, money only has exchange-value. At this stage, Locke and Marx come apart. For Marx, money's uselessness makes it bad, whereas Locke accepts that whilst money is not 'truly useful', the exchange-relation it facilitates can function to preserve life or enhance comfort. With Locke and Marx so separated, Marx explains that non-money objects can assume an abstract, mediating character. Provided it is not materially destroyed immediately upon use, we can treat any object as having an independent concrete form. And, Marx says, any instrumental relation that takes this form is reified, for the function of the object is independent from our present desires or ends. If this relation is universal, Marx says, alienation will be total, for we would exist in a near-total distance from ourselves, others and nature.

To appreciate Marx's worry, we must develop a distinction drawn by Charles Taylor between 'original' and 'derivative' purpose.[41] To claim, as Marx does, that the purposes of objects always originally depend on our desires or ends is not necessarily to say that objects cannot later possess purposes separately from this originating desire or projection. We could internalise the idea that there is no inherent purpose embodied in nature, whilst also making sense of the idea that objects can have purposes apart from what we desire and pursue. Even if we create all meaning, as Marx argues, it is conceptually possible that we do not have immediate control over all that we create, as Marx explains. For even if man is the root of all, even if we recognise or believe that only we have original purposes, that the concrete forms of objects are derivative does not mean that they always depend for their continued existence on exercises of original constituting desires or ends. That we name objects, give them their identities, does not necessarily mean that their names only endure when we say them out loud – that they cannot, through 'fetishism', assume the 'fantastic form' of 'autonomous figures',[42] existing apart from our consciously willed activities.

In some respects, fetishism is more sensible than the alternative. To think that the identity of objects can only be sustained through the continued attribution of purpose can generate the kind of counterintuitive conclusion that is postulated by Christine Korsgaard in her *Self Constitution*. In that book, she adopts a metaphysic of activity that overlaps with the ontological expressivism of Marx. Just as Marx's 'garment becomes a real garment only in the act of being worn',[43] so on the logic of Korsgaard's metaphysic, a vacuum cleaner in the closet does not really exist as such: it is a mere 'entity that, when properly incorporated by you, makes *you* into a vacuum cleaner'.[44] On this model, concrete forms not only emerge from original desires or ends, they only endure if we continue to use them to satisfy or realise them. Ultimately, objects exist for us, to be absorbed or incorporated by us. Like Korsgaardian vacuum cleaners, nothing concrete exists apart from us. In Marx's idiom, the world revolves around man since it is just an extension of him.

Even if the implications of this ontology are counterintuitive, it does not mean that it is right to treat the purposes of objects as being independent of our existing desires and ends. Much that was once odd, after all, later seems obvious. To judge matters in the present either way, we must interrogate further the nature of this relation.

We have been speaking about reified instruments in epistemic terms. For the relation to form, we must believe that an object has a purpose apart from existing desires or ends. This belief is not enough. One can hold it but, like Herbert Marcuse tells us to do, 'refuse', or at least try to refuse, to relate to objects in this way.[45] In fact, much opposition to capitalism starts by first recognising that it actually exists – as Marx puts it, that reified relations 'appear as what they are'.[46] Thus, in addition to belief, we must also affirm the purposive independence of objects.[47] This affirmation has two constitutive attitudes: caution and self-control. To reveal this, let us consider a deservedly famous polemic by a youthful Marx:

> Self-denial, the denial of life and of all human needs, is [capitalism's] cardinal doctrine. The less you eat, drink and read books; the less you go to the theater, the dance hall, the public-house; the less you think, love, theorize, sing, paint, fence, etc., the more you *save* – the *greater* becomes your treasure which neither moths nor dust will devour – your *capital*. The less you *are*, the more you *have*; the less you express your own life, the greater is your *alienated* life – the greater is the store of your estranged being.[48]

Marx claims a conceptual unity between capital formation and its alienating effects. This unity is rooted in his model of the person. By 'throwing' potentially useful objects 'again and again' into markets for the sake of making more money,[49] he says later, rather than being consumed by him for the sake of expressing his existing desires or ends, the capitalist betrays his real self. In other words, it is always bad for persons to renounce the satisfaction of their existing desires, to delay and stymie the realisation of their ends, for the sake of future ones, that is, something other than what is desired and pursued in the present.[50] For to sacrifice 'the lusts of his flesh to the fetish of gold', to live by the 'gospel of abstinence',[51] to be cautious rather than 'spontaneous',[52] to bring under control instead of living out his desires and ends, Marx says, is for man to exist in a form and appear in a relation that does violence to his true self.

Marx tells us why caution and self-control conflict with expression: they limit its spontaneity. How do these attitudes constitute reified instruments? Relating to objects as reified instruments entails an affirmation of concrete forms that exist independently from existing desires and ends. For this independence to hold in fact, a condition must be met: durability.[53] Only if the object's 'independent use-shape' can endure over time can it have a purpose independently of the existing desires or ends of subjects. If it were 'used up' immediately, or dissolved when we stopped using it, it could not retain and possess purpose apart from that which we give it when using it.[54] If this were the case, the distinction between original and derivative purpose would collapse. Therefore, to affirm the existence of reified objects and to affirm the relations of which these objects form a constitutive part, is necessarily to commit to the act of preserving the object's concrete form. To do this, to structure action in the present by regard for the future, is to adopt in one's relations the attitudes of caution and self-control. In Arendt's idiom, it is to live as *homo faber*, a creature who builds today for the sake of tomorrow.[55]

Let us conclude by noting two things that do not follow from these attitudes. First, one need not judge these attitudes as good for their own sake (GP3). We can endorse only the instrumental value of reifications, as Hayek does, who thinks them essential to the accumulation and dispersal of information by the market process, which he thinks essential to maximise satisfaction of what matters in the last resort: our preferences (GP5). Second, caution and self-control are consistent with a humanist, disenchanted stance towards the world. The existence of reified instruments is not dependent on our 'forgetting' that their concrete meanings originally derive from our desires or ends.[56] We can recall this, whilst also treating objects as having concrete functional forms that exist independently of what we desire or pursue in the present. We can think of ourselves as the root of all, but decline Marx's plea that we always assert ourselves as lords. For all that is required for reified instruments to exist, is for our attitudes towards objects to be cautious and self-controlled. The relation's attitudinal basis is captured by Max Weber's notion of 'this worldly asceticism',[57] described by Taylor as a kind of 'caring and not caring'.[58] This is an attitude that is possessed by persons who hear future concerns calling and respond by resisting their urge to satisfy or realise immediately their existing desires or ends. When instrumental relations to objects are constituted by this ascetic attitude, a relation is formed in which persons, rather than being self-absorbed and absorbing objects, are detached from their present selves and detach the world from these selves. The result is reified instruments.

This Worldly Asceticism

Caution and self-control (DA2) make possible diverse goods (DA1). Tradition reveals two: security and markets. For both, reified instruments are essential. Thus, each good necessitates a formally similar set of property rights (DA3). As with consumer relations, when we articulate in more concrete terms the rights needed to facilitate the more particular forms realised through and in the relation, logical incompatibilities emerge. To see this, we begin with their formal overlap: liberty, claim, power and immunity.

Whereas consumables are always used immediately for present desires and ends, reifications are distinguished by their independence from these present desires or ends – that is, they mediate between them, making possible the satisfaction or realisation of desires or ends that are external to the present relation to the object, namely, desires and ends we may have in the future. Reified instruments, though, are not limited to this mediated use. Mediation is necessary, but the relation might also satisfy or realise existing desires or ends. 'Joint uses are always possible',[59] as David Harvey puts it, say, when you use the street to transport commodities to markets and I use it to take a Sunday stroll. Not only independent use by different individuals, the same activity by the same person can serve both immediate and mediated forms of use. Hard work, initiative, thrift, temperance, exchange, and so on, we are often told, need not exist only as 'stepping-stones to success', they can also be 'their own reward' (GP3).[60] And the competitive element that is constitutive of the exchange-relation, according to Francis Fukuyama, means that markets can be sites in which individuals satisfy their desire for social recognition.[61] Immediate use, though, must not frustrate the essential mediating function that is served by the reified instrument.[62] Marx puts this point as follows:

> If commodities could speak, they would say this: our use-value may interest men, but it does not belong to us as objects. . . . Our own intercourse as commodities proves it. We relate to each other merely as exchange-values.[63]

Let us develop this internal limit on forms of use. Caution and self-control are internal to the logic of reified instruments. The object-relation is structured by, as Taylor explains, 'a caring and not caring',[64] a commitment to preserve its concrete form for the sake of a non-existing desire or end.[65] This future-orientation means that present use may not render reified objects materially or spiritually unfit for purpose; present use that frustrates future utility is prohibited. Only if use is structured by this concern,[66] do we act cautiously, controlling our present selves for the sake of something in the future. For example, whilst so-called 'wear and tear' and capital depreciation is permissible,[67] wanton destruction is not;[68] whilst storing reserves may sometimes be necessary,[69] Scrooge-like hoarding can never be allowed.[70] These internal limits on permissible forms of use are one reason for zoning regulations, targeted inflation, and duties of departing tenants to restore premises to their original condition, 'fair wear and tear excluded'. Whereas the duties of tenants ensure that premises remain fit for use, factories in suburbs threaten their spirit, and inflationary targets are thought to incentivise those with money to keep it in circulation. The concrete form of this limit will depend on the liberty's purpose, but we can articulate its general structure:

> I. A liberty to use objects for the sake of satisfying or realising in a mediated way their desire or end – but also, if they want and can, in an immediate way, provided that this does not render the object unfit for its essential mediating purpose.

This liberty is necessary to realise Hegelian or Hayekian markets, as well as Benthamite security. Without it, these goods cannot be made real. For unless we structure present use by our essential regard for the future, we cannot be secure nor can we participate in markets. Whatever else they do, without this liberty Bentham's men cannot secure themselves against their uncertain future, for they cannot reasonably expect to have future control of objects and so cannot build up stores of objects that will offer protection if a social or natural threat occurs; nor can Hegel or Hayek's men treat objects as being possessed of exchange- rather than use-value, necessary to constitute their interpersonal relations in the market form.

For these purposes to be realised, we must protect the exercise of this qualified liberty. Those in whom we vest it must not be frustrated in exercising it:

II. A claim against others frustrating the exercise of (I), in circumstances where (I) is being exercised.

This claim prevents others from interfering with use, for the correlative of any claim is duty. By vesting in the liberty-holder a claim, Bentham can say to others who try to seize his stock, and Hegel and Hayek can say to those who object to their trips to the market: 'The object is mine to use as I please, let me be.' In this way, the claim has the same protective function as a consumer claim. What distinguishes them is what each claim protects. Whilst the latter protects consumer liberties, reified claims protect mediated use and immediate use consistent with its mediated use, say, market relations and social recognition. If the object is not appropriately used, though, then others have no duty not to use it. This fact is reflected in the qualifying clause: 'in circumstances where (I) is being exercised'. If the right-holder abandons the object, or uses it in the wrong way, for example, non-instrumentally, she has no-claim against it being used by someone else.

Let us move to the remaining Hohfeldian incidents: power and immunity. Here, the goods we have been describing, formed by instrumental reified relations, come apart. Whilst the market, in its Hegelian and Hayekian forms, requires that the holder of the liberty (I) and claim (II) have the power to alter the rights (DA3), Benthamite security does not. When security is our concern, what is essential is that the liberty and claim be immune from alteration (DA3). Whilst markets require an immunity, this property right shines brightest when security is our concern. To see this, let us start with Hegelian and Hayekian markets.

To facilitate markets, holders of the liberty (I) and claim (II) must have the power to alter the rights if this constitutes an exercise of the liberty:

III. A power to alter the liberty in (I) or claim in (II), if this constitutes an exercise of (I).

This power has the same purpose as consumer powers: it allows the holder of the liberty (I) and claim (II) to alter their content. Moreover, both of the powers can be exercised in the same ways: annulling, creating or waiving rights. They differ in content, though, for their qualifying clauses tie their exercise to their respective liberties. Whilst exercises of consumer powers must satisfy or realise immediately existing desires or ends, reified powers must mediate between desires or ends. For example, whereas consumer powers can facilitate practices like gift-giving, the reified power can facilitate the practice of contracts. With both powers, a person alters her rights for the sake of some desire or end. What distinguishes the powers is the relation between the exercise of the power and the desire or end. With consumer powers, this relation is immediate; with reified powers, it is mediated. It is mediated since the desire or end is external to the power's exercise: it is not satisfied or realised through and in the exercise of the power itself. The reason for altering rights by concluding a contract is not the exchange itself. Rather, the reason for the exchange is the desire or end that the exchange will facilitate.

As explained, this does not mean that the exchange cannot be accompanied by an immediate benefit. The exchange might enhance your status. Rather, the point is that the exchange must be for the sake of a desire or end not realised through and in the act. It is this externality to present desires and ends, one's essential orientation towards the future, that makes relations reified. The alteration of rights is for the sake of something other than the exchange, like the plan to expand your business operations using the profits that you make through today's sale.

When security is our structuring concern when allocating property, it is not the power to alter rights, but their protection that is essential. In the idiom of chapter 3, whereas Hegel and Hayek look to open borders through the movement of rights, Bentham builds walls to protect men from future threats. For Bentham, in modern cities where resources are scarce and production requires hard or boring work, or where work is not available, our relations are structured by a constitutive uncertainty. Timid and alone, people try to maximise their control over useful objects. To avoid a self-destructive free-for-all, existing rights must be secured. This is done by giving immunities to their holders, which limit or disable the power of others to alter rights. In doing this, immunities protect reified instruments, because security is an essentially future-oriented concern. Security is about expectation; it concerns how desires or ends may be frustrated in the future.

If this security were all that mattered, we would allocate absolute immunities. Few advocate such a right. The reason why is that security is usually understood as a means to facilitate goods, either instrumental or which matter for their own sake (GP3). For Bentham, this good is pleasure, but it could be others, like Hegelian unity or Hayekian efficiency, each made possible by reified instruments. Even if security is important for its own sake, however, the immunity would still be qualified to permit alterations to facilitate other goods:

IV. An immunity against others altering (I), (II) or (III), save when [. . .].

Here, Bentham stands out relative to Hegel and Hayek. He reduces the content of the qualifying clause to almost nothing, but not nothing at all. Whilst the insecurity generated by empowering authorities to alter rights against expectations is bad, starvation and death are worse. Apart from avoiding these bads, though, the immunity must be absolute. If not, our diminished expectations will destroy society itself. We need not go this far. Hegel and Hayek recognise a greater role for the state in altering rights, but they both understand that giving too much power to the state will render markets impossible, frustrating the goods each thinks is essential. If we followed them, we would allocate immunities, but we would define their content in accordance with their particular concerns. And, so, the incompatibilities (GP1, GP4) accumulate further.

RISE OF THE ESSENTIAL WORKER

A comprehensive Lockean and Marxian consumerism might have been attractive in the milieu of seventeenth-century Western expansion or in the optimism rooted in the rapid technological development of the nineteenth century,[71] but few today advocate without qualification its constitutive attitudes: eros and indifference.[72] Virtue is seen in caution and self-control, with many recognising their role in facilitating other goods or mitigating the humanistic hubris shared by some strands of liberal and Marxian thought. Because consumption is bound up with goods like life and expression, though, many embrace both sets of attitudes. Such an embrace, however, will generate conflicts when we are allocating property. There is the conflict between consumer and reified relations: because they are constituted by incompatible attitudes, the rights needed to facilitate life and expression are incompatible with those needed to facilitate Hegelian or Hayekian markets and Benthamite security. Conflict is also internal to each relation: Locke and Marx's consumerism potentially conflict, but the reified relations advocated by Bentham, Hegel and Hayek always conflict. These contingent and logical conflicts between and internal to diverse relational forms mean that we cannot realise all that many of us consider good. This is not just a spatio-temporal truth (GP1), it is also a logical one (GP4).

Revealing this is one of the reasons we must ask DA3. It makes plain what is still possible to occlude when we just identify (DA1) and describe (DA2) the qualitative structures of our diverse relational forms. In chapter 8, we consider the tragic attitude appropriate to this fact, and in part III we see how this feeds into concrete allocative choices, say, when expropriating property and fixing compensation. This section, though, considers a related question: If we cannot have it all, then who should decide what to do? Or since we disagree about the answer, as Raymond Geuss puts it, who does what to whom for whose benefit?[73] This is an issue concerning authority, which raises difficult questions with many conflicting answers that we cannot go into here, save for one answer that we have to consider, since it is bound up with our subject: instrumentality. As we did with consumables and reified instruments, let us describe its qualitative structure.

Circumspection: An Unwitting Alliance

One response to the fact of conflict between and within instrumental categories is to allocate property in a way that creates mixed instruments, that is, afford to individuals or groups the power to decide in which of these ways to relate to objects. Doing this would facilitate a distinct good, choice (DA1),[74] and would thereby enable what was first called European, then Western, but is now known as the globalised system of property,[75] for this liberty would go towards constituting the structure of consumer capitalism.[76]

Facilitating a system of mixed instruments (DA2) requires (DA3) the following right:

I. A liberty to use an object for the sake of satisfying or realising, immediately or in a mediated way, a desire or end.

This liberty permits immediate and mediated relations. In this way, it is like a reified liberty, but it is distinguished by its lack of any qualifying clause: it does not require mediated use, nor does it prohibit use that renders objects unfit for purpose. The right-holder can choose in which way to use objects, they have a discretion: consume or save, burn or bank.

Where consumables and reifications exist 'alongside' and 'in opposition to' each other,[77] as Marx puts it, a liberty-holder may adopt either erotic and indifferent, that is, consumer, or cautious and self-controlling, for example, capitalist, attitudes. Whilst the attitudes are incompatible,[78] at a higher level of abstraction they share the attitude which Heidegger calls 'circumspection',[79] in the sense of 'surveying', 'deliberating' and 'envisaging',[80] that is, 'looking around for a way to get something done . . . a kind of awareness in which one looks around before one decides just what one ought to do next'.[81] Here the only rules limiting use are the background ones that regulate interpersonal relations, say, laws against murder or defamation.

To facilitate a system of property constituted by mixed instruments, we need, in addition to a liberty (I), the following claim:

II. A claim against other people frustrating the exercise of (I), in circumstances when (I) is being exercised.

This claim prevents others from interfering with use, for the correlative of any claim is duty. So, like consumer and reified claims this mixed claim affords protection. What distinguishes it is the scope of this protection. Consumer and reified claims protect only their two qualified liberties. A mixed claim protects both immediate and mediated use. It protects them when each is exercised individually and also when they are exercised at the same time. By vesting in holders of mixed liberties a claim, they can say to persons who attempt to interfere with their chosen form of use: 'It is not your business to tell me what to do with my property, let me be.'

We will also require the following power:

> III A power to alter the liberty in (I) or claim in (II), if doing so is an exercise of (I).

This power permits most forms of alterations: gifts, contracts, donations, inheritance, and so on. All are permissible exercises of power since the qualifying clause ties the power to the liberty (I), which is correspondingly inclusive. The only limit is categorical: the power only includes instrumental use. If the alteration has a non-instrumental function, like those we describe in chapter 7, then the liberty- and claim-holder may not alter their rights. Given the goods that are constituted through and in non-instrumental object-relations, like artworks, memorials and ancestral land, it is likely that we will not be happy with this categorical limit. In a community that is pure in its embrace of the logic being described here, however, it must exist.

Lastly, we must afford to the holder of the liberty (I), claim (II) and power (III) an immunity. This immunity is not required by the peculiar logic of mixed instruments but rather by a concern for the relation as such. Immunities limit the power of others to alter existing rights and thereby serve a protective function against authority. If we want to protect the good of choice, enabled by this mixed relation, then we must disable others from altering the rights needed to actualise this relation. Just as few people concerned with security would have us allocate absolute immunities, though, so few people who are concerned with choice are absolutist. They almost always provide for exceptions:

> IV. An immunity against others altering (I), (II) or (III), save when [. . .].

The immunity's logic does not dictate a particular content for the qualifying clause. Provided the alteration is consistent with the logic of the relation – treat objects as means to satisfy and realise existing or future desires and ends, chosen by the rights-holder – there is no further internal limit on the qualification. Apart from obvious rights-alterations needed to fund the state through tax,[82] therefore, the qualification is compatible with alterations that enable original and ongoing capital accumulation,[83] prevent dependency on others,[84] improve the expectations of the least well-off,[85] rectify past injustice,[86] promote resource equality,[87] maximise capabilities,[88] or ensure relational justice.[89] This does not mean that advocates of these principles are consumer capitalists,[90] rather it means that the mixed object-relation can absorb them, since the open qualifying clause in (IV), 'save when [. . .]', permits the construction of property systems according to (I), (II) and (III), which privilege choice, that are consistent with each distributive principle.

Here is one source of the power that the logic of consumer capitalist relations, constituted in part by mixed instruments, seems to exert in the present. It is a broad church that welcomes most stripes. Indeed, this church is broader than our sketch suggests. For the relation is not only liberal or neoliberal in its origin. Whilst liberalism's concern for negative freedom and its privileging of choice, lends itself to it, concern for this good is not exclusive to it, for no great logical gap exists between liberal freedom and concerns about power that sit in the heart of those schools that stem from liberalism's most powerful critic: Marx. To reveal this fact, let us contrast Marx with one of consumer capitalism's high priests: Hayek.

The logical gap separating Hayekian preference-satisfaction, a consumer capitalist ideal, and Marxian ontological affirmations of being, is narrow. For both, what matters is that individuals can satisfy their desires and realise their ends. They also agree that the ideally situated individual has privileged epistemic access to these desires and ends. And they agree further that all desires and ends are rooted in the material world: theatres, TVs, pubs, cars and so on, if it matters to you, then ideally you should experience and have it. So, they conclude, to structure life in accordance with this ideal is required by a true individualism. Of course, Marx, owing to his ontology, thinks that desires do not, but for some artificial limit, conflict. However, if someone loyal to Marx's materialist and expressivist ethics lost faith in the goal of realising ontological unity, if they were to 'declare' together with Max Horkheimer that 'basically we cannot bring about change',[91] then there would remain no practical distinction between her individualism and Hayek's.

After utopia, when the real, practical commitment to unity no longer exists,[92] there might still be opposition to consumer capitalism. Whilst their individualism structurally overlaps with this relation, these lapsed, or 'pessimistic' as Perry Anderson puts it,[93] Marxians could couple their expressivist ethics with criticism of Hayekian markets. They may not articulate an alternative,[94] but as they and others explain, not all criticism is constructive.[95] Provided that these critics are not destructively nihilistic, though, for so long as their negation does not entail the contesting of everything positive, then the consumer capitalist form will happily open its doors to them.

It will do this because they share the same positive truth: the consumer is always right. Having retained the materialist and expressivist commitments of Marx, their relation to the world is constitutively consumptive: a relation in which the practical ideal is, as Theodor Adorno puts it, an 'unshackled reality'.[96] And since 'money has no smell', since all that matters is 'effective demand', of what it is irrelevant provided 'the consumer . . . can pay',[97] who better to induct into the broad church of consumer capitalism than new consumers.

At first, the liberals already in the church may struggle to understand these new arrivals, who come from a foreign tradition, so use strange new words or old words in strange new ways. This is hardly a problem. Like good Hayekians, they are skilled in decoding signals. Sometimes doing so will require private study, where the liberal will 'go educate' themselves. Other times, it will call for interpersonal engagement where they sit or kneel and 'listen and learn'. But no matter the technique, they will act in this way, they will 'do the work', since what their critics feel, think or desire is important to them. In fact, it cannot really be questioned, for it is their truth, experiences that they have lived, the consumer is always right. Whatever initial struggles the original liberal churchgoers have in understanding, they eventually learn the right words, and where appropriate substitute them for their own: preference may become authenticity,[98] its revelation now known as lived experience. They adapt, though, not only because the consumer is always right, but also because all these words or engagements do not really threaten the relation's structure. For a 'politics of deference', which centres and thus equalises 'marginalised' 'voices',[99] as Olúfẹ́mi O. Táíwò puts it, and in general merely critical 'discourse',[100] as Ellen Meiksins Wood argues, and indeed the latent ideal that structures this politics and criticism, what Jean Baudrillard calls 'the play' of 'inessential' or 'marginal differences',[101] is only expressive in form and effect. At bottom, the critics, their hopes exhausted, exist now only as disenchanted consumers desperately searching for a new 'home',[102] that is, for the simplifying comforts offered by a model.

The consumers in this church, therefore, take diverse forms. The Hayekian consumer, whilst essentially concerned with her preferences, lends support to the whole she believes enables their satisfaction: the market. Therefore, she values a collective good, albeit an instrumental one, that exists outside her contingent desires. Not so with the lapsed Marxian, who no longer believes in Marx's immediate unity and also rejects Hayek and Hegel's mediated alternatives. Without Hayek or Hegel's self-control in the present, or Marx's structured direction of the present for the sake of a radically different future, the lapsed Marxian exists in a fragmented and fleeting succession of nows.[103] Free to do what he wants, when he wants and for how long he wants, but not willing or unable to imagine Marx's hoped-for unity, or reconcile himself to the unity offered by Hegel and Hayek, his expressive materialism devolves into a form of 'solipsistic narcissism',[104] in which all exists to revolve about himself, and himself alone.

Nothing internal to the logic of narcissism precludes those who embody it from desiring and striving together. As Christopher Lasch explains, narcissism is not selfishness, it is the elevation of the desires or ends of the present self, separated from others or the world, and the denial of the independence or legitimacy of what is not this immediately experienced self.[105] So, the narcissist can perceive and think about or act in the world with others, he can belong to groups.[106] Whether he forms alliances or solidarities is contingent, a product of the intersecting expressive events of history, to be chosen or rejected in the present as he wants and is able. These contingencies aside, because the consumer is always right, the ultimate arbiter of what is good and bad will always be the simple lived fact of how the narcissist experiences himself, others or the world, and therefore what he happens to desire or pursue in the present. Marcuse tells us why: 'Eros redefines reason in his own terms. Reasonable is what sustains the order of gratification.'[107]

The world now revolving around these unwitting converts to consumer capitalism,[108] some of them may start to take steps to remake it in their own self-image. The problem, though, is that at the bottom of this self-image there lies 'a hungry, enraged, empty self, full of impotent anger at being frustrated, and fearful of a world which seems as hateful and revengeful' as themselves.[109] Thus, faithless but still demanding change, if what they encounter does not conform to what they want at this stage in the fleeting succession of nows, their identity,[110] it must be liquidated: burnt, removed, torn down. As Marcuse once remarked, however, from their perspective, these 'powers are conceived not as destruction but as peace, not as terror but as beauty'.[111]

This response and self-understanding is not contingent. Rather, it is internal to the logic of all consumer relations. In Marcuse's idiom, perpetually seeking 'the redemption of pleasure, the halt of time, the absorption of death; silence, sleep, night, paradise',[112] the lapsed Marxian cannot but experience their loss of control as shameful, and that which frustrates their desires or ends always will become the object of disgust.[113] In their anarchistic world-of-becoming, if something that is external to them does not meet their demands, they will suffer an existential death – their world, having long-ago melted into air, not crumbling but evaporating. Aware of this lurking possibility, there will immediately swell up from inside their empty selves a narcissistic and often collective cry. Representatives not of the will to power, but of the will to consume, it is a cry to cancel any part of the present that embodies any part of the past that is not experienced as their own; a cry to reclaim present embodiments of time and space from people who illegitimately, given their now incorrect identity-configuration, intrude upon them. Whilst the particular form of this fathomless cry from nothing into nothing,[114] this 'euphoric destruction or ritualistic devouring of objects and gestures',[115] will vary, it will always have the same aggressive-passive structure: 'Fuck you',[116] they will wail, 'Just let me exist',[117] they will plead.

In reply, you will hear, as Marx puts it in a related context, the 'applause' of allies, 'dripping with the milk of human kindness',[118] intoning about the need for change and respect. The reply is not novel, for capital is used to sweeping away outmoded rules in the name of progress. But what is all too often neglected by the critics of capital is that Marx's lapsed heirs, for whom the past is 'a nightmare',[119] are the vanguard now demanding its liquidation. Imprisoned in an 'interminably recurrent present',[120] lusting after 'immediate gratification', and thus living in a 'state of restless, perpetually unsatisfied desire',[121] the 'bad infinity' of capital accumulation will have created its near-ideal vehicle.[122] For it will now have a consumer who has internalised as good the precarity of living hand to mouth, confusing its immediacy, its lack of duties rooted in the past or reaching back into the present from the future,[123] as the 'realm of freedom'.[124]

Surveying this, the practical capitalist will let forth a 'hearty laugh',[125] for what is swept away must be replaced, and who better to satisfy the always new, since always fleeting, desires of these licentious all-destroyers than capital's productive and liquid supply chains. In any event, with all its critics providing no alternative, there is nobody else who can perform the existentially urgent task of 'affirming' or 'celebrating' their faithless and fluctuating world-of-becoming. This, in turn, reveals that their constitutive anarchistic narcissism, their idealisation of 'consumption power',[126] is at the same time one that is all too easily managed by the power of capital. As Baudrillard puts it: 'perfectly emancipated, perfectly servile'.[127]

Catastrophe: Working from Home

Though rooted in Marx, much of the above is snatched from Horkheimer, Adorno, Marcuse, Baudrillard and Lasch. Whatever their merits as social criticism, if we read them as qualitative descriptions of consumer capitalism, they offer a great deal. In this qualitative sense, this chapter ends by describing what would happen if the unwitting alliance amongst liberals, narcissists and capital were to fixate on an ancient concern. In the present's idiom, we call it vulnerability, but in the past's more impersonalised idiom, it is known as security.

In Bentham, we saw that when fear or a sense of vulnerability structures how we think about or experience the world, life is not just characterised by conflict, it is related to in warlike terms. For Bentham, the war is social: he imagines himself surrounded by masses of men who will, but for some risk that they judge too great, opportunistically lunge for control over resources. This is due not to their unique or chosen moral failings; it is a product of a contingent structural feature of the world: mass society. There is nothing special, however, about this origin of vulnerability. A threat might be rooted in other structural features of the world. It could be political, economic, cultural or biological: like a lingering effect of now-rejected relations between races or sexes, or something that is internal to the logic of a form, like families; or it might be the predicted effects of climate change, a novel virus or increased immigration; or it might be a mixture of these real or perceived threats. No matter its source, though, the form of the response must be the same. To defeat the threat or to mitigate its effects, we have to follow Bentham: take control, regulate what exists and protect those whom we think vulnerable,[128] that is, we must strive for security.

What social form will this striving for security take if the unwitting alliance amongst liberals, narcissists and capital becomes fixated by its material or social vulnerability? The alliance would, through and in their use of the Hohfeldian incidents constitutive of consumer capitalism, strive to overcome their ultimate bads: death and pain. That these bads will become ultimate follows from their shared truth: the consumer is always right. When present desire is the font of all values, the immediate self the reference point of all reason, the determinate instance of all actions, then loss of life and intense suffering, which forecloses the experience of desire itself, becomes bound up with the loss of value.[129] When our fears define us, such that we 'no longer dream of overcoming difficulties but merely of surviving them',[130] then life-preservation and avoidance of pains (AS1) inevitably assert themselves as privileged (AS2) goods.

With this, consumer capitalism is transformed. Not called to work to make a living, to obtain the means to satisfy desires or pursue ends, we will be expected to work to preserve life or lessen the risk of pain. Not mine, yours or ours, but life and pain as universally equivalent, disembodied abstractions – in Baudrillard's idiom, 'statistical shadows' represented on 'screens',[131] and thus each susceptible to control, regulation and protection. Whilst those property theorists who direct our attention to vulnerability and dependency,[132] resilience,[133] sustainability,[134] and so on, often do this because they rightly want us to grapple with our shared limits, when the consumer capitalist form fixates on this concern, what emerges is a system that is consumed by limits, but which is wholly unable to reconcile itself to them. Not *animal laborans* or *homo faber*, we would get a frightened and pathetic mixture: the essential worker.

Conquered by fear, public life would be saturated by the narcissist's wartime idiom. Skilled in the art of liquidation, they would traduce critics and dissenters, anyone who does not embrace the ethics and the model of the essential worker, as sceptics and denialists. Existing now in what Lasch calls a 'state of siege',[135] or what Giorgio Agamben refers to as 'the state of exception',[136] what will become privileged (AS2) is not the goods and services declared essential for particular women and men, but rather the goods and services themselves; or more exactly, the system by or conditions in which these are produced (AS3). As Judith Butler, a high priestess of this strand of thought, puts it:

> . . . the very idea of precariousness implies dependency on social networks and conditions, suggesting that there is no 'life itself' at issue here, but always and only the conditions of life, life as something that requires conditions in order to become liveable life and, indeed, in order to become grievable. . . . To sustain life as sustainable requires putting those conditions in place. . . . Our obligations are precisely to the conditions that make life possible, not to 'life itself'.[137]

By means of the model of the essential worker, we would be led by Benthamite fear to Lockean workhouses, but with a modern twist. With our homes functioning as workspaces, the workhouse would not just be outsourced, the boundary lines between work and free time would effectively disappear – and with this, the modern struggle over the limits of the working day, catalogued in quite horrifying detail by Marx,[138] would be decided in capital's favour, through its exploitation of the 'annihilation of space by time' enabled by the roll-out of remote working.[139]

Now, there might be the appearance of free time, where we would not be subject to our line manager's call. During this time, we will be encouraged to relax, look after our mental health by baking bread, watching Netflix or doing yoga.[140] Your health restored, you might also celebrate our real heroes, the essential and therefore disposable ones, who cannot work from home since somebody needs to grow our food, drive our trucks, pack our shelves to keep us fed, produce our goods and deliver our parcels to keep us busy or entertained, staff our lobbies to keep us safe, or enter our hospitals to keep us breathing. Like some, you might make the case for 'fiscal support', 'bringing homeless people into shelter' or 'eviction bans' whilst the threat lasts.[141] Or if you, like Butler, were of the view that the threat is permanent, you might, in the spirit of 'communities of care',[142] advocate 'guaranteed income',[143] to secure all lives (AS1), present and future. Given the open immunity (IV) constitutive of consumer capitalism (AS3), however, these are ideals (AS2) that can be accommodated by it – illustrated by the fact that Hayek,[144] Milton Friedman,[145] along with other neoliberals, as Anton Jäger and Daniel Zamora Vargas explain, 'established' the idea of a guaranteed 'basic income'.[146]

Whether Butlerian or neoliberal, however, Adorno is right: 'Underlying [your fixation with] health is death. All the movements of health reflect the reflex-movements of beings whose hearts have stopped beating.'[147] Therefore, celebration of the essential worker will not be rooted in your belief that something other than bare life, such as community and valour, has ultimate worth. The sacrifices of, for example, healthcare workers, will be celebrated because it reaffirms your belief that life is what matters. Nor will baking or binging or Bikram exist as realised forms of ultimate good. Rather, these acts of consumption will function as 'enforced idleness',[148] as Marx puts it, or 'enforced enjoyment',[149] as Baudrillard writes after him, just obligatory ways to spend your time and recharge your batteries, for the sake of your next Zoom meeting – that is, to reproduce those conditions that make this system possible.

Unshaven, clad in comfy clothing, waiting for others inside this no-space to click 'Admit', the black mirror separating you from reality will be at its most transparent. This infinite abyssal moment, before you 'Join' your colleagues, will be your best chance of seeing the truth: reduced to a mere 'consumer unit',[150] in Friedman's idiom, and thus just a 'carcase of time',[151] as Marx explains, your time will never truly be free.

When survival (AS1) is our ultimate (AS2) concern, 'which in principle should override' all others,[152] as the philosopher Benjamin Bratton argues it should, when 'catastrophe' becomes our orienting attitude,[153] when we go so far beyond the due recognition of our shared vulnerabilities that they become the starting point of politics,[154] with humanity finding 'the shadow of fatality' everywhere it turns,[155] so that rather than the diversity of goodness we have 'a wounded species and its wounded habitat',[156] we will do what for some might appear contradictory: we will open society up for capital by locking its people down (AS3). With the social distancing internal to the logic of consumer capitalism now state policy and elites revelling in a 'delicious confinement',[157] applauding themselves and each other for working from home, their greatest fear being that they might one day have to leave, the Lockean dream, with the efficient aid of Hayekian information systems and their enraged enforcement by lapsed Marxians, will finally become real.

Embodying a new form that is something in the nature of Arendt's 'society of jobholders',[158] Baudrillard's system of '*reproductive* consumption',[159] Lasch's 'culture of survivalism',[160] or the political form that Agamben argues lies at the 'root' of modernity itself,[161] the resulting property system, 'lives and livelihoods' (AS3), will be a more totalising whole than consumer capitalism. It will be more total since it will have absorbed more from our ethical tradition and thereby will have neutered more avenues of external ethical critique.

If you find the idea of this totalising whole the stuff of nightmares, and if you thought it real, you would probably want to escape it. But how? For Locke, Bentham, Hayek, Hegel and Marx, each of whom is an orienting strand in our tradition, offer the theoretical ballast for this structure. It is them, or parts of them, that the whole will have absorbed. Our tradition apparently exhausted, we would find ourselves unhappy, but seemingly with nowhere to go.

In chapter 7, we reveal that this diagnosis is too despairing. Despite the global assault on the diversity of goodness during the pandemic, to which we shall return in a South African context in chapter 9, there exist resources to describe another world. For our world is not so 'subsumed' under the logic of this whole,[162] so 'one-dimensional' and 'totally administered',[163] so 'colonized' in all thought and appearance,[164] so 'obsessed' with the 'production, calculation and functionality' of a 'systematic' 'homogenous material' and 'cultural' world,[165] so dominated by the 'hegemony of the code' of 'consumption',[166] so 'hollowed out' by the 'gale of market forces',[167] so wholly 'fragmented' and 'subject to a proliferation of senseless choices',[168] as its countless critics like to imagine. 'The way these guys write', Marshall Berman once said, 'it's as if the world has passed them by'.[169] Indeed, for as he puts it: 'Reading *Capital* [or another great work by our prescriptive anthropologists] won't help us if we don't also know how to read the signs on the street.'[170] If we look more closely at what really exists, we will discover a veritable pageantry of object-relations that escape the modes, attitudes, concepts and categories of what was described above. For there exist forms of being in which we do not relate to objects as instruments, but rather relate to them as modes of spirit. These forms will not be presented, nor do they exist, as absolute alternatives to those instrumental ones just described. They exist alongside them as yet further incompatible possibilities on our ever-expanding list of goods. As always, we must look to add to the picture, not try to replace it.

Before turning to these relations, let me conclude this chapter by admitting my hope. Even if you think that critics of our society, culture, politics and economic system are close to the truth in their descriptions of reality or its internal tendencies, the description of these non-instrumental forms will be one way to resist it. For if these non-instrumental structures are grasped in thought, even those who do not judge anathema the whole just described, and find quite comfortable and secure a routine structured by Zoom, Amazon, Netflix and Uber Eats, might begin to wonder if there is more to life than this totalising whole. This primitive wonder would offer an opportunity. For the fact that the possibility of something has appeared to us in thought is evidence that there is already a way out in practice. All that we would have to do is choose or affirm it – conscious, like always, of the limits, spatio-temporal and logical, that structure all decisions, and therefore always sensitive to the consequences that any resulting action would entail.

NOTES

1. John Gardner, *Law as a Leap of Faith* (2012). This chapter is indebted to the influence and insights of Jacob Reynolds.
2. Aristotle, *The Nicomachean Ethics* (tr. D. Ross, 2009) 1098b28–30.
3. Gardner (n 1) v.
4. Michael Walzer, *Spheres of Justice: A Defense of Pluralism and Equality* (1983) 3.
5. Hannah Arendt, *The Human Condition* (2ed, 1998) 303.
6. Martin Heidegger, *Being and Time* (tr. J. Macquarrie and E. Robinson, 1962) 97.
7. Arendt (n 5) 79–174.
8. On preference- and freedom-based conceptions of efficiency, see Amartya Sen, *Development as Freedom* (1999) 116–20.
9. For Jean Baudrillard, *The System of Objects* (tr. James Benedict, 2005) 217–24, consumption is an essentially 'idealist' not 'material practice'.
10. Sigmund Freud, *Civilization and its Discontents* (tr. D. McLintock, 2014): 'Eros [is] the drive . . . by the narcissistic libido' that 'turns towards objects . . . to preserve the living substance and bring it together in ever larger units' (79–80). See also Herbert Marcuse, *Eros and Civilisation: A Philosophical Inquiry into Freud* (2ed, 1969).
11. By affixing 'ultimate' to 'lack of concern', I leave open the possibility that other attitudes, like those that constitute the religious or ritualistic preparation, offering or consumption of food, may be consistent with the logic of consumer relations. See Jean Baudrillard, *Symbolic Exchange and Death* (tr. Iain Hamilton Grant, rev. ed, 2017) 158–59.
12. On 'productive consumption', Marx says: 'It consumes the objective character of the object', that is, an 'indifference towards the form' of the matter used-up in the process (GFCPE 300–01). As Nussbaum writes: 'Appetites are always directed toward a certain sort of object from which they never diverge . . . and the appetite itself does not contain any further thought of the value or goodness of the object. They are, then, both *object-fixated* and *value indifferent.*' (UT 130).
13. Baudrillard (n 9) 224 and Jean Baudrillard, *The Consumer Society: Myths and Structures* (tr. Chris Turner, 1998) 76–78.
14. Christopher Lasch, *The Culture of Narcissism: American Life in an Age of Diminishing Expectations* (1979) 21–25.
15. CVI 283. See GFCPE 90–94, where the same process is described.
16. EPR § 67 and 67A.
17. PhS § 194.

18. CVI 549–50.

19. Consumption of 'signs', in its structuralist or semio-linguistic sense, in contrast to the practical use of matter that includes material consumption, is a theme in Baudrillard (n 9) and (n 13). On their conceptual differences, see Jean Baudrillard, *For a Critique of the Political Economy of the Sign* (tr. Charles Levin, 1981) 66–67.

20. CVII 300. The 'stomach or the imagination makes no difference' (CVI 125).

21. Lasch (n 14) 22 and 71–74.

22. Heidegger (n 6) 396–400.

23. Theodor Adorno and Max Horkheimer, *Dialectic of Enlightenment* (tr. John Cumming, 2016) 120.

24. Guy Debord, *The Society of the Spectacle* (tr. Fredy Perlman, 2021) and John Gray, *Heresies: Against Progress and Other Illusions* (2004) 202–09.

25. Baudrillard (n 9) 142 and 223.

26. Baudrillard (n 13) 41–47 and 60–68.

27. Christopher Lasch, *The True and Only Heaven: Progress and Its Critics* (1991) 518–22.

28. John Gray, *Straw Dogs: Thoughts on Humans and Other Animals* (2023) 162–66.

29. John Gray, *False Dawn: The Delusions of Global Capitalism* (2009) 38.

30. Barbara Ehrenreich, *Fear of Falling: The Inner Life of the Middle Class* (2020) 27.

31. For an analysis of the logic of 'conformity', the 'formal innovation' of 'models', and 'social differentiation and prestige', see Baudrillard (n 19) 38–52.

32. For similar, critical points, see Theodor Adorno, *Minima Moralia: Reflections on a Damaged Life* (tr. EFN Jephcott, 2005) 118–19.

33. TTG II § 27.

34. GFCPE 300.

35. GFCPE 706.

36. On Marx's 'use-value fetishism', see Baudrillard (n 19) 130–42, which critique is developed in *The Mirror of Production* (tr. Mark Poster, 1975).

37. Arendt (n 5) 96–101 and 126–35.

38. CSF 380.

39. Section 26(3) of the Constitution.

40. Section 25(1) of the Constitution.

41. Charles Taylor, *Philosophical Papers: Volume 1, Human Agency and Language* (1985) 99.

42. CVI 165.

43. GFCPE 91.

44. Christine Korsgaard, *Self-Constitution: Agency, Identity, and Integrity* (2009) 37.

45. Suggested in Herbert Marcuse, *One-Dimensional Man: Studies in the Ideology of Advanced Industrial Society* (2ed, 1991) 66–67, 74 and 261 and developed in *An Essay on Liberation* (1972).

46. CVI 166.

47. On how beliefs and attitudes 'tend to merge' in the constitution of forms, see Joseph Raz, *The Morality of Freedom* (1986) 350–51.

48. EPM 84.

49. CVI 254–55.

50. On 'time horizons', see Hartmut Rosa, *Social Acceleration: A New Theory of Modernity* (tr. Jonathan Trejo-Mathys, 2013).

51. CVI 231.

52. EPM 52–55. Defined by practical reason, his men are spontaneous, not impulsive. They satisfy immediately existing desires but through plans (CVII 390), considering potential future facts, not desires or ends. Ideal production requires objects that outlast concrete use (CVII 241), producing enough to cater for possible disasters (CVII 256–57), to insure against natural accidents, to keep up with new needs that arise and increases in population (CVIII 958), and withdrawing objects from immediately useful operations if planning requires (CVII 434).

53. Durability is a quality both of Marx's 'means of labour' and its capitalist form 'fixed capital' (GFCPE 710–71 and CVII 237–40), and of Arendt's 'world' (Arendt (n 5) 93–96 and 136–74).

54. CVII 237 and 246–48.

55. Arendt (n 5) 136–44.

56. When Marx writes about 'the conversion of things into persons and the conversion of persons into things' (CVI 209), what he means is that it takes place 'behind [our] backs' (CVI 201–02), in that we do not control it. In CVIII 965–70, when he deals with 'reification' and 'mystification' of the 'source' of value, his concern is with the 'autonomy' of objects: they appear as 'natural laws, governing [us] irrespective of [our] will'. On 'forgetting', see Axel Honneth, *Reification: A New Look at an Old Idea* (2007) 52–63 and Heidegger (n 6) 388–89.

57. Max Weber, *The Protestant Ethic and the Spirit of Capitalism* (tr. Talcott Parsons, 2005) 118.

58. Charles Taylor, *Sources of the Self: The Making of Modern Identity* (1989) 222–23.

59. David Harvey, *The Limits to Capital* (2018) 229.

60. Lasch (n 14) 57.

61. Francis Fukuyama, *The End of History and the Last Man* (1992).

62. When Marx says the 'valorization of value [is] the determining purpose, the driving motive', of industrial capital (CVII 180), and that 'appropriation of ever more wealth in the abstract is the sole driving force of the capitalist', he means use-value is not 'the immediate aim' (CVI 254). In CVI 738–46, he criticises the 'abstinence theory' of accumulation.

63. CVI 176–77.

64. Taylor (n 58) 222–23.

65. CVII 215–17.

66. The objects are 'destined to play the same role' again and again (GFCPE 711), so 'while usage is bound to use up these objects, this end is not their destiny in the same way as destruction is the inherent end of all things for consumption. What usage wears out is durability' (Arendt (n 5) 137).

67. CVI 528 and CVII 248–61.

68. Destroying part of the instrument may be required to preserve the whole, for example, control inflation (Harvey (n 59) 307–15), or in crises after 'overaccumulation' where 'value destruction' is needed to sustain the capitalist mode of production (190–203).

69. For Bentham, its necessity is due to mass psychology. For Marx, it is internal to capitalism's logic (CVI 227–32 and CVII 157–58, 162–66, 200–02, 214–25, 423, 476, 526 and 565–71), but is a 'dead weight' on capital's flow, that is, the realisation of surplus value, which is why the 'credit system' is a necessary feature of capitalism (CVII 574).

70. Generally, see CVII.

71. On the relation between culture and political economy, see Joel Mokyr, *A Culture of Growth: The Origins of the Modern Economy* (2016).

72. On the conquest of scarcity, see Marcuse (n 10) and Aaron Bastani, *Fully Automated Luxury Communism* (2019).

73. Raymond Geuss, *Philosophy and Real Politics* (2008) 25–26.

74. Freedom to choose (AS1) is the privileged (AS2) good that informs the neoliberalism (AS3) in Milton Friedman's *Capitalism and Freedom* (2002).

75. Generally, see Eric Hobsbawm, *The Age of Capital: 1848–1875* (1977), David Harvey, *A Brief History of Neoliberalism* (2007), Quinn Slobodian, *Globalists: The End of Empire and the Birth of Neoliberalism* (2018), Branko Milanovic, *Capitalism, Alone: The Future of the System That Rules the World* (2019) and Grace Blakeley, *Vulture Capitalism: Corporate Crimes, Backdoor Bailouts and the Death of Freedom* (2024).

76. For Marxians, the rights outlined below are necessary but not sufficient features. Also needed are: (i) the vesting in a minority of rights used to produce instruments; (ii) exercise of these rights must be structured by market imperatives, for example, increase profit through competitive development of productive forces; and (iii) non-right-holders of producer rights must depend, in order to live, on markets to sell their labour-power. On some of the qualitative differences between capitalist and commercial societies, like whether market-exchange is an 'imperative' or 'opportunity', see Ellen Meiksins Wood, *The Origin of Capitalism: A Longer View* (2017).

77. CVII 487.

78. CVI 743, where Marx refers to 'the awful conflict between the desire for enjoyment and the drive for self-enrichment'.

79. Heidegger (n 6) 98.

80. Ibid 410.

81. Ibid 98 fn 2.

82. Cass Sunstein and Stephen Holmes, *The Cost of Rights: Why Liberty Depends on Taxes* (1999).

83. CVI 873–76 and 927–40, and David Harvey, *The New Imperialism* (2005) 137–82 and *Spaces of Global Capitalism: A Theory of Uneven Geographical Development* (2019) 41–50 and 90–95.

84. According to Arthur Ripstein, *Force and Freedom: Kant's Legal and Political Philosophy* (2009), Kantian property ultimately refers to things individuals freely use as they choose.

85. John Rawls, *A Theory of Justice* (rev. ed, 1999) begins with primary goods. These are rights, liberties, opportunities and income and wealth, namely, things that we generally want in order to achieve our chosen and contingent ends.

86. Robert Nozick, *Anarchy, State and Utopia* (1974) couples a Kantian political philosophy that prohibits aggression with a Lockean right of original acquisition to produce a property theory in which instruments, control and choice are dominant concepts.

87. Ronald Dworkin, *Sovereign Virtue* (2000), conceptualises resources as private income, wealth, land, raw materials, and other impersonal and personal instruments. Equality of resources entails people having control over the same external resources, corrected for natural, unchosen talents or handicaps, to use as they choose. Use, however, must fit within the framework of an abstractly determined baseline system, which has a strong presumption in favour of choice and includes a principle of security.

88. Sen (n 8) is liable to absorption since his idea of freedom is an all-purpose good, in which income and wealth are likely sufficient. With Nussbaum (see references in chapter 8), it is less clear. Her talk about property, coupled with her political liberalism and attempt to identify basic goods that enable people to choose amongst diverse ways of life, suggests instrumental relations are adequate. Such a reading is consistent with her view that Rawls' concept of primary goods is essentially right: her recasting of primary goods as capabilities means that we must look beyond income and wealth, but many of her capabilities can be met with instruments. The closest that we get to a non-instrumental account is with animals: they have their own dignity, so cannot be treated in a purely instrumental way, that is, without regard to their rights.

89. Hanoch Dagan, *A Liberal Theory Property* (2021), says that the ultimate value of property, to or by which non-ultimate goods like independence, personhood, community and utility should be directed or constrained, is autonomy-enhancement. This means we should afford people rights so that they have private authority over resources, which exist as means, to choose to act in ways that they judge best, but always consistently with our shared autonomy.

90. One way to resist absorption, from a Marxian perspective, will be to argue that the advocated principle proscribes the structural features listed in note 76.

91. Theodor Adorno and Max Horkheimer, *Towards a New Manifesto* (tr. Rodney Livingstone, 2019) 61.

92. Adorno (n 32) 38: 'the individual as individual, in representing the species of man, has lost the autonomy through which he might realize the species'.

93. Perry Anderson, *Considerations on Western Marxism* (1979) 88–94. On this attitude's roots, see Anderson (42–48 and 92–93) and Anton Jäger and Daniel Zamora Vargas, *Welfare for Markets: A Global History of Basic Income* (2023) 55–125.

94. Horkheimer and Adorno (n 91) 72: 'The horror is that for the first time we live in a world in which we can no longer imagine a better one.'

95. Philosophy, writes Max Horkheimer, *Critique of Instrumental Reason* (trs. MJ O'Connell et al, 2012), 'cannot prescribe how people are to escape from the charmed circle of the status quo; it can only seek to give the charm a name'. (32) See the essay 'Must Criticism be Constructive?' in Raymond Geuss, *A World Without Why* (2014) 68–90.

96. Adorno and Horkheimer (n 91) 14.

97. CVI 205 and CVII 486.

98. For Marx-inspired criticisms of the authentic self, see Adorno (n 32) 152–55 and Baudrillard (n 9) 77–90.

99. Olúfẹ́mi O. Táíwò, *Elite Capture: How the Powerful Took Over Identity Politics (And Everything Else)* (2022) 61–84.

100. Ellen Meiksins Wood, *The Retreat from Class: A New 'True' Socialism* (rev. ed., 1998). On the constitutive compatibility of identity politics with capitalism, see her Ellen Meiksins Wood, *Democracy Against Capitalism: Renewing Historical Materialism* (2016) 238–83.

101. Baudrillard (n 9) 150–53 and 166–68 and Baudrillard (n 13) 87–98. See also Jean Baudrillard, *Impossible Exchange* (tr. Chris Turner, 2001) 132–33.

102. Adorno (n 32) 112: 'To a child returning from a holiday, home seems new, fresh, festive. Yet nothing has changed', and so will 'the world one day appear', when free of 'the law of labour, and when for home-comers duty has the lightness of holiday play'.

103. David Harvey, *The Condition of Postmodernity* (1990) 52–54.

104. On this concept, see Christopher Lasch, *The Minimal Self: Psychic Survival in Troubled Times* (1985) 245–53. See also Nussbaum's analysis in PE 168–74.

105. Lasch (n 105) 193. For example, Debord (n 24) advocates an 'authentic communism' that will 'abolish[] everything that exists independently of individuals' (90–91).

106. Chantal Delsol, *The Unlearned Lesson of the Twentieth Century: An Essay on Late Modernity* (tr. R. Dick, 2006) 123–35.

107. Marcuse (n 10) 180.

108. As explained by Jäger and Zamora Vargas (n 94) 92–125 and 174–79, though, sometimes not so unwitting.

109. Otto Kernberg, quoted in UT 344.

110. On this 'situational' form of identity, see Rosa (n 50) 224–50.

111. Marcuse (n 10) 135.

112. Ibid.

113. On the roots of these emotions, see UT 196–207 and 220–22 and PE 359–64.

114. On the 'predicateless' self (nothing), which accompanies the perpetual 'liquefication' of material social structures (nothing), see Rosa (n 50) 242.

115. Baudrillard (n 9) 144.

116. Judith Butler, *Frames of War: When is Life Grievable?* (2016) 182. Conjoined with her belief that to be a human is to be 'partially formed through violence', that is, we exist in a world in which not all is determined by our 'will' (167), she is almost our archetype. She is saved by her tentative remark that she is 'not at all sure' (169) that all norms are violent.

117. Their 'telos', writes Marcuse (n 10) 136, is 'just to be what they are, being-there, existing'.

118. CVI 347 and 404.

119. EB 480. What is needed, writes Debord (n 24) 66, is a 'revolution embodying the permanent domination of the present over the past and a total critique of separation'. On this shared feature of capitalist and Marxian thought, see Marshall Berman, *All That Is Solid Melts Into Air, The Experience of Modernity* (1983) 98–105.

120. Perry Anderson, 'Modernity and Revolution', NLR I/44, March-April 1984, 109.

121. Lasch (n 14) xvi.

122. David Harvey, *Marx, Capital and the Madness of Economic Reason* (2019) 173.

123. Rosa (n 50) 145–48.

124. Baudrillard (n 13) 84.

125. CVI 300. He laughs since a limit on his profit-making potential, that is, the 'restriction' imposed by 'the consumer needs of society' (CVII 391 fn 1), will almost be overcome – only almost since 'every . . . need has a limit' (CVI 201), meaning even the dominant capitalist must accept that for all his power, 'a material substratum is always left' (CVI 133) that constrains his actions. If his lapsed heirs were also to abandon his materialism, their consumerism may assume the 'unlimited character' described in Baudrillard (n 13) 60–66.

126. Baudrillard (n 19) 85.

127. Baudrillard (n 102) 75. In Baudrillard (n 19), he says that the 'adherence to these values [of consumption] acts as a new morality for slaves' (61).

128. On these aspects of biosecurity, see Frédéric Gros, *The Security Principle: From Serenity to Regulation* (tr. David Broder, 2019) 135–70.

129. Lasch (n 14) 207–17.

130. Ibid 49.

131. Baudrillard (n 102) 139.

132. Martha Fineman, 'The Vulnerable Subject: Anchoring Equality in the Human Condition' 20(1) *Yale Journal of Law and Feminism* (2008) 1–23, 'Equality, Autonomy, and the Vulnerable Subject in Law and Politics' in *Vulnerability: Reflections on a New Ethical Foundation for Law and Politics* (eds. Martha Albertson Fineman and Anna Grear, 2016) 13–27, and 'Vulnerability and Inevitable Inequality' 4(3) *Oslo Law Review* (2017) 133–49. For criticism, see Nina A. Kohn, 'Vulnerability Theory and the Role of Government' 26(1) *Yale Journal of Law and Feminism* (2014) 1–27.

133. Lorna Fox O'Mahony and Marc L. Roark, *Squatting and the State: Resilient Property in an Age of Crisis* (2022) 203–30.

134. Bram Akkermans, 'Sustainable Ownership – New Obligations towards Achieving a Sustainable Society' 10(2/3) *European Property Law Journal* (2021) 277–303 and 'Sustainable Property Law: Reckoning, Resilience, and Reform' *Eleven International Publishing*. 24 *Maastricht Law Series* (2022) 7–22.

135. Lasch (n 104) 94.

136. Giorgio Agamben, *Homo Sacer, Sovereign Power and Bare Life* (tr. D. Heller-Roazen, 1998) 148. For extended discussion, see Giorgio Agamben, *The State of Exception* (tr. Kevin Attell, 2005).

137. Butler (n 117) 22–23. In Judith Butler, *The Force of Nonviolence: An Ethico-Political Bind* (2021) the logic of life (45–46) is carried all the way through: the duty to preserve life is extended 'not only [to] persons, but animals; and not only [to] living creatures, but living processes, the systems and forms of life' (58).
138. CVI 340–416.
139. GFCPE 524 and 539. On the social-technological roots of this 'space-time compression', see Rosa (n 50) 161–74.
140. On the 'ethics of pressured performance', see Baudrillard (n 13) 151–58.
141. Fox O'Mahony and Roark (n 134) 386–405.
142. Judith Butler, *What World Is This? A Pandemic Phenomenology* (2022) 27 and 86.
143. Ibid., 27, 48 and 52.
144. RS 124–26.
145. Friedman (n 74) 190–95.
146. Ibid., 176.
147. Adorno (n 32) 59. Max Horkheimer, *The Eclipse of Reason* (2004) 84: 'the apotheosis of the ego and the principle of self-preservation as such culminate in the utter insecurity of the individual, in his complete negation'.
148. CVI 403.
149. Baudrillard (n 13) 80.
150. Friedman (n 74) 193.
151. PP 57.
152. Benjamin Bratton, *The Revenge of the Real: Politics for a Post-Pandemic World* (2021) 33.
153. On the catastrophic attitude, see Gros (n 129) 185–87.
154. As in Bratton and Butler's texts cited above. For another illustrative text, see Judith Butler, *Precarious Life: The Powers of Mourning and Violence* (2020).
155. Butler (n 138) 204.
156. Bratton (n 153) 143.
157. Bernard-Henri Levy, *The Virus in the Age of Madness* (2020) 39–54.
158. Arendt (n 5) 322.
159. Baudrillard (n 11) 50.
160. Lasch (n 105) 23–59.
161. Agamben: 1995 (n 137) 119–25 and 166–80.
162. CVI 1019–38.
163. See the references to Marcuse in note 45.
164. Debord (n 24) 12–20.
165. Baudrillard (n 9) 28–29, 47–49 and 66.
166. Baudrillard (n 36) 121 and 126.
167. John Gray, *Endgames: Questions in Late Modern Political Thought* (1997) 184.
168. Gray (n 29) 38.
169. Marshall Berman, *Adventures in Marxism* (1999) 260.
170. Ibid., 169.

Chapter 7

Spirit and Its Modes

Not all relations to objects are instrumental. Sometimes, we can relate to objects directly, not as a means to some end but for the sake of what is constituted through and in the relation itself. When we do, we do not face objects as things more or less useful in efforts to satisfy or realise desires or ends. Rather, we meet them as embodiments of spirit: sources of expressive purpose, meaning, significance.

Direct meetings can take at least two functional forms. They can be access-points to already-existing purpose, or they can constitute originally this purpose. With both, we relate to objects as embodiments of spirit. They are distinguished by the mode spirit takes in meeting it. It can exist in the mode of actuality or potentiality. When the meeting offers access to an actualised purpose, we adopt a passive and contemplative stance towards the spirit embodied in the object: whatever purpose we bring to the relation, it comes after and is subordinate to our duty to care reflectively for its purpose. In meetings where we originally constitute purpose, where spirit's mode of existence is potentiality, our stance is active: whilst objects exist as sources of purpose, their constitution as such depends on our being consciously open to the fact that we also exist as sources of purpose. When we directly but passively meet an actual object, it exists as a reified expression; a meeting constituted by activity and potentiality entails relating to an object as living spirit. Distinguishing these relations is important, since they constitute diverse goods. With reified expressions (DA2), we can constitute aesthetic, interpersonal and intergenerational goods (DA1), whilst living spirit (DA2) constitutes the good of possibility (DA1). As we shall see, the property necessary (DA3) for each are incompatible (GP4), and both are incompatible (GP4) with that which is necessary (DA3) for consumables, reified instruments and mixed instruments.

BEING WORLD-GUIDED

The idea that spirit can be embodied in objects is an old one. Indeed, we have seen variations of it in Locke, Hegel and Marx: men who mix labour in objects, form the world in their own image and humanise nature. The lineage of the idea is impressive. Not all purpose, though, is embodied instrumentally, for spirit can inhere in objects we relate to directly. When we do, when we meet rather than use the world, with our words or deeds structured and directed by objects in ways not under our purposive control, we are guided by reified expressions.

Care

There is a formal, structural overlap between reified expressions and reified instruments. In the temporal idioms of Hegel and Marx, they share an orientation towards past and future. With both, objects have concrete forms, identities, that pre-exist and can outlast the existing desires or ends of subjects. As explained in chapter 6, this does not mean that they have an original purpose emanating from themselves, which they strive on their own to actualise. Whilst they pre-exist the present and exist independently of what a subject desires or pursues, the purpose may be derived from past desires or ends. So, to say that objects have purposes that pre-exist and outlast existing desires or ends, means that they do not rely for their existing or future existence on the conscious attribution of any original purpose. Formally put, reified instruments and expressions exist in the mode of actuality. In this way, we see later, they differ from living spirit, which relation exists in the mode of potentiality.

Despite this formal overlap in their modes of existence, the two reifications are incompatible. They are incompatible because they are constituted by logically opposed attitudes, concepts and categories. As we saw in chapter 6, this logical incompatibility entails incompatible demands for property. To reveal this fact, we must distinguish two ways in which the present can embody the past: dependently and independently.

When unbundling Marx and describing consumer relations, we explained how gifts can exist as embodiments of love. The genesis of the object's form – the fact that someone who loves you shaped it – can constitute its meaning, say, as an anniversary gift. In these cases, the concrete form is tied to and dependent on its origin. Therefore, if your relationship with the person changes, say, if they betray you and you become estranged, the object may take on a new meaning. Rather than existing as an expression of love, it will now mean something else, say, it might be an artefact of anger or anguish. Adorno writes: 'He who has loved and who betrays love does harm not only to the image of the past, but to the past itself.'[1] Dependence on interpersonal ties is basic to Marx's ontology: man is root and lord of all. Not all purpose, though, is embodied in this way. An object can embody a purpose other than its creator's – author, sculptor, painter, and so on. Spirit can inhabit the structure of the object itself, autonomously and independently of anyone who shaped it. When it does, the object exists as a reified expression. To unpack its nature, we start below by stipulating some representative examples of reified expressions, then articulating more concretely the different ways in which these objects can embody spirit.

Let artworks,[2] statues and land act as our representative examples. In *Upheavals of Thought*, Martha Nussbaum explains, in the context of an analysis of literature and music, that when we relate to reified expressions, the meeting can manifest in various more concrete general forms.[3] Whilst what she says concerns music and literature, it has a general application. It applies to other forms of art, like poetry or paintings, and non- or less-traditionally artistic forms, like buildings, statues or land.[4] Below, we shall see that this structural generality is essential to property theory because it means that despite important concrete differences between the relations that constitute these more concrete forms of reified expressions, formally speaking, the same rights are required to facilitate them.

Nussbaum outlines four general forms that relations to reified expressions can take. First, the relation can be with the parts of the object, to its particular qualities, such as a novel's characters, which together with other qualities, similar or different, structure and unify the object as a whole. Second, the relation can be to the whole itself, say, the story, where the object of attention is not particular qualities but the unity constituted through and in the relation amongst the qualities. In both cases, whether we relate to the object's parts or as a whole, we can identify empathetically with, or we can react sympathetically or critically to, the parts or the whole: we can share in the hero's turmoil, recognise her motives, condemn her enemy's conduct, or experience or make any of these emotions or judgements about the story itself: 'I identified with the protagonists, but the plot really did not affect me at all.'

A third relation to reified expressions, Nussbaum says, is to meet the object in a way that we see in it a world of possible forms,[5] be they already-existing but faintly grasped, or possibilities not previously understood at all. The possibility can be an 'idealized form of . . . life',[6] as Roger Scruton explains, or as Nussbaum remarks, a form that we would ideally avoid: 'When we have emotions of fear and pity toward the hero of a tragedy and his reversal, we explore aspects of our own vulnerability in a safe and pleasing setting, apprehending general possibilities for human life.'[7] Here, recall what was said in chapter 5, where we considered how a strong goods pluralist can strive to persuade the weak pluralist to adopt her perspective on the world. We explained that the faculty of imagination and the capacities to empathise or sympathise are essential, and that to activate and exercise these, our primary mode of argument is persuasion rather than deduction or induction, with the technique shifting from analytical reason to rhetorical flourish, and the style of presentation being more like storytelling than formal treatise. In telling stories, we explained, we must be sensitive to our audience, for what we say will differ depending on our purpose. But sometimes, we must tell stories that disclose the depth and the complexity, that is, the qualitative distinctiveness (GP4), of diverse relational forms. Another way of putting all of this is to say that we can sometimes grasp in artworks, memorials or ancestral homes general possibilities for life, diverse and conflicting options for how we might live in the future or accounts of how others live in the present or have lived in the past.

Here is a fourth general form that our relations to reified expressions can take. Through and in the relation, we can disclose a fact or quality about ourselves, others or the world, for the first time, or about something that we already know but have 'forgotten'[8] or prefer to 'ignore'.[9] Since the object tells us something new, or refreshes our memory, the relation functions to expand our understanding. Nussbaum explains that these experiences can be exhilarating or delightful, but as Berlin observes in a different context, not all revelation is pleasurable: 'Whether ignorance is or is not bliss . . . is an empirical question.'[10]

What unites each form is its self-referential character. With each, in the search for spirit, we do not go beyond the relation to the object for the form to be realised. To use a favourite example of Nussbaum, without knowing anything about Sophocles' intentions when writing *Antigone*, we can empathise and sympathise with Antigone, or we can criticise Creon or the city's laws that led to Antigone's reversal; this tragedy can present possible but unfamiliar forms of life, like honour or patriotic duty; and in watching its performance we can learn and understand better something about ourselves, like how we treat the dead. In each of these cases, that with which we empathise, sympathise or criticise, what our eyes set upon, or what we understand, all this exists within the object. Each of these relations to the spirit embodied in the object is realised through and in our meeting directly its expressive content. This is not to say we can effectively approach the play in the absence of any training in the tragic literary tradition, or that we can be totally clueless about the cultural or historical context in which it is set. It just means that when striving to identify the spirit embodied in the object, rather than referring to any purpose external to it, our attention must be directed towards discovering the meaning that inhabits its structure.

The self-referential nature of each relation suggests a fifth relation. Sometimes, we relate to embodiments of spirit in a way that the object refers outside itself to a past exercise of purpose. When we do, the relation is not structured by attention that is directed to the object's parts or as a whole, nor does the object present to us possibilities or keep us in its thrall. Rather, it tells a story about an external exercise of expressive significance, be it by a person, a group or another reified expression. With external references, objects can embody spirit indirectly or directly. It embodies spirit indirectly if the referent is not responsible for the object's concrete form, that is, when the object refers to words or deeds that had no role in shaping it. Examples are how we can relate to land or statues, where these objects direct our attention to past events, like the lives of ancestors or the losses incurred in the struggle for freedom. Here, when objects embody the 'spirit of one's ancestors' or 'freedom fighters', they do so not because these individuals shaped the land or built the statue, but because the objects remind us of them – they memorialise them.

An object embodies external spirit directly when the purpose to which it refers is the purpose responsible for its concrete form. One example of direct, referential embodiment is how we can relate to paintings. We sometimes think their origin matters. When we do, it becomes important to distinguish originals from copies, even if they are indistinguishable. To attach significance to origins does not necessarily mean that we are reverting to a Marxian dependent picture of things. We may be interested in the painting's origin and also judge that it is irrelevant to interpreting its meaning. Scruton articulates these ideas when he, in a discussion of the 'detached' conception of music, where sounds are 'emancipated from their causes',[11] says that:

> Even if we are aware that the music is a performance, and that in listening to music we are hearing the real actions of real people, putting themselves into the sounds that they produce, this awareness must be registered in the musical movement if it is to be musically significant.[12]

In another idiom, even if we grant the author's 'death' when it comes to questions of meaning,[13] the object can still be the 'legacy' of what they said or did.[14] For we can admit that objects embody the desires or purposes of their creators, whilst also thinking that the products of their works embody ideas, desires, moods, and so on, that stand alone, independently of their creators. As Arendt puts it: 'Works of art are thought things, but this does not prevent their being things.'[15]

All this is possible because purpose can be embodied in one object in multiple ways: the four ways identified by Nussbaum, and directly and indirectly. So, the examples of indirect and direct external reference are not fixed. Artworks can embody the past indirectly, reminding us of facts external to their forms, like events surrounding their creation. Land and statues can embody the past directly, like when land is shaped through agriculture, or statues exist as a community's expression of respect for the dead. Just as one object can embody external purpose directly and indirectly, it can embody purpose in one or more of Nussbaum's self-referential ways.

Identifying these distinctions and overlaps is important, for the concrete form that a particular reified expression takes determines the proper way to relate to it: what beliefs, feelings, attitudes, and so on, are proper in response to the object we meet. For example, right relations to war memorials are constituted by recognition of a particular form: the belief that a soldier's actions were noble; regret that they sacrificed their life or well-being; but awe at the fact that they made this sacrifice for the sake of an important belief; and reverence for the fact that they did this for other people or some ideal. Other beliefs, feelings, attitudes, and so on, are proper for artworks – and there will be more differences depending on the artwork's nature. Likewise with places: if the land is a family home or site of religious significance, the appropriate response will vary. Important here, though, is what these concrete forms of embodiment share: the attitude we must have towards them. This attitude is one of 'care',[16] that is, concern for the fate of concrete forms that exist outside of the control of our will.[17] To make its necessity plain, let us contrast it with the attitudes constitutive of consumables and reified instruments.

With consumption, subject is centre: all is defined in relation to her, and what ultimately matters is what she desires or pursues. If she wants to eat or dance, then she must be free to take from the world's objects what she needs. The world serves her, it revolves about her, just an extension of her willing self. The function of objects is fixed by their capacity to satisfy her fleeting demands: she is the root of all and their lord. So, if an object is destroyed by eating it, she ultimately cares not. If a clothing item loses its aesthetic appeal, she will confidently discard it, for having lost its spiritual significance, it is just a disposable heap of matter. Fulfilment and realisation of existing desires and ends, not a concern for the concrete forms of objects, define relations constituted by eros and indifference. These attitudes are impermissible with reified expressions. This relation is formed by the treatment of objects as having purpose that exists independently of existing desires or ends. It entails treating an object as having a concrete form, an identity, not tied to but severed from what we desire or pursue in the present.

In this way, the structures of reified expressions and reified instruments overlap: both treat an object as having a purpose external to present desires or ends. Their structures differ, though, by virtue of how this link is severed. With reified instruments, externality of purpose is rooted in the subject's orientation towards the future. Her attitude is cautious and self-controlled, structured by non-existing desires or ends, for example, tomorrow's hunger. Reified instruments answer the calls of our future selves, for we still or stymie the self's present desires and ends for the sake of future ones. Whilst consumables and reified instruments are distinguishable temporally – the former concern the present, the latter the future – both privilege the subject's desires and ends. But with a reified expression, no subject is privileged, for the self is displaced or decentred: this is how the purpose of the reified expression is severed from the present. Present desires or ends are not set aside for future ones, nor are future ones set aside for present ones. You *qua* subject are displaced because you are *subject to* the demands expressed through and in the object.[18] This is Walter Benjamin's meaning when he writes that:

> there is in the life of a [book] collector . . . a relationship to objects which does not emphasize their functional, utilitarian value . . . but studies and loves them as the scene, the stage, of their fate.[19]

Unlike, say, the 'authentic' *Dasein* of Heidegger, which 'throws itself primarily' into its own ends instead of seeking to 'understand itself in terms of the world',[20] for Benjamin books are their own sources of meaning and so make demands on him. They do not exist as for Heidegger 'primarily' to be 'utilize[d]',[21] for their 'fates' are not just to be read,[22] say, to disclose 'possibilities' we can choose for ourselves.[23] And unlike those 'collections' described by Baudrillard, which by being 'possessed . . . allows me . . . to recognise myself in the object as an absolutely singular being',[24] and thereby existing as a 'narcissistic equivalent[] of the ego',[25] it is in the nature of Benjamin's books to be treasured (GP3), studied and loved in their own right (GP5), as the scene, the stage, of their own fate.

Benjamin's vision is anathema to Marx, for whom our right relation to the world is essentially consumptive in character. As the Marxist István Mészáros explains, 'after consumption the work of art remains as it was before – but only as a physical being; its aesthetic substance is constantly recreated in the *activity of consumption*. The work of art has no strictly "independent" aesthetic being'.[26] With reified expressions, contrarily, independence of being is central, as revealed in the fact that they make demands on us. The right response to them is not within our control, and this lack of power is constitutive of their identity. For internal to the experience is that the tragic play *moves* us, the sacred ground *inspires* us, and the war memorial *humbles* us. The object's concrete form is such that it calls for an emotional response, expresses honour or merits respect. We might affirm its demand, we might identify it as our own, but this endorsement comes after the fact, for the demand is not based on, nor does it ultimately rely on, an affirmation of its source or content. As categorical requirements, they exist apart from existing desires and ends. They emerge from laws internal to the object itself – from the 'compulsion of its structure',[27] its 'indwelling soul',[28] its 'semantic substance' that 'stands opposed' to what we desire or pursue in the present.[29]

When we relate to reified expressions, there is always a practically significant sense in which the object's power eludes our grasp. Whether an artwork, memorial or ancestral land, the spirit of the object is not tied to and exhausted by what we now desire or pursue, or by what we desired or pursued in the past, or by what we might desire or pursue in the future. The object itself demands a particular response from us, it calls for an action not chosen or affirmed but given to us from without, by an actual expression of spirit. We might disagree about what is demanded, for our interpretations of the expression might differ. So, whilst our relation to reified expressions is passive in one sense, it is the object's purpose that matters, not ours, it is active in another, for in meeting the object we must strive to understand its purpose. Despite this active capacity, it is still the case that what we think, feel, say or do is structured by an object that we meet in an already-existing world, that is, a world that does not revolve about us but rather guides or directs us.

We must draw attention to one way in which we are world-guided, and link it to the attitude of care discussed above. Reified expressions are non-substitutable; we meet them as particulars. When visiting ancestral land, it is necessary that you travel to a particular place, not another part of the country. If you go to the theatre to see *Antigone*, it will not do if another play is performed. To honour war heroes, you must visit their memorial, not some unrelated party's. These particular objects, as embodiments of spirit, are essential. This is not necessary with reified instruments, for they are substitutable. It does not matter which coin is in my wallet or knife is in my hand, only that it has exchange-value or can cut my sandwich. This substitutability means that I can replace them with alternatives if doing so is convenient or efficient. With reified expressions, substitution is not an option. When relating to them, it is always a particular, unique object that matters: this artwork, this memorial, this land is irreplaceable.

Because all reified expressions exist as non-substitutable particulars, if we think that the spirit that is embodied in an object is significant, we must comport ourselves towards it in a particular way. Whatever other feelings, emotions, beliefs, and so on are demanded by the object, internal to the logic of all relations to reified expressions is concern for their continued existence. This caring is internal to the logic of the relation because if the object is destroyed or dissolves through neglect, the spirit that inhabits its structure will go with it. Whilst the spontaneity internal to consumption entails acting how and when we please, indifferent to the world's fate, it is only by our caring for objects (DA2), materially and spiritually, that we can secure the scene, the stage through and in which something meaningful can express itself (DA1). With reified expressions, we do not lord over things, we humble ourselves before them, devote ourselves primarily to understanding what is expressed by and disclosed in them, and embrace and thereby let ourselves be guided by their independent power over the present.

Preservation and Access

The structure of the Hohfeldian incidents needed (DA3) for reified expressions differs from those needed for instrumental relations. With the latter, we started with the liberties that we need to facilitate the goods they make possible, then moving to claims, powers and immunities. With reified expressions, the liberty is shifted down the list, and we begin not with a claim but with a duty. The reason for this change, we shall see, is the displacement of the self that is constitutive of the relation to objects as reified expressions.

The concrete form of the duty depends on the concrete form of the reification. The particular shape the duty takes depends on whether the object is a painting, burial ground, statue, and so on. That said, the duty will always have the following general structure:

I. A duty to preserve the concrete form of an object that embodies concrete expressive significance, i.e., which reifies particular desires, beliefs, emotions, etc.

This duty distinguishes reified expressions from consumer relations. The latter is constituted by actions that negate the material or spiritual form of an object, whilst the former is constituted by its preservation. Only by preserving its form can the significance embodied in an object express itself. Consumption and preservation are logically incompatible. And whilst this duty resembles the reified liberty and claim in chapter 6, this is illusory. To see this, let us turn from the attitude constitutive of reified expressions, care, to its basic category or concept: directness.

With reified instruments, the duty not to alter the concrete form of an object prohibits words and deeds that affect the object's utility, that is, its capacity to mediate the fulfillment of desires and ends. The duty in (I) differs in its content. Relations to reified expressions are only possible absent the functional, utilitarian value that we attach to instruments, consumable and reified. In adopting a caring attitude towards an object, this may serve instrumental functions, but we fail to care for it in the required way if we apply instrumental concepts and categories. War memorials can enable a sense of community, reading Greek tragedies can facilitate catharsis, and protecting communal land can lessen the rootlessness that often blights modern life. Facilitating these ends can even be the purpose of those who create, commission or concern themselves with preserving these objects.[30] But if we approach memorials, plays and ancestral land for these reasons, we do not, since we cannot, meet them as embodiments of spirit. We only honour heroes if our relation to the memorial is guided by recognition of their greatness, expressed by the statue, not by the fact that it improves cohesion; we only appreciate an artwork if our response to it is governed by the qualities inhabiting its structure, instead of its healing potential; and we disrespect 'the deceased' and fail to act with 'respectful solicitude' if we treat their remains as objects of use.[31] To employ instrumental concepts or categories, in which we treat an object's function as lying in 'something other than' its expressive significance,[32] in its capacity to realise an external good, is to fail to act with honour, appreciation or respect. For instead of humbling ourselves before and being-guided by what is disclosed through and in the object itself, we elevate our present or future selves and subordinate the object to this self's desires or ends.

This self-displacement is reflected in the duty (I). Whilst the right necessary to enable reified instruments is formulated as a claim, the right in (I) is a duty. Sure, we must specify its content, and this content will be fixed in part by the nature of the expression: whether it is a painting or a play, a burial ground or a home, a memorial or a monument. Generally, however, each of us will have a negative duty not to alter the object's concrete form. In practice, the duty will take diverse forms, depending on the object's material or spiritual qualities, or both. Familiar laws of the first kind are those that prohibit malicious damage to property and remedies in criminal and private law against those who breach it. As for the second, one function that can be served by copyright law is to protect the spirit of an artwork from being degraded by imitations and copies. And laws that protect both matter and spirit include regulations that direct or constrain the architecture and construction of buildings. It is an open question, though, as to who must have the more concrete, positive duty of care: who must be tasked with restoring the fading painting, who must attend to the garden in the burial grounds, or who must keep the memorial free from bird droppings?[33] The answers to these questions turn on ethical matters external to the logic of the relation, meaning that they are political in nature and so must be settled through ordinary processes. At the formal level, though, we can state the direction of this positive duty, which is the same no matter its concrete content. Instead of persons having a claim against others, like with instruments, here the duty is owed to the object: to restore its colours, tend to its surrounds, make it clean again. As odd as it might sound to our disenchanted ears, because the duty (I) is owed to the object itself, it is the artwork, land or memorial that is vested with a claim.

We have journeyed far from the erotic and indifferent attitudes that form consumer relations, and the caution and self-control of reified instruments, but to say that these attitudes conflict with reified expressions is not to say that we cannot derive any immediate or mediated benefit from an artwork, land or memorial. It means that whatever present or future benefits we may obtain, they cannot be at the expense of our duty to preserve the scene, the stage of the object. The conceptual space for immediate benefit is well put by Adorno:

> No moral terrorism can control the fact that the face the work of art turns towards the viewer gives him pleasure . . . But consumption, and with it complicity in the bad sense, are not smuggled in on the side through the primacy of the aesthetic as an object of pure construction. For while the moment of pleasure always recurs in the work's effect even if it has been extirpated from it, the principle that governs autonomous works of art is not effect but their inherent structure. They are knowledge in the form of a nonconceptual object. In this lies their dignity.[34]

Writing about the third way of relating to reified expressions, that is, containing possibilities for the future, he says: 'As pure artifacts, products, works of art, even literary ones, are instructions for the praxis they refrain from: the production of life lived as it ought to be.' For this reason, whilst the inherent 'dignity' of the artwork precludes it from being used, for example, as a mere means to pursue some 'real or ostensible progressive politics', we can still be moved by the vision that it expresses to act in some or other way.[35] Whilst these remarks concern artworks, they apply to objects like memorials and ancestral land. If goods external to them can be realised consistently with our caring for their spirit, this is permissible.[36]

Grasping this possibility reveals the second Hohfeldian incident that is necessary for reified expressions. It is not just permissible to experience these goods, in one sense this is required. As objects that have in their internal structures expressive significance, facilitating these experiences is their purpose. If the artwork does not inspire, if the land does not induce respect, if the statue is an embarrassment, it does not live up to its own internal standard. To fulfil its purpose, the object must be experienced: seen, heard, felt, tasted or touched. As Scruton puts it: 'The earth is not just a heap of objects; it has its own subjectivity, and it achieves this subjectivity in me.'[37] Therefore, to enable this experience, the following right is necessary:

> II. A liberty to access an object, for the sake of relating to it in a way that actualises a good that is constituted through and in this relation.

For each expression, there must be someone to see, hear, and so on, what is expressed by the object and thereby interpret its meaning. Beauty, respect and honour are all made possible through and in our meeting the artwork, land and memorial. Spectatorship is necessary. To facilitate the goods made real in these objects, we may not allocate rights in a manner that precludes access by those whom we would like to benefit. For example, it is not permissible to grant control of a memorial to one person or group to the exclusion of others, we must not censor artworks, and trespass laws must be formulated in ways that access to ancestral land is not wholly foreclosed. Some access limits, though, are necessary. Whilst a liberty (II) to access the object is essential, it is subordinate to the duty (I). It is a conditional exemption since access must not frustrate the preservation of the object's concrete form. The duty has priority since without the memorial there can be no honour, without the artwork there can be no appreciation, without the land there can be no pilgrimage. Nietzsche forthrightly explains: 'The spectator without a spectacle is a nonsense.'[38]

For Marx, contrarily, these limits and duties are anathema. Of course, he knows that we often experience objects in this way. That is his point: what we have to do is break the chains that bind us. Sometimes, to escape externally imposed limits and imagined duties, a revolution in spirit, a change in ideas or beliefs, will be enough. Criticism, for example, can strip a law of its authority and therefore can imperil the law's existence as such. Spirit, though, is often tied more deeply to objects, such that reified expressions will exert power over the present for so long as they exist in their concrete form. This can happen with statues – of Cecil John Rhodes, Confederate generals, slave traders – that we cannot detach from their pasts. Here, when the object is too deeply laden with meaning, when the spirit inhabiting its structure appears to be inseparable from its concrete embodiment, we must tear it down, move it, reconstitute its setting. It is only by altering its form, sometimes materially but always spiritually, that we will be free from its external power.

This antagonistic attitude towards the past is antithetical to the careful, conservative one that is constitutive of reified expressions. This difference is reflected in the power that is necessary to enable them. For example, apart from Marx's criticism of markets, he spent time attacking norms of inheritance.[39] Advocates of reified expressions will ally with Marx in opposing market power. Whatever else one believes about all their talk of the 'culture industry', Adorno and Horkheimer are right that when we treat an artwork instrumentally, we risk reducing it to a mere commodity. Advocates of reified expressions who recognise this, though, will have less difficulty with their intergenerational transfer.[40] For example, according to Benjamin:

> inheritance is the soundest way of acquiring a collection. For a collector's attitude towards his possessions stems from his feeling of responsibility towards his property. Thus it is, in the highest sense, the attitude of an heir, and the most distinguished trait of a collection will always be its transmissibility.[41]

Benjamin's point is that the transfer of rights in reified expressions, for him books, must function to preserve them. He thinks that this is best done by vesting rights in individuals, rather than by promoting 'public collections',[42] but this is a contingent claim and since what matters is preservation of the object, we must be open to different ways in which this can be done.

Just as the duty to preserve has logical priority over the right of access, so the power to alter rights must be exercised for the sake of, or at least it must always be consistent with, the duty to preserve and promote access:

III. A power to alter the duty in (I) or the liberty in (II), provided doing so would not frustrate the duty in (I) or the exercise of the liberty in (II).

Often, which form of alteration is appropriate will depend on the good in question. If the good is the intergenerational bond and respect facilitated through access to land, familial inheritance may be suitable. If it is the honour embodied in and expressed through memorials, alterations placing them in public trust may be appropriate. If the good is an artwork, like a painting, transferring it to a museum may be a good fit. So, typical alterations of rights that would be consistent with the power (III) are those facilitated by bequests to children or museums, donations, or non-reciprocal gift-giving. In each case, the institutions – family, public trust, museum – exist, or at least ought to do so, for the sake of preserving reified expressions and facilitating access.

The final necessary Hohfeldian incident is an immunity:

IV. An immunity against others altering the content of (I), (II) or (III).

Immunities serve a protective function against authority by limiting the power of others to alter rights. So, if we want to protect the goods constituted through and in reified expressions, then we must disable others from altering the rights required to realise them. South Africa's Constitution offers examples of how this may be done. It is one function of the right to have the environment 'protected, for the benefit of present and future generations'.[43] This purpose is also facilitated by the right to security of tenure in land for persons who suffered from past racially discriminatory laws.[44] And it informs the idea that since a home is more than just a shelter from the elements, it should be protected by judicial oversight from arbitrary loss.[45] So, to facilitate goods like natural beauty, intergenerational ties and belonging, we have to allocate property rights consistently with the constitutive structure of reified expressions. This requires protecting (IV) the rights (I, II, III) of people striving to realise these goods.

Having displaced or decentred ourselves, thereby letting the world disclose itself, we are not free to alter property for the sake of present or future concerns. For the reified expression is not formed by various ways of 'in-order-to'. It possesses its own dignity (GP5), it exists as the scene, the stage, of its own fate. Having unpacked this relation, we see yet again the need for choice and sacrifice, not just between our model philosophers' privileged goods, but also between these and various aesthetic, interpersonal and intergenerational goods. The formal rights articulated in this section are incompatible with the rights necessary for life and expression: the duty to preserve (I) is incompatible with the consumer liberty necessary to make Locke and Marx's goods real. The liberty (II) and power (III) are also incompatible with Hegelian and Hayekian markets, as well as Benthamite security, for they preclude the mediated use essential to these goods. And, lastly, the immunity (IV) is incompatible with both consumables and reified instruments, because all reified expressions are non-instrumental in nature.

THE SOUL OF THE WORLD

In this section, we describe the relation of living spirit. The good that is realised through and in this relation is possibility. Like reified expressions, it is non-instrumental. The two relations are distinguished by their modes of existence and attitudes. Reified expressions, like all consumables and reified instruments, always exist in the mode of actuality, which is to say, they always have a concrete form: food, commodity, house, artwork, memorial, and so on. Living spirit, contrarily, exists in the mode of potentiality, meaning it never has a concrete form. And whereas reified expressions are constituted by an attitude of care, living spirit is formed in an attitude of openness. To reveal and clarify the nature of living spirit as a relation to objects, in this section we consider perhaps its most prophetic advocate: Martin Buber.

Openness

'To man the world is twofold', Buber starts his delightful *I and Thou*, 'in accordance with his twofold attitude'. Each attitude, he says, partly constitutes a relation to other people and objects. The relations 'do not describe something that might exist independently of them', but rather they bring a 'world' into 'existence', in which the person holding the attitude 'takes his stand'.[46] The two basic relations that constitute the worlds of man are 'I-It' and 'I-Thou'. The first includes the relations we described in chapter 6 and reified expressions: 'I perceive something. I am sensible of something. I imagine something. I will something. I feel something. I think something.'[47] The experiences can extend to relations to persons and objects. If somebody relates to another person or an object in this way, his 'experiences . . . present him . . . with a world composed of *It* and *He* and *She* and *It* again'.[48] Whilst the I-It relation is often instrumental,[49] it is not always so, for this relation includes reified expressions. To see this, let us start to contrast the relation of I-It with the relation of I-Thou.

Buber: 'The life of human beings is not passed in the sphere of [I-It] alone', since 'the realm of *Thou* has a different basis'. As explained, one way in which it differs is that the relation is not instrumental in nature. What is important to understand is why it cannot be instrumental. 'When *Thou* is spoken', he says, 'the speaker has no thing for his object . . . he has indeed nothing. But he takes his stand in relation'.[50] We do not meet an object as a means to an end, rather we meet it directly, for the purpose of the meeting is constituted through and in the relation itself:

> The relation to the *Thou* is direct. No system of ideas, no foreknowledge, and no fancy intervene between *I* and *Thou*. The memory itself is transformed, as it plunges out of its isolation into the unity of the whole. No aim, no lust, no anticipation intervene between *I* and *Thou*. Desire itself is transformed as it plunges out of its dream into the appearance. Every means is an obstacle. Only when every means has collapsed does the meeting come about.[51]

In this relation, objects are not defined by their biological material or physical laws, which can be classified and located within the natural world.[52] Such knowledge about an object, he says, using a tree as an example, can be retained when relating to objects, but in 'considering the tree',[53] we can relate to it 'in a different way'.[54] To reveal the nature of this difference, let us contrast the I-Thou relation, which I am referring to as living spirit, with the relation to objects that I have been calling reified expressions.

Like reified expressions, relations to objects as living spirit are non-instrumental. Rather than having their purpose given to them, we meet these objects as bearers of spirit. Unlike relations to artworks, memorials, and so on, however, when we relate to objects as living spirit, the world is without all 'particulars'.[55] This is the meaning of the line quoted: 'When *Thou* is spoken, the speaker has no thing for his object . . . he has indeed nothing.'[56] As we saw above, reified expressions always exist as non-substitutable particulars: each has a concrete form through and in which its meaning is articulated. This is never so with the objects of living spirit, for lacking concrete 'qualities',[57] they are without limit: '*Thou* has no bounds.'[58] Further, unlike reified expressions, the spirit that inhabits the structures of its objects is not independent of, isolated from,[59] persons. For objects to be possessed with living spirit, they must rather stand in a 'mutual' relation with subjects,[60] they must be equal 'partners',[61] engaged in a 'conversation . . . without words'.[62]

Apart from Buber's unfamiliar idiom, it is unclear how all that has been said can be true. How can spirit – purpose, meaning – inhabit an object's structure in a way that it lacks instrumentality, particularity and limit, whilst also depending for its existence as spirit on its mutual relation with persons? To clarify things, we have to identify a (non-concrete) quality that objects and subjects possess, and so makes them alike. Let us start by distinguishing three ways in which objects and subjects can be alike.

We have come across the first and second of these ways, for they belong to Hegel and Marx. Hegel sees purpose in all, for all that exists develops towards its own essential end. This purpose first takes proto- or petrified forms, moving according to the natural laws embodied in inorganic and organic objects. In time, however, Hegelian spirit assumes rational form in the conflict that constitutes civil society and between this social form and the family form. When we understand the necessity of conflict, Hegel tells us, we come to see objects as the products of the purposive work of persons, living and dead. When objects are permeated by agency in this way, the world formed in our self-image, it is intelligible to say objects are like subjects. Whilst all objects stand apart from and can frustrate us, they exist as our creations, as reified instruments or expressions. When object-relations take this form, they are like subjects, since in constituting them, we define them, and in this rational way they become united with us. For Marx, this rational reconciliation is deficient. When the world exists as obstacle and reification, we lack unity. Luckily, Marx says, capitalism broke nature's chains: objects need not stand against us as obstacles or reifications. If we use the power available to us, we can close the gap between man and world. Man's capacity to control nature means he can use it freely. The immediacy of this relation between subject and object is the key to understanding how they are alike. If we take collective control of the world, it will not do justice to our relations to describe objects either as obstacles or as mere instruments. Our power establishes an intimacy neglected by these terms. With 'natural material transformed into organs of the human will over nature, or of human participation in nature',[63] objects will be experienced as extensions of our willing selves: consumables. Man being root and lord of all, it is intelligible to collapse, at least partially, the distinction between subject and object.

For Marx, the collapse seems to be necessarily partial: whilst technological development and social organisation narrow the gap between man and nature, it cannot obliterate it, for whilst we are lords, rooted in nature we are constitutionally limited.[64] In directly confronting this limitation, Buber distinguishes himself from Hegel and Marx, articulating a third way in which objects are like subjects, that is, when both exist in the relation of living spirit. Like Hegel but unlike Marx, Buber reconciles himself with the fact that a divide exists between subject and object.[65] But like Marx and unlike Hegel, rather than as obstacles or instruments, he sees in the world a bounty of opportunities. Objects can limit the will, but they never exist as crosses to bear. Nature is not our captor nor an unreliable neighbour. Rather, it is a partner with a shared non-concrete quality: this quality is that neither subject nor object has essential functions.

Living spirit is incompatible with all relations in which concepts like 'causality', 'teleology', 'process' and 'growth' are constitutive parts,[66] that is to say, both the instrumental rationality of men like Bentham, Locke and Hayek, as well as the 'organic' model of the self that informs the models of Hegel and Marx.[67] So, whereas Marx criticises instilling objects with subjectivity, not objectification itself, Buber's claim is that all objectification is 'not valid for spirit',[68] for neither man nor world are essentially 'functional' in nature.[69] As regards man, our willing faculty vests us with a freedom to choose between diverse (GP1, GP4) forms of life, so we are not determined, fated through an unfolding of either natural or normative laws, to live in a prescribed way. What about objects? From one perspective, they are so determined, for they follow natural causal laws, and indeed we can relate to objects in ways that take advantage of this fact, which allow us to use them to benefit ourselves.[70] What Buber explains, though, is that we do not always have to relate to objects in this way. We can see them in a different 'light',[71] adopting another attitude towards them. Instead of the erotic and indifferent attitudes that are constitutive of the consumer relation, or the controlling and cautious ones that define reified instruments, or the caring disposition that characterises reified expressions, we can relate to objects as a 'whirlpool' of possibility.[72] In this form of being, where our 'effective power streams out',[73] the world's objects are always waiting to be constituted in the concrete forms we choose. This latent possibility embodied in the world, the fact that objects are not formed or destined to be formed for any given end, as a consumable or a reification of either form, but rather await the effective power of our freely willed actions, is the constitutive non-concrete quality shared by subjects and objects.[74]

For object-relations to be characterised by living spirit, we must treat ourselves and world as undetermined in this way, as 'embodied possibility'.[75] Therefore, by living spirit Buber does not mean that objects have transcendent or immanent personalities. Buberian objects do not have any original desire or end, as Charles Taylor distinguishes them from derivative ones,[76] which strive by themselves to become actual. Buber is not a mystic. He does not dispute formal and empirical knowledge. He just points to their limitations.[77] Nor does he call for an 'absurd' return to the pre-modern ontic logos,[78] a world without instruments and filled with its own and inherent particular meanings, that preceded modernity's disenchantment of the world. His anti-teleological attitude precludes this interpretation. Rather, he can talk of objects as subjects, about world being 'living personality',[79] because it is intelligible to see objects as embodied possibility. The reason why is that the constitution of man as a possibility-bearing being is dependent on him relating to objects as equally bearing this possibility, and because for an object to exist as embodied possibility, it is necessary that we treat it as such. Before we articulate this admittedly difficult concept of mutual dependence in formal terms, let us continue the contrast with Hegel and Marx.

Like Hegel and Marx, Buber sees unity as ultimately good (GP5). His unity, however, is not formed instrumentally, through consumption (Marx) or in conflict (Hegel).[80] Rather, unity comes into being directly, through and in the relation of living spirit. For this to happen, we must adopt a particular attitude: openness. Whenever we act, we face and constitute limits. Not just natural objects, but consumables, reified instruments and expressions necessarily limit the will. We can alter their concrete functions, but the presence of some or other function is permanent. This fact is a 'melancholy of our fate'.[81] It means that we have a willing faculty, we know it,[82] but cannot actualise it fully. There is no 'solution' to the 'riddle' of history.[83] The worlds of I-Thou and I-It are 'irreconcilable',[84] their constitutive relation is one of 'essential and indissoluble antinomy'.[85] Despite this constitutive feature of our reality, we need not despair, since there is more than one way to relate to objects. We can relate to them as functional particulars. If we do, however, they will always exist apart from us as dead matter potentially or actually opposed to our willing self. We can escape this 'alienation',[86] though, if we relate to objects as beings equally vested with a quality that is possessed by man. We must see that world like man *is* possibility. We must realise that objects are given to us to fashion however we will. They are 'gifts',[87] which we must receive with 'grace' and thanks,[88] that out of nowhere,[89] and by no right at all,[90] we have been given the material through and in which we can externalise our willing selves.[91]

Formally put, objects are constituted by radical indeterminacy, in the sense that we can shape them into whatever concrete forms we choose or affirm. Objects are given to us unconditionally, not in exchange for something or with strings attached. What we do with them, the concrete form any object takes in our hands, is essentially up to us. Thus, any object's function in any moment is contingent, or rather it is contingent if two conditions are satisfied. First, we must recognise or 'believe' in reality's radical indeterminacy.[92] Second, we must be open to – 'love',[93] embrace – the indeterminacy and therefore diversity of concrete forms that can be given to the objects that exist in, and can be constituted by the persons who create and live in, this world.[94] Whilst spirit is always embodied in particular matter, it is never defined by any particular end, for spirit exists in or inhabits the structure of the world itself. It makes possible all the concrete forms described thus far. As Scruton puts it, it is 'the moment of pure intersubjectivity, in which nothing concrete appears, but in which everything hangs on the here and now'.[95] Formally put, lacking functional and therefore concrete 'content',[96] its mode of existence is potentiality.

With possibility's mode of existence as potentiality revealed, we can state more formally the idea that I-Thou exists as mutual relation, in which subject and object depend on each other to be their true or real selves. To exist as embodied possibility, man is dependent on world, subject on object,[97] since without its material we cannot externalise our wills. We would always be without the actuality internal to the logic of possibility. Actuality is a logical correlate of, it is entailed by, possibility because internal to it is the potential for diverse forms to be made actual through word or deed. This reveals the dependence of man on world. Its objects, in turn, depend on subjects to be embodied possibility, because for possibility to become real the movement from potentiality to actuality must be effected through choice. Absent choice, objects follow their own causal laws towards the ends to which they were determined from the start. If choice is not present, when the movement from potentiality to actuality unfolds by itself, what exists is not possibility but rather 'necessity'.[98] Like actuality, choice is a logical correlate of, it is entailed by, possibility.

Because actuality is internal to the logic of possibility, the existence of man as a possibility-bearing being depends on the existence of world, and since choice is also internal to possibility, the existence of world as embodied possibility depends on the existence of man, vested as he is with a capacity to choose. In Buber's idiom, together these facts mean: 'You need God, in order to be – and God needs you, for the very meaning of your life.'[99]

Fallen and Falling, Forever

When possibility is valued as a form of being (DA1), with living spirit understood as the way of relating to objects that actualises it (DA2), it follows that property rights must be allocated in certain ways (DA3). Two Hohfeldian incidents, a liberty and a duty, are necessary to facilitate this relation and actualise this form.

With Buber's living spirit, we are not limited when allocating property in the ways that Marx and Hegel are limited. Living spirit privileges unity (DA1), but this unity is not formed through consumption or conflict – rather by treating all that exists as embodied possibility. So, instead of treating objects as being formed for particular purposes, we must treat them as always-waiting to be formed by our chosen, effective actions. If we follow Buber, we will not allocate rights to use objects for the sake of satisfying or realising immediately or mediately desires or ends, nor will we create a duty to preserve objects. We must be free to actualise whatever relation and form we please. We must be free to consume objects, use them as tools, create art and discover new ways of relating to or with each other or the world – free to identify forms not previously imagined and not before actualised. This total lack of limit on possible relational forms, this constitutively open possibility of man and world, defines relations to objects as living spirit.

Before articulating this vision in Hohfeldian terms, it is worth noting how easy it would be to move from living spirit as a mutual relation to a model where objects do not depend on relations with subjects. On this model, objects are constituted by potentiality but 'unfold' into actuality in their own way and time, not in Hegel's petrified form but fully so. From this, it is a small step to say that this process not only matters for its own sake (GP3), but that the source of the goodness of the unfolding of the being of an object lies in itself (GP5). And we can imagine someone who has taken these steps then taking a third – judging, like the South African environmental lawyer Cormac Cullinan, that when we do intervene in this process and thereby destabilise the 'life force that flows through us all and drives the [sacred] evolutionary process' that 'defines' all,[100] when we fail to act in a 'benign or mutually enhancing' and 'common' way when relating to objects,[101] and thereby frustrate the 'glorious expression'[102] of its 'differentiated', 'self-ordering', 'dynamic' and 'balanced' 'whole',[103] we interfere with the harmony, the 'cyclical ebb and flow of energy or spirit',[104] of this 'greater unfolding reality' (GP5).[105] If we took these steps, we would move from a vision that, like Hegel, Marx and Buber, sees man as being bound up with the good, to one that envisions us, whenever we do not subject ourselves (AS3)[106] to the 'primary' (AS2) authority of nature's unfolding reality (AS1),[107] as the root of all evil.

Even if we do not adopt this misanthropic vision of 'Gaia',[108] which rather than lifting nature up (GP5), humiliates humanity, brings us low so that we fit within a deeper underlying order, and just take the first two steps by decentering ourselves when evaluating what is good,[109] we will see why theory must start, as I said in chapter 1, by asking about forms of being, not experiences. To facilitate the good of untouched nature (GP3, GP5), this requires property being allocated to limit actions that interrupt its processes. Not nature reserves, but spaces (DA1) closed-off (DA2) from man, protected areas we have no right (DA3) to access or impact at all.

With living spirit, contrarily, rather than excluding humanity from nature, each person must be given free rein:

I. A liberty to relate to objects in whatever way is judged worthwhile.

This right contemplates a liberty not just to hunt, fish, and so on, at different times of the day. It includes a liberty to use instruments, create art and build homes, as well as to act in ways necessary to form families, associations, teams or protected areas, or to enter markets, *poleis*, offices or assemblies. It contemplates our being free to form relations to and with objects how we like or when we like. In Hohfeldian terms, it is an unconditional discretion. We see again how models which privilege (AS2) different forms (AS1) require incompatible rights (AS3). Facilitating one relation through the necessary allocation of rights excludes (GP4) relations that require incompatible ones, which in turn frustrates forms we think good (GP3, GP5).

It will suffice here to draw attention to one such logical conflict. It is between this discretion, wholly unconditioned and therefore open to exercise by any person at any time, and the security that sits in the heart of Bentham's property theory. Buber writes:

> The prophets of Israel have never announced a God upon whom their hearers' striving for security reckoned. They have always aimed to shatter all security and to proclaim in the opened abyss of the final insecurity the unwished-for God who demands that His human creatures become real, they become human, and confounds all who imagine that they can take refuge in the certainty that the temple of God is in their midst.[110]

Through and in its constitutive attitude of openness, by 'shattering [all] security',[111] the relation of living spirit renders unthinkable the closed-off society demanded by Bentham.

Let us end this chapter by pointing to another conflict. It is also logical, but the conflict is not with another good; rather, it is internal to the relation of living spirit. The conflict is between the discretion (I) and a duty that is also required by this relation. To relate to an object as living spirit is to meet it as embodied possibility. We have seen, though, that internal to possibility's logic is choice and actuality. Only if any situation is constituted by these qualities can possibility exist: hence the discretion (I). The exercise of this right, however, conflicts with possibility's open attitude. All words or deeds that strive to satisfy desires and realise ends will necessarily limit, for a while at least, the possibilities of the actor and the objects through and in which she can externalise her will. For example, in reaching out for an object as food, she becomes a consumer and the object a consumable and thereby she frustrates living spirit.[112] Rather than being open to the possible, in choosing or acting, she limits what is and what can be. This means that living spirit also calls for inaction, a stilling of desire and purpose, or at least a refusal to act on or a resistance to acting on, desires and purposes.[113]

Formally put, we have the following Hohfeldian duty:

II. A duty not to exercise the liberty in (I).

The relation of living spirit, therefore, is structured by internal contradiction. Its nature precludes it from being fully actualised. This is reflected in (I) and (II). Whereas (I) provides us a discretion, (II) prohibits its exercise.

Despite this conflict, living spirit can function as a regulative ideal. Living spirit is impossible to realise fully, but we could always strive towards it. We could, as Roger Scruton, whose work is influenced by Buber, explains, adopt certain ritualistic practices like those familiar in religion.[114] Or as Buber writes, we could cultivate an open attitude in the 'field of work or field of battle'.[115] Or we could either make or identify an image or an object,[116] through and in which we can 'look at Him'.[117] Or we could build places 'where the faithful can encounter God',[118] become 'united' with him,[119] that is, can freely (I) gather in contemplation or meditation or prayer,[120] for the sake of performing our duty (II) to be open to the world.

Such places would be open to all, for as sites of possibility they cannot make any distinctions or allow any exclusions. All must have a 'license to dwell' within them.[121] Buber articulates their function and necessity as follows:

> Only now can man, confident in his soul, build again and again, in a special conception of space, dwellings for God and dwellings for men, and fill swaying time with new hymns and songs, and shape the very community of men . . . But . . . if a culture ceases to be centred in the living and continually renewed relational event, then it hardens into the world of *It* . . .[122]

Even after building these places, Scruton explains, possibility can only be revealed through and in a lack of content, for 'he is also hidden there, concealed in the inner sanctum, or in rituals . . . The temple reveals God by concealing him'.[123] Since the good of possibility exists in the mode of potentiality, Buber tells us, its presence in the world, though real, lacks a concrete form: 'Man receives, and he receives not a specific "content" but a Presence, a Presence as power.'[124] Whilst for man particularity is all-pervasive, these places offer us structures in which we can meet what Scruton calls the 'soul of the world' (GP5).[125]

If we try to obtain from them 'more than' this,[126] though, we will find ourselves fallen into a world of concrete functions, where these places and images exist not as meeting sites or vantage points, but as reifications – idols – that frustrate the realisation of living spirit. Even when rightly entered, though, the meeting is temporary. Eventually, we must leave spirit's dwelling and return to the world of things. As embodied beings, we 'must continually' choose or act,[127] even if only to eat and drink. So, living spirit is perpetually transformed through words and deeds. What first exists as potential is always made actual through and in particular relations. In striving to satisfy desires or realise ends, we construct a world of 'hardened' objects,[128] concrete forms, defined by diminished possibility.[129] When we sacrifice 'endless possibility' on 'the alter of form',[130] Buber tells us, we inescapably move from the world of I-Thou to the world of I-It.

The world of I-It need not weigh on us like a nightmare, for it is not 'evil',[131] but it is a fallen state, 'sunk' in the world of things.[132] We constitute living spirit, but through our actions we dim its 'flame',[133] thereby frustrating what would be ultimately good: the penetration of all existence with living spirit's 'blaze'.[134] Except fleetingly, we cannot live in the whirlpool of possibility. By 'nature' compelled to act,[135] forced to live in some or other way, all are eventually drawn under, into the world of actuality. And since words or deeds cannot be undone, and roads not taken are forever closed, we are always-already trapped in and by the past. There is no way, on this model of the person, to escape this truth, nor our role in violating what is ultimately (GP5) good (AS1). We are all 'guilt[y]',[136] even those who privilege (AS2) possibility. Born to live in contradiction (AS3), compelled to choose and act and thus transform potentiality into actuality, is our original 'sin'.[137] Fallen and falling, forever – our melancholic fate.

NOTES

1. Theodor Adorno, *Minima Moralia: Reflections from Damaged Life* (tr. EFN Jephcott, 2005) 166. This chapter would not exist were it not for the many theoretical insights of, and countless conversations with, Rachel Robinson.
2. The concept of art described here is of the autonomous, kind, in which the 'work concept' is central (Roger Scruton, *Understanding Music: Philosophy and Interpretation* (2016) 8–12). Cf. Gene Ray, 'Dialectical Realism and Radical Commitments: Brecht and Adorno on Representing Capitalism' *Historical Materialism 18* (2010) 3–24, 12.
3. UT 271–79.
4. Roger Scruton, *The Soul of the World* (2014) 130–36 and Gregory Alexander, *Property and Human Flourishing* (2018) 145–47 and 236–58.
5. For defences of this function, see Theodor Adorno, *Notes to Literature* (combined ed., ed. Rolf Tiedemann, tr. Shierry Weber Nicholson, 2019) 348–63 and Louis Althusser, *For Marx* (tr. B. Brewster, 2005) 131–51.
6. Scruton (n 2) 78.
7. UT 272.
8. Martin Heidegger, *Being and Time* (tr. J. Macquarrie and E. Robinson, 1962) 388–89.
9. Scruton (n 2) 94.
10. Isaiah Berlin, *Liberty* (ed. Henry Hardy, 2002) 275.
11. Scruton (n 2) 22.
12. Ibid., 7. In Scruton (n 4) 145, he describes musical movement as 'an expression of intention', but 'not necessarily a private intention of the composer's'.
13. Roland Barthes, 'The Death of the Author' in *Image, Music, Text* (tr. Stephen Heath 1977) 142–48 and Michel Foucault, 'What is an Author?' in *Aesthetics, Method, and Epistemology, Volume 2* (ed. James D. Faubion, tr. Josué V. Harari, 1998) 205–22.

14. Scruton (n 2) 7.

15. Hannah Arendt, *The Human Condition* (2ed, 1998) 168–69.

16. Hannah Arendt, *Between Past and Future: Eight Exercises in Political Thought* (2006) 197–226.

17. On art as a form of play that enables people to care for, not control, the external world, see PE 177–82.

18. Scruton (n 2) 49–56.

19. Walter Benjamin, *Illuminations* (ed. Hannah Arendt, tr. Harry Zohn, 1969) 60.

20. Heidegger (n 8) 186, 219–24 and 264.

21. Ibid., 381.

22. Ibid., 440.

23. Ibid., 444–49.

24. Jean Baudrillard, *The System of Objects* (tr. James Benedict, 2005) 96–97.

25. Ibid., 105.

26. István Mészáros, *Marx's Theory of Alienation* (4ed, 1975) 209.

27. Adorno (n 1) 70.

28. EPR § 64R.

29. Jean Baudrillard, *The Consumer Society: Myths and Structures* (tr. Chris Turner, 1998) 107.

30. On cultivating 'public emotions', see PE 257–313.

31. Heidegger (n 8) 282.

32. Baudrillard (n 31) 108.

33. Elizabeth Spelman, *Repair: The Impulse to Restore in a Fragile World* (2003).

34. Adorno (n 5) 361–62.

35. Ibid., 362–63. See also Herbert Marcuse, *Counter-Revolution and Revolt* (1972) 110–15.

36. Scruton (n 4) 137.

37. Roger Scruton, *The Face of God* (2012) 126.

38. Friedrich Nietzsche, *The Birth of Tragedy and Other Writings* (ed. R. Geuss and R. Speirs, 1999) 38.

39. CHPR 97–111.

40. Baudrillard (n 31) 100-102.

41. Benjamin (n 21) 66.

42. Ibid., 67.

43. Section 24(b) of the Constitution.

44. Section 25(6) of the Constitution.

45. *Port Elizabeth Municipality v Various Occupiers* 2005 (1) SA 217 (CC) para. 17, dealing with Section 26 of the Constitution.

46. IT 3–4.

47. IT 4.

48. IT 5. 'He' and 'She' designate interpersonal relations within the realm of I-It, for they refer to persons with particular and, thus, limited identities.

49. IT 7–8.

50. IT 4.
51. IT 11–12.
52. IT 7.
53. IT 7.
54. IT 8.
55. IT 29.
56. IT 4.
57. IT 17 and 30–31.
58. IT 4.
59. Whilst Buber criticises the idea that God, the eternal Thou, lacks 'independence', he means by this that God like every Thou is distinct from, is not absorbed by, persons. God, like you and me, 'exists independent of as well as related to the human subject' (EG 68).
60. IT 8.
61. IT 22.
62. IT 27. EG 37: 'I-Thou finds its highest intensity and transfiguration in religious reality, in which unlimited Being becomes, as absolute person, my partner.'
63. GFCPE 706.
64. CVIII 958–99.
65. As he explains in IT 18–22 and 24–28, the I-Thou relation can only exist because of this split.
66. IT 51–58.
67. IT 57.
68. IT 58.
69. IT 23 and 29.
70. IT 7–8, 31–34 and 38.
71. IT 8.
72. IT 9.
73. IT 10.
74. IT 26.
75. EG 112.
76. Charles Taylor, *Philosophical Papers: Volume 1, Human Agency and Language* (1985) 99.
77. It is in this sense that we must understand his talk of 'mystery' (IT 15, 39) and the idea that we 'live our lives inscrutably within the streaming mutual life of the universe' (IT 16).
78. IT 47–48.
79. EG 42. Whilst Buber is writing here of 'God', for him the Eternal Thou, which constitutes and permeates all reality, is God.
80. On contrast with Napoleonic consummation, see IT 67–69.
81. IT 16, 23 and 98.
82. This knowledge is not propositional, that is, know-that, but appears to be a form of knowledge by acquaintance (EG 24–26).
83. IT 111.
84. IT 96.

85. IT 95.
86. IT 58, 70–72, 100 and 119.
87. IT 89 and 116.
88. IT 7, 11, 53, 61, 76, 101 and 131.
89. EG 62: 'The Coming One came of his own will out of the mystery of his withdrawnness; we did not cause Him to come.'
90. IT 129–30.
91. IT 109–12.
92. IT 58–61.
93. IT 14–17, 45–46, 85, 94 98–99 103 and 108–09.
94. IT 76–78 and 99–101.
95. Scruton (n 4) 23.
96. IT 31.
97. IT 50–51.
98. IT 52–53.
99. IT 82. See also EG 50 and 63. If you struggle with a religious idiom: 'But when he, too, who abhors the name [God], and believes himself to be godless, gives his whole being to addressing the *Thou* of his life, as a *Thou* that cannot be limited by another, he addresses God.' (IT 76).
100. Cormac Cullinan, *Wild Law: A Manifesto for Earth Justice* (2ed, 2011) 30.
101. Ibid., 49 and 151–52.
102. Ibid., 72.
103. Ibid., 79–84 and 115–17.
104. Ibid., 116.
105. Ibid., 94.
106. For his views on property, see Ibid., 103, 106 and 138–45.
107. Ibid., 82, 100, 162 and 165–66. On nature's rights as 'trumps', see Ibid., 108–09.
108. Ibid., 159–60.
109. An example of this way of treating 'Gaia' is found in John Gray, *Endgames: Questions in Late Modern Political Thought* (1997) 161–70.
110. EG 61.
111. IT 34.
112. IT 16–18 and 61–65.
113. IT 100.
114. Scruton (n 4) 195–96.
115. EG 30–31.
116. IT 7–8.
117. EG 38.
118. Scruton (n 4) 123.
119. IT 114.
120. EG 109.
121. Scruton (n 4) 134.
122. IT 54.
123. Scruton (n 4) 123.

124. IT 110.
125. Scruton (n 4) 198.
126. EG 38.
127. IT 9, 17, 33, 38, 42, 98–99 and 112.
128. IT 40.
129. IT 13 and 39–43.
130. IT 10.
131. I-IT is evil if it 'overruns' man, 'robs him of the reality of his own *I*', foreclosing I-Thou's salvation (IT 46).
132. IT 47 and 50.
133. IT 83.
134. IT 40.
135. IT 17.
136. IT 38.
137. IT 38.

Chapter 8

The Tragedy of Goodness

In the introduction to part II, I said that this book could be understood as a sustained effort to try to persuade you to adopt a therapeutic attitude towards all prescriptive anthropology. By this, I meant that we should understand the problems that accompany the anthropological approach to property as pseudo-problems. They only appear to us as problems because we presume a need to construct models. But if there were no need, if we resisted the temptation to say what we in fact are, then the problems that follow in the wake of any interpretation of man would never arise. I also noted, though, that in philosophy matters are never so simple. For the solutions we imagine to old problems always generate or reveal new problems. The time has now come to confront the problem: tragedy.

NUSSBAUM: FINITUDE, NARROWNESS AND DILEMMA

Over several decades, Martha Nussbaum has written extensively, impressively and sensitively on tragedy. First articulated in detail in her magisterial book, *The Fragility of Goodness*, she situates tragedy in the heart of her ethics, politics, and legal and policy proposals. For this reason alone, it is sensible to devote some time to her ideas on the issue. But there is another more critical reason to begin with her, for the phenomenon of tragedy that arises in a strongly plural world is different to the tragedy that she explores. Whereas she has in mind an external conception of tragedy, SGP means that we require an internal one too. We need it not to replace her conception but because it is logically different, which difference has deep implications for property. So, the hope is that by first articulating the contours of her conception of tragedy, we might illuminate better the tragedy that is internal to a strongly plural theory of property.

Nussbaumian tragedy concerns circumstances that, whilst avoidable conceptually or technically, manifest in ways that stop people from living good lives. This tragedy concerns 'the essential nature of the human soul in its attempts to live well',[1] and the predicaments, 'the worst disasters in life',[2] that befall women or men, foreclosing or frustrating their attempts at living well. Her conception of tragedy is external, for it is contingent.[3] To reveal this, let us stipulate some sources and forms of foreclosure and frustration on Nussbaum's scheme of tragedy, then unpacking them by way of an exegetical overview of her work.

Nussbaum identifies three origins of this form of tragedy: finitude, narrowness and dilemma. Because we are embodied, *finite* beings, we are vulnerable to threats posed by others, physical or emotional, and natural threats, like illness and chance natural events. This finitude also manifests in our cognitive and emotional powers and activities. We are often blind to important facts about ourselves, others and the world, and we often fail to see clearly or at all important conceptual and moral truths. Moreover, when we make conceptual and moral claims, we often do so in one-sided ways, failing to consider other perspectives. When we suffer this *narrowness*, conflicts arise with the result that people will come to grief. Finally, we sometimes face apparent *dilemmas*, where a person is thought to have two or more duties, or many people have these duties, but the words or deeds required to satisfy each pull in different directions, rendering full performance impossible. When, because of our vulnerability and limits, someone is harmed, or our one-sided perspectives produce conflict, or our duties seem incompatible, there is tragedy. But none of this is necessary, Nussbaum says, as each source of loss is contingent. Yes, the 'world can intervene',[4] frustrating or foreclosing good, but this is not a constitutive part of our condition. Tragedy can 'come upon' us from 'outside'.[5] It destroys 'life, loved ones, freedom, nourishment, mobility, bodily integrity, citizenship, shelter'.[6] Life is plagued by 'rape, war and material deprivation'.[7] Outside of natural necessity or real luck, though, not choice that is disguised as such,[8] this is not our inevitable lot. Ultimately, these losses are due to bad institutions, bad people or bad ideas. This proposition is why her conception of tragedy is external in form, since it involves events that can be avoided, at least in theory. This external conception of tragedy informs all her work: political philosophy, ethics and that which is written 'with a view to shaping public policy'[9] and laws.[10] Let us begin with the first and third areas: political philosophy and policy or law.

The concept that structures these areas of her work is the 'capabilities approach'. In a Rawlsian spirit, she articulates political principles that she says must be adopted by 'all nations',[11] by 'the entire system of global justice'.[12] Nussbaum's theoretical ambition to design 'the basic structure of society',[13] is ultimately framed by this question: 'What is each person able to do and to be?'[14] In answering it, she identifies ten central capabilities or primary goods, such as life, play, emotions and practical reason,[15] which she says each person needs no matter their conception of the good.[16] For justice to be done, she says, people must be empowered to a minimum degree to choose among and realise these goods.[17] When empowered, we possess these capabilities. Their provision is required by justice, with the 'ultimate political goal',[18] therefore, being to 'secure to all citizens at least a threshold level' of the specified capabilities.[19] Only in doing this do we treat persons with equal dignity.[20] To realise this goal, we must entrench capabilities as 'constitutional guarantees' on which all can effectively rely.[21] When this 'fully universal' goal is not pursued or is ineffective,[22] when the threshold level of capabilities is not met, the result is a 'waste' of human potential,[23] which is to say, it is 'unjust and tragic'.[24]

This serving as Nussbaum's normative frame, she says: 'Sometimes social conditions make it seem impossible to deliver this threshold amount of all ten capabilities to everyone: two or more of them may be in competition [GP1, GP4].'[25] Because this competition affects goods that 'have intrinsic value and importance' (GP3), there is an injustice, for 'the situation produced when two of them collide is tragic: any course we select involves doing wrong to someone'.[26] Later, I will resist the idea that tragic choice is coterminous with injustice, but for now what is important is to recognise the contingent nature of her tragic predicaments. Tragic choice, she says, involves 'a cost of a distinctive sort, one that in a fully just society no person has to bear'.[27] It always entails injustice, which is why the failure to secure for every person the minimum level of their entitled capabilities is not just a cause for us to grieve, it is wrong. We are all vulnerable and finite beings, but in 'realizing that we cannot make ourselves or our nation immortal, we can, and must, try for the available goal of making it equal and free'.[28] If we realise that the central goods 'support and complement one another',[29] instead of pulling in different directions, all that stands in the way of a 'tragedy-free future' is coordination.[30] With enough 'ingenuity and effort',[31] the apparent need to choose 'between two evils',[32] or to make do with 'trade-offs',[33] will be revealed as an illusion that disguises injustice as natural or inevitable.[34]

What is the root of this conception of tragedy? When it comes to her capabilities theory, it has two basic features. First, it is a result of her tying the thesis to political liberalism, in its Rawlsian sense, where the ambition is an 'overlapping consensus among all the reasonable comprehensive doctrines',[35] which eschews all controversial metaphysical, epistemological, ethical, and so on, ideas.[36] Second, it is rooted in her Aristotelian and Marxian-inspired conception of justice, according to which politics must strive to provide each person a minimum level of capabilities.[37] By limiting the domain of reasons for action, in the sense of excluding controversial views, and by limiting the goal, in the sense of realising a floor rather than maximal flourishing,[38] it follows that loss is contingent. It is contingent because consensus is conceptually possible, even if it is empirically difficult, and securing the conditions in which persons can choose between and actualise distinct goods is likewise contingent, since it only depends on having enough resources and the adoption of appropriate distributive criteria.[39]

We also find this conception of tragedy, however, in her thicker ethical prescriptions, within and without her capabilities thesis. The source of this fact is her Aristotelian attitude to conflict, already noted, namely, her belief that the capabilities 'support and complement one another'.[40] Despite the forms in which dignity is made real being distinct, 'the capabilities are understood as a coherent overall set, not as conflicting among themselves [GP4]'.[41] Such an approach is like 'Aristotle's way of defining each virtue: in doing so he considers the implications for accounts of other virtues.'[42] So, when it comes to political philosophy and policy, it is not just that she strives for a minimum rather than a maximum of flourishing and excludes comprehensive conceptions of the good as reasons relevant to public actions. Equally important is that Nussbaum's ten central goods are all coherent: 'it is to *avoid* the need to make trade-offs that we might look across to the other capabilities, making sure that the whole set is coherent and can be delivered as a whole'.[43] What has to be understood, she says, is that the 'field of human capabilities should not be seen as a tragic "either-or" . . . it is, instead, a "both-and"'.[44]

In striving for this 'whole', Nussbaum does not extirpate difference. She is acutely sensitive to qualitative particularity and separateness. Nor does she neglect the 'tension' that often arises from it.[45] She still, however, sees basic conflict as 'unacceptable',[46] so as calling for 'reform'.[47] If goods and duties, such as concern for equality and for people with whom we have attachments, religious tradition and individual choice,[48] solidarity and individuality,[49] or patriotism and critical freedom,[50] appear to conflict, she does not think that these dilemmas mean we are necessarily faced with tragic situations. Faced with conflicts, the 'structure[s]' of what we judge good or duty-creating can be altered.[51] This can be done by amending our conception of one to bring it into line with others,[52] adjusting both for the purpose of arriving at a 'balance',[53] or repudiating one entirely.[54] The reason for Nussbaum's stance, where she looks for a 'way out of the problem' of conflict,[55] is that criticism can only take us so far. Without a 'positive proposal', 'solutions' to the problems of 'social justice' will evade us,[56] which means that any adequate social and political theory must 'offer a definite approach' and 'political proposal'.[57] So, she articulates 'normative criteria',[58] or 'orienting principles',[59] which function as the ground of all political morality. To 'strike the right balance', she says, 'we need an adequate political conception of the person'.[60] The conception of the person that Nussbaum articulates is one according to which 'any child of human parents who [though vulnerable] is capable of some type of agency or striving . . . is fully equal in worth and entitlement to every other human being'.[61]

Therefore, whilst Nussbaum's work is structured by a concern for particularity, she retains the idea that 'there is a best conception of the good human life.'[62] The role she gives to particularity means that the conception should be open to debate. A 'cosmology of our finitude and imperfection' lends itself to democratic politics,[63] for it points to the 'flawed particular',[64] that is, the fact that we are all 'equally needy and finite and mortal'.[65] Ultimate (GP5) conflict (GP4), though, can be stilled. By way of a 'perfectly good human argument',[66] with the right 'quality' and a sufficiently enlarged perspective, we can 'show' at an abstract level what is right and what is wrong.[67] In the last analysis, therefore, threats to the good only come from the outside, as 'forces that bear down upon' us,[68] pushing us hither or thither, or in some way impeding our path to the good.

Similarly, whilst Nussbaum does discuss 'qualitative distinctiveness', the sense in which she means it is wholly different to the Taylorian and Razian sense articulated in chapter 1: 'Consider snowflakes. Each is qualitatively distinct, or so we are told.'[69] Even in this narrow sense, though, she still thinks that 'separateness', in its Rawlsian sense, namely, that we all 'have distinct bodies and lives, and lives that are [our] own to live', is more 'significant'.[70] In privileging separateness of this kind, the logical incompatibility (GP4) between forms recedes into the background.[71] This descriptive occlusion positions her to employ two Rawlsian methodological devices: overlapping consensus,[72] albeit supplemented by more 'reasonable political psychology',[73] and also reflective equilibrium, where ideas are abstractly balanced to render them 'coherent'.[74] With these devices, she designs principles about which persons with diverse conceptions of the good could agree. To make their agreement 'stable',[75] though, we need a community rooted in 'love' and 'democratic reciprocity',[76] in which usually 'narrow sympathy'[77] and 'concern' are extended outwards,[78] and harmful emotions like 'disgust, shame, and fear' are managed.[79] This community will strive after 'transcendent ideals',[80] but will not demand their final realisation. In a world of 'inconstancy and imperfection',[81] filled with so many 'quirky, idiosyncratic',[82] 'odd', 'mess[y]', and 'uneven'[83] individuals, this effort cannot but lead to failure and quite often 'cynicism'.[84]

When focussed more on ethics, Nussbaum adopts a similar reconciliatory method. When she articulates, for example, a conception of love which incorporates all that is good and discards all that is bad in our different conceptions of it, she advises us to 'climb the ladder [towards an ideal love] and yet, at times, to turn it over, looking at a real person in bed or on the chamber pot'.[85] In this remark, she seems to echo Hegel's dialectical movement between the sky of universal ideas and the cave of appearances. Indeed, she sometimes compares her own approach to Hegel's. Writing about Sophocles' *Antigone*, where the eponymous character is forced to choose between positive law and sacred law, she says that this conflict 'is a sign that society has gone wrong somewhere'. As such, this conflict must be 'removed (in the Hegelian sense *aufgehoben*)', which she says can be done with 'the creation of societies that honour each individual's free exercise of [reasonable] religion as a part of what constitutes the political sphere and its basic values'.[86] His dialectic, she argues, entails 'denying and rising above contradictions', as opposed to situations where 'internal tensions [are] present and acknowledged'.[87] For Hegel's project is to 'cancel' the 'possibility of conflict or tension between spheres of value',[88] by appropriately balancing them.[89] Like him, we must ask: 'Is there a rearrangement of our practices that can remove the tragedy?'[90]

This may be the best reading of *Antigone*, or even the best reading of Hegel on *Antigone*, but it is not Hegel's dialectics as applied to ethics. This dialectic is not a form of Rawlsian reflection. He does not identify his most considered judgements, test them against each other and his existing theories to see if they conflict, adjusting one or both when this seems right, all the while 'seeking consistency and fit in theory and judgments taken as a group'.[91] Hegel does not aim for the 'best overall coherence and fit'.[92] Not equilibrium after 'dialogue',[93] but recognising reason as the rose in the cross of the present, Hegel tells us to delight (GP5) in the necessity of the conflicts (GP4) between goods (GP3). The world's conflict, he argues, is not due to 'stupidity, or selfishness, or laziness, or malice'.[94] Life is defined by either-or options: this is the cross of the present. In other words, there is no fabricating 'a world in which such conflicts do not confront citizens',[95] 'well-intentioned' or otherwise,[96] since no higher principle that strives to avoid conflict can in theory succeed. However, when we recognise the constitutive necessity of this conflict, Hegel says, we will reconcile ourselves to it by reducing the conflicting either-or (GP4) options (GP3) to modes of an ultimate good (GP5). It is by his abstracting from and recognising the constitutive relations between spirit's conflicting embodied moments that he reconciles the conflict between them, not by 'better planning' that reveals conflict to be contingent.[97] So abstracted and modally reduced, even when we must choose and thus sacrifice goods, or suffer failure or reversal in our relations with others, we will accept that this loss is internal to the logic of constituting and thus sustaining spirit: this is reason's rose. His dialectic does not entail denying and rising above contradictions, but rather rising above each (GP5) by embracing both (GP3).

Nussbaum replaces 'either-or' with 'both-and', but it is Hegel's project to explain that 'either-or' is 'both-and'.

These differences, however, should not obscure what unites Nussbaum and Hegel. As Walter Kaufmann writes about Hegel, both 'prefer happy endings'.[98] Their paths to this ending differ – for Hegel, modal reduction; for Nussbaum, methodological and conceptual rejection – but each tries to avoid the force of logical conflict. Neither path is available to strong pluralists.

Beginning with Nussbaum, her ideal of 'both-and' neglects the logical nature of conflict. The good is not just fragile, exposed to external calamity, it is internally divided. To identify internal conflict is not to deny the significance of its external form. Vulnerability is real, and an emphasis on external limits – finitude, temporality – is important. Many reasons why have been given: for Hegel, facing up to the possibility of dying is constitutive of individual freedom[99] and political sovereignty;[100] for Heidegger, 'anticipating' death or 'finitude' is necessary for any truly authentic existence;[101] for Baudrillard, only by rooting our social relations in the 'cycle' between life and death,[102] rather than a 'linear' and progressive 'accumulation' of instruments,[103] might we escape political economy's structuring categories; for Martin Hägglund, recognising limits is '*necessary* for motivating ethical, political, and filial commitments';[104] and for yet others still, it is needed to develop the virtuous self,[105] mitigate the delusions of wishful thinking,[106] ground the 'humanity' of 'the profoundly disabled',[107] or tame the Freudian 'drive to destruction' in the 'service of life' itself,[108] not just in its bare sense but also for the sake of enjoying its 'sunshine' more 'keenly'.[109] Nussbaum provides yet further reasons to emphasise fragility, many of which can be, and have in related forms been, adopted by property theorists.[110] She paints diverse and compelling portraits of how acknowledging fragility assists in cultivating the compassion necessary for a healthy and stable community. Its acceptance can also ward off the narcissism, disgust, envy or shame rooted in helplessness or fear. And only by confronting neediness and interdependence, she argues, can we develop our sympathetic faculties, which is necessary to extend our ordinarily narrow circles of concern outwards to neighbours and strangers.[111]

We ought to embrace much of what Nussbaum and others say on these fronts. However, even if we realised her politically just society by making life 'safe for well-disposed people',[112] even if we faced our finitude and cared for what matters in this life, tragedy would still remain because its roots run deeper. Yes, life is imperfect, messy and incongruous but we face a deeper problem: loss can come from the outside, but it also necessarily comes from within. Whilst conflict is often due to the narrowness of our perspectives, or can be the result of a naïve treatment of the content of our duties, or can be due to distorted emotional structures, this is not always so. Often, conflict emerges from the incompatible structures of diverse goods themselves. Whilst Hegel recognises this reality, he escapes its practical implications by reducing incompatible (GP4) goods (GP3) to modes of one ultimate good (GP5). However, if Hegel's 'happy ending', his fantastic speculative attempt to tame tragedy by conceptualising 'either-or' as 'both-and', does not persuade, then we must admit the truth that conflict is internal to ultimate goods. And because conflict is internal to the good, life is necessarily constituted by choice and sacrifice. As Berlin puts it, if 'ends collide the very concept of an ideal life, a life in which nothing of value need ever be lost or sacrificed . . . is not merely Utopian, but incoherent'.[113] In other words, to turn Nussbaum's thesis inside out, this is the tragedy of goodness.

To endorse an internal conception of tragedy does not require rejecting Nussbaum's external version. Whilst George Steiner is correct to distinguish 'temporal' conflict that 'can be resolved through technical or social means', from losses that cannot be avoided or that cannot be undone, we need not demote the former to 'serious drama',[114] or follow Sidney Hook in calling it merely 'pitiful'.[115] Loss has many roots and causes, and meaning matters more than labels, so there is no difficulty in making sense of both external and internal tragedy. Distinguishing them, however, is important, since it bears on how we should approach and respond to the fact that our choices and actions inevitably result in the loss of something worthwhile.

RESPONSIBILITY AND REGRET

What is the proper attitude to tragedy? It is tempting to offer the attitude that we found in Buber: melancholy. As I explained in chapter 7, he recognises that life demands choices and sacrifices, which he says generates responsibilities for how we must act and relate with others.[116] Whatever its plausibility as a response to tragedy, though, it is ultimately inadequate.

Buber is a monist who wrote at length about Kant's anthropological question.[117] Like others he provides an answer: we are living spirit. This answer shapes his understanding of and attitude to choice and sacrifice. For Buber, choice is not between diverse ultimate (GP5) goods, as it is for the strong pluralist, nor is it between goods (GP3) that are mere modes of a more ultimate (GP5) one, as it is for Hegel. It is between diminished versions of a single good. Choice or action does not result in the loss of something good for the sake of another good nor for a more ultimate one. Rather, it effects a falling away from *the* good, since in the place of unlimited potentiality we get limited actuality. On Buber's monistic premise, it is difficult to fault his melancholic attitude. The loss of hope and the vain wish that the 'facts had been otherwise',[118] as Bernard Williams writes in an essay on the nature of ethical conflict, is understandable when confronted by an inescapable non-ideal reality. The strong goods pluralist's condition, however, differs from a Buberian man's in two constitutive respects. First, unlike the Buberian man, who always-already finds himself in a fallen state, the strong pluralist must choose what to sacrifice. Second, his choice is not among diminished forms of a single good, but rather among diverse logically incompatible (GP4) goods that ultimately (GP5) all matter for their own sake (GP3). For this reason, wishing that the facts had been otherwise is incompatible with recognising that conflict is between goods. What Buber laments as 'limits' are the 'conditions' that constitute this world of goods.[119] The conditions are not poor substitutes for living spirit, with us 'corrupting' the good when we act in this world.[120] They constitute independently good forms. To suffer from Buberian lament, therefore, is to wish away these conditions, to wish away good, not just in agonising cases, when we cry out wishing that matters were simpler, but absolutely and forever. As excusable as this cry might sometimes be, however, to commit to this wish as a way of life is to repudiate the logically diverse nature of what is good, contrary to the starting point of the strong goods pluralist.

Moving from potentiality, a situation constituted by the need to choose between incompatible goods, to actuality, where particular goods are sacrificed for the sake of others, can be agonising even for persons who do not privilege the relation of living spirit. It is agonising not necessarily because the decision is difficult, for agony is experienced even if we know immediately what we should do. It is agonising because the choice is between forms, each of which is ultimately (GP5) important for its own sake (GP3), that despite their goodness – rather, due to their uniquely good natures – exclude each other (GP4). In such cases, when goods collide, no matter how we choose or act, no matter the resources we have at our disposal or the purity of our heart, something truly worthwhile will always be lost. Buber is correct to stress these difficulties. His error is to see the movement initiated by choice and realised in sacrifice as bad. This does not capture what occurs through and in the transformation of modes of existence. Whilst life for us late moderns calls for choice and sacrifice, this does not mean that we are fallen – that in our present condition ultimate good is never realised. It just means that even when we do realise any ultimate good, we cannot but leave other goods behind. Sacrifice is necessary not because our 'structure' is 'perverse' and 'wretched'.[121] We are not broken or crooked, an abyss does not separate us from what is True or Good or Real. Not from a constitutive lack, our difficulties emerge from the other direction: we have imaginative access to 'too many' goods. Marx and his followers mistake the conflicts that arise therefrom as 'Faustian' in nature. They also underestimate its range. The reality of strongly plural goods means that more than '[t]wo souls . . . dwell within [man's] breast',[122] which is to say, we have many more than two natures. The potentialities of our nature are as plural as there are goods. This fact, captured well by Nietzsche's talk of the 'superabundance of life',[123] is what generates conflict, agony, choice and sacrifice – that is, tragedy.

In a 'certain frame of mind',[124] Williams writes, tragedy can move us to question or doubt or long for simpler times, but in being so moved we should guard against the temptation to interpret these activities and experiences as meaning that we are fallen in the way described. Historically, this image may have made sense of life, but today it is an illusion. This does not mean that the sense of fallenness never has pockets of appropriateness in the present. For those oriented by Buberian, Christian or similar monistic ideals, it plays an important, even defining, role. Even for those not so inclined, it can have phenomenological purchase. It will often be compelling, for example, in our personal lives – when we suffer heartbreak, when a loved one dies, when we are betrayed – when we experience a sense of absolute disorientation, with time itself standing still, our whole world crumbling. Less significantly, which is not to say less vividly felt, it can capture what life is like the morning after a 'big night out', when nothing in the world fits and everything appears about two inches to the left. In public life too, the sense of fallenness can be a proper response to the sudden recognition that one's unexamined belief that other people are committed to a shared ideal is mistaken, especially when one also concludes that the belief was a naïve faith. In general, however, it does violence to reality to say, together with Buber, that the experience of choice and action is evidence that we are perverse, broken, crooked, corrupt or sunken. We cannot be fallen, for our world is radically and therefore tragically good.

If so, how should we respond to tragedy? To answer this question, we must take up a point I put aside earlier: Nussbaum's claim that tragic loss, outside of natural necessity or luck, overlaps with injustice and wrongfulness. This is often true with external tragedy, but it is never true with its internal form. Whatever justice requires, it does not require what is impossible. And whatever our reasons for action, the standards justifying them do not demand the performance of mutually exclusive words or deeds. As Williams explains, 'no agent, conscious of the situation of conflict, in fact thinks that he ought to do *both* of the things. What he thinks is that he ought to do *each* of them'.[125] As such, when allocating property rights to facilitate one good will necessarily frustrate another, we err in describing the resulting loss as wrongful and unjust. Because what is lost is not due to the failure to act as reason, all things considered, requires, there is nothing about which we can fairly be blamed, nor anything from which we might ideally like to hide. As Chantal Delsol explains, 'a villain is nowhere to be found. The difficulty is just inherent in the circumstances'.[126] Because our hands are clean, guilt, shame and any sense of injustice is never appropriate, nor is it right to experience interpersonal emotions like resentment and indignation.

Kaufmann says something like this when considering Hegel's concept of tragedy, for whom the distinction between 'tragic guilt' and 'moral fault' is important.[127] This distinction, however, 'does not go far enough', for guilt 'is not the right word when guilt feelings are not appropriate; and we do not really admire those who harbor such feelings in a situation in which they are not to be blamed'. Kaufmann then offers an alternative: 'not tragic guilt but *tragic responsibility*; for responsibility, like pride, is something one can *take*'.[128] Because loss emanates from our choices and actions, we should agree with Kaufmann that taking responsibility is an appropriate response to internal tragedy. Having rejected as illegitimate the authority of philosophers to tell us what to do, we become responsible for what we choose and sacrifice. Recognition of this reality matters, for the freedom bound up with this responsibility is a constitutive feature of politics as a distinct sphere of life. To do justice to the tragedy internal to the good, however, taking responsibility in this way is necessary but not sufficient. We must couple this attitude with another: tragic regret. This is a technical term, so let us take a little time to unpack it.

For Hegel, regret is not a proper response to the loss suffered through and in conflict because nothing of ultimate importance is actually lost: all is subsumed within spirit. As strong pluralists, we reject this solution, since we experience the full impact of the loss suffered through and in the conflict (GP4) between ultimate (GP5) goods (GP3). Kaufmann writes: 'Hegel's concepts do not plumb the depths of [tragic] despair. . . . In the end righteous indignation and retributive justice is called into question, and the impact is shattering.'[129] We must be careful, though, for whilst loss can be shattering, when we take responsibility, tragic regret not despair is right. Regret is right for the reasons earlier given by Kaufmann: 'The tragic poet confronts us with the claim that what he relates is worthy of not being forgotten; that it is of great significance.'[130] Or as he later puts the same point: 'the necessary condition of a play's being a tragedy is not that it ends badly but that it represents on the stage suffering so intense and immense that no conclusion can eradicate this impression from our minds'.[131] In a different idiom, which talks in the language of reasons rather than memory and phenomenology, John Gardner says likewise:

> That a reason is defeated does not mean that it is undermined or cancelled. It still continues to exert its rational appeal. It may indeed be a matter of bitter regret . . . that, thanks to reasons which justified one's actions, one nevertheless acted against the prima facie reasons for avoiding that action.[132]

Recognition of the fact of tragedy means that we should not forget the significance of what is lost, we should regret it in the sense that it should exert rational power over our future actions.[133] This regret, I explain in chapter 10, is central to the idea of 'compensation in kind' that structures the exercise of the state's power to expropriate in South Africa's Constitution. What is important to grasp at the moment, however, is that regret does not entail imagining our choices and actions unjustified. Tragic regret is not remorse. Since we think ourselves justified, we will not feel guilt or shame or suffer melancholy. These attitudes or emotions or moods are defined by their wish to avoid what has to be done or undo what cannot be undone. Strong pluralists repudiate this wish. A strong pluralist should regret the fact that good is or will be lost, he should take responsibility, but he should never wish for a world in which he had acted otherwise, nor one that is structured in a way that the potential for loss cannot present itself. The first is inconsistent with his concrete ranking of goods and the second entails wishing for a world where certain ultimate goods do not exist. Instead, he must embrace past and present, affirm his choices and actions, and take pride in his judgements and efforts,[134] all the while recognising that the particular path he has chosen was not fixed by abstract reason – by any model – but rather, as Raz explains, by contingent 'factors which make it attractive' and thus right for him.[135] In doing so, he will come to see that sacrifice is proper, and he will grow to accept that for us late moderns, with our imaginative access to the superabundance of goods that constitute our shared reality, it is only through agonising conflicts and regrettable losses that we achieve anything worthwhile.

We must not only have the courage to choose and act, knowing that whatever we decide and do, something good will be lost; after this tragedy unfolds, we must also experience tragic regret. In Buber's idiom, but against his meaning, it is only in mourning what is lost that we honour the sacredness of that which is sacrificed.

HOPE WITHOUT REDEMPTION

As we illustrated in chapters 6 and 7, only when we recognise the strongly plural character of our world and the tragedy internal to it can we make sense of our options, choices and their practical implications. This theoretical clarity and practical empowerment is why we must learn to let go of the anthropological structure. Despite the limits of this structure, a prescriptive anthropologist may reply, there is still good reason to retain it. It is a reason that we have alluded to throughout. Models purport to offer two goods that the deflated alternative seemingly does not: certainty and hope. Theories structured by models provide more certainty than the deflated alternative because models function as abstract rules against which we can evaluate concrete options. Models allow us to answer 'What is to be done?' with a degree of confidence. If we reject models, therefore, it is likely that this confidence will be undermined – and as theorists like Judith Shklar and Russell Jacoby explain,[136] this loss of confidence is often followed by a loss of hope that humanity might someday be redeemed, that is, restore or realise, or at least perpetually and progressively strive to restore or to realise, the ideal of reconciliatory perfection.

Let us first recognise this position's merits. As human life is complex, to make possible lives that possess the practical qualities of efficiency, coherence or enduring success, we need abstract and stable rules, such as laws, that function to regulate diverse and fluctuating particulars. Shklar and Jacoby are also right that if we let go of comprehensive rules, we risk nihilism, resignation, irony or apathy, rooted as these emotions, attitudes or moods tend to be in bitterness or the often-desperate desire to protect ourselves from luck, chance or other forms of contingency. We should not neglect these concerns. What is important to grasp, though, is that these are ethical concerns (GP3), just like those that inform Locke, Nussbaum and all in between. Certainty and the search for final meaning, the longing for 'a singular ontological type', the logic of which can explain the goodness or badness of all,[137] though goods themselves, must pit themselves against all our other goods as yet further antagonists in our strongly plural world.

Few now seriously argue that certainty has absolute or abstract priority, so let us put it aside. Let us rather wade into deep waters by offering a few tentative remarks about the spectres of resignation, nihilism, irony and apathy. Considered from the standpoint of SGP, it seems to me, none could justifiably entrench themselves. Just as melancholy is not consistent with facing honestly the fact that goods (GP3) will often demand conflicting (GP1, GP4) words or deeds, we neglect their ultimate (GP5) status if we fail to take the choice amongst them and their potential losses seriously – if we allow ourselves to think that what was not chosen was not important, resign our wills to choose or act, shrug our shoulders, or go with the flow and let come what may. When reflection is grounded in a sense of tragedy, in recognition of the fact that some goods will not come to pass because we must sacrifice them for the sake of others, this will not be accompanied by any deep-seated form of melancholia, nor will it produce a characteristic nihilism, resignation, irony or apathy. Moods, emotions or attitudes of this nature will not entrench themselves because we will have rejected as normative ideals two related conceptions of redemption, each rooted in a Kantian anthropology: the first absolutist, the second aspirational or regulative.

First, we will have rejected the old eschatological hope exemplified beautifully in Marx, and the tendency towards theodicy so spectacularly embodied in Hegel, that we can restore or realise perfection, attain completeness, through a reconciliation with ourselves, others or the world. Few today openly espouse this ideal, but it seems to me to exert force through many crude, one-sided theories of property. Second, we will have rejected the 'more modest',[138] some say 'etiolated',[139] form of this hope, so persuasively articulated by liberals like Nussbaum. This hope, she explains, is embodied in the idea that humanity, despite our 'inconstancy and imperfection',[140] is capable of perpetual, albeit not 'complete and final',[141] 'progress' towards certain specified 'transcendent ideals'.[142] We will reject each conception of redemption because in the tragic world described by strong pluralists, they are incoherent, for even 'beckoning to a resolution that is deferred, not yet available',[143] is incompatible with an ethics that considers sacrifice inevitable.

Loss of this form of hope will not be accompanied by nihilism, nor will we sink into apathy, resign our wills or ironically withdraw from life.[144] For strong pluralists, only sensitive to context can we coherently decide what to realise and sacrifice, and what we realise and sacrifice is in fact good, for its own sake (GP3) and ultimately so (GP5). There is simply no space here for nihilism, irony, resignation or apathy. For only an 'Enlightenment fundamentalist',[145] as John Gray puts it, a recycler of the ancient 'narrative of sin and redemption',[146] albeit in 'secular clothes',[147] could impute, like Samuel Moyn does, to philosophers who reject the idea that 'history is . . . progress', a belief that it is 'meaningless'.[148] Gray gives the real alternative: 'The meaning of life is a touch, a scent, which comes by chance and is gone before you know it.'[149] Or as Gray writes elsewhere: 'Meaning shows itself in intimations . . . the shadow that reminds of mortality; the sudden vista that reveals an unimagined loveliness; the brief glance that opens a new page.'[150] In chapter 10, we return to this issue – the plurality, contingency and tragedy of meaning – when unpacking the role of money as a substitute for goods that we sacrifice when expropriating property. Let us end part II, however, by pushing back a little against the familiar philosophical assumption that only models can provide hope to finite, imperfect, messy beings such as ourselves.

From recognition of the reality that life is essentially tragic, it does not follow that it must be lived in a way that is wholly tragic. Whether it does depends on how we approach and respond to this recognition. We can flee from tragic reality, look away from the diversity of what is good, building models that strive to avoid conflict and the choice and sacrifice that it requires. If we do, tragedy internal to the good will necessarily be accompanied by avoidable tragedy external to it. The refusal to face tragedy always makes matters worse. Social exclusion, political domination and avoidable material loss, these are the prices that we must pay for those simplifying comforts offered by models. Here is an alternative: we can look at tragedy in the face, we can tarry with it, we can meet it open-eyed, with humility and courage, by taking responsibility for all that we do, experiencing tragic regret and therefore in the future striving to make amends. If we lived in this way, internal tragedy would remain, but we could at least coherently hope for a world in which its external forms would not.

Here, the power of Nussbaum's external conception of tragedy exerts itself:

> The world as it is is beautiful, but it is also a mess, and much of the suffering it contains can be ameliorated by a wiser use of our time in the world. A creative reach towards something better is a key feature of most societies that strive for decency and justice and that striving needs a vision of its goal.[151]

It is true that Nussbaum errs in thinking that theorists, not 'we the people' through our agonistic and political choices, can offer this future vision, but she is right that a 'balance' between 'aspiration and acceptance' is essential.[152] The strong goods pluralist, who starts out from their awareness of the superabundance of conflicting goods, strives to facilitate as many of these goods as possible, whilst also ameliorating as far as possible all the bad that necessarily comes with doing so – even when the form of this bad 'only' includes those lost possibilities of our community striving after and realising other ultimate goods.

Is there scope here for a reformed conception of redemption, which incorporates the internal conception of tragedy; one according to which we could say that, if ever, it would be during all those necessarily fragile moments, which by nature would require a constant and active renewal, when the tragic sensibility manifests itself in a liveable reality, that we would be redeemed? I do not think so. Even this reformed, purportedly tragic, conception of redemption remains entangled in the anthropological structure that we must let go. For only a despairing or melancholic being, who suffers under the illusion that she is fallen in just the way that SGP obliges us to disavow – wretched, perverse, sunken – and therefore longs for an emancipation from this corrupted world, or thinks that because prevailing forms of life exist in tension we must work to make them whole again, or lusts after the consummated oneness of man with man and men with nature, or wonders whether our forms of life are damaged, incomplete, worth living at all, would think it plausible, not base and insulting, the notion that life itself – filled as it is with a superabundance of goods – stands in need of redemption.

Instead of trying to reform this old idea, we must learn to hope without it. We must trust that our world is essentially good but also remain 'vigilant' in our commitment to making,[153] as far as it is possible, all that is bad good again. We must adopt an attitude according to which we remain willing to choose and act, to 'see things through', even when it appears that things will not 'work out for the best'.[154] Absent this attitude, this dual conviction that whilst every effort to transform the world into an ultimately non-antagonistic whole is incoherent, we should still strive to realise the ultimate but incompatible goods that constitute it, we risk not just resignation, nihilism, irony and apathy. There is a more primitive danger. Gray writes: 'At its worst human life is not tragic but unmeaning. The soul is broken, but life lingers on. As the will fails, the mask of tragedy falls aside. What remains is only suffering.'[155] He is right. Whilst there is never a need for redemption from being human, long overdue indeed is the need to face this vale of tears naked, with genuine compassion, rather than with sword or shield or salve that secures us from or numbs us to all the suffering cries of our sisters and brothers.[156]

NOTES

1. UT 684.
2. UT 352.
3. TFG 6–7, she identifies three threats to the good. First, activities and relationships that make up the good life. Second, the connections amongst the constituents of the good life. Third, the internal makeup of persons, that is, appetites, emotions and feelings. Each is external, in the sense that I am using it, because the apparent conflicts that they generate are all conceptually and/or technically capable of resolution or avoidance.
4. UT 383–84.
5. UT 411.
6. UT 374.
7. UT 371.
8. UT 419 and THJ 215–22. When death is not due to avoidable causes, it is tragic in nature, but it is not necessarily wrong (PE 384–85).
9. WHD xiii.
10. FJ 70.
11. WHD 5.
12. FJ 250.
13. FJ 139.
14. CC 18.
15. CC 33–34.
16. The capabilities are not merely instrumental, for they are 'ways of realizing a life with human dignity, in the different areas of life in which human beings typically engage' (FJ 161).
17. CC 36.
18. WHD 74.
19. CC 33.
20. FJ 161–62.
21. WHD 74.
22. WHD 6 and FJ 78.

23. WHD 13 and 83.
24. WHD 71.
25. CC 36.
26. CC 37.
27. CC 37.
28. UT 677.
29. CC 186.
30. CC 45.
31. CC 38.
32. CC 163.
33. CC 37.
34. THJ 213–41.
35. CC 169.
36. CC 89–93.
37. WHD 70–74 and 244.
38. WHD 6.
39. FJ 174–75.
40. CC 186.
41. FJ 175.
42. FJ 432 fn 16.
43. FJ 175–76.
44. WHD 296.
45. PE 131–32.
46. FJ 175.
47. UT 478–81.
48. WHD 211–12, 221 and 235–40.
49. PE 104–09.
50. PE 211–19.
51. UT 14.
52. WHD 270–83.
53. UT 578. The balancing is conceptual: conflict is avoided by adjusting the content of each idea to fit the other. We also find the balancing metaphor in TFG 79–82, in the context of the virtues. When it comes to capabilities, she rejects balancing, that is, the idea that one can be sacrificed for the sake of another, for all must delivered as a whole set (FJ 85 and 173–76).
54. PE 158–59.
55. PE 87.
56. UT 612.
57. PE 108.
58. UT 478–81 and 525.
59. WHD 187–98.
60. UT 580.
61. PE 120.
62. UT 581.
63. UT 661.

64. UT 709.
65. UT 662.
66. UT 581.
67. CC 32.
68. UT 409.
69. UT 481.
70. UT 480–81.
71. In TFG 74–75, she talks of conflicting attitudes that necessarily oppose each other. There is also a tentative acknowledgement of the losses arising when the modern value of choice conflicts with traditional ways of life (WHD 235–40). These are rare exceptions, though, which fact is rooted in her valuing of choice and focus separateness and distinctness.
72. PE 127–34.
73. UT 402.
74. FJ 175–76.
75. PE 1–24.
76. PE 37. The idea is developed later in the book (378–83).
77. PE 59.
78. PE 164–65, 173, 176–82 and 190.
79. PE 122. She refers to these emotions as 'Compassion's Enemies' (314–77).
80. PE 51.
81. PE 50.
82. PE 66.
83. PE 16, 21, 46 and 53.
84. PE 385.
85. UT 713.
86. FJ 401.
87. TFG 75.
88. TFG 68.
89. THJ 226–28, reciting her arguments in TFG.
90. PE 271.
91. FJ 174.
92. FJ 300.
93. PE 157.
94. PE 271.
95. PE 272.
96. AAF 134.
97. PE 269.
98. Walter Kaufmann, *Tragedy and Philosophy* (1992) 72 and 285–87.
99. PhS § 194–96.
100. EPR § 324R.
101. Martin Heidegger, *Being and Time* (tr. J. Macquarrie and E. Robinson, 1962) 304–11, 378–09 and 435.
102. Jean Baudrillard, *Symbolic Exchange and Death* (tr. Iain Hamilton Grant, rev ed, 2017) 174–79.

103. Ibid., 218–25.

104. Martin Hägglund, *This Life: Why Mortality Makes Us Free* (2020) 10.

105. Chantal Delsol, *Icarus Fallen: The Search for Meaning in an Uncertain World* (tr. R. Dick, 2003) and Patrick J. Deneen, *Why Liberalism Failed* (2018) 125–30.

106. John Gray, *Straw Dogs: Thoughts on Humans and Other Animals* (2023) 145–49.

107. Jeremy Waldron, *One Another's Equals: The Basis of Human Equality* (2017) 240–53.

108. John Gray, *The New Leviathans: Thoughts After Liberalism* (2023) 146 and 158.

109. John Gray, *Gray's Anatomy: Selected Writings* (new ed, 2016) 499–501.

110. For example, Martha Fineman, Bram Akkermans, Lorna Fox O'Mahony, and Marc L. Roark. References can be found in chapter 6.

111. For discussions, see generally PE and UT 297–454.

112. THJ 220.

113. Isaiah Berlin, *Liberty* (ed. Henry Hardy, 2002) 43.

114. George Steiner, *The Death of Tragedy* (1980) 8. Better to follow Kaufmann (n 100) 307–08: 'there is no essence of the tragic . . . merely different ways of using' the term.

115. Sidney Hook, 'Pragmatism and the Tragic Sense of Life' 33 *Proceedings and Addresses of the American Philosophical Association* (1959) 5–26, 11.

116. For Buber's reflections on responsibility, see PTW, where he addresses, *inter alia*, education, economics, politics, leadership and philosophy.

117. BMM 118–205.

118. Bernard Williams, *Problems of the Self, Philosophical Papers 1956–1972* (1973) 172.

119. For this distinction, see Kei Hiruta, *Hannah Arendt & Isaiah Berlin: Freedom, Politics and Humanity* (2021) 72–75.

120. Giorgio Agamben, *The Kingdom and the Garden* (tr. Adam Kotsko, 2020) 115–18.

121. Stephen Mulhall, *Philosophical Myths of the Fall* (2005) 6, 10, 118 and 123.

122. CVI 741, quoting Goethe.

123. Friedrich Nietzsche, *The Birth of Tragedy and Other Writings* (ed. R. Geuss and R. Speirs, 1999) 22 and 98. This idea is an organising concept of the book (4).

124. Williams (n 120) 172.

125. Ibid., 181.

126. Delsol (n 107) 207.

127. Kaufmann (n 100) 208–10.

128. Ibid., 210.

129. Ibid., 212.

130. Ibid., 154.

131. Ibid., 268.

132. John Gardner, 'Justifications and Reasons' in *Harm and Culpability* (eds. A.P. Simester and A.T.H. Smith, 1996) 108.

133. John Gardner, *From Personal Life to Private Law* (2018) 142.
134. Joseph Raz, *The Morality of Freedom* (1986) 383–90.
135. Ibid., 388.
136. Judith N. Shklar, *After Utopia: The Decline of Political Faith* (2020) and Russell Jacoby, *The End of Utopia: Politics and Culture in an Age of Apathy* (1999).
137. Leif Wenar, 'The Development of Unity' 21(3) *Journal of Human Development and Capabilities* (2020) 211–22, 214.
138. Christopher Lasch, *The True and Only Heaven: Progress and Its Critics* (1991) 42.
139. Raymond Geuss, *Outside Ethics* (2005) 14. See also the essay 'Adorno's Gaps' (234–47).
140. PE 50.
141. PE 67.
142. PE 51 and 54–81.
143. PE 104.
144. Williams (n 120) 178: 'The notion of a moral claim is of something that I may not ignore: hence it is not up to me to give myself a life free from conflict by withdrawing my interest from such claims.'
145. John Gray, *Enlightenment's Wake: Politics and Culture at the Close of the Modern Age* (2007) xvi–xvii.
146. John Gray, *Heresies: Against Progress and Other Illusions* (2004) 13–14.
147. Ibid., 31.
148. Samuel Moyn, *Liberalism Against Itself: Cold War Intellectuals and the Making of Our Times* (2023) 77.
149. John Gray, *Feline Philosophy: Cats and the Meaning of Life* (2021) 111.
150. John Gray, *The Soul of the Marionette: A Short Inquiry into Human Freedom* (2015) 101.
151. PE 117.
152. PE 117.
153. Delsol (n 107) 219–23.
154. Lasch (n 140) 80–81.
155. Gray (n 108) 101.
156. Kaufmann (n 100) 182.

Part III

THE CHOSEN WAY

Noting the 'radical indeterminacy' that is constitutively bound up with the 'irreducibly different concerns arising from' the 'diversity of relevant value' that characterises our lives, John Gardner says that the 'common hope' that the philosopher can offer 'uniquely' right answers to any of our many practical questions 'is not a reasonable hope'. What to do in these situations? Gardner tells us to 'hire a lawyer'.[1]

Gardner recalls Hegel's memorable criticism of Plato and Fichte for their attempts to advise nurses and design passport regulations.[2] This resemblance is superficial. The reason for Hegel's criticism is that he understands that reality's fluctuating and fleeting particulars render futile all efforts to prescribe principles to regulate in advance all concrete situations. The material through and in which the abstract emerges into its contingent concrete form is always new and different, and this movement is always performed by particular persons, each always new and different. It is this double particularity, the world's and our own, which renders fantastical the effort to draw a neat line between the abstract and concrete. The relation between principle and its application is defined not by deduction, but rather by indeterminate judgement or interpretation, where we try to derive concrete, context-appropriate rules from abstract principles.

With much of this Gardner agrees, but for him philosophers face a more ultimate constraint. Hegel is a weak pluralist: he recognises the reality of diverse (GP1), acceptable (GP2) goods that matter for their own sake (GP3), which logically conflict (GP4), but by reducing each to a mode of one rational, expressive and relational whole, he denies them ultimate status (GP5). Gardner, contrarily, is an 'intellectual squirrel',[3] who recognises logical conflict between ultimate goods, and since theory cannot rank (GP6, GP7) these goods, he understands that no system of abstract principles can possess the internal coherence or hierarchy needed for it to function prescriptively. Therefore, it is not just that we cannot deduce concrete rules from abstract principles, we cannot derive them either. Hegelian interpretation is not available to strong goods pluralists, for there is no system to interpret, no coherent or ordered set of principles from which to derive anything at all. So, whilst it is true that theory is incomplete since it depends on the input of contingent real-world facts, and because interpretative output is likewise contingent, its limits run deeper. When theory reflects reality, it should confront the logical conflict between ultimate goods. This means that its practitioners – philosophers – who by nature abstract from concrete relations, cannot have any ultimate insight into realising what is good. This is the reason why there is almost no point in asking them 'What is to be done?'

If theorists cannot help us, where must we turn when deciding how to allocate property? We must look to ourselves and each other, for the decisions are political: concrete and conflictual. As many others explain,[4] the implications of pluralism for how we understand politics and structure our institutions are profound. Given the limits of philosophy when it comes to ethics, it is urgent we theorise those institutions that will empower persons to identify, construct, express and judge conflicting forms and relations, and thereafter, of course, empower them to take steps that will in general make their judgements of good a reality. I do not contribute to this vital task in this book. Rather, in part III, I consider the tool through and in which conflict is resolved: law.

One of law's functions, Gardner reminds us, is to settle, at least for now, the conflicts theory cannot. After we speak through law, we move from theory and politics to legal practice. Once we are there, if we want to know what to do, we should hire a lawyer. We must consult a lawyer not because she knows in some transhistorical way what should be done. Law is always downstream of politics: the sphere of conflict, agony, choice and sacrifice. Therefore, law always embodies a contingent settlement of conflict, 'the sacrificial reduction of a plurality to oneness'.[5] We hire the lawyer not because she is an expert on 'What is to be done'. Such experts do not exist. Indeed, if SGP is true, the idea otherwise is incoherent. We hire the lawyer because her job, for which a life of formal learning and practical training ideally equips her, is to interpret the practices or texts – laws – in which past political judgements about conflicting goods are embodied.

There is an enormous literature on legal interpretation, none of which I can explore. To make sense of what follows, though, I must stipulate two points considered trite in South Africa. First, to say that we must interpret the judgements embodied in laws is not to say that we must look for the subjective intentions of lawmakers. Whether we must is an ethical not a conceptual question. Second, South African law has little interest in intentions, for it adopts a functional or purposive approach to interpretation. When interpreting the law, the ultimate criterion is the 'spirit, purport and objects' of the

Constitution, its foundational values and rights. Therefore, when determining what a law requires in any particular case, we must first determine the concrete ethical judgement embodied in the Constitution. Then, we must adopt the interpretation of the Constitution or other law that best promotes this judgement (subject to reasonable textual constraints). Articulating the content of this judgement is rarely easy, and interpretations of it will almost always be the subject of reasonable disputes. If we want to know what political authorities should do when allocating property, however, what ultimately matters is this concrete ethical judgement.

In chapter 9, I provide an interpretation of this judgement. I shall argue that the Constitution, conscious of the diversity of goodness, recognises and embraces strong goods pluralism, together with an awareness of the inevitability of conflict, agony, choice and sacrifice. Rooted in history, forged in the ruins of exclusion, domination and avoidable loss, the Constitution looks at tragedy in the face. Instead of looking-away from the diversity of what is good, by constructing a model that strives to avoid conflict and the choices and sacrifices that it requires, it tarries with tragedy. It obliges us to take responsibility for what we do, to experience regret when our actions result in the loss of something that is good, and therefore to take steps to make up for what has been done and cannot be undone. Whatever other communities and systems of law decided to do when they first bore witness to our strongly plural reality, its embrace is South Africa's chosen way.

In chapter 10, I consider what this embrace means for property. I focus on the state's power, embodied in Section 25 of South Africa's Constitution, to expropriate property and its correlative duty to provide all affected parties just and equitable compensation when it exercises this power. In doing this, I make the case for interpreting this power and duty in a way that brings to the fore their transformative and therefore radical potential.

NOTES

1. John Gardner, *From Personal Life to Private Law* (2018) 13–14.
2. EPR 21.
3. John Gardner, *Law as a Leap of Faith* (2012) vi.
4. Joseph Raz, *The Morality of Freedom* (1986), John Gray, *Two Faces of Liberalism* (2000), Chantal Mouffe, *The Democratic Paradox* (2000) and *The Return of the Political* (2005), Chantal Delsol, *Icarus Fallen: The Search for Meaning in an Uncertain World* (tr. R Dick, 2003), Lawrence Hamilton, *Freedom is Power: Liberty Through Political Representation* (2014) and Michael Lind, *The New Class War: Saving Democracy from the Metropolitan Elite* (2020).
5. Johan van der Walt, *Law and Sacrifice: Towards a Post-Apartheid Theory of Law* (2005) 204.

Chapter 9

A Constitution of Possibilities

This short chapter was not planned to be written, but after the state's political-economic response to the threat posed by Covid, the argument made in this chapter, that South Africa's Constitution embodies the commitment to strong goods pluralism, calls for articulation and defence. That the Constitution embraces SGP is its most original normative truth. During the pandemic, though, it was neglected by those with power. Authorities had a duty to situate the diversity of goodness in the heart of the Covid response, by respecting, protecting, promoting and fulfilling all the goods that make life worth living. Their political-economic response, lives and livelihoods,[1] described in chapter 6, was constitutively incompatible with this duty.

TWO CONCEPTS OF DIVERSITY

'We, the people of South Africa', the Constitution's preamble tells us, 'believe that South Africa belongs to all who live in it, united in our diversity'. This statement prompts two questions. What is meant by diversity? How can unity be realised given this diversity? In this chapter, I answer the first, and I gesture at an answer to the second, which I make concrete in chapter 10.

Before starting, we must distinguish two conceptions of diversity. In the idiom that I adopted in chapter 1, I shall call them the 'spatio-temporal' and 'logical' conceptions of diversity. Recall, when articulating the concept of SGP, I distinguished two ways in which relational forms can be incompatible: spatio-temporal (GP1) and logical (GP4). GP1 refers to the self-evident truth that diverse forms sometimes cannot be realised simultaneously, diachronically or synchronically. It admits the obvious: we often cannot do two things at once, for example, scarce resources can compel us to choose between dialysis machines and antiretroviral drugs. Logical incompatibility makes a stronger claim: there exist relational forms that, by virtue of their constitutive qualities, exclude each other. Here, it is not a contingent fact that we cannot actualise both forms at the same time, since the impossibility is rooted in the forms' structures. To actualise one is to frustrate the other. Chapters 6 and 7 revealed the breadth of this conflict, and chapter 8 dealt with the attitudinal and practical implications of structuring life in accordance with it.

When the Constitution refers to diversity, is it referring to the spatio-temporal form, or does it also contemplate its logical form? Only if the logical form is also included will the door be open to interpreting the Constitution as embodying SGP.

SOOBRAMONEY AND PORT ELIZABETH MUNICIPALITY

Let us start by contrasting two judgements of South Africa's Constitutional Court: *Soobramoney* and *Port Elizabeth Municipality*. The first illustrates that the Court grasps and accepts GP1, with the second revealing that it grasps and appears to accept GP4.

The tragic facts that gave rise to *Soobramoney v Minister of Health* are quite well known. Mr Soobramoney, 41 years old, unemployed and in the final stages of chronic renal failure, went to a state hospital for dialysis treatment, but the hospital lacked the resources to provide the treatment to all who needed it. Given the irreversibility of Mr Soobramoney's illness, it declined to provide him this life-saving service. He challenged the constitutionality of the decision, on the basis that it breached his rights to life and healthcare services.[2] After Chaskalson P set out these sad facts, he soberly described the state of South African society as one in:

> . . . which there are great disparities in wealth. Millions of people are living in deplorable conditions and in great poverty. There is a high level of unemployment, inadequate social security, and many do not have access to clean water or to adequate health services. These conditions already existed when the Constitution was adopted and a commitment to address them, and to transform our society into one in which there will be human dignity, freedom and equality, lies at the heart of our new constitutional order. For as long as these conditions continue to exist that aspiration will have a hollow ring.[3]

Chaskalson P, however, rejected Mr Soobramoney's application, so sent him home to die. He did this because the right to healthcare is always dependent on the availability of resources. Since the resources available are limited, often difficult allocative choices between different constitutional needs (GP1) must be made. Whilst expressing 'sympathy' for Mr Soobramoney, he reasoned that there 'will be times when' the state will have to 'adopt a holistic approach to the larger needs of society rather than to focus on the specific needs of particular individuals within society'.[4] Sachs J had a similar rationale: 'However the right to life may come to be defined . . . there is in reality no meaningful way in which it can constitutionally be extended to encompass the right indefinitely to evade death', so there will always be a need for 'agonising' and 'tragic' choices.[5]

Our second case is equally famous. In *Port Elizabeth Municipality*, the Court was faced with a conflict between the exclusive claims and liberties thought central to the idea of ownership, and the immunity against arbitrary evictions embodied in Section 26(3) of the Constitution. Writing for a unanimous Court, Sachs J held:

> the Constitution . . . counterposes to the normal ownership rights of possession, use and occupation, a new and equally relevant right not arbitrarily to be deprived of a home. The expectations that ordinarily go with title could clash head-on with the genuine despair of people in dire need of accommodation.[6]

We must distinguish between two forms of opposition contemplated in this extract. The first is between 'the normal ownership rights of possession, use and occupation' (GP2, GP3) and the 'new right not arbitrarily to be deprived of a home' (GP2, GP3). The 'counter-position', as Sachs J puts it, is logical (GP4). The opposition is logical since ownership rights and housing rights are distinct, in the sense that a claim to exclude and a protective immunity enable distinct relations to objects.[7] That these rights are distinct, however, does not mean they will necessarily 'clash head-on' in practice. Whether this second form of opposition manifests depends on how the rights are allocated and exercised. When vested in one person, they will complement, not conflict with, each other. And if the holder of ownership rights is happy with the possession, use and occupation of their house by the person who holds the immunity, conflict might not arise. They might not want to evict their paying, conscientious tenant. In both ways, whether the logical distinctness referred to by Sachs J will manifest in conflict is contingent. That said, the Court is well aware that when it comes to property, there always exists the possibility of 'dilemmas',[8] that is, conflicts between 'diametrically opposed [GP4] fundamental interests [GP2, GP3]'.[9]

Equally significant is how the Court has decided to deal with logical conflicts between rights. It explains that we must not abstractly elevate one set of rights above others (GP6, GP7). When a conflict arises, its resolution must always be contextual. It entails the concrete relative ranking of conflicting goods, say, between the economic security that rights of ownership might bring (GP2, GP3) and the security and belonging (GP2, GP3) often made real in having a home. The 'judicial function', Sachs J explains:

> . . . is not to establish a hierarchical arrangement between the different interests involved, privileging in an abstract and mechanical way the rights of ownership over the right not to be dispossessed of a home, or vice versa. Rather it is to balance out and reconcile the opposed claims in as just a manner as possible taking account of all the interests involved and the specific factors relevant in each particular case.[10]

Port Elizabeth Municipality grants not just spatio-temporal, *Soobramoney*-type conflict (GP1), it also recognises its logical form (GP4). Further, it rejects the theoretical ranking (GP6, GP7) of goods (GP2, GP3) as a model for judgement. Reason should always be practical: context always matters, that is, we must concretely rank conflicting goods. This will be familiar to South African lawyers in the context of the judicial function, but in chapter 10, we shall see that this same exercise is a constitutive feature of transformation that is effected through legislation. For now, though, what is important to grasp is that *Port Elizabeth Municipality* and *Soobramoney*, with their recognition of the diversity of goodness and their rejection of theoretical reason in favour of practical reason, take us most of the way to SGP. All that we still require is GP5: goods that matter for their own sake are also ultimately good, in the sense that they are the source of their own goodness.

Before confronting GP5, I must explain why, given these cases, I said the Court only appears to accept logical diversity. In short, because there are counterexamples. There are judgements that seem to say that conflict is not internal to the Constitution but is an illusion that must be resolved through judicial reasoning. The counterexamples can be sat in two categories: apparent and real. The first is apparent because they make the separate point that, when possible, we must strive to reconcile conflict, a position that is logically compatible with strong goods pluralism, and none of the judgements that populate it concern conflicting goods.

In *S v Rens*, which concerned the right of appeal of an accused and the power of the state to regulate appeals, Madala J makes this separate point: 'It is not to be assumed that provisions in the same constitution are contradictory and the two provisions should, if possible, be construed in such a way as to harmonise with one another.'[11] The critical words are, 'if possible', for they hardly insist on the necessity of harmony or the abstract rejection of logical conflicts. Similarly, the Court in *United Democratic Movement* observes:

> It would be extraordinary to conclude that a provision of the Constitution cannot be enforced because of an irreconcilable tension with another provision. When there is tension, the courts must do their best to harmonise the relevant

provisions, and give effect to all of them. Sections 157(1) and (3) must thus be read together in the context of the Constitution and the section as a whole.[12]

The language is a little stronger, but the Court still does not insist on harmony. We find the same approach in *Doctors for Life*, where Ngcobo J held that when constitutional provisions 'appear to be in conflict', the 'proper approach' will always be to 'examine them to ascertain whether they can reasonably be reconciled'.[13] In *Gauteng Development Tribunal*, Jafta J goes further. Citing *United Democratic Movement*, Jafta J writes that courts must not only do their best to harmonise constitutional provisions, they should, in fact, realise it: 'It is the duty of this Court, and indeed the other courts as well, to construe the sections of the Constitution in a manner that strikes harmony between them and gives effect to each and every section.'[14] Likewise, in *S v Boesak*, it was held by Langa DP that 'a purposive approach to the harmonising' of provisions in the Constitution is always necessary.[15]

Even if we granted the extensions of Jafta J and Langa DP, though, none of these cases act as authority for the proposition that the Constitution does not embody SGP. The reason why is that all involved structures of public power, rather than a conflict between constitutional rights. *Rens*, whilst it concerned an accused's right of appeal, was about reading the state's power to regulate appeals in conformity with that right. To the extent that political rights were addressed in *United Democratic Movement*,[16] the issue was whether they were affected by law empowering Members of Parliament elected under a system of proportional representation to 'cross the floor', it did not concern a conflict of rights. And the context of the reference to striving for harmony was an issue concerning non-Bill of Rights provisions.[17] *Doctors for Life*,[18] *Gauteng Development Tribunal*,[19] and *Boesak*,[20] likewise all concern non-Bill of Rights provisions. Because none of the cases were about conflicts between constitutional rights and the goods that they facilitate, they are of no help when deciding what to do when rights appear to conflict.

Not so with the judgement of Madlanga J in *New Nation Movement NPC*,[21] our single second category case. There, the Court was concerned with Section 19(3)(b) of the Constitution,[22] which protects a citizen's right to stand for public office and, if elected, to hold the office. The question was whether it is constitutional to channel the right's exercise through membership of a political party.[23] Madlanga J held that it is not constitutional,[24] as this would conflict with Section 19(1)(a) of the Constitution, which entrenches the right to choose to form (or not) a political party, that is, a discretion. Citing *Doctors for Life*, Madlanga J held that this conflict 'must be avoided',[25] which premise he leveraged to sustain his finding.[26]

Let us put aside the atomic individualism driving his conceptions of politics and democracy. This individualism is evident in his view that the

Section 19(1)(a) discretion would be diminished if individuals are 'forced' or 'coerced' to exercise the Section 19(3)(b) right by joining a party,[27] that is, a collective body, and in the overwhelming interpretative weight put on the right to freedom of association in Section 18 of the Constitution,[28] where his driving concern was with individual 'choices'[29] that can advance individual interests.[30] It seems to me that Froneman J, in his minority judgement, has already done enough to alert us to these difficulties.[31] More relevant here are three points. First, in *Doctors for Life*, the Court held that the proper approach is to determine whether constitutional provisions can reasonably be reconciled, not that they must be. Second, that matter was not about rights but rather the structures of public power, so even if it were authority for the proposition that we must avoid conflict, it is only authority for it in that wholly different context. Third, the idea that conflicts between 'distinct' rights must be avoided,[32] by a process of 'abstract . . . balancing' that brings them 'into harmony',[33] is incompatible with the contextualised method of interpretation long-ago articulated by Sachs J in *Port Elizabeth Municipality*.

I do not mean to be too critical. Though deeply consequential, his mistakes are familiar. He is just guilty of that 'vice' common to the analytically minded,[34] lawyers and philosophers alike: to ease the burden of his obligation to engage in substantive practical reasoning, he waves the wand of conceptual necessity. This formalism emerges quite clearly when he says:

> The Constitution is one composite whole. As such, it could not have been framed to be contradictory. That is exactly why this court has held that '(i)t is not to be assumed that provisions in the same Constitution are contradictory'.[35]

Owing to our close study of Hegel in chapter 4 and the Marxian conception of consumer capitalism in chapter 6, though, we know that this conceptual claim is not correct. That a whole or unity exists does not preclude it from being structured by constitutively contradictory parts. So, even if we endorsed formal over practical reason, Madlanga J's interpretation of the political rights in Section 19(3)(b) of the Constitution still does not follow.

After these varied errors, though, Madlanga J repeats the point made in *Rens*. When possible, we must strive to avoid conflict: 'To the extent that there may be tensions between its provisions, everything possible must be done to harmonise them.'[36] Nobody can avoid the reality of conflict forever. Ultimately, the question is not whether rights and the goods or bads that they facilitate or frustrate conflict. The question is: What is to be done given this conflict?

NO RIGHT IS ABSOLUTE

The Constitutional Court has on numerous occasions told us that it is a 'truism' that no one right is 'absolute'. Is this judicial recognition of GP5? I think so. Since diverse goods not only matter for their own sake but are equal in status (GP5),[37] no single right (GP2, GP3) may breach its own borders and export its constitutive qualities (GP4) to other rights,[38] or declare imperial dominion over them (GP6, GP7).[39] During the pandemic, though, leading South African constitutionalists said otherwise: 'Individual rights are important. But life is a paramount right. Keeping us alive is the most important function of government [GP7].'[40] This proposition structured the Executive's political-economic response to the Covid threat: its abstract privileging (AS2) of bare life (AS1), its normatively violent 'effacement' of the diversity of goodness,[41] and its predictably physically violent enforcement of the policy of lives and livelihoods (AS3).

How did these constitutionalists justify their biopolitics? One method was either to cultivate or contribute towards a culture of catastrophism, by substituting for the 'pageant of diversity', as the Constitutional Court once put it, a 'parade of horribles'.[42] For example, in January 2021, the Supreme Court of Appeal, presumably conscious of the scale of the devastation that was, and is still being, wrought by HIV/AIDS, wrote the following:

> The seriousness and the magnitude of the threat to life brought about by the pandemic cannot be exaggerated. It is not melodramatic to say that it posed, and continues to pose, the biggest threat to this country since the Spanish influenza pandemic of the immediate post-World War I years a century ago. It had the potential, and continues to have the potential, to cause devastation on a scale that, only a short while ago, people could not have begun to imagine.[43]

At a normative level, it was common to cite Chaskalson P's remark in *Makwanyane* that 'life and dignity are the most important of all human rights, and the source of all other personal rights in Chapter Three'.[44] However, even if we ignored the context of the judgement, which concerned the constitutionality of the death penalty, that is, the 'conscious extinction' of persons,[45] Chaskalson P's words do not bear the meaning that was provided to them by those who relied on them. What matters, it was common cause before Covid, is not simply being alive but dignified living: a life that is filled with meanings, where the diverse possibilities of goodness are actualised in some or other form. This normative feature of the Constitution, that is, the fact that it is a constitution of possibilities, is captured well by O'Regan J in her concurring judgement in *Makwanyane*:

> It is not life as mere organic matter that the Constitution cherishes, but the right to human life: the right to live as a human being, to be part of a broader community, to share in the experience of humanity. This concept of human life is at the centre of our constitutional values.[46]

Once this primitive legal truth is recalled, we see that the claim that keeping us alive trumps rights is, constitutionally speaking, incoherent. Because the function of rights is to afford people the power to act in ways that make possible the constitution of meaning, that is, to serve ultimate goods, it is only by respecting, protecting, promoting and fulfilling rights that Chaskalson P and O'Regan J's shared vision, expressed in *Soobramoney* and *Makwanyane*, of a truly transformed South African society can be made real. For absent a continued realisation of the ultimate goods promised in rights, the mere fact of being alive and living securely, the Constitutional Court tells us,[47] matters little. There are no exceptions to this 'supreme' legal truth,[48] no conceivable state of our world in which it is not binding. To suspend this ideal, to say 'may everything perish so long as man remains',[49] is to suspend the Constitution itself.

Therefore, at least in its pre-Covid jurisprudence, the Constitutional Court repudiated not just the idea that any right, abstracted and isolated from others and the conditions for their realisation, has priority (GP6, GP7). It regarded it a truism that no right is absolute: all rights are equal, since all the goods (GP2, GP3) facilitated by rights are uniquely (GP1, GP4) ultimate (GP5).

In *Midi Television*, a judgement of the Supreme Court of Appeal, Nugent JA gathered together all these features of the Constitution:

> Where constitutional rights [GP2, GP3] themselves have the potential to be mutually limiting – in that the full enjoyment of one necessarily [GP1, GP4] curtails the full enjoyment of another and vice versa – a court must necessarily reconcile them. They cannot be reconciled by purporting to weigh the value of one right against the value of the other and then preferring the right that is considered to be more valued [GP6, GP7], and jettisoning the other, because all protected rights have equal value [GP5]. They are rather to be reconciled by recognising a limitation upon the exercise of one right to the extent that it is necessary to do so in order to accommodate the exercise of the other (or in some cases, by recognising an appropriate limitation upon the exercise of both rights) according to what is required by the particular circumstances [concrete relative ranking] and within the constraints that are imposed by [the limitation clause in] s 36.[50]

The Constitution embraces strong goods pluralism. It embodies a concrete ethical judgement that the state should, in all that it does, respect, protect, promote and fulfil the diversity of goodness.[51] In the idiom of legal theorists, these duties are the 'ultimate' normative 'criteria of validity' of all state action,[52] including anything pertaining to property.

Is unity possible where there exist logically diverse ultimate goods? Hegel says it is not, and that to pretend otherwise 'must certainly give rise to a conflict whereby either the whole is destroyed or unity is restored by force'.[53] He is wrong to think that a form of unity cannot exist, but is right to warn that this unity contains within itself a deep conflict that has the potential to explode into violence. To obtain unity in the midst of logically diverse ultimate goods, whilst avoiding, or at least mitigating, the inherent danger about which Hegel warns us, we must embrace the tragedy of goodness. In chapter 8, we saw that this embrace entails the following: with humility, we must courageously confront the reality of conflict and the need for choice; we must take responsibility for what we sacrifice; we must regret what is lost whilst always holding firm to our choices; and for us to do justice to all of this, we must, going forward, always try to make up for that which cannot be undone, always doing our best to make amends.

Thus, the form of this unity is not a shared consensus – either actual or built-into laws – like that presumed by all prescriptive anthropologists. Rather, as Gray explains, it takes the form of a *modus vivendi*, 'a political project' committed to upholding 'common institutions' structured by a concern to 'mediate' peaceably and fairly conflict amongst 'permanently divergent' goods and bads.[54] In the next chapter, we see how in South Africa this unity – as made possible by its most basic common institution, the Constitution – can be realised through and in the application of its transformative and therefore radical property clause.

NOTES

1. The model for the political-economic response was the 'Risk adjusted strategy for economic activity' 6 (www.cesa.co.za/wp-content/uploads/2020/04/Untitled.pdf). It prescribed (AS2) and ordinally ranked (GP7) three criteria (AS1) for decision-making (AS3): (a) risk of Covid transmission; (b) impact of lockdown on an affected business sector; and (c) economic value of the sector. This is the essential worker. The Executive, in *Esau and others v Minister of Co-operative Governance and Traditional Affairs and others* [2021] 2 All SA 357 (SCA) paras. 122–29, confirmed that lives and livelihoods was its model. The Court too understood this to be so (para. 132), which model it found 'rational' (para. 142). I am indebted to Quentin du Plessis for his comments on an early draft of this chapter.

2. *Soobramoney v Minister of Health (Kwazulu-Natal)* 1998 (1) SA 765 (CC) paras. 1–7.

3. Ibid., para. 8.

4. Ibid., para. 31.
5. Ibid., paras. 57 and 59.
6. *Port Elizabeth Municipality v Various Occupiers* 2005 (1) SA 217 (CC) para. 23.
7. Ibid., paras. 20–21 and 33.
8. Ibid., para. 38.
9. Ibid., para. 33.
10. Ibid., para. 23.
11. *S v Rens* 1996 (1) SA 1218 (CC) para. 17.
12. *United Democratic Movement v President of the Republic of South Africa and Others* (No 2) 2003 (1) SA 495 (CC) para. 83.
13. *Doctors for Life International v Speaker of the National Assembly* 2006 (6) SA 416 (CC) para. 48.
14. *Johannesburg Metropolitan Municipality v Gauteng Development Tribunal* 2010 (6) SA 182 (CC) para. 61.
15. *S v Boesak* 2001 (1) SA 912 (CC) para. 15.
16. *United Democratic Movement* (n 12) paras. 48–52.
17. Sections 157(1) and (3) of the Constitution.
18. Sections 167(4)(b) and (e) of the Constitution.
19. Sections 41, 151 and 155 and schedules 4 and 5 of the Constitution.
20. Sections 167(3)(a) and (b) and 168(3) of the Constitution.
21. *New Nation Movement NPC and Others v President of the Republic of South Africa and Others* 2020 (6) SA 257 (CC).
22. Ibid., para. 4.
23. Ibid., para. 2.
24. Ibid., para. 120.
25. Ibid., para. 18. In footnote 24, he cites *United Democratic Movement* and *Gauteng Development Tribunal*, but neither is relevant for the reasons given. He also cites *Matatiele Municipality and Others v President of the RSA and Others (No 2) [*]* 2007 (6) SA 477 (CC) para. 36, but this is about interpreting constitutional provisions in the context of the Constitution as a whole.
26. *New Nation Movement* (n 21) paras. 106–111.
27. Ibid., paras. 14, 18 and 52.
28. Ibid., para. 59.
29. Ibid., paras. 48, 52, 53, 54 and 58.
30. Ibid., paras 49 ('free spirited. . . element of self; the idea of a free self; one's idea of freedom'), 52 ('one's inner core . . . personal situation'), 53 ('constrained . . . shackles'), 54 ('choices by an individual may well define her or him'), 57 ('encumbrances of party politics . . . free will'), 60 ('inner self'), 61 fn 84 ('right to be different') and 109 ('compulsion . . . against their will').
31. Ibid., paras. 211–232.
32. Ibid., para. 214.
33. Ibid., para. 109, quoting a journal article by Chaskalson P.
34. HLA Hart, *The Concept of Law* (3ed, 2012) 129.
35. *New Nation Movement* (n 21) para. 63.

36. Id.
37. *Midi Television (Pty) Ltd t/a E-TV v Director of Public Prosecutions (Western Cape) [*]* 2007 (5) SA 540 (SCA) paras. 9–11.
38. *Bernstein v Bester and Others NNO* 1996 (2) SA 751 (CC) para. 67.
39. *Economic Freedom Fighters v Minister of Justice and Correctional Services* 2021 (2) SA 1 (CC) para. 3.
40. The identity of the writer is not important. It is the idea that matters.
41. Russell Jacoby, *Dialectic of Defeat: Contours of Western Marxism* (2002) 120.
42. *MEC for Education, KwaZulu-Natal v Pillay* 2008 (1) SA 474 (CC) para. 107.
43. *Esau* (n 1) para. 140.
44. *S v Makwanyane and Another* 1995 (3) SA 391 (CC) para. 144.
45. Ibid., para. 357.
46. Ibid., para. 326.
47. *Daniels v Scribante and Another* 2017 (4) SA 341 (CC) para. 2.
48. Section 2 of the Constitution.
49. Chantal Delsol, *The Unlearned Lesson of the Twentieth Century: An Essay on Late Modernity* (tr. R Dick, 2006) 154.
50. *Midi Television* (n 37) para. 9.
51. Section 7(2) of the Constitution.
52. Hart (n 34) 100–23.
53. EPR § 272A.
54. John Gray, *Two Faces of Liberalism* (2000) 25–33, 121 and 133–39.

Chapter 10

Radical Transformation

In a plurality judgement for the Constitutional Court,[1] *Shoprite Checkers*, Justice Froneman makes a plea for articulated openness when dealing with property:

> Whether articulated or not, each decision on whether to protect a particular property interest or not rests on some assumption as to why it merits, or does not merit, constitutional protection. Better then to articulate the underlying reasons for the protection in order to ensure that these often unarticulated premises fall within the constitutional framework.[2]

Earlier in this judgement, Froneman J tells us why:

> The question of property is fiercely contested in South African society. There is, as yet, little common ground on how we conceive of property under [section] 25 of the Constitution, why we should do so, and what purpose the protection of property should serve.[3]

Whilst some disagreement is fine, he suggests,[4] the lack of at least some kind of agreement on the issue 'exposes a potential fault line that threatens our constitutional project'.[5] On the back of this concern, he offers us a 'constitutional conception of property'.[6] On its face, his method for giving content to this conception is to direct attention to the Constitution's values and rights.[7] When read more closely, though, we discover that he draws inspiration for this conception from another source: a model of the person. Drawing on decisions of the Court, foreign case law and academic work, he articulates his model and connects it to his conception of property: 'The function that the protection of holding property must thus, broadly serve, is the attainment of . . . socially situated individual self-fulfillment.'[8]

In this chapter, I echo Froneman J's plea that we evaluate openly the reasons for protecting certain property interests over others, but I resist his conception of property, arguing that when we articulate the reasons relevant to the allocation of property, we cannot accept his method for giving content to his conception of property: his reliance on a model of the person. In fact, this method is inadequate for the reason that motivated him in *Shoprite*. As argued in this book, and as I explain again in this chapter, models by nature artificially manage or exclude from practical reason logically diverse goods, and therefore necessarily frustrate the transformative power that is latent in the Constitution's property clause.

To make these claims more concrete, I draw on another judgement by Froneman J, one more radical than *Shoprite Checkers*. That judgement is his ingenious concurrence in *Agri SA*.[9] The key idea there, which I unpack in the second section of this chapter, is 'compensation in kind'. This idea does justice to the need to articulate the reasons for protecting some property interests over others, whilst being free from *Shoprite Checkers*' method. Because *Agri SA* does not rely on any model, it enabled the implementation of large-scale transformative legislation in a concrete context (minerals), in a way that does justice to the diverse goods that constitute South African life. More important here, however, is that Froneman J also clarifies the nature of transformation: alteration of the rights that attach to or obtain in objects to a logically different set of rights, which thereby alters the possible relations that can be had through and in objects. With this clarification of the nature of transformation, Froneman J offers us a framework, albeit only in outline, for effecting equivalent diversity-respecting structural changes in substantively different contexts.

THE PROBLEM WITH SHOPRITE CHECKERS

In *Shoprite Checkers*, Froneman J endorses a model of the person: a socially situated individual striving for self-fulfilment. In doing this, he draws on Gregory Alexander,[10] a U.S. progressive property theorist.[11] Following *Shoprite*, Alexander wrote a book unpacking this model, in which he not only promises 'an entirely novel theory of ownership',[12] but argues it is the 'most morally attractive justification of property' in general.[13] His theory is not novel, and when we understand why, we see that despite its many merits, it is not one that South Africans can endorse.

Socially Situated Individual Self-Fulfilment

Property exists, Alexander says, to enable 'human flourishing'.[14] For an individual to flourish, they must actualise their basic 'capabilities'.[15] The basic capabilities include autonomy, security, privacy, personhood, self-expression, self-determination, self-definition, community, individual freedom, life, equality, responsibility, sociability and practical reason.[16] If the individual does not actualise these capabilities, their life is diminished. This is regardless of personal preferences,[17] for the capabilities refer to objective goods, so to recognise this, Alexander argues, is to grasp the true nature of things.[18] This does not mean that our capabilities must be exercised uniformly. The more concrete ways in which our general capabilities are actualised must be up to each person.[19] One reason for this is that the basic capabilities are plural. The capabilities cannot be reduced to a super-good, nor can these irreducible goods be totally ordered, so each individual must be free to choose to actualise their capabilities as they judge best.[20]

Froneman J articulates the essence of Alexander's ideas when he writes:

> The objective normative values of . . . dignity, equality and freedom necessitate a conception of property that allows . . . for individual self-fulfilment in the holding of property. . . . The function of personal self-fulfilment in this sense is not primarily to advance economic wealth maximisation or the satisfaction of individual preferences, but to secure living a life of dignity in recognition of the dignity of others.[21]

The above overview of Alexander only captures half of his theory: individual self-fulfilment. It does not address the other half: the interconnected and socially situated nature of life. The quoted words of Froneman J do speak to this issue in his talk of living a life of dignity in recognition of the dignity of others. To see how this living takes place, let us continue with Alexander.

The development of our capabilities, Alexander argues, depends on there being a 'matrix of social structures and practices'.[22] The communities in which we live provide the material goods, institutions and infrastructure necessary to develop our capabilities. Because the development of our capabilities is essential to being human, at an 'ontological level' we are communal in nature.[23] Indeed, he continues, life is given meaning by striving to and in fact actualising our 'objectives, desires, preferences, wishes'.[24] Because this purposive striving cannot be realised in isolation, it is wrong to conceive of persons as being formed outside of social relations. As a matter of logic, therefore, we must strive to belong to communities.[25] It is an obligation each individual owes to themselves as a rational, autonomous and self-conscious being.[26] He continues, arguing that the duty to develop our capabilities generates a second duty: to support institutions, associations and infrastructure that enable our self-development. This obliges us to establish and maintain a police force, a national security system, legal and administrative systems, communication and transport networks, a clean environment, and affordable and accessible healthcare.[27] From the first duty to develop our capabilities and the second duty to support the conditions that make the fulfilment of the first duty possible, Alexander deduces a third: facilitate the development of the capabilities of all members of one's community. And to satisfy this duty, we must allocate property rights in a way that each individual has the means to actualise their capabilities.[28]

Alexander's argument here overlaps with Froneman J's that self-fulfilment can only be made real when we secure for others a life of equal dignity. Since 'the individual is not an island unto itself',[29] Froneman J says, drawing on the concept of ubuntu, we must grant that the 'holding of property also carries with it a social obligation not to harm the public good'.[30] By recognising the necessity for social coordination and interdependence, whilst doing justice to the dignity of each individual, we reconstitute their relation as one of 'complementarity' (Alexander),[31] and thereby we resolve abstractly the apparent 'tension' between 'individual' and 'society' (Froneman J),[32] in favour of the ideal of socially situated individual self-fulfilment.[33]

Such is Alexander's property theory and Froneman J's constitutional conception of property. Alexander claims that his theory is entirely novel, whilst Froneman J says that this conception of property conforms to the Constitution's internal normative structure.[34] Neither of these claims is sustainable. This is for the same reason: their theories form part of a settled tradition of thinking about property, the anthropological one I have criticised throughout this book. Since they belong to this tradition, Alexander's claim to novelty is mistaken. And more importantly, the tradition's structure, its use of models, is why Froneman J's conception is incapable of measuring up to the Constitution's transformative demands. In the rest of this section, I explain why.

The Flight from Diversity and Conflict

In *Shoprite Checkers*, Froneman J also draws inspiration from German law, again following Alexander. After noting that insights gained from other jurisdictions should not unreflectively be transplanted into our own,[35] he approvingly cites a decision of Germany's Federal Constitutional Court:

> The image of humankind in the Basic Law is not that of isolated, sovereign individuals. On the contrary, the Basic Law has *resolved* the tension between *individual and society* in favour of coordination and interdependence with the community without touching the intrinsic value of the person.[36]

For our purposes, the essential words are those that I have italicised, which contain two premises that we must historically situate and criticise. The first premise is that when we are theorising about property, we must strive to resolve tensions. The second is that the basic objects of this task are individual and society. Whilst each premise has an impressive pedigree, neither is suited to South Africa's constitutional context.

In chapter 4, we explained how the great German poets and philosophers of the eighteenth and nineteenth centuries united around an effort to reconcile two seemingly incompatible models. The first sees persons as essentially social; the second sees each person as being free to chart their destinies as they deem fit. Formally put, what unites this tradition is the shared commitment to the premises just noted: resolving the tension between the individual and society. The greatest representatives of this tradition are Hegel and Marx, and it is a moment in Hegel's thinking that Froneman J and Alexander endorse. Like this stage in his thinking, both try to realise the project of reconciliation in the same way. They prescribe coordination and interdependence amongst individuals within a community but without touching on their intrinsic value, for the sake of ensuring that the 'pieces' (individuals) 'fit together' into the 'ongoing process' of one 'whole life' (community),[37] thereby making them complementary, that is, 'mutually supporting'.[38] It is because their theory is structured by a Hegelian narrative, communal model of the self,[39] rooted in the ancient desire to 'reconcile' conflicting demands,[40] that Alexander's theory is not novel. And for similar reasons, the method of Froneman J is unsuited to the Constitution. As argued in chapter 9, the Constitution embraces SGP, which means it does not: resolve tensions; situate individual and society in the heart of its internal normative structure; or call on us to give content to the Constitution's property clause by designing a model of the person. To make this proposition persuasive, a helpful place to begin is to recall the nature of the method: models.

In part I, we explored the anthropological question. Inspired by Isaiah Berlin, we formalised it as AS1, AS2 and AS3, with chapters 2 to 4 offering interpretations of Locke, Bentham, Hayek, Hegel and Marx that pivoted on this characterisation. There, I argued that to claim that traditional theoretical disagreements about property are rooted in a more ultimate one about man, is to claim that despite fierce doctrinal divides, all of these philosophers unite in the triadic structure of their prescriptive theories. One function of these critical interpretations, which unbundle and separate out disparate 'thoughts that have been regarded, mistakenly, as part of some package deal',[41] is to reveal the parochial content of models. Whilst an historical awareness of this kind can dissolve the prejudices of the present, it alerts us to another problem, tragedy, whose nature we unpacked in chapter 8. For when disagreement is at the level of models, there might be hope for resolution: one model, we assure each other, might really be right. If disagreement is rooted in diverse (GP1, GP4) ideas about what matters (GP3, GP5), this hope is diminished. For on what abstract basis, for example, can we choose between the experience of being your own person, which underlies individualism, or being part of a relational whole, which is communalism's basis?

Many philosophers offer sophisticated answers to this question, so it is hardly a surprise that Froneman J does so too. He manages this conflict by means of his model of the socially situated individual. This method, however, fails to grasp the character of the conflict between individual and society. It is not only logical (GP4), but the conflict is between ultimate (GP5) goods (GP3). Their modes, attitudes, concepts and categories, which alone mean little but together constitute relational forms, actualised diachronically or synchronically (GP1), are mutually exclusive. For this reason, their conflict cannot be resolved through coordination since the forms are mutually exclusive (GP4). Conflict also cannot be resolved, like Madlanga J did in *New Nation Movement* with political rights, by abstractly balancing forms, for gerrymandering ideas in this way always functions to bring a new form into being, defining out of existence the other. As illustrated by the result of that case, namely, the transformation of political democracy from a common enterprise into an atomically individualistic one, rather than reconciling individuals (GP3, GP5) and society (GP3, GP5), this method always compromises the internal logical structures, and thus the reality, of one or both of the conflicting forms. And finally, conflict cannot be resolved by treating forms as complementary in either of its two senses. Conflict cannot be resolved by making these forms complementary in Nussbaum's 'both-and' sense, once again because they are mutually exclusive (GP4). And conflict also cannot be resolved by making the forms complementary in Froneman J and Alexander's sense of fitting them into the pattern of a community's whole life. For this neo-Hegelian method of modal reduction only works by suppressing diversity, which it does by giving 'primacy' (GP5) to one of the incompatible (GP4) relational forms,[42] that is, society as a whole,[43] and reducing the other, that is, particular individuals, to 'constituent members' (GP3) of this ultimate good.[44]

Like the method adopted by Froneman J, each of these traditional solutions to the logical conflict between ultimate but incompatible goods is not adequate to the Constitution's internal normative structure. Recall what part I revealed: the diverse concerns that inform the theories of our model philosophers. So revealed, we see that individual and society are not the only ways to categorise property theories. In fact, doing so is often unhelpful. What matters is often not whether a theory is individualistic or social in character. More important are the practical concerns that inform the theoretical framework itself. With our model philosophers, the goods that they strive to facilitate are life, security, information, and so on, which themselves are informed by experiences like struggle, vulnerability, ignorance, and so on. Even if we must begin giving content to the Constitution's property clause by constructing a model, therefore, why adopt individual and society as its basic 'building blocks'?[45] The Constitution's property clause does not use these words, so why not use struggle, vulnerability, ignorance or alienation? Why not those forms that give life meaning: love, family, play, friendship, faith, art, spontaneity, education, and so on?

After all, as Froneman J himself notes,[46] the Constitution obliges the state to respect, protect, promote and fulfil diverse rights,[47] each of which, I argued in chapter 9, embody ultimate (GP5) goods (GP3). These goods include religion, the media, art and science, assemblies, associations, politics, trades and professions, trade unions, employer organisations, the environment, homes, the state's modes, citizenship, childhood, language or culture and their constitutive communities, and so on. Absent real distortion, however, many of these rights cannot be categorised as individual or social. It seems plain to me that only by us flattening out their internal diversity, thereby effacing their qualitatively distinct structures and therefore making it impossible to think clearly about the Hohfeldian incidents required to facilitate them, is it conceptually possible to reduce these rights to anything so homogenously simple as the individual/social binary.

If so, why does Froneman J begin as he does? The answer, I suspect, is that the unrecognised power of our tradition – the project of reconciliation – suggests it as natural. The rootedness and content of this approach revealed, though, it appears to me that it, like all the other many abstract binaries that populate the field of South African theory,[48] is not suited to the Constitution. For as I explained in chapter 9, internal to its normative structure is a concern for diversity and context, but when it comes to property rights, Froneman J writes elsewhere, it is especially 'supple'[49] and opposed to 'ahistorical' 'obfuscation'.[50] I recognise that this is just the beginning of an argument. If part II revealed anything, though, it is that the relational forms that many of us think important are constituted by qualitative structures so radically diverse as to resist all efforts to reduce them to abstract binaries – at least insofar as, and this is what matters, they are intended to function as tools for dealing with concrete conflicts between goods.

No matter one's thoughts about this point, however, there is a deeper problem with Froneman J's method. For it is not only that the use of individual and society, rather than other concepts, as our original building blocks when we are creating a model grates against the pageant of diversity that is embodied in constitutional rights. The method itself, the use of models, is constitutionally intolerable. Recall their function: they eliminate or artificially manage diversity (GP1, GP4). Our tradition reveals different ways of doing this, which in chapter 5 we called: linguistic reduction, modal reduction, rejection and ranking. Without some such strategy, men like Locke, Bentham, Hayek, Hegel and Marx could never avoid or manage conflict between diverse interests, thereby frustrating the prescriptive ambition that motivates all model-building. Without models, we will be aware of diverse concerns, for example, struggle, ignorance and expression, many of which implicate qualitative structures incompatible in the same way that individual and society are incompatible: logically. Absent models, though, we have no theoretical tool to resolve, in detail or in structured principle, their conflicting demands. This is why models attract: they offer a measure of certainty and control. Froneman J's model is so appealing because it provides clarity about what to do in concrete situations. It thereby empowers authorities to determine, structurally and often actually, 'What is to be done' in the face of the diversity of goodness. Its function, however, is to obscure or repudiate diversity, as is revealed in his claim that it resolves the tension between individual and society. In other words, his model serves to still the conflict between goods, thereby freeing up people with power to manage, contain or cabin disagreement. It always achieves this, though, at the expense of real difference – in Marx's idiom, by forcing contradictions to embrace – and also the context that is necessary to rank what is essentially different.

In practice, a choice must be made: structural certainty and control, but at the expense of real diversity; or diversity, but knowing that this will render property open to structural contest. That older approaches to property were proper for the times in which they were adopted, Froneman J says in a different judgement,[51] does not make them right for us. That another community prefers structural certainty and control should not detract from the fact that our Constitution does not. As I argued in chapter 9, the Constitution is incompatible with the belief that we need a 'foundation' to prescribe in principle what to do.[52] It might be that other legal communities do not 'subscribe to foundational value pluralism', but our Constitution does, since it embraces, 'all the way up',[53] the diversity of goodness (GP1 to GP5), it accepts that this inevitably results in conflict that calls for choice and sacrifice, and it says that these choices cannot be made in the abstract (GP6, GP7), but rather require concrete, contextual judgements.

These structural qualities of the Constitution mean that we should resist the temptation to flee from diversity and conflict by using models when thinking about property. And in doing this, we must accept three conclusions that follow. First, the incompatible demands made on property by diverse goods means that facilitating one good will always result in the loss of other goods: their relation is not inclusive, symbiotic, complementary or creative; rather, it is exclusionary, agonal, conflictual and tragic. Second, the problems that this generates are not wicked, nor are there any solutions to them, for they are internal to the logic of our strongly plural world. And third, whilst disagreements need not be fierce, in the sense that worries Froneman J, they must be passionate, for we are arguing about facilitating and sacrificing goods that make life worth living.

But if we reject models, where does this leave us? In short, we are back to where Froneman J, before he built his model, told us to start. We must articulate the reasons for different allocations of property and then, as I shall argue in the epilogue, decide concretely and democratically what to do. Put otherwise, we must engage in practical not theoretical reason. Sure, some will resist an approach that so deflates theory's prescriptive pretensions, but if we accept the limits of theory to prescribe, we will receive a practical benefit. In exchange for the simplifying comforts offered by models, we will get an unshackled transformative property clause. Let us see it in action.

GRASPING MATTERS AT THE ROOT

Having rejected the methodology of models, whilst endorsing Froneman J's plea to state openly the reasons for different allocations of property, we are in a position to reveal the radicalism that is inherent in the Constitution's property clause. We do so in two stages. First, we consider the concurring judgement of Froneman J in *Agri SA*, a matter that concerned legislation that effected institutional change to the legal regime that regulates property in minerals. This points towards a framework, grounded in practical, not theoretical, reason, for addressing property issues without a model. Second, we unpack this framework, clarifying how it empowers transformation by way of legislation and further revealing that Section 25 of the Constitution contemplates a passionate and pluralistic radicalism directed towards facilitating diverse goods and frustrating diverse bads, but which, beyond that, is limited only by the democratic imagination of 'we the people'.

Agri SA: The MPRDA as Transformative Legislation

The legislation that effected institutional change was the Minerals and Petroleum Resources Development Act 28 of 2002 (MPRDA). This law drastically altered the law regulating minerals. One class of rights affected were the rights of those not exploiting them. The MPRDA froze the power to sell or lease unused rights, until they were converted into either a prospecting or mining right.[54] To obtain conversion, old right-holders had to apply to the state within a year of this law taking effect. During this year, nobody else could apply. If they did not apply, the old right would lapse.[55] If they successfully applied, they received a right to mine or prospect. This right, though, is conditional, for if they fail to use it appropriately, it can be annulled.[56]

The legislative changes that were effected by the MPRDA are profound. Before the MPRDA was enacted, the holders of unused rights had a liberty either to exploit or not exploit minerals in which they held rights, they had a claim against others doing so even if they were not,[57] and they had the power to transfer these rights to others.[58] By imposing a time limit on the right to convert, and attaching particular conditions to the exercise of the new prospecting right or mining right, the MPRDA annulled these old rights.[59]

Reform and Transformation

The MPRDA is radical and therefore transformative. To recognise this, it will help to start by clarifying the function or purpose served by its alteration of rights.[60]

Historically, people had a liberty to use minerals to satisfy immediately their desires or ends, to prospect or mine, but the failure to exercise this liberty would not result in its loss. Neglecting to use minerals did not return them to nature or to the state for others to use or obtain the right to use. The holder of the right, therefore, was free (productively) to consume them, to store them, or to not use them at all. Parliament, though, decided that the nonexploitation of profitable minerals whilst so many millions continue to languish in poverty is bad. Therefore, Parliament decided to amend the law that regulates minerals.

The purpose of the MPRDA helps us to make sense of the changes that it effected. It tells us that we may now only treat minerals as consumables. It did this by altering the structures of what is a permissible relation to minerals. In the past, we could treat minerals as being objects capable of being consumed, stored or let alone. Now just the first is allowed: we must search for minerals, and if we find them, we must sever them from the ground and carry them away. Our relations to minerals are now constituted exclusively by use, and only use of a particular kind. For we are not allowed not to use them and we may not delay use to a future time that we consider best. The old right-holder could exploit or not; the new right-holder is only free to exploit immediately. Rather than having a discretion like old right-holders, new right-holders have an exemption to prospect or mine, which they must appropriately exercise. In the categories articulated in chapters 6 and 7, the MPRDA transformed object-relations from ones in which people could treat objects as mixed instruments, reified expressions or forms of living spirit, into a strictly consumptive one.

The MPRDA effected four structural changes to the legal regime regulating minerals:

1. It annulled the discretion to exploit or not exploit unused minerals.
2. It granted the person deprived of the discretion in (1) an exclusive discretion to apply or not apply, within a prescribed period, for a prospecting or mining right.

3. If the person exercised the discretion in (2) and was granted a new prospecting or mining right, the right is in the form of an exemption. This right, however, can be annulled if it is not appropriately exercised.
4. It created a state power to grant the exemption in (3) to the holder of the discretion in (2), or if the holder did not exercise it within a prescribed time period, or if the exemption in (3) is annulled, to grant it to the first qualifying applicant.

Whenever the law effects change of this nature – by altering the liberties, claims, powers and/or immunities that attach to or obtain in objects – it is radical. It is radical because, by changing the rights, it transforms the relations that lawfully can be had through and in objects and thereby the possible forms of being that can be constituted through and in them. As a result of the MPRDA, people can now only relate to minerals as consumables, thereby making possible present profits. They can no longer relate to minerals as objects to be stored or left alone.

To clarify better the radical nature of this structural change, let us contrast it with non-radical forms of change. We should distinguish transformation, which is always radical in character, and reform, which is never radical. Reform essentially concerns a quantitative question: How much should an individual and/or group get? Within the negative limits and positive duties prescribed by the values and rights in the Constitution, the answer to this question is determined through the political process. But always, the form of the change, if it is to be reformist, is limited. It may not alter the structures of what currently exists. For example, the Constitution envisages changes that transfer, improve access to or control of existing property, and the adoption of law or policy that concerns taxation, remedial equality and welfare.[61] Whatever the merits of these changes, or the form that they take after transition to democracy, they are reformist, not transformative, in nature. They are effected by changing the identities of right-holders by redistributing the rights amongst persons. They do not alter the structural makeup of existing sets of rights.

Transformation, however, always alters these structures. It is concerned with our horizons of possibility, with what is done not just to whom or for whom it is done, which necessarily entails not just a quantitative change, but also a qualitative one. And as Marx understands, all qualitative change requires grasping matters at the root, that is, the alteration of the logic of the relations that are facilitated and frustrated by property rights, by altering an existing set of rights to a 'mutually exclusive',[62] logically different, set of rights.

Pointing the Way: A Framework for the Exercise of Practical Reason

The MPRDA was met with reaction. In *Agri SA*, the applicant contended that because the law expropriated property, it was entitled to just and equitable compensation. In delivering judgement, the Constitutional Court split. Froneman J held that there was an expropriation, but Mogoeng CJ, for the majority of the Court, did not agree. Whilst the MPRDA deprived the applicant of rights,[63] Mogoeng CJ held, it did not expropriate rights,[64] since the state did not 'acquire' rights that had a 'substantial similarity' to what was lost.[65]

Even if Mogoeng CJ is correct that expropriation does entail acquisition,[66] he is incorrect that the state did not acquire rights. As Marx demonstrates, original acquisition is still acquisition.[67] There is a link between the loss of the discretion in (1) and the state's new power in (4) to grant the exemption in (3) to the holder of a new discretion (2) or to the first qualifying applicant. Like Froneman J, it 'seems as plain and simple as that to me'.[68] Mogoeng CJ is correct that the power in (4) is not 'substantially similar' to the discretion in (1), but he offers no argument for why this is required. More importantly, however, this requirement contradicts the logic of transformation. Transformation by its nature will always alter the structures of relations, which means that it will always generate rights that are not substantially similar to those lost in the expropriation. Driving his error is the concern that if compensation is required when we are effecting structural change, the scarcity of resources may frustrate transformation.[69] Limits should inform our interpretation of Section 25, but his solution gets matters backwards. We should not shy away from talking about expropriation.[70] Indeed, given our prevailing socio-economic conditions, it appears to me to be, ethically speaking, a non-discretionary power. As Froneman J explains, rather than us relying on 'formalistic' reason by endorsing a definition of expropriation that excludes a particular class of rights-alterations from Section 25,[71] our practical concerns about limited resources must be dealt with by adopting a conception of compensation that considers context.[72]

Due to limited precedent on the meaning of compensation in Section 25,[73] Froneman J found himself free to pose a first-order question: Must compensation be monetary?[74] In answering this question in the negative, he points us to the words 'just and equitable' found in Section 25(3) of the Constitution, which sets the standard of compensation required when expropriating property. When fixing the compensation awarded, Section 25 says, we have to balance the public interest, that is, the diversity of goodness, with the interests of the affected party, that is, the concrete goods that are presently facilitated by rights. To do so, we must consider all the relevant facts, including the current use of the object, the history of its acquisition and use, and the purpose of expropriation. Drawing attention to the MPRDA's purpose and to historical injustice around the acquisition and use of minerals,[75] he turned to the effect of the expropriation. Despite effecting a radical change, old rights-holders could still act in a way that facilitates the actualisation of goods made possible by the old system: if they applied, they could prospect or mine. Sure, they cannot sterilise minerals, but given the MPRDA's aims and past injustice, the provision of an exclusive discretion to apply for a conditional exemption (use it or lose it) is just and equitable. The form of the compensation is 'in kind',[76] which is to say, compensation is not monetary; rather, it entails granting a right that is similar to what existed prior to the passage of the MPRDA.[77]

Froneman J's approach is ingenious. He tells us that compensation can take the form of non-monetary rights that facilitate the realisation of existing goods. His approach mitigates the worry of Mogoeng CJ about limited resources. Further, it suggests a more general approach, grounded in practical, not theoretical, reason, to transformation. It tells us to ask these three questions: what ends do we want to facilitate or frustrate (DA1); what relations constitute these ends (DA2); and what rights are needed to facilitate or frustrate these relations and ends (DA3)? After we answer each question, we may decide to effect a change to existing sets of rights. If the resulting change makes possible the realisation of new goods, like equality or growth, whilst also providing rights to the affected party that affords them the means to do what they could do before, such as exploit minerals, the result will be just and equitable. It will satisfy the compensation standard stipulated in Section 25(3) of the Constitution because it will respect, protect, promote and fulfil, as far as it is possible in fact and logic, the rights in the Bill of Rights.

Froneman J, therefore, articulates a conception of compensation *as* transformation, for when expropriation alters an existing set of property rights to a logically different set of rights, which new set of rights better respects, protects, promotes and fulfils the diversity of goodness than the old set of rights, compensation will be just and equitable.[78] In the rest of this chapter, I clarify the structure and practical implications of Froneman's 'new and fresh' method.[79]

Compensation in Kind

Froneman J's framework has two pillars: transformation and compensation. Each directs our attention to three questions: what forms (DA1), what relations (DA2), what rights (DA3)? After asking the first question, we may answer: love, play, family, art, and so on. If we did, this would require a complex set of answers about the relations that constitute these forms. And after identifying the relations, we will then have to identify the liberties, claims, powers and immunities necessary to facilitate them. In asking and answering these questions, we will always be performing the same task that Parliament did when enacting the MPRDA, just on other goods. Because the MPRDA is concerned with economic growth and equality, it requires immediate use and grants an exemption conditional on appropriate use. If we identify love, play, belonging, and so on, as desired ends, we will identify different relations and rights, but the structured approach will be the same.

We saw in chapter 5 that because the ends and relations, and the rights necessary to facilitate or frustrate them, are logically incompatible, context is always necessary when evaluating them. Only when historically situated, in possession of the facts relevant to our options, can we exercise our practical reason, sensibly deciding what to do. Enter Section 25(3) of the Constitution:

> The amount of the compensation and the time and manner of payment must be just and equitable, reflecting an equitable balance between the public interest and the interests of those affected, having regard to all relevant circumstances, including:
>
> (a) the current use of the property;
> (b) the history of the acquisition and use of the property;
> (c) the market value of the property;
> (d) the extent of direct state investment and subsidy in the acquisition and beneficial capital improvement of the property; and
> (e) the purpose of the expropriation.

Only with these facts can we coherently evaluate whether changes conform to our existing views on the Constitution's transformative demands. Only with this information can we decide whether alterations to property rights comply with the state's duty to respect, protect, promote and fulfil the rights in the Bill of Rights. To see what this means, it is necessary to consider each category. As I shall explain below, we must first look at paragraphs (a) and (e), then at paragraph (c), after which we must return to (a) and (e) and consider them alongside both (b) and (d).

Facilitating Existing/Old and Proposed/New Goods

The function of transformative legislation is to facilitate better than existing sets of rights the realisation of diverse ends that South Africans judge good. So, first prize is always to restructure rights in a way that facilitates both existing/old and proposed/new goods.[80] As we saw above, the MPRDA illustrates how this can be done. If we are to tie compensation to this restructuring, then when awarding compensation, we must start with paragraphs (a) and (e). We begin there because they concern the current use and purpose of the expropriation, that is, the functions that existing and proposed rights facilitate. Later, I explain that facts about functions are also relevant to concrete rankings of goods, but initially (a) and (e) concern the goods and bads facilitated or frustrated by rights-allocations, for the ideal is to restructure rights in a way that does justice to both.

Current use of the property: When we are fixing compensation, we must start by establishing the ends towards which the affected party puts the expropriated object. How does she relate to it? Is it as a consumable or as an object of capital? Or does she relate to it in a mixture of these ways depending on the circumstances? Or is the relation non-instrumental? If it is non-instrumental, is the relation such that it constitutes an expression of creative energy or a reminder of past words or deeds? More concretely, we must first figure out what ends the rights facilitate or frustrate. If the affected party relates to the object as a consumable, is consumption for the sake of leisure or survival? If she relates to it as capital, is it fixed like a factory or interest-bearing like a mortgage held over a home? If it is not an instrument, is it an artwork or memorial? If it is not related to in any particular way, is this because she has not yet identified any end with which she associates it, or is it because she relates to it as a bearer of living spirit or as a protected area?

Identifying the relations and ends enabled by existing allocations is essential to determine the nature of the compensation. Only with this information can we establish whether the proposed scheme of rights better fulfils the Constitution's transformative agenda. Sometimes, however, the need for particularity can be diminished. The MPRDA is an example of how: the right to sterilise was extinguished and the holders of unused rights were afforded an exclusive right to apply for a liberty to prospect or mine. This strategy has merits, one being its general form. Expropriation is only lawful when authorised 'in terms of' a general law,[81] so the power is always general at this level, but the MPRDA is also general at the level of compensation. Because the expropriation in *Agri SA* concerned the right to sterilise, Froneman J made a general finding about compensation. If an affected party relates to minerals as exploitable material, he held, granting them a discretion to apply for a conditional exemption is just and equitable compensation.

This strategy, however, only reduces the cases in which we must ask after relations and ends, it does not eliminate it. It reduces them because it excludes a class of expropriated persons from the requirement to ask after further facts, namely, people who relate to minerals as objects to be exploited. If this is how they relate to minerals, that is all that we need to know. There is nothing about this approach that is blunt. To argue otherwise conflates the levels at which evaluation occurs: legislative and adjudicative. When passing the MPRDA, Parliament evaluated the interests of the affected class of right-holders and it then decided to award them compensation in the form of an exclusive discretion to apply for an exemption to prospect or mine.[82] When a dispute later arose, this award was considered and 'approved' by Froneman J as just and equitable.

The reason that this strategy does not eliminate the need to ask after further facts, is that not all holders of unused mineral rights relate to them as objects of exploitation. Minerals lie in land, but not all who have rights in land want to mine. It may be profitable, but money isn't everything. There are other goods, like visiting graves to pay respect to your ancestors, or fishing at the river with your children like your dad did with you. To realise these goods, a discretion not to exploit is necessary. If so, then the MPRDA, by extinguishing this right, imperilled these goods. This may be justified, but recognising these goods means it is less likely that the MPRDA's restructuring of rights is just and equitable.[83] Having a discretion to apply for an exemption either to prospect or mine does not facilitate the goods that matter to the affected party: respect or tradition. Thus, even with an MPRDA strategy, we will often have to enquire after the current use of the affected objects. In doing so, we must always construct forms of compensation sensitive to the facts, that is, facts concerning the goods or bads affected by the expropriation.

This need for context means that it is difficult to articulate anything in general terms that will always be useful in particular cases. Whilst context is always essential, we can still illustrate how to go about approaching the facts. Let us continue with our imperilled goods: respect and family tradition. In effecting transformation, the state should enable both old and new goods. Given the MPRDA's aims, it restructured rights in a way that facilitates the actualisation of access or economic growth. Whilst this is legitimate, we must also strive to facilitate goods like respect and tradition. This requires three rights. First, descendants or a family will need a liberty to access land: to visit graves or to fish. Second, they need a claim against others frustrating their exercise of the liberty, say, a claim protecting them from mining firms that want to construct buildings that will prevent access to the graves or produce pollution that kills life in the river. Third, they need an immunity against others annulling their rights. Whilst these rights are needed to actualise goods like respect and tradition, the power to transfer the rights in the market is not – but the holders of these rights will need the fourth Hohfeldian incident, a power, if transferring their liberty, claim or immunity to their heirs or family members is necessary to keep the goods alive.

If the outcome of the expropriation reflects sensitivity to these goods, such that the rights are restructured in a way that facilitates both old and new goods, the legislation will afford just and equitable compensation because it will facilitate a greater actualisation of the diversity of goods that constitute South African life. To repeat, the function of transformation is to realise more that we think good: the more, the better.

Purpose of the expropriation: Paragraph (e) directs us to the purpose of the expropriation and therefore draws our attention to the ends that expropriation is meant to facilitate or frustrate. Just as knowledge of current use is relevant when determining what rights are necessary to facilitate existing goods, so information about the ends pursued through expropriation is needed to decide how to restructure rights to facilitate them. For example, two aims of the MPRDA are to promote access to resources and diminish poverty. To facilitate such goods, it was not judged necessary to abolish all existing rights in minerals. Parliament only judged it necessary to remove the right to sterilise. As such, the total deprivation of rights would have been unjust, on this picture of things, because it would have deprived persons of the means to actualise existing goods. In the idiom of Section 36(1)(e) of the Constitution, a clause that regulates conflicts between rights and requires that we concretely balance them, the purpose of the expropriation was achievable through a less restrictive set of means. The MPRDA's restructuring of rights, therefore, facilitated the possible realisation of more that we judge good.

To sum up, expropriation must be sensitive to existing and proposed ends. And as Froneman J revealed in *Agri SA*, this requires paying attention to the relations and property rights required to actualise these ends. Transformative expropriation must facilitate as many goods, and it must frustrate as many bads, as possible. Sometimes, though, it is not possible to have it all. This may be for contingent reasons, say, if the minerals are located under graves. Or it could be for logical reasons, say, if existing rights create a protected area that by nature only exists if not intervened in by humans. If so, then no restructuring can avoid the loss of something that is good. Every real 'pageant',[84] as the Constitutional Court once called the diversity of goodness, will have a winner and a loser. When the pageant concerns the diverse conflicting goods that make life worth living, the loss is tragic. In these situations, when for contingent or logical reasons we cannot have it all, Section 25(3) of the Constitution tells us that we must resort to the market.

Markets as Substitutes

The concept of compensation in kind frees our thinking about property from unduly narrow and economic forms of thought, which distort the exercise of practical reason. This, in turn, frees us to conceptualise clearly the role of markets in Section 25(3)(c) of the Constitution.

It is widely accepted by courts and academics that the market value of expropriated property has no decisive weight when we are fixing compensation. It is one factor amongst many. To this extent, they are free from the hegemony of a narrowly economic form of thought. Following this recognition, however, one of two approaches is then proposed.[85] The first says that whilst market value is not decisive, we should always begin by determining the market value of the property, after which we then consider other relevant factors and adjust the amount payable. The second objects that starting in this way in practice privileges markets. Even if we do not privilege market value in theory, considering it first produces a tendency to use it as a default. To avoid this outcome, it is said, we must adopt a *gestalt* approach, considering all the relevant facts together and from this then determine an amount that is appropriate.

Both approaches are captured by an essentially economic framework, and therefore neither is capable of thinking in truly transformative terms. Recall, on Froneman J's approach, we structure our thinking about property around forms and their constitutive relations. This form of thought is qualitative, not quantitative. Rather than numbers, measurements or calculations, we identify and describe the modes, attitudes, concepts, and so on, that constitute diverse relational forms. This shift in conceptual orientation alters how we understand the function of market value. We do not look to the market first, nor do we consider it alongside other facts. Markets matter only if the ideal – to respect, protect, and so on, both existing and proposed goods – is impossible. For example, to provide housing to South Africa's millions of homeless and inadequately housed individuals, new homes have to be built. This construction, though, will often be incompatible, contingently or logically, with other goods. When building homes, this might frustrate goods facilitated by the property's current use. A communal paired liberty over someone's land may be necessary to build an access road. The effect of this might frustrate the realisation of goods that come with privacy and quiet, or the presence of humans may result in the loss of unspoiled nature. In such cases, when there is no way to facilitate both goods, we must choose and sacrifice. To do so, we need the information in (a) and (e), for they tell us what goods are implicated, with the choice that we make reflecting our concrete ranking of these conflicting goods. When we act on our choice, a good is lost, and in these circumstances, but not before, we must resort to the market.

The reason we rely on the market has two parts: ethical and instrumental. Ethically, when we sacrifice a good, we fail to do it justice if we do not take its actual loss with the seriousness that it deserves. Rather than with indifference, we must respond to its loss with a sense of regret.[86] This sense of regret, though, is not sufficient to do justice to what is lost. To make this regret real, we must not just 'mourn the ruins' that accompany all sacrificial choice.[87] We should also take steps to 'make up' for what is lost in a 'second best' way. This is because, in John Gardner's idiom,[88] the original reasons for facilitating the realisation of the sacrificed good continue to exert rational force, even after they are defeated by the reasons for realising another good. Indeed, the experience of this continued force is just what it means to regret.[89] Because these reasons still exert rational force, they have a practical bearing on what we ought to do. Even after we sacrifice one good for the sake of another, we still have reason to facilitate actualisation of this sacrificed good, albeit in an alternative concrete form. Whilst sacrifice is required, only by acting on the defeated reasons do we do justice to that which is lost. Only then do we 'make amends'.

That is the ethical part of the reason we rely on markets, but markets can only function in this way if there exists a class of objects which, though being instrumental in nature, do not satisfy or realise immediately existing desires or ends. In Marx's idiom, the instruments must be 'universal equivalents',[90] or in Amartya Sen's, they must be 'general-purpose means'.[91] So, what is needed is a set of rights in objects that enable their holders to obtain rights in other objects, which rights in turn either facilitate goods or frustrate bads. This is why market value is important, for value is often a good guide when we fix how much money is required to make up for the sacrificed good, that is, how much we must offer an affected party to achieve an 'equitable balance' and thereby make amends.

This is a lot. To make it more real, let us return to our housing example. Sometimes, building a house will conflict with existing goods, say, respect and tradition. That the latter goods in their current form will be lost does not mean that we can forget about them. We should try to facilitate the actualisation of all goods, old and new. If a good in its existing concrete form is lost, then we must facilitate it in some other form. It might be possible, for example, for a disappointed family to obtain property rights equivalent to the rights that were expropriated, that is, new land to (re)bury their dead. To acquire these rights and to actualise these goods, they will need money – and only with a monetary award that corresponds to what rights of this kind go for on the market can they realise, albeit in an alternative form, the good that is sacrificed through expropriation. Therefore, it is not just that market value has no special significance. The point is analytical, not quantitative. The market is a tool of last resort. This is what the two traditional approaches to Section 25(3) do not grasp. We turn to markets only when we cannot restructure rights in a way that will facilitate both old and new goods. Like money, markets are substitutes, they function as second-best tools that we use when concrete relations cannot realise particular ends.

We must notice here a logical feature of this approach, which is key to a coherent exercise of practical reason. Property facilitates goods and frustrates bads. If what matters is goods and bads, not every right lost through expropriation merits compensation. The reason why, as we saw in part II, is that diverse goods require different Hohfeldian rights. For contingent reasons, an asymmetry often exists between rights and goods: we have rights not required to facilitate the ends towards which we put objects. For example, gift-giving is a way in which people express love or respect. To facilitate such goods, we do not need the power to exchange gifts in the market. In fact, as we know from that feeling we get when we learn that a friend returned our gift to the store for credit, this exchange betrays gift-giving as a practice. As such, if expropriating the power will facilitate another good, then we should. Whilst expropriation often requires consideration of market value, this value is irrelevant here. Because the loss of this right is not accompanied by loss of a means to some good, monetary compensation is not necessary as a substitute. Ordinarily, though, value is relevant. Which is not to say compensation must correspond with it. That is an open question, the answer to which depends on our concrete ranking of conflicting goods.

Adjusting for Concrete Rankings

We resort to market value only when we cannot accomplish the ideal: facilitating old and new goods. If we can, then not only is value (c) irrelevant, so is any past state investment and subsidy (d), as well as the history of its acquisition or use (b). These facts only become relevant when we cannot facilitate the ideal, and when we do resort to the market, the current use (a) and purpose of the expropriation (e) become relevant again, albeit for reasons different to those discussed above. Before unpacking all this, let us make explicit what the facts have in common. We know market value is not special, for we can have reason to deviate from this value. This reason takes distinct forms. Below, I categorise them temporally, according to whether they concern the past, present or future. Whilst differing in their temporal dimensions, each is structured by concern for conflict, choice and sacrifice, for they reveal facts relevant to concretely ranking goods (practical reason) and therefore concern information critical to the allocation of limited resources.

Present and future. Paragraphs (a) and (e) concern the ends that property rights enable. This information, as explained above, is initially relevant to legislative efforts to restructure rights in a way that facilitates both old and new goods. If this ideal is not possible, though, this information becomes relevant for another reason: concretely ranking goods.

When there is conflict between the rights needed to facilitate old and new goods, we resort to markets. At this stage, we must concretely rank conflicting goods. Ranking is required because resources, in all times and places, are limited. Because resources are limited, to award monetary compensation for an expropriated right will always be at the expense of other uses to which this universal equivalent can be put. Every cent that is put towards facilitating the second-best form of the concrete good sacrificed through expropriation reflects a relative ranking of this and other goods that the state has a duty to facilitate through legislative or other measures. If the use that is facilitated by the expropriated right is judged relatively unimportant, the award must be adjusted downwards; and if it is judged relatively important, it must be adjusted upwards. Either way, the market value of the right is not decisive. What matters are the goods or bads we want to facilitate or frustrate and our ranking of them, which means monetary awards must be sensitive to existing and proposed ends, their constitutive relations, and our concrete relative rankings.

History of acquisition: In the rest of the section, I consider three ways that the past might be relevant to the determination of awards: acquisition, use, and investments or subsidies. We shall begin with the history of acquisition. Here, we must draw distinctions. We must first distinguish unjust and just acquisitions. If unjust, we must distinguish further between general and particular forms of injustice. An unjust acquisition is general when effected through laws that have general application, like those before or during apartheid regulating property rights. Injustice is particular if effected absent the authority of law or policy, like with theft, enrichment or contractual breach. Whenever possible, we respond to both forms of injustice by restoring the property to the affected person. Sometimes, however, for epistemic reasons, say, the difficulties of tying present holdings to past injustices, or for pragmatic reasons, like large-scale injustices which render ineffective or inefficient restitutionary tools, this response is difficult if not impossible.[92] This is not the end of the road, though, for the fact of historical injustice is relevant not just to questions of corrective justice, it is also relevant to distributive justice. For our purposes, it can still exert practical force when we are determining what is just and equitable compensation.

Above, we saw that past discrimination around mineral rights was relevant to the MPRDA's justification. We also saw that it was relevant to the application by Froneman J of his concept of compensation in kind. Usually, we attach less significance to a good if the rights that facilitate its actualisation were acquired in an unjust way, either generally or in a particular way. This is why Froneman J said that discrimination around minerals rendered just the new system of rights. The MPRDA deprived people of their capacity to realise the economic goods enabled by the liberty to sterilise minerals or to exchange them in the market. On Froneman J's framework, this would ordinarily entitle them to a monetary award. General historical injustice around minerals, though, diminished their concrete significance. According to Froneman J, so much so that the decision by Parliament to adjust market value downwards to nil was just and equitable.

Below we touch on injustice again, but first we consider how forms of just acquisition can be relevant when awarding compensation. Some property is the conscious creation of the lawmaker, brought into being *ex nihilo* for an instrumental, policy-based reason. One favourite example of theorists is an exemption, for example, to sell alcohol. When property rights are acquired in this way, we are often less worried about their later deprivation. The reason why is not, as is often argued, that 'just as the state giveth, it can taketh away'. It is not a question of state largesse, nor is it because government must be free to adopt new policies. Rather, it is because concerns about the security of holdings or expectations seem less urgent. They seem less urgent because, ordinarily, holders know, or they can be expected to know, that the rights were contingent on government not later changing the policy that moved it to create these rights. In short, these rights were always a little insecure. Whilst this fact is not decisive, justice and equity require less in such cases. Sometimes, if we afford affected parties reasonable notice of, and an opportunity to participate in, the process resulting in the decision to alter their rights, this will ensure that justice is done.

What about where property rights were acquired justly, but through relations with non-state actors? Are these facts relevant to compensation? Yes. The form of the relation is crucial. If the property was acquired through market exchange, our response to expropriation will be different than if it was acquired as inheritance, as a gift, by donation, or originally. The relevant question is: Does the history of acquisition tell us anything about the goods or bads that are facilitated or frustrated by these rights? If so, history matters – and monetary awards, grounded in the exercise of practical, not theoretical, reason, must be sensitive to this form of acquisition.

History of use: Turning now to the history of use. This information may be relevant from the perspective of the right-holder, as evidence of how important this use is to them. Long-standing use may be evidence, for example, of the fact that the existing set of rights facilitates a good that has constitutive, not fleeting, importance to their life. Whilst relevant to compensation, we focus here on a different role performed by this use-aspect of paragraph (b). When (b) asks after use, it focusses attention on the ends to which persons who once held rights, but no longer do, put them. The concern for historical use displays sensitivity to two facts. First, our past is stained by unjust acquisitions. Second, there are epistemic or pragmatic hurdles to restitution. With compensation, though, such hurdles matter less. This is because, with Section 25(3), the aim is not restoring rights but promoting good and frustrating bad. To realise this function, establishing direct ties between persons, or determining the exact scope of an injustice, is unnecessary. What matters are the ends towards which property was put by the victims of injustice. If the ends are good, facts about this use are relevant when, through the exercise of our practical reason, we fix compensation.

Let us make this more concrete through examples. On a family holiday, you drive past your childhood home. You stop, knock on the front door, and ask the occupiers if you can show your children around, to see where mom grew up. These experiences matter, for they offer us a link to our past. Therefore, if your request is denied, you would be disappointed, but you would probably let the matter go. Let us complicate the example. For some, ties to property go deeper, having a constitutive, identity-defining significance. This is sometimes the case with land. A white South African like me is sometimes told by black South Africans that this is what is meant by phrases like, 'We want the land' or 'The land is ours'. If legislation answers these calls by expropriating land, historical use is relevant to the compensation awarded. It is relevant because it will allow us to rank concretely conflicting goods.

To see this clearly, consider how an existing right-holder may respond to legislation the goal of which is to expropriate rights to facilitate access to graves. He might complain that granting a third party a liberty to access land will impinge on his privacy or complain about the risk of damage to the land or attached property. If bona fide, these concerns matter. For expropriation to be just, we must be sensitive to them. Legislation can cater to them by making the liberty to access land conditional on first giving reasonable notice to the occupier and by affording the right-holder a claim against people who, when exercising the liberty, cause damage. But even with these efforts, privacy and security will still be diminished, even if not a lot. This is unavoidable since privacy and security for one person conflict with access by another. In these cases, we must consider the market value of the lost rights. At this point, historical use becomes relevant. The fact of limited resources means we must concretely rank goods. After we do, if we conclude that the importance of, say, a sense of belonging exceeds, in the prevailing context and therefore at this point in time, goods like privacy and security, then we must adjust downwards the money paid.

Past investments and subsidies. Section 25(3)(d) concerns the extent of state investment and subsidies in the acquisition and beneficial capital improvement of property. Why is this relevant? AJ Van der Walt says: 'Obviously it would make no sense to compensate someone at full market value for land that was originally acquired or subsequently developed with state assistance.'[93] It is not obvious, though, for assisting people is the state's job, so if we benefit 'twice',[94] in the past and present, all the better. For state provision is not largesse, but rather a fulfilment of duty. When the state expropriates it is not owed anything. What it has historically provided, however, is relevant when the incompatibility of goods calls, through the exercise of practical reason, for choice and sacrifice.

To grasp why, we must recognise that the function of paragraph (d) is not restitutionary, nor does it concern retribution or reward. These issues all concern the past. Their essential question is: What was done? Expropriation, contrarily, both reformist and transformative, is always future-oriented.

It asks: What should be done? To answer this, however, and to do right by those living in this world, our thinking must be structured by our awareness of wrongs done in a world that is no more. This is not to reverse wrongs. Nor is the reason derived from the fact that their legacies endure. When we expropriate and compensate, what matters is not the effect of a wrong, but the wrong itself. Even then, only derivatively. Wrongs matter because they are accompanied by loss of something good. This loss is part of what makes a wrong bad. With expropriation, it is why its relevance is rooted in good. Wrongs matter since they concern our non-conformity to the reasons that we had to bring a good into the world. It is to do justice to goods that did not come to be that we must, when fixing compensation, consider the wrongs responsible for this fact.

In doing so, the fact of limited resources is relevant, for it means that the state's investing in and subsidising one good will always be at the expense of another. To choose between goods is not to deny the significance of what is sacrificed, but it does communicate a relative ranking of goods. Past benefits matter when fixing compensation because these benefits evidence concrete rankings. They evidence past rankings because the deemed 'value' of the benefitted object will have been a reason for the investment or subsidy. For us, what matters is how we respond to the fact that a benefit was given, for our response likewise evidences a concrete ranking, albeit what it now evidences is how goods are ranked in the present. Critical is whether our past and present judgements diverge. If they do, then the award must be adjusted. The quantity that is awarded can either be increased or decreased. It must be increased if the past judgement is now thought to have 'undervalued' the relative significance of the good facilitated by the investment or subsidy. If its 'extent' was inadequate, if the benefits were too small, or if no benefits were provided at all, then the affected party will be entitled to payment exceeding market value. Contrarily, if the judgement 'overvalued' the good, then the award should be decreased, with the affected party awarded less than market value. To make this more tangible, recall the apartheid state's discriminatory laws in this regard. For example, whilst white agricultural areas received significant state funding, areas zoned for black agriculture were given little. This past divergence evidences a concrete judgement about the relative importance of the agricultural activities of blacks and whites. Of course, there is now a shared recognition that this past ranking was wrong. And this judgement must feed into how we fix monetary awards when or if agricultural property is expropriated.

In a strongly plural world, constituted by diverse goods, life is necessarily structured by both choice and sacrifice. To do justice to these conflicting demands, we must rank them. This entails the exercise of practical, not theoretical, reason. When we fail in the judgements that structure these rankings and thereby do wrong, this must inform what we do going forward. It is to discover the past failure of reason that we must look at subsidies or investments. When we find failure, Section 25(3)(d) tells us this: What is done is what remains, but living between past and future, we should always strive to make amends. And as Walter Benjamin remarks in a related context: 'That claim cannot be settled cheaply.'[95]

NOTES

1. An earlier version of the second section of this chapter was published in Matthew Kruger, 'Compensation as Radical Transformation' *Potchefstroom Electronic Law Journal* 27 (June 2024): 1–33.
2. *Shoprite Checkers (Pty) Ltd v MEC for Economic Development, Eastern Cape and Others* 2015 (6) SA 125 (CC) para. 39.
3. Ibid., para. 4.
4. Ibid., paras. 35–36.
5. Ibid., para. 4.
6. Ibid., paras. 36 and 51.
7. Ibid., paras. 4, 42–49 and 60–63.
8. Ibid., para. 50.
9. *Agri SA v Minister for Minerals and Energy* 2013 (4) SA 1 (CC).
10. Gregory Alexander, 'Property as a Fundamental Constitutional Right? The German Example' (2003) 88 *Cornell Law Review* 733. This article is cited six times by Froneman J.
11. On progressivism, see G. Alexander et al., 'A Statement of Progressive Property' (2009) 94 *Cornell Law Review* 743 and Jane B. Baron 'Contested Commitments of Property' 61(4) *Hastings Law Journal*(2010) 917–67.
12. Gregory Alexander, *Property and Human Flourishing* (2018) xi.
13. Ibid., 3.
14. Ibid., 4–6.
15. Ibid., 6–9.
16. Ibid., 5–7, 220–22 and 231ff.
17. Ibid., 225.
18. Ibid., 26–28.
19. Ibid., xiv and 269.
20. Ibid., 6–7 and 10–14.
21. *Shoprite Checkers* (n 2) para. 50.
22. Alexander (n 12) 7.
23. Ibid., 47–53.
24. Ibid., 49.
25. Ibid., 53–55.
26. Ibid., 73.
27. Ibid., 56–57.
28. Ibid., 58–62.

29. *Shoprite Checkers* (n 2) para. 47.
30. Ibid., para. 50.
31. Alexander (n 12) 28–35.
32. *Shoprite Checkers* (n 2) para. 53.
33. Ibid., para. 50.
34. Ibid., paras. 36, 44, 46 and 52.
35. Ibid., para. 52. On this issue, see A.J. Van der Walt, *Constitutional Property Law* (3ed, 2011) 23–29.
36. *Shoprite Checkers* (n 2) para. 53, quoting *Investment Aid* Case *4 BVerfGE 7* [1954] (emphasis added).
37. Alexander (n 12) 32–35, 201–06 and 265–66, read with the chapters on communities (75–100) and intergenerational communities (103–33). In *Shoprite Checkers* (n 2), Froneman J cites *Affordable Medicines Trust and Others v Minister of Health and Others* 2006 (3) SA 247 (CC) para. 59, and *Hamburg Flood Control* 24 BVerfGE 367 [1968], where a narrative model of the self is adopted (paras. 45 and 53). See also the reference to 'human personality as a whole' (para. 64).
38. Alexander (n 12) 66.
39. His theory has three pillars: (a) the social thesis (Ibid., 45–55), (b) the capabilities thesis (6–9); and (c) temporally extended fittingness (32–33). When combined, we get a model that in its basic structure is Hegelian in form.
40. Ibid., 202–03 and 206.
41. John Gardner, *Law as a Leap of Faith* (2012) v.
42. Alexander (n 12) 52.
43. For Alexander, the 'whole just is the concept of ownership itself, including its moral foundation' (Ibid., 204), which is to enable the temporally extended flourishing of 'the community as a whole' (209). This is why he can argue that: 'Property rights and their correlative obligations are cognizable as social goods, worthy of vindication by the state, only insofar as they are consistent with community and human flourishing more generally' (215), and that 'the state should protect property only to the extent that the owner fulfills this social responsibility. . . [because the] social obligation norm . . . is conceived as internal to the concept of ownership itself' (222). Primacy of the community also structures his analysis of self-expression and destruction of art (255–27).
44. Ibid., 61.
45. *Shoprite Checkers* (n 2) para. 48.
46. Ibid., paras. 42–43.
47. Section 7(2) of the Constitution.
48. Some examples: change/stability (A.J. Van der Walt, *Property in the Margins* (2009) 1–26); public/private (Theunis Roux, 'Property' in Woolman and Bishop (eds) *Constitutional Law of South Africa* (2014) ch. 46); conquest/conquered (Joel Modiri, 'Conquest and constitutionalism: first thoughts on an alternative jurisprudence' (2018) *South African Journal of Human Rights* 300); exclusion/sharing (Z Boggenpoel and B Slade, 'Where is Property? Some Thoughts on the Theoretical Implications of *Daniels v Scribante*' (2020) *Constitutional Court Review* 379); and

agency/repression (Stuart Wilson, *Human Rights and the Transformation of Property* (2021) 27–33).

49. *Tshwane City v Link Africa* 2015 (6) SA 440 (CC) para. 106.

50. *Daniels v Scribante* 2017 (4) SA 341 (CC) paras. 115 and 138.

51. Ibid., para. 134.

52. Cf. Sue-Mari Viljoen, 'Property and "Human Flourishing": A Reassessment in the Housing Framework' PER / PELJ 2019(22) 20–21.

53. Hanoch Dagan, *A Liberal Theory of Property* (2021) 37.

54. *Agri SA* (n 9) para. 2.

55. Item 8 of schedule II to the MPRDA.

56. Section 51(4) of the MPRDA.

57. *Agri SA* (n 9) paras. 41–46.

58. Ibid., para. 50.

59. Ibid., paras. 51–52 and 66.

60. Section 2 of the MPRDA.

61. For property, see sections 25(4)(a), (5), (6), (8) and (9) of the Constitution; for other rights, see sections 9(2), 26(2), 27(1)(b) and 27(2) of the Constitution.

62. *Holcim (South Africa) (Pty) Ltd v Prudent Investors (Pty) Ltd* [2011] 1 All SA 364 (SCA) para. 23.

63. *Agri SA* (n 9) paras. 50–53.

64. Ibid., paras. 67–68.

65. Ibid., paras. 58–59, 68 and 71.

66. Ibid., paras. 48, 58–59 and 67. Cameron J (paras 77–78) and Froneman J (paras 100–05) think that it is a hallmark of expropriation, but not a necessary condition.

67. As Marx explains, 'systematic colonization' (CVI 939) or 'expropriation' (CVI 932–34, 940), as a method of 'original' (CVI 714*) or 'primitive accumulation' (CVI 873) was effected by means of 'government set[ting] an artificial price on the virgin soil' (CVI 938), that is, creating a state power to allocate, through sale, exclusive property rights in land over which people previously had a discretion to use.

68. *Agri SA* (n 9) para. 81.

69. Ibid., paras. 60–65 and 69–70.

70. Ibid., para. 81.

71. Ibid., paras. 86–90, 92–95 and 104.

72. Ibid., paras. 87, 90 and 99.

73. Ibid., para. 91.

74. Ibid., para. 88.

75. Ibid., paras. 82–84 and 99.

76. Ibid., paras. 88, 90, 94, 99 and 107–08.

77. Ibid., para. 107.

78. The standard reading of Section 25(3) is that it is 'protective' (Van der Walt (n 34) 28–31) or 'defensive' (Jackie Dugard, 'Unpacking Section 25: What, If Any, Are the Legal Barriers to Transformative Land Reform?' (2019) 9 *Constitutional Court Review* 135, 144), with sections 25(5) to (9) reformist.

79. *Agri SA* (n 9) para. 91.

80. Compensation can be fixed before or after expropriation (*Haffejee NO and Others v Ethekwini Municipality* 2011 (6) SA 134 (CC)), hence my alternate use of old/existing and new/proposed in the main text that follows.

81. Section 25(2) of the Constitution.

82. Items 2(b) and 8 of schedule II to the MPRDA.

83. *Agri SA* (n 9) para. 108.

84. *MEC for Education, KwaZulu-Natal v Pillay* 2008 (1) SA 474 (CC) para. 107.

85. The disagreement is captured in *Du Toit v Minister of Transport* 2006 (1) SA 297 (CC) paras. 37 and 84.

86. A point well-made by JW Singer, *Entitlement: The Paradoxes of Property* (2000) 39 and 205, in the context of property.

87. Johan van der Walt, *Law and Sacrifice: Towards a Post-Apartheid Theory of Law* (2005) 191–231.

88. John Gardner, *From Personal Life to Private Law* (2018) 98–102.

89. Ibid., 142.

90. CVI 162–63.

91. Amartya Sen, *Development as Freedom* (1999) 14.

92. On these and other difficulties, see Alexander (n 11) 135–68.

93. Van der Walt (n 34) 513.

94. Jeannie Van Wyk, 'Compensation for land reform expropriation' (2017) *Tydskrif vir die Suid-Afrikaanse Reg* 21, 29.

95. Walter Benjamin, *Illuminations* (ed. Hannah Arendt, tr. Harry Zohn, 1969) 254.

Epilogue

In the hope of reconciling us to the conflict between the goods that constitute modern life, Hegel takes up the flower as a symbolic call for intellectual activity: '*Here* is the rose, dance *here*.'[1] In criticising Hegel, Marx adopts but inverts the symbol, for the sake of prescribing a revolutionary form of change: 'cast off the chain and gather the living flower'.[2] In chapter 4, we revealed that the contents of their symbols and property theories are rooted in answers to the anthropological question: What is Man? In this book, I have argued that their schemes – indeed, all such abstract prescriptions – are unavailable to the strong goods pluralist, for the diversity of goodness renders them arbitrary and incoherent.

The symbol, however, is worth keeping. Polish novelist Olga Tokarczuk, in her melancholic, haunting, yet playful book, *Drive Your Plow Over the Bones of the Dead*, deploys this symbol to powerful effect. She does so in a way that South Africans, but I think all who reside in a strongly plural community, should take seriously when thinking about property:

> I grew up in a beautiful era, now sadly in the past. In it there was great readiness for change, and a talent for creating revolutionary visions. Nowadays no one still has the courage to think up anything new. All they ever talk about, round the clock, is how things already are, they just keep rolling out the same old ideas. Reality has grown old and gone senile; after all, it is definitely subject to the same laws as every living organism – it ages. Just like the cells of the body, its tiniest components, the senses, succumb to apoptosis. Apoptosis is natural death, brought about by the tiredness and exhaustion of matter. In Greek this word means 'the dropping of petals'. The world has dropped its petals.[3]

The world has indeed dropped its petals; or, in the more prosaic idiom of theorists, for some time we have been living at the end of history, where our elites can see no alternative to the prevailing arrangement of things. Yet, it is in this fact that we can find hope, a chance for revivification, and through this a way of overcoming the melancholy of Tokarczuk and indeed of late modernity in general. By virtue of the petals having been dropped, they lie all around us, at our feet, waiting to be gathered and arranged in the ways we judge best. The petals include those ultimate goods that inspired the originally revolutionary visions of Locke, Bentham, Hayek, Hegel and Marx, and so also those parts of the resulting formal structures found in their works. As I have not yet tired of stressing in these pages, however, they would form just part of the arrangement, a mere selection of the superabundance of goods that constitute our lives.

Ever since Karl Klare's influential paper on transformative constitutionalism,[4] though, theory in South Africa on the constitutional need for and process of legal change has been characterised by three key features. First, emphasis on the judicial function. Second, identification of common law defects. Third, efforts to articulate more concretely the abstract content of the Bill of Rights. Perhaps this restricted focus can be explained by the fact that lawyers, in education and practice, are primarily exposed to issues of this kind. Or perhaps it is the product of a latent prejudice, as Jeremy Waldron puts it, against the 'dignity of legislation', rooted in their distrust of politics and its '*all too human*' unpredictability or foibles,[5] its 'fickle and capricious nature',[6] as two eminent South African lawyers see it – a prejudice possibly rooted in the role that legislation, as sustained by a compliant judiciary that employed formal over substantive reasoning, played in constituting and implementing apartheid rule. Whatever the reasons, and as understandable as they might be, the legal and theoretical battles around these issues have been settled. It is time that we move on, at least when it comes to efforts to transform property.

Certainly, judicial law-making and discretion are legitimate, common law must be developed in line with constitutional values, and it is critical that we give concrete content to abstract rights by fixing their Hohfeldian structures and thereby augmenting the authority of the foundational law of South Africa. When it comes to property, however, courts and common law must take a back seat to Parliament and legislation, and theorists must learn to humble themselves and limit their work to diverse descriptions of what can be done, rather than forever beneficently prescribe to us what they believe ought to be done. By now, it is hopefully clear why, but let us put the reason in constitutional terms.

The Constitution obliges us to respect, protect, promote and fulfil diverse goods. These basic commitments express the Constitution's spirit, purport and objects. With property, they entail the deflated, descriptive alternative to the anthropological structure, where we ask after the forms we want to facilitate or frustrate, the constitutive relations of the forms, and the Hohfeldian incidents that we must allocate to facilitate or frustrate these relational forms. In deciding what to facilitate or frustrate, the Constitution non-exhaustively stipulates some answers in the Bill of Rights, with the theorist's task being to describe their constitutive relations and the property rights that enable them, as I tried to do in chapter 10 with the MPRDA. After we answer these questions, however, we learn that they are often incompatible. Which means that we must rank the conflicting goods to establish whether we must restructure existing rights for the sake of facilitating or frustrating goods or bads in accordance with our rankings. It is here, when we are choosing which goods to make possible and which goods to sacrifice, when selecting which bads to battle and which to let manifest, that the Constitution offers no answer to the question, 'What is to be done?'

This ultimate indeterminacy is why our theorists must learn to humble themselves. Because it is not just, as Klare writes, that the particularity of the materials with which judges work and the particularity of their backgrounds allows for diverse outcomes. He is right. We have known since at least Hegel,[7] and much important work on this issue has been done by legal philosophers since then, that the relation between a principle and its application entails not a mechanical deduction but derivation, that is, the exercise of interpretation and judgement, which activity and outcome are necessarily indeterminate. The Constitution, however, embodies a more radical openness. When effecting structural change to the legal regime that regulates property, the Constitution's embrace of the diversity of goodness means that we are sometimes faced with conflicts between ultimate but incompatible goods. When we are, the indeterminate interpretation pointed to by Klare does not assist decision-making. The difficulty in these cases, like when we are transforming existing property relations, is not the presence of gaps in the system but the total absence of any system, for when we are deciding 'What is to be done', there is no absolute principle, nor any coherent or ordered set of principles, to interpret at all.

Therefore, at least in the South African context, the yearnings of the socialist for a 'coherent and organic conception of ends, means, social processes, and historical possibilities',[8] is just as incoherent as the more modest wish of liberals or progressives for a 'theory of improvement',[9] or 'moral guidelines' to be 'legally implemented' in particular cases,[10] or 'parameters' to 'guid[e]' those with power,[11] or 'maxims' that are sensitive to 'local' facts that empower the capable to get on with the technical art of government.[12] Each is incoherent because we live in a strongly plural world, which means that when we are deciding what to do, we are confronted with incompatible options, the practical significance of which is relative and contextual. This is why philosophers have no privileged insight when it comes to deciding what to do. Their ignorance is why there is no point in turning to them in these situations. Rather than telling us what to do, they must satisfy themselves with describing existing or possible worlds by answering one of the three questions posed by Froneman J in *Agri SA*: what forms, relations and rights? In doing so, they may let our allocative options be seen more clearly, but that is all that they can do. The philosopher is not an architect; their job is not to provide us with blueprints. Whatever we or they might wish, they are constitutionally incapable of prescribing how this world should be changed, not just at the level of details but structure too.

All of their blueprints, paradigms, templates and lenses, no matter how ingeniously they have been rethought, reframed, redesigned or reimagined, reveal a failure either to grasp or accept the radical nature of the Constitution. Before a decision is made, every attempt, by people with titles before their names or letters after them, to prescribe what we should do, as opposed to describing what we can do, is always a result of their theoretical naïveté, a function of their political hubris, or an articulation of their illegitimate power. When there exists conflict between good and good, each bearing the seal of constitutional law, authority decides. This is one reason why law exists: there are no experts to trust, so it functions to settle authoritatively and for the time being all the questions that theory cannot. And since our ultimate law is democratic, this power is reserved for 'we the people', acting directly and through Parliament. Thus, it is only after we together decide what to do that a transformed property system can be justified and just. Waldron explains: 'That is the logic of legislation.'[13] And only once legislation of this kind exists, is it ever permissible to empower judges to evaluate concretely and contextually, like Froneman J did in *Agri SA*, matters that become embroiled in dispute.

Whilst it is true and important that the Constitution leaves unanswered questions open to the input of contingent facts,[14] its non-prescriptiveness runs far deeper. Its normative content is not a seamless web. It does not progressively unfold by means of legislative and judicial discernment of its immanent content, a perhaps never-ending process, but one that still strives to work the text pure. The refusal to prescribe is internal to the Constitution itself. Thus, not just an 'interpretive openness',[15] requiring legislators or judges to make 'the impossible passage between the rule and its application',[16] when we are faced with incompatible goods, we have a true discretion, a radical choice, where we the people are free to choose as we judge fit.

Whilst transformation talk often exists at the level of abstraction, using, as Marx once put it, a 'pompous catalogue' of five-dollar words, in legal practice it is quite 'modest'.[17] Legislatively, it entails an originally free choice to, for example, annul (or not) a discretion to sterilise minerals and create (or not) a new power to allocate exemptions to exploit minerals to the first qualifying applicants. That is all. That is what any act of transformation entails. Provided these changes are not arbitrary, and provided that they are accompanied by just and equitable compensation, which evaluative questions when disputed we allow judges to decide or approve, there is a convergence between constitutionalism and radicalism – that is, in the idiom of political economists, between the political and social questions. Reduced to these formal features, we now see that the common refrain that a 'paradigm of private property' or 'absolute' conception of property dominates our legal practice and that we live in the grip of an 'ownership model' that privileges 'individualism and exclusion' does not accurately describe our reality. Whilst correct to direct focus to property structures and not just their distribution, those who make these claims tilt at windmills. For, as the MPRDA illustrates, their refrains do not faithfully describe our present. Still haunted by the past, as understandable as this may be, it is not us but them who remain captured by these phantom – tired and exhausted – forms of thought.

Law is an authoritative institution. It settles questions theory cannot. It does this by creating rights: liberties, claims, powers or immunities. In this way, it helps to make goods possible. And because South Africa's ultimate law embraces the diversity of goodness, its people live, or ought to live, in a world of possibilities. In *Agri SA*, Froneman J discovered the radical potential of this truth. That the majority of the Court did not see this, however, reveals two related tragic truths. First, and inescapably, since possibility is constituted by indeterminacy and choice, the movement from what can be to what is cannot be guaranteed. Second, and intolerably, we hanker after change but fail to see that the Constitution is a constitution of possibilities. The results of this failure will be evident to all who look. We live in a world, a structure of political-economic and legal practices, in which, as Heidegger once wrote, our horizons of possibilities have been 'closed off', few 'new possibilities are willed', and much that is still willed is often little more than 'wishful' thinking.[18] The gap that separates what can be and what is has become all but abyssal.

To some extent, this situation is explicable. Absorbed by more immediate, pressing concerns, many have little time or space to reflect on the radical possibilities inherent in any situation. But even if we identified all the causes and excused all particular persons, the threatening abyss – the possibility that all will always be essentially the same – would still exist as a constitutive feature of the present conjuncture. Were South Africans to grasp the fact that the Constitution's property clause embodies a call for a pluralistic radicalism, however, they would come closer to grasping the import of its transformative nature. Section 25 of the Constitution is transformative, meaning it is also radical, for it rejects prescriptive anthropology in favour of the diversity of goodness. It understands that the conflict internal to all rights-allocations means there will often be a need for new exercises of power to settle disagreements. And it recognises that the exercise of this power will often result in change, effected by grasping matters at the root – by altering the logic of the relational forms facilitated or frustrated by the property rights that attach to or obtain in objects, by altering these rights to some mutually exclusive set.

Whilst transformation entails moving from what exists to something that is incompatible with it, it does not entail the embrace of extremes, hubris or vanity. The Constitution calls on us to act, but having embraced the diversity of goodness, it ultimately and for the most part keeps silent on what to do. So situated, we must evaluate our diverse possibilities with humility and courage, we must take responsibility for what we choose and sacrifice, and we must regret what is lost whilst holding firm to our choices – a way of relating incompatible with extremism, hubris and vanity. Transformation obliges us to do justice to all sides of conflicts between goods, to discover and to accept the limits that the conflicts impose, and to keep each incompatible good within its rightful bounds. This requires recognising all involved and facilitating a fair decision-making process – that is, democratically, by virtue of our status as free and equal bearers of dignity, each united in our diversity. And it equally requires that we strive to make up for all the goods that will always be lost whenever the law performs its authoritative, allocative function.

The power of this tragic yet hopeful commitment, it appears to me, makes itself felt nowhere more compellingly than in the setting of Parliament's original power to expropriate property and its correlative duty to compensate all affected parties when it does.

NOTES

1. EPR 22.
2. CCHPR 132.
3. Olga Tokarczuk, *Drive Your Plow Over the Bones of the Dead* (tr. Antonia Lloyd-Jones, 2019) 57.
4. Karl Klare, 'Legal Culture and Transformative Constitutionalism' 14 *South African Journal of Human Rights* (1998) 146.
5. Jeremy Waldron, *The Dignity of Legislation* (1999) 24.
6. Michelle le Roux and Dennis Davis, *Lawfare: Judging Politics in South Africa* (2019) 172.
7. In fact, as explained by Gregory Alexander, *Property and Human Flourishing* (2018) 28–33, we have known this since at least Aristotle.
8. Ellen Meiksins Wood, *The Retreat from Class: A New 'True' Socialism* (rev. ed., 1998) 90–91.
9. Ronald Dworkin, *Sovereign Virtue* (2000) 162–64.
10. WHD 202–03.

11. Alexander (n 7) xvi.
12. Hanoch Dagan, *A Liberal Theory of Property* (2021) 17–18.
13. Waldron (n 5) 91.
14. Stuart Wilson, *Human Rights and the Transformation of Property* (2021) 34.
15. Henk Botha, 'Freedom and Constraint in Constitutional Adjudication' 20 *South African Journal of Human Rights* (2004) 249, 276.
16. Johan van der Walt, *Law and Sacrifice: Towards a Post-Apartheid Theory of Law* (2005) 224.
17. CVI 416.
18. Martin Heidegger, *Being and Time* (tr. J. Macquarrie and E. Robinson, 1962) 239–40.

Bibliography

Adorno, Theodor. *Minima Moralia: Reflections on a Damaged Life*. Translated by E. F. N. Jephcott. London: Verso, 2005.

———. *Notes to Literature*. Edited by Rolf Tiedemann. Translated by Shierry Weber Nicholson. New York: Columbia University Press, 2019.

Adorno, Theodor, and Max Horkheimer. *Dialectic of Enlightenment*. Translated by John Cumming. London: Verso, 2016.

———. *Towards a New Manifesto*. Translated by Rodney Livingstone. London: Verso, 2019.

Affordable Medicines Trust and Others v Minister of Health and Others 2006 (3) SA 247 (CC).

Agamben, Giorgio. *Homo Sacer: Sovereign Power and Bare Life*. Translated by Daniel Heller-Roazen. Stanford: Stanford University Press, 1998.

———. *The Kingdom and the Garden*. Translated by Adam Kotsko. London: Seagull Books, 2020.

———. *The State of Exception*. Translated by Kevin Attell. Chicago: University of Chicago Press, 2005.

Agri SA v Minister for Minerals and Energy 2013 (4) SA 1 (CC).

Akkermans, Bram. 'Sustainable Ownership – New Obligations Towards Achieving a Sustainable Society'. *European Property Law Journal* 10, no. 2/3 (2021): 277–303.

———. 'Sustainable Property Law: Reckoning, Resilience, and Reform'. *Eleven International Publishing. Maastricht Law Series* 24 (2022): 7–22.

Alexander, Gregory. *Property and Human Flourishing*. New York: Oxford University Press, 2018.

———. 'Property as a Fundamental Constitutional Right? The German Example'. *Cornell Law Review* 88, no. 3 (2003): 733–78.

Alexander, Gregory, Eduardo M. Peñalver, Joseph William Singer, and Laura S. Underkuffler. 'A Statement of Progressive Property'. *Cornell Law Review* 94, no. 4 (2009): 743–44.

Althusser, Louis. *For Marx*. Translated by Ben Brewster. London: Verso, 2005.

Anderson, Perry. *Considerations on Western Marxism*. London: Verso, 1979.
———. 'Modernity and Revolution'. *New Left Review* I/44 (March–April 1984): 96–113.
Arendt, Hannah. *Between Past and Future: Eight Exercises in Political Thought*. London: Penguin Books, 2006.
———. *The Human Condition*. Chicago: University of Chicago Press, second edition, 1998.
———. *Lectures on Kant's Political Philosophy*. Edited by Ronald Beiner. Chicago: University of Chicago Press, 1989.
———. *The Promise of Politics*. Edited by Jerome Kohn. New York: Schocken Books, 2005.
———. 'Thinking'. In *The Life of the Mind*. New York: Harcourt Brace Jovanovich, one-volume edition, 1978.
Aristotle. *The Nicomachean Ethics*. Translated by David Ross. Oxford: Oxford University Press, 2009.
Avineri, Shlomo. *Hegel's Theory of the Modern State*. Cambridge: Cambridge University Press, 1974.
———. *The Social and Political Thought of Karl Marx*. London: Cambridge University Press, 1968.
Avineri, Shlomo, and Avner de-Shalit, eds. *Communitarianism and Individualism*. Oxford: Oxford University Press, 1992.
Baron, Jane B. 'Contested Commitments of Property'. *Hastings Law Journal* 61, no. 4 (2010): 917–67.
Barthes, Roland. 'The Death of the Author'. In *Image, Music, Text*. Translated by Stephen Heath. London: Fontana Press, 1977.
Basso, Luca. *Marx and Singularity: From the Early Writings to the Grundrisse*. Translated by Arianna Bove. Chicago: Haymarket Books, 2012.
Bastani, Aaron. *Fully Automated Luxury Communism*. London: Verso, 2019.
Baudrillard, Jean. *The Consumer Society: Myths and Structures*. Translated by Chris Turner. London: Sage Publications, 1998.
———. *For a Critique of the Political Economy of the Sign*. Translated by Charles Levin. St Louis: Telos Press, 1981.
———. *Impossible Exchange*. Translated by Chris Turner. London: Verso, 2001.
———. *The Mirror of Production*. Translated by Mark Poster. St Louis: Telos Press, 1975.
———. *Symbolic Exchange and Death*. Translated by Iain Hamilton Grant. London: Sage, revised edition, 2017.
———. *The System of Objects*. Translated by James Benedict. London: Verso, 2005.
Beiser, Frederick C. *Enlightenment, Revolution and Romanticism: The Genesis of Modern German Political Thought, 1790–1800*. Cambridge, MA: Harvard University Press, 1992.
Benjamin, Walter. *Illuminations: Essays and Reflections*. Edited by Hannah Arendt. Translated by Harry Zohn. New York: Schocken, 1969.

Bentham, Jeremy. 'An Essay on Language'. In *The Works of Jeremy Bentham: Vol. VIII*, published under the Superintendence of his Executor, John Bowring. Edinburgh: William Tait, 1838–1843.

———. 'A Fragment on Government'. In *A Comment on the Commentaries and A Fragment on Government*, edited by J. H. Burns and H. L. A. Hart. Oxford: Oxford University Press, 2008.

———. 'A Fragment on Ontology'. In *The Works of Jeremy Bentham: Vol. VIII*, published under the Superintendence of his Executor, John Bowring. Edinburgh: William Tait, 1838–1843.

———. *An Introduction to the Principles of Morals and Legislation.* Oxford: Clarendon Press, 1907.

———. 'Principles of Legislation'. In *Theory of Legislation.* Translated from the French of Etienne Dumont by Richard Hildreth. London: Kegan Paul, Trench, Trübner & Co., Ltd, 1896.

———. 'Principles of the Civil Code'. In *Theory of Legislation.* Translated from the French of Etienne Dumont by Richard Hildreth. London: Kegan Paul, Trench, Trübner & Co., Ltd, 1896.

Berlin, Isaiah. *Concepts and Categories: Philosophical Essays.* Edited by Henry Hardy. Princeton: Princeton University Press, 1999.

———. *Liberty.* Edited by Henry Hardy. Oxford: Oxford University Press, 2002.

———. *The Proper Study of Mankind: An Anthology of Essays.* Edited by Henry Hardy. London: Vintage Publishing, 2013.

Berman, Marshall. *Adventures in Marxism.* London: Verso, 1999.

———. *All That Is Solid Melts Into Air, The Experience of Modernity.* New York: Penguin Books, 1988.

Bernstein v Bester and Others NNO 1996 (2) SA 751 (CC).

Blakeley, Grace. *Vulture Capitalism: Corporate Crimes, Backdoor Bailouts and the Death of Freedom.* London: Bloomsbury Publishing, 2024.

Boggenpoel, Zsa-Zsa, and Bradley Slade. 'Where is Property? Some Thoughts on the Theoretical Implications of *Daniels v Scribante*'. *Constitutional Court Review* 10 (2020): 379–99.

Botha, Henk. 'Freedom and Constraint in Constitutional Adjudication'. *South African Journal of Human Rights* 20 (2004): 249–83.

Bratton, Benjamin. *The Revenge of the Real: Politics for a Post-Pandemic World.* London: Verso, 2022.

Braver, Lee. *A Thing of This World: A History of Continental Anti-Realism.* Evanston: Northwestern University Press, 2007.

Brooks, Thom. *Hegel's Political Philosophy: A Systematic Reading of the* Philosophy of Right. Edinburgh: Edinburgh University Press, 2007.

Buber, Martin. *Between Man and Man.* Translated by Ronald Gregor Smith. New York: The MacMillan Company, 1947.

———. *Eclipse of God: Studies in the Relation between Religion and Philosophy.* Princeton: Princeton University Press, 2016.

———. *I and Thou.* Translated by Ronald Gregor Smith. Edinburgh: T&T Clark Ltd, second edition, 1958.

———. *Pointing the Way: Collected Essays*. Translated by Maurice Friedman. New York: Haper, 1957.

Burns, J. H. 'Jeremy Bentham: From Radical Enlightenment to Philosophic Radicalism'. *Bentham Newsletter* 8 (June 1984): 4–13.

Butler E. M. *The Tyranny of Greece over Germany: A Study of the Influence Exercised by Greek Art and Poetry over the Great German Writers of the Eighteenth, Nineteenth and Twentieth Centuries*. Boston: Beacon Press, 1958.

Butler, Judith. *The Force of Nonviolence: An Ethico-Political Bind*. London: Verso, 2021.

———. *Frames of War: When is Life Grievable?* London: Verso, 2016.

———. *Precarious Life: The Powers of Mourning and Violence*. London: Verso, 2020.

———. *What World Is This? A Pandemic Phenomenology*. New York: Columbia University Press, 2022.

Chang, Ruth. 'Against Constitutive Incommensurability or Buying and Selling Friends'. *Philosophical Issues* 11, no. 1, *Social, Political, and Legal Philosophy* (2001): 33–60.

———. 'Are Hard Cases Vague Cases?' In *Value Incommensurability Ethics, Risk, and Decision-Making*, edited by Henrik Andersson and Anders Herlitz. New York: Routledge, 2022.

———. 'Are Hard Choices Cases of Incomparability'? *Philosophical Issues* 22, *Action Theory* (2012): 106–26.

———. 'Hard Choices'. *Journal of the American Philosophical Association* 3, no. 1 (2017): 1–21.

———. 'Introduction'. In *Incommensurability, Incomparability, and Practical Reason*, edited by Ruth Chang. Cambridge, MA: Harvard University Press, 1997.

———. 'Parity, Imprecise Comparability and the Repugnant Conclusion'. *Theoria* 82, no. 2 (2016): 182–214.

———. 'Value Pluralism'. In *International Encyclopedia of the Social and Behavioral Sciences*, edited by James Wright. Oxford: Elsevier, second edition, Volume 25, 2015.

Chernilo, Daniel. *Debating Humanity: Towards a Philosophical Sociology*. Cambridge: Cambridge University Press, 2017.

Cohen, G. A. *Karl Marx's Theory of History: A Defence*. Princeton: Princeton University Press, expanded edition, 2001.

———. *Self-Ownership, Freedom, and Equality*. Cambridge: Cambridge University Press, 1995.

Constitution of Republic of South Africa, 1996.

Crimmins, James E. *Secular Utilitarianism: Social Science and the Critique of Religion in the Thought of Jeremy Bentham*. New York: Clarendon Press, 1990.

Cristi, Renato. 'Hegel on Property and Recognition'. *Laval Théologique et Philosophique* 51, no. 2 (June 1995): 335–43.

Cullinan, Cormac. *Wild Law: A Manifesto for Earth Justice*. Cambridge: Green Books, second edition, 2011.

Dagan, Hanoch: *A Liberal Theory Property*. Cambridge: Cambridge University Press, 2021.

Daniels v Scribante 2017 (4) SA 341 (CC).

Day J. P. 'Locke on Property'. *The Philosophical Quarterly* 16, no. 64 (July 1966): 207–20.

Debord, Guy. *The Society of the Spectacle*. Translated by Fredy Perlman. Montreal: Critical Editions, 2021.

De Champs, Emmanuelle. *Enlightenment and Utility: Bentham in French, Bentham in France*. Cambridge: Cambridge University Press, 2015.

Delsol Chantal. *Icarus Fallen: The Search for Meaning in an Uncertain World.* Translated by Robin Dick. Wilmington: ISI Books, 2003.

———. *The Unlearned Lesson of the Twentieth Century: An Essay on Late Modernity*. Translated by Robin Dick. Wilmington: ISI Books, 2006.

Demsetz, Harold. 'Toward a Theory of Property Rights'. *The American Economic Review* 57, no. 2 (May, 1967): 347–59.

Deneen, Patrick J. *Why Liberalism Failed.* New Haven: Yale University Press, 2018.

Doctors for Life International v Speaker of the National Assembly 2006 (6) SA 416 (CC).

Du Plessis, Quentin. 'A Hohfeldian Analysis of the Bill of Rights'. *South African Law Journal* 139, no. 3 (2022): 577–622.

Du Toit v Minister of Transport 2006 (1) SA 297 (CC).

Dugard, Jackie. 'Unpacking Section 25: What, If Any, Are the Legal Barriers to Transformative Land Reform?'. *Constitutional Court Review* 9 (2019): 135–60.

Dworkin, Ronald. *A Matter of Principle*. Cambridge, MA: Harvard University Press, 1985.

———. *Sovereign Virtue: The Theory and Practice of Equality*. Cambridge, MA: Harvard University Press, 2000.

Economic Freedom Fighters v Minister of Justice and Correctional Services 2021 (2) SA 1 (CC).

Ehrenreich, Barbara. *Fear of Falling: The Inner Life of the Middle Class*. New York: Twelve, 2020.

Engels, Friedrich. *The Condition of the Working Class in England.* Oxford: Oxford University Press, 1993.

Esau and others v Minister of Co-operative Governance and Traditional Affairs and others [2021] 2 All SA 357 (SCA).

Eskom Holdings SOC Ltd v Vaal River Development Association (Pty) Ltd and Others 2023 (4) SA 325 (CC).

Ethekwini Municipality v Mounthaven (Pty) Ltd 2019 (4) SA 394 (CC).

Ex parte President of the Republic of South Africa: In re Constitutionality of the Liquor Bill 2000 (1) SA 732 (CC).

Feuerbach, Ludwig. 'Principles of the Philosophy of the Future'. In *The Fiery Brook: Selected Writings*. Translated by Zawar Hanfi. London: Verso, 2012.

Fineman, Martha. 'Equality, Autonomy, and the Vulnerable Subject in Law and Politics'. In *Vulnerability: Reflections on a New Ethical Foundation for Law and*

Politics, edited by Martha Albertson Fineman and Anna Grear. London: Routledge, 2016.
———. 'Vulnerability and Inevitable Inequality'. *Oslo Law Review* 4, no. 3 (2017): 133–49.
———. 'The Vulnerable Subject: Anchoring Equality in the Human Condition'. *Yale Journal of Law and Feminism* 20, no. 1 (2008): 1–23.
Foster, Michael Beresford. *The Political Philosophies of Plato and Hegel*. New York: Russell & Russell, 1965.
Foucault, Michel. *Archaeology of Knowledge*. Translated by A. M. Sheridan Smith. London: Routledge, second edition, 2002.
———. 'What is an Author?'. In *Aesthetics, Method, and Epistemology, Volume 2*, edited by James D. Faubion. Translated by Josue V. Harari. New York: The New Press, 1998.
Fraser, Ian. *Hegel and Marx: The Concept of Need*. Edinburgh: Edinburgh University Press, 1998.
Freud, Sigmund. *Civilization and its Discontents*. Translated by David McLintock. London: Penguin Classics, 2014.
Friedman, Milton. *Capitalism and Freedom*. Chicago: University of Chicago Press, fortieth anniversary edition, 2002.
Fromm, Erich. *Marx's Concept of Man*. London: Continuum, 2004.
Fukuyama, Francis. *The End of History and the Last Man*. London: Hamish Hamilton, 1992.
Gamble, Andrew. *The Iron Cage of Liberty*. Boulder, Colorado: Westview Press, 1996.
Gardner, John. *From Personal Life to Private Law*. Oxford: Oxford University Press, 2018.
———. 'Justifications and Reasons'. In *Harm and Culpability*, edited by A. P. Simester and A. T. H. Smith. Oxford: Clarendon Press, 1996.
———. *Law as a Leap of Faith: And Other Essays on Law in General*. Oxford: Oxford University Press, 2012.
Gerstle, Gary. *The Rise and Fall of the Neoliberal Order: America and the World in the Free Market Era*. Oxford: Oxford University Press, 2022.
Geuss, Raymond. *Outside Ethics*. Princeton: Princeton University Press, 2005.
———. *Philosophy and Real Politics*. Princeton: Princeton University Press, 2008.
———. *A World Without Why*. Princeton: Princeton University Press, 2014.
Google. 'Risk Adjusted Strategy for Economic Activity'. Accessed 18 August 2024. www.cesa.co.za/wp-content/uploads/2020/04/Untitled.pdf.
Gray, John. *Endgames: Questions in Late Modern Political Thought*. Cambridge, Polity Press, 1997.
———. *Enlightenment's Wake: Politics and Culture at the Close of the Modern Age*. London: Routledge Classics, 2007.
———. *False Dawn: The Delusions of Global Capitalism*. London: Granta Books, revised edition, 2009.
———. *Feline Philosophy: Cats and the Meaning of Life*. London: Picador, 2021.
———. *Gray's Anatomy: Selected Writings*. London: Penguin, new edition, 2016.

———. *Hayek on Liberty*. London: Routledge, third edition, 1998.
———. *Heresies: Against Progress and Other Illusions*. London: Granta Books, 2004.
———. *The New Leviathans: Thoughts After Liberalism*. London: Allen Lane, 2023.
———. *The Soul of the Marionette: A Short Inquiry into Human Freedom*. London: Allen Lane, 2015.
———. *Straw Dogs: Thoughts on Humans and Other Animals* London: Granta Publications Ltd, 2023.
———. *Two Faces of Liberalism*. Cambridge: Polity Press, 2000.
Gros, Frédéric. *The Security Principle: From Serenity to Regulation*. Translated by David Broder. London: Verso, 2019.
Haffejee NO and Others v Ethekwini Municipality 2011 (6) SA 134 (CC).
Hägglund, Martin. *This Life: Why Mortality Makes Us Free*. London: Profile Books, 2020.
Hamburg Flood Control 24 BVerfGE 367 [1968].
Hamilton, Lawrence. *Freedom is Power: Liberty Through Political Representation*. Cambridge: Cambridge University Press, 2014.
———. *The Political Philosophy of Needs*. Cambridge: Cambridge University Press, 2003.
Hampshire, Stuart. *Justice is Conflict*. Princeton: Princeton University Press, 2000.
Hardimon, Michael O. *Hegel's Social Philosophy: The Project of Reconciliation*. Cambridge: Cambridge University Press, 1994.
Harrison, Ross. *Bentham*. London: Routledge, 1999.
Hart, H. L. A. *The Concept of Law*. Oxford: Oxford University Press, third edition, 2012.
———. *Essays on Bentham: Studies in Jurisprudence and Political Theory*. Oxford: Clarendon Press, 1982.
Harvey, David. *A Brief History of Neoliberalism*. Oxford: Oxford University Press, 2007.
———. *A Companion to Marx's Capital: The Complete Edition*. London: Verso, 2018.
———. *The Condition of Postmodernity: An Enquiry into the Origins of Cultural Change*. Oxford: Basil Blackwell, 1990.
———. *The Limits to Capital*. London: Verso, 2018.
———. *Marx, Capital and the Madness of Economic Reason*. London: Profile Books, 2019.
———. *The New Imperialism*. Oxford: Oxford University Press, 2005.
———. *Spaces of Global Capitalism: A Theory of Uneven Geographical Development*. London: Verso, 2019.
Hayek, Friedrich. *The Constitution of Liberty*. Chicago: University of Chicago Press, 1978.
———. *The Counter-Revolution of Science: Studies on the Abuse of Reason*. Glencoe: The Free Press, 1952.
———. 'The Fatal Conceit: The Errors of Socialism'. In *The Collected Words of F. A. Hayek Volume I*, edited by W. W. Bartley III. London: Routledge,1988.

———. *Individualism and Economic Order*. Chicago: University of Chicago Press, 1948.

———. *Law, Legislation and Liberty: A New Statement of the Liberal Principles of Justice and Political Economy*. Oxford: Routledge Classics, 2013.

———. *New Studies in Philosophy, Politics, Economics and the History of Ideas*. London: Routledge, 1990.

———. *The Road to Serfdom*. Oxford: Routledge Classics, 2001.

———. *Studies in Philosophy, Politics and Economics*. London: Routledge & Kegan Paul, 1967.

Hegel, Georg Wilhelm Friedrich. *Elements of the Philosophy of Right*. Edited by Allen W. Wood. Translated by H. B. Nisbet. Cambridge: Cambridge University Press, 1991.

———. *On Christianity: Early Theological Writing by Friedrich Hegel*. Translated by T. M. Knox. New York: Harper Torchbooks, 1961.

———. *Phenomenology of Spirit*. Translated by A. V. Miller. Oxford: Oxford University Press, 1977.

Heidegger, Martin. *Being and Time*. Translated by John Macquarrie and Edward Robinson. Oxford: Blackwell Publishing, 1962.

Heller, Agnes. *The Theory of Need in Marx*. London: Verso, 2018.

Hiruta, Kei. *Hannah Arendt and Isaiah Berlin: Freedom, Politics and Humanity*. Princeton: Princeton University Press, 2021.

Hobsbawm, Eric. *The Age of Capital: 1848–1875*. London: Abacus, 1977.

Hohfeld, Wesley Newcomb. 'Some Fundamental Legal Conceptions as Applied in Judicial Reasoning'. *Yale Law Journal* 23 (1913): 16–59.

Holcim (South Africa) (Pty) Ltd v Prudent Investors (Pty) Ltd [2011] 1 All SA 364 (SCA).

Honneth, Axel. *Reification: A New Look at an Old Idea*. New York: Oxford University Press, 2007.

Hook, Sidney. *From Hegel to Marx: Studies in the Intellectual Development of Karl Marx*. Ann Arbor: University of Michigan Press, 1962.

———. 'Pragmatism and the Tragic Sense of Life'. *Proceedings and Addresses of the American Philosophical Association* 33 (1959): 5–26.

Horkheimer, Max. *Critique of Instrumental Reason*. Translated by Matthew J. O'Connell and others. London: Verso, 2012.

———. *The Eclipse of Reason*. London: Continuum, 2004.

Jacoby, Russell. *Dialectic of Defeat: Contours of Western Marxism*. Cambridge: Cambridge University Press, 2002.

———. *The End of Utopia: Politics and Culture in an Age of Apathy*. New York: Basic Books, 1999.

Jäger, Anton, and Daniel Zamora Vargas. *Welfare for Markets: A Global History of Basic Income*. Chicago: University of Chicago Press, 2023.

Johannesburg Metropolitan Municipality v Gauteng Development Tribunal 2010 (6) SA 182 (CC).

Kaufmann, Walter. *Tragedy and Philosophy*. Princeton: Princeton University Press, 1992.

Klare, Karl E. 'Legal Culture and Transformative Constitutionalism'. *South African Journal of Human Rights* 14, no. 1 (1998): 146–88.

Kley, Roland. *Hayek's Social and Political Thought*. Oxford: Clarendon Press, 1994.

Knowles, Dudley. 'Hegel on Property and Personality'. *The Philosophical Quarterly* 33, no. 130 (January, 1983): 45–62.

Kohn, Nina. 'Vulnerability Theory and the Role of Government'. *Yale Journal of Law and Feminism* 26, no. 1 (2014): 1–27.

Korsgaard, Christine M. *Self-Constitution: Agency, Identity, and Integrity*. Oxford: Oxford University Press, 2009.

———. 'Two Distinctions of Goodness'. *The Philosophical Review* 92, no. 2 (April, 1983): 169–95.

Kramer, Matthew H. *John Locke and the Origins of Private Property: Philosophical Explorations of Individualism, Community, and Equality*. Cambridge: Cambridge University Press, 1997.

Kresge, Stephen, and Leif Wenar, eds. *Hayek on Hayek: An Autobiographical Dialogue*. London: Routledge, 1994.

Kruger, Matthew. 'Compensation as Radical Transformation'. *Potchefstroom Electronic Law Journal* 27 (June, 2024): 1–33.

Kukathas, Chandran. *Hayek and Modern Liberalism*. Oxford: Oxford University Press, 1989.

Lasch, Christopher. *The Culture of Narcissism: American Life in an Age of Diminishing Expectations*. New York: W. W. Norton & Company, 1979.

———. *The Minimal Self: Psychic Survival in Troubled Times*. London: Picador, 1985.

———. *The True and Only Heaven: Progress and Its Critics*. New York: W. W. Norton & Company, 1991.

Law Society of South Africa and Others v Minister for Transport and Another 2011 (1) SA 400 (CC).

Le Roux, Michelle, and Denis Davis. *Lawfare: Judging Politics in South Africa*. Johannesburg: Jonathan Ball Publishers, 2019.

Leopold, David. *The Young Karl Marx: German Philosophy, Modern Politics, and Human Flourishing*. Cambridge: Cambridge University Press, 2007.

Levy, Bernard-Henri. *The Virus in the Age of Madness*. New Haven: Yale University Press, 2020.

Lind, Michael. *The New Class War: Saving Democracy from the Metropolitan Elite*. London: Atlantic Books, 2020.

Locke, John. *The Clarendon Edition of the Works of John Locke: An Essay Concerning Human Understanding*. Edited by Peter H. Nidditch. Oxford: Oxford University Press, 1975.

———. *Two Treatises of Government*. Edited by Peter Laslett. Cambridge: Cambridge University Press, student edition, 1988.

Löwith, Karl. *From Hegel to Nietzsche: The Revolution in Nineteenth-Century Thought*. Translated by David E. Green. New York: Columbia University Press, 1991.

Lukács, Georg. *History and Class Consciousness*. Translated by Rodney Livingstone. London: Merlin Press, 1971.

Lukes, Steven. *Liberals and Cannibals: The Implications of Diversity*. London: Verso, 2017.

MacIntyre, Alasdair. *After Virtue: A Study in Moral Theory*. Notre Dame: University of Notre Dame Press, third edition, 2007.

Mack, Mary P. *Jeremy Bentham: An Odyssey of Ideas 1748–1792*. London: Heinemann, 1963.

Macpherson, C. B. *The Political Theory of Possessive Individualism: Hobbes to Locke*. Oxford: Oxford University Press, 1964.

Mandel, Ernest. *The Formation of the Economic Thought of Karl Marx: 1843 to Capital*. Translated by Brian Pearce. London: Verso, 2015.

Manning D. J. *The Mind of Jeremy Bentham*. New York: Barnes & Noble, 1968.

Marcuse, Herbert. *Counter-Revolution and Revolt*. Boston: Beacon Press, 1972.

———. *Eros and Civilisation: A Philosophical Inquiry into Freud*. London: Sphere Books, second edition, 1969.

———. *An Essay on Liberation*. London: Penguin Books, 1972.

———. *One-Dimensional Man: Studies in the Ideology of Advanced Industrial*. Oxford: Routledge, second edition, 1991.

———. *Reason and Revolution: Hegel and the Rise of Social Theory*. London: Routledge & Kegan Paul Ltd, second edition, 1955.

Marx, Karl. *Capital: A Critique of Political Economy, Volume I*. Translated by Ben Fowkes. London: Penguin Classics, 1990.

———. *Capital: A Critique of Political Economy, Volume II*. Translated by David Fernbach. London: Penguin Classics, 1992.

———. *Capital: A Critique of Political Economy, Volume III*. Translated by David Fernbach. London: Penguin Classics, 1991.

———. 'The Class Struggles in France: 1848–1850'. In *The Political Writings*, translated by Paul Jackson. London: Verso, 2019.

———. 'A Contribution to the Critique of Hegel's "Philosophy of Right"'. In *Critique of Hegel's "Philosophy of Right"*, translated by Annette Jolin and Joseph O'Malley. Cambridge: Cambridge University Press, 1977.

———. *Critique of Hegel's "Philosophy of Right"*. Translated by Annette Jolin and Joseph O'Malley. Cambridge: Cambridge University Press, 1977.

———. 'Critique of the Gotha Programme'. In *The Political Writings*, translated by Joris de Bres. London: Verso, 2019.

———. *Early Texts*. Translated by David McLellan. Oxford: Basil Blackwell, 1972.

———. 'The Eighteenth Brumaire of Louis Bonaparte'. In *The Political Writings*, translated by Ben Fowkes. London: Verso, 2019.

———. *The German Ideology, Part One with selections from Parts Two and Three and, Together with Marx's "Introduction to a Critique of Political Economy"*. Edited by C. J. Arthur. London: Lawrence & Wishart, second edition, 1974.

———. *Grundrisse: Foundations of the Critique of Political Economy*. Translated by Martin Nicolaus. London: Penguin Books, 1993.

———. 'On James Mill'. In *Early Texts*, translated by David McLellan. Oxford: Basil Blackwell, 1972.

———. 'On the Jewish Question'. In *Early Texts*, translated by David McLellan. Oxford: Basil Blackwell, 1972.

———. *The Poverty of Philosophy*. Translated by Harry Quelch. New York: Cosimo Classics, 2008.

———. 'Theses on Feuerbach'. In *The German Ideology, Part One with Selections from Parts Two and Three and, Together with Marx's "Introduction to a Critique of Political Economy"*, edited by C. J. Arthur. London: Lawrence & Wishart, second edition, 1974.

———. 'Wage Labour and Capital'. In *Essential Writings of Karl Marx*. St Petersburg: Red and Black Publishers, 2010.

Marx, Karl, and Friedrich Engels. 'The Communist Manifesto'. In *The Political Writings*, translated by Samuel Moore. London: Verso, 2019.

———. *Economic and Philosophic Manuscripts of 1844*. Translated by Martin Milligan. Blacksburg: Wilder Publications Inc, 2011.

Matatiele Municipality and Others v President of the RSA and Others (No 2) [*] 2007 (6) SA 477 (CC).

McLellan, David. *The Young Hegelians and Karl Marx*. New York: Frederick A. Praeger, 1969.

MEC for Education, KwaZulu-Natal v Pillay 2008 (1) SA 474 (CC).

Merrill, Thomas W. 'Property and the Right to Exclude'. *Nebraska Law Review* 77 (1998): 730–55.

Merrill, Thomas W., and Henry E. Smith. 'Optimal Standardization in the Law of Property: The Numerus Clausus Principle'. *The Yale Law Journal* 110 (2000): 1–70.

———. 'What Happened to Property in Law and Economics?'. *The Yale Law Journal* 111 (2001): 357–98.

Mészáros, István. *Marx's Theory of Alienation*. London: Merlin Press, fourth edition, 1975.

Midi Television (Pty) Ltd t/a E-TV v Director of Public Prosecutions (Western Cape) [*] 2007 (5) SA 540 (SCA).

Milanovic, Branko. *Capitalism, Alone: The Future of the System That Rules the World*. Cambridge, MA: Harvard University Press, 2019.

Mill, John Stuart. 'Bentham'. In *Essays on Ethics, Religion and Society (Collected Works of John Stuart Mill, Vol. 10)*, edited by John M. Robson. London: Routledge & Kegan Paul, 1969.

———. 'Utilitarianism'. In *On Liberty and Other Essays*, edited by John Gray. Oxford: Oxford University Press, 1998.

Mineral and Petroleum Resources Development Act, 2002.

Modiri, Joel. 'Conquest and Constitutionalism: First Thoughts on an Alternative Jurisprudence'. *South African Journal of Human Rights* 34, no. 3 (2018): 300–25.

Mokyr, Joel. *A Culture of Growth: The Origins of the Modern Economy*. Princeton: Princeton University Press, 2016.

Mouffe, Chantal. *The Democratic Paradox*. London: Verso, 2000.

———. *The Return of the Political*. London: Verso, 2005.

Moyn, Samuel. *Liberalism Against Itself: Cold War Intellectuals and the Making of Our Times*. New Haven: Yale University Press, 2023.

Mulhall, Stephen. *Philosophical Myths of the Fall*. Princeton: Princeton University Press, 2005.

Mulhall, Stephen, and Adam Swift. *Liberals and Communitarians*. Oxford: Blackwell, 1992.

Munzer, Stephen R. *A Theory of Property*. Cambridge: Cambridge University Press, 1990.

New Nation Movement NPC and Others v President of the Republic of South Africa and Others 2020 (6) SA 257 (CC).

Nietzsche, Friedrich. *Beyond Good and Evil: Prelude to a Philosophy of the Future*. Translated by R. J. Hollingdale. London: Penguin Classics, 2014.

———. *The Birth of Tragedy and Other Writings*. Edited by Raymond Geuss and Ronald Speirs. Translated by Ronald Speirs. Cambridge: Cambridge University Press, 1999.

Nozick, Robert. *Anarchy, State and Utopia*. Oxford: Blackwell, 1974.

Nussbaum, Martha. *Anger and Forgiveness: Resentment, Generosity, Justice*. Oxford: Oxford University Press, 2016.

———. 'Bernard Williams: Tragedies, Hope, Justice'. In *Reading Bernard Williams*, edited by Daniel Callcut. London: Routledge, 2009.

———. *Creating Capabilities: The Human Development Approach*. Cambridge, MA: Harvard University Press, 2011.

———. *The Fragility of Goodness: Luck and Ethics in Greek Tragedy and Philosophy*. Cambridge: Cambridge University Press, revised edition, 2001.

———. *Frontiers of Justice, Disability, Nationality, and Species Membership*. Cambridge, MA: Harvard University Press, 2007.

———. 'Mill between Aristotle and Bentham'. In *Economics and Happiness: Framing the Analysis*, edited by Luigino Bruni and Pier Luigi Porta. Oxford: Oxford University Press, 2005.

———. *Political Emotions: Why Love Matters for Justice*. Cambridge, MA: Harvard University Press, 2013.

———. *Upheavals of Thought: The Intelligence of Emotions*. Cambridge: Cambridge University Press, 2001.

———. *Women and Human Development: The Capabilities Approach*. Cambridge: Cambridge University Press, 2001.

Oakeshott, Michael. *Hobbes on Civil Association*. Indianapolis: Liberty Fund, 1975.

———. *Morality and Politics in Modern Europe*. Edited by Shirley Robin Letwin. New Haven: Yale University Press, 1993.

———. *Rationalism in Politics and Other Essays*. Indianapolis: Liberty Fund, new and expanded edition, 1991.

Olivecrona, Karl. 'Locke's Theory of Appropriation'. *The Philosophical Quarterly* 24, no. 96 (1974): 220–34.

Ollman, Bertell. *Alienation: Marx's Conception of Man in Capitalist Society*. Cambridge: Cambridge University Press, second edition, 1971.

O'Mahony, Lorna Fox, and Mark L. Roark. *Squatting and the State: Resilient Property in an Age of Crisis*. Cambridge: Cambridge University Press, 2022.

Pierson, Christopher. *Just Property: A History in the Latin West Volume One: Wealth, Virtue, and the Law*. Oxford: Oxford University Press, 2013.

———. *Just Property: Volume Two: Enlightenment, Revolution, and History*. Oxford: Oxford University Press, 2016.

Pinkard, Terry. *German Philosophy 1760–1860: The Legacy of German Idealism*. Cambridge: Cambridge University Press, 2002.

———. *Hegel: A Biography*. Cambridge: Cambridge University Press, 2000.

Plant, Raymond. *Hegel*. London: George Allen & Unwin Ltd, 1973.

———. 'Hegel and Political Economy—I'. *New Left Review* I/103 (1977): 79–92.

———. 'Hegel and Political Economy—II'. *New Left Review* I/103 (1977): 103–13.

Polanyi, Karl. *The Great Transformation: The Political and Economic Origins of our Times*. Boston: Beacon Press, 2001.

Popper, Karl. *The Open Society and Its Enemies, Vol. II: Hegel and Marx*. London: Routledge, 2002.

Port Elizabeth Municipality v Various Occupiers 2005 (1) SA 217 (CC).

Posner, Richard A. *The Economics of Justice*. Cambridge, MA: Harvard University Press, 1983.

Radin, Margaret Jane. *Reinterpreting Property*. Chicago: Chicago University Press, 1993.

Rawls, John. *A Theory of Justice*. Cambridge, MA: Harvard University Press, revised edition, 1999.

Ray, Gene. 'Dialectical Realism and Radical Commitments: Brecht and Adorno on Representing Capitalism'. *Historical Materialism* 18, no. 3 (2010): 3–24.

Raz, Joseph. *The Morality of Freedom*. Oxford: Clarendon Press, 1988.

Ripstein, Arthur. *Force and Freedom: Kant's Legal and Political Philosophy*. Cambridge, MA: Harvard University Press, 2009.

Rorty, Richard. *Philosophy and the Mirror of Nature*. Princeton: Princeton University Press, 1979.

Rosa, Harmut. *Social Acceleration: A New Theory of Modernity*. Translated by Jonathan Trejo-Mathys. New York: Columbia University Press, 2013.

Roux, Theunis. 'Property'. In *Constitutional Law of South Africa*, edited by Stuart Woolman and Michael Bishop. Cape Town: Juta Law, second edition, revision service 6, April 2014.

Ryan, Alan. *Property and Political Theory*. Oxford: Blackwell, 1984.

Sandel, Michael. *Liberalism and the Limits of Justice*. Cambridge: Cambridge University Press, 1982.

Sciabarra, Chris Matthew. *Marx, Hayek and Utopia*. Albany: State University of New York Press, 1995.

Scruton, Roger. *The Face of God*. London: Bloomsbury, 2012.

———. *On Human Nature*. Princeton: Princeton University Press, 2015.

———. *The Soul of the World*. Princeton: Princeton University Press, 2014.

———. *Understanding Music: Philosophy and Interpretation*. London: Bloomsbury, 2016.
Sen, Amartya. *Development as Freedom*. New York: Alfred A. Knopf, 1999.
Shklar, Judith. *After Utopia: The Decline of Political Faith*. Princeton: Princeton University Press, 2020.
———. *Political Thought and Political Thinkers*. Edited by Stanley Hoffmann. Chicago: University of Chicago Press, 1998.
Shoprite Checkers (Pty) Ltd v MEC for Economic Development, Eastern Cape and Others 2015 (6) SA 125 (CC).
Singer, Joseph William. *Entitlement: The Paradoxes of Property*. New Haven: Yale University Press, 2000.
Skinner, Quentin. *Liberty before Liberalism*. Cambridge: Cambridge University Press, 2012.
Slobodian, Quinn. *Globalists: The End of Empire and the Birth of Neoliberalism*. Cambridge, MA: Harvard University Press, 2018.
Soobramoney v Minister of Health (Kwazulu-Natal) 1998 (1) SA 765 (CC).
Spelman, Elizabeth. *Repair: The Impulse to Restore in a Fragile World*. Boston: Beacon Press, 2003.
Sreenivasan, Gopal. *The Limits of Lockean Rights in Property*. New York: Oxford University Press, 1995.
Steiner, George. *The Death of Tragedy*. New York: Oxford University Press, 1980.
Sunstein, Cass, and Stephen Holmes. *The Cost of Rights: Why Liberty Depends on Taxes*. New York: W. W. Norton & Company, 1999.
S v Boesak 2001 (1) SA 912 (CC).
S v Makwanyane and Another 1995 (3) SA 391 (CC).
S v Rens 1996 (1) SA 1218 (CC).
Táíwò, Olúfẹ́mi O. *Elite Capture: How the Powerful Took Over Identity Politics (And Everything Else*. Chicago: Haymarket Books, 2022.
Taylor, Charles. *The Ethics of Authenticity*. Cambridge, MA: Harvard University Press, 1991.
———. *Hegel*. Cambridge: Cambridge University Press, 1977.
———. *The Language Animal: The Full Shape of the Human Linguistic Capacity*. Cambridge, MA: Harvard University Press, 2016.
———. 'Marxism and Empiricism'. In *British Analytic Philosophy*, edited by Bernard Williams and Alan Montefiore. London: Routledge & Kegan Paul, 1966.
———. *Philosophical Arguments*. Cambridge, MA: Harvard University Press, 1995.
———. *Philosophical Papers: Volume 1, Human Agency and Language*. Cambridge: Cambridge University Press, 1985.
———. *Philosophical Papers: Volume 2, Philosophy and the Human Sciences*. Cambridge: Cambridge University Press, 1985.
———. *Sources of the Self: The Making of Modern Identity*. Cambridge, MA: Harvard University Press, 1989.
———. 'The Opening Arguments of the Phenomenology'. In *Hegel: A Collection of Critical Essays*, edited by Alasdair MacIntyre. Notre Dame: University of Notre Dame Press, 1976.

Tebble, A. J. *F. A. Hayek*. New York: Continuum, 2010.

Tokarczuk, Olga. *Drive Your Plow Over the Bones of the Dead*. Translated by Antonia Lloyd-Jones. London: Penguin Publishing Group, 2019.

Tshwane City v Link Africa 2015 (6) SA 440 (CC).

Tucker, Miles. 'Two Kinds of Value Pluralism'. *Utilitas* 28, no. 3 (2016): 333–46.

Tully, James. *A Discourse on Property: John Locke and his Adversaries*. Cambridge: Cambridge University Press, 1980.

United Democratic Movement, Gauteng Development Tribunal and Matatiele Municipality and Others v President of the RSA and Others (No 2) [*] 2007 (6) SA 477 (CC).

United Democratic Movement v President of the Republic of South Africa and Others (No 2) 2003 (1) SA 495 (CC).

Van der Walt, A. J. *Constitutional Property Law*. Cape Town: Juta, third edition, 2011.

———. *Property in the Margins*. Oxford: Hart Publishing, 2009.

Van der Walt, Johan. *Law and Sacrifice: Towards a Post-Apartheid Theory of Law*. London: Routledge, 2005.

Van Wyk, Jeannie. 'Compensation for Land Reform Expropriation'. *Tydskrif vir die Suid-Afrikaanse Reg* 1 (2017): 21–35.

Viljoen, Sue-Mari. 'Property and "Human Flourishing": A Reassessment in the Housing Framework'. *Potchefstroom Electronic Law Journal* 22 (August, 2019): 1–27.

Waldron, Jeremy. *The Dignity of Legislation*. Cambridge: Cambridge University Press, 1999.

———. *God, Locke, and Equality: Christian Foundations in Locke's Political Thought*. Cambridge: Cambridge University Press, 2002.

———. *One Another's Equals: The Basis of Human Equality*. Cambridge, MA: Harvard University Press, 2017.

———. *The Right to Private Property*. Oxford: Clarendon Press, 1988.

Walsh W. H. *Hegelian Ethics*. London: Macmillan and Co Ltd, 1969.

Walzer, Michael. *Spheres of Justice: A Defense of Pluralism and Equality*. New York: Basic Books, 1983.

Weber, Max. *The Protestant Ethic and the Spirit of Capitalism*. Translated by Talcott Parsons. London: Routledge, 2005.

Wenar, Leif. 'The Development of Unity'. *Journal of Human Development and Capabilities* 21, no. 3 (2020): 211–22.

———. 'The Nature of Rights'. *Philosophy and Public Affairs* 33, no. 3 (2005): 223–52.

———. 'Rights'. In *The Stanford Encyclopaedia of Philosophy*, edited by Edward N. Zalta. Accessed 18 August 2024. https://plato.stanford.edu/entries/rights/.

Williams, Bernard. *Ethics and the Limits of Philosophy*. London: Routledge Classics, 2011.

———. *Problems of the Self: Philosophical Papers 1956–1972*. Cambridge: Cambridge University Press, 1973.

———. *The Sense of the Past: Essays in the History of Philosophy*. Princeton: Princeton University Press, 2006.

———. *Truth and Truthfulness: An Essay in Genealogy*. Princeton: Princeton University Press, 2002.

Wilson, Stuart. *Human Rights and the Transformation of Property*. Cape Town: Juta Law Publishers, 2021.

Wood, Allen W. *Hegel's Ethical Thought*. Cambridge: Cambridge University Press, 1990.

———. *Karl Marx*. New York: Routledge, 2004.

Wood, Ellen Meiksins. *Democracy Against Capitalism: Renewing Historical Materialism*. London: Verso, 2016.

———. *Empire of Capital*. London: Verso, 2005.

———. *The Origin of Capitalism: A Longer View*. London: Verso, 2017.

———. *The Retreat from Class: A New "True" Socialism*. London: Verso, revised edition, 1998.

———. *A Social History of Western Political Thought*. London: Verso, 2022.

Index

About the Author

Matthew Kruger is an advocate at the Johannesburg Bar in South Africa. He has a PhD in law and philosophy from King's College London and is a former research clerk at South Africa's Constitutional Court.

www.ingramcontent.com/pod-product-compliance
Ingram Content Group UK Ltd.
Pitfield, Milton Keynes, MK11 3LW, UK
UKHW012118150926
475560UK00002B/163

9 781666 96839